D1577253

Planning Public Library Buildings

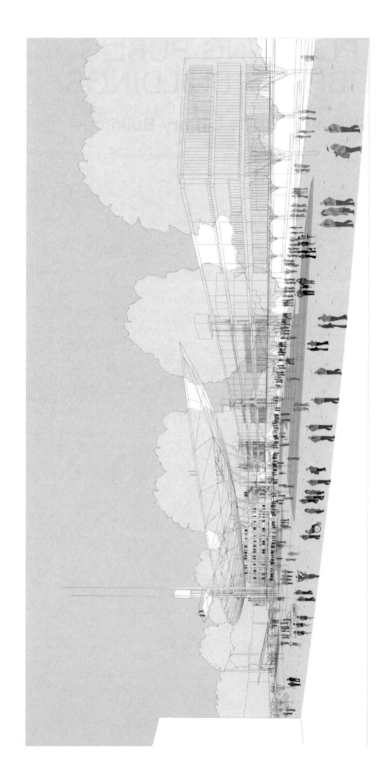

Frontispiece The Library of Birmingham: design concept
Source: Richard Rogers Partnership/Photo Libraries

PLANNING PUBLIC LIBRARY BUILDINGS

Concepts and Issues for the Librarian

Michael Dewe

ASHGATE

Published by
Ashgate Publishing Limited
Gower House
Croft Road
Aldershot
Hants GU11 3HR
England

Ashgate Publishing Company
Suite 420
101 Cherry Street
Burlington, VT 05401-4405
USA

Ashgate website: http://www.ashgate.com

British Library Cataloguing in Publication Data
Dewe, Michael
  Planning public library buildings : concepts and issues for
  the librarian
  1. Public libraries 2. Public libraries - Planning 3. Library
  planning
  I. Title
  027.4

Library of Congress Cataloging-in-Publication Data
Dewe, Michael.
  Planning public library buildings : concepts and issues for the librarian /
  by Michael Dewe.
      p. cm.
  Includes bibliographical references and index.
  ISBN 0-7546-3388-8
    1. Library buildings--Design and construction. 2. Public libraries--Planning. 3. Library architecture. 4. Library buildings--Great Britain--Design and construction. 5. Public libraries--Great Britain--Planning. 6. Library architecture--Great Britain. I. Title.

  Z679.5.D49 2006
  022'.3--dc22

                                                          2005017269

ISBN 0 7546 3388 8

Printed and bound in Great Britain by TJ International Ltd, Padstow, Cornwall.

Contents

To Karen, Robert and Deborah who have
learned to live with library buildings

List of Figures

Preface

The opportunity to be involved in the creation of a library building must be one of the most exciting and rewarding features of a librarian's career, especially when the project is over and the library is being well-used by an appreciative public. Some public librarians have considerable experience of building projects, including conversions and refurbishments, although not perhaps of erecting a large or very large library, while others have none or little at all. For everyone, however, there is a first time, and while the librarian may well look forward to the pleasure and the challenge of such an enterprise, they may also feel less than well-prepared. In part this may be because the planning and design of libraries was not addressed by the librarian's professional education, at least not in recent years. Librarians are unlikely, therefore, to be familiar with the building planning and design process, the management of such projects, the business of writing an architect's brief, interpreting plans and drawings, writing furniture specifications, and for a large building, completing facility data sheets for each space in the proposed library.

The aim of this book is to make up for the lack of a recent UK publication specifically concerned with the planning and design of public libraries. It is intended principally to provide a point of departure and guide for those librarians and architects embarking on a public library building project for the first time. It will also be a useful aide-mémoire for more experienced individuals, as well as offering information on issues that may not have arisen before.

The basic principles and practices of the planning and design of public library buildings have been described at various times in the past but necessarily need to be reiterated for today's librarians. This book brings these principles and practices together, along with the various professional concepts, ideas, issues and controversies which are likely to be examined in the course of the planning and design process.

This book is not, however, a 'how-to-do-it' manual on planning and designing public library buildings nor a technical guide to construction and other matters that must concern the librarian but are the remit of other experts. It endeavours to raise issues without necessarily resolving them as their resolution depends very much on local circumstances.

The work is intended primarily for a British audience and records concepts and issues that relate to that UK context. However, the experiences and library buildings of other countries are drawn on and a number highlighted as case studies. This wide-ranging coverage should broaden its appeal to an international audience. The book demonstrates that the UK continues to create public library service points, both big and small, that enliven and shape its local communities and that this is part of the worldwide public library scene.

It would have been impossible to write this book without access to the unrivalled resources of the Thomas Parry Library, University of Wales Aberystwyth. I am extremely grateful to the Librarian, Alan Clark, for providing me with research accommodation and facilities and the staff for their help on numerous occasions. The National Library of Wales in Aberystwyth, too, has been a useful source of information, as well as a place for quiet reflection and frantic re-writing.

I owe a particular debt to Rob Froud, County Librarian of Somerset, who has supported my interest in public library buildings since his days as editor of *Public library journal*, and to Malcolm Tunley my good friend and ex-colleague at the College of Librarianship Wales (now the Department of Information Studies, University of Wales Aberystwyth). Both have read the draft of this book and made many useful comments and necessary corrections. Huw Evans, Head of Advice and Support at CyMAL (Museums, Archives and Libraries Wales), and Tony Durcan, Head of Libraries, Information and Lifelong Learning at Newcastle upon Tyne have also looked at some chapters and offered some helpful observations. Tony also hosted an informative visit to Newcastle, enabling me to look at some library buildings both old and new.

My thanks are due also to a number of friends and colleagues who have helped me in a variety of ways: Jacqui Durcan, Mike and Anne Wells (who provided help with accommodation and library visits), Norma McDermott of the Library Council of Ireland, Jane Schaedel, Veronica Wellington, Library Services Manager of Peterborough Libraries, and Derek English, Divisional Manager (North) Durham Libraries. I would also like to thank the many librarians in the UK and abroad who have been kind enough to respond to my request for information about their library buildings, as well as for plans and photographs.

Since its inauguration in 1995, I have been fortunate enough to be a member of the judging panel for the Public Library Building Awards scheme. My thanks are due to the Public Libraries Group of the Chartered Institute of Library and Information Professionals (CILIP) for enabling me to enjoy this privilege and for the opportunities to visit many public libraries in both the UK and the Republic of Ireland. Such visits provided plenty of evidence that library services and their buildings continue to inspire the long-standing public library ideal. Thanks are due to my colleagues on the judging panel, especially those who chaired the group on different occasions (Pearl Valentine, Philippa Harper and Mandy Hickens) for fruitful hours of discussion. The many librarians who prepared profiles of their library buildings for the award scheme and, when shortlisted, took time to show the judging panel round their libraries, also deserve the grateful thanks of the panel and the author. As described in Chapter 2, the awards scheme and its categories have been revised for the 2005 competition.

The commissioning editor at Ashgate, Suzie Duke, has put up with the usual author delays and changes to structure and content in an understanding way. My thanks are due for her support for the idea of the book in the first place and later encouragement and suggestions. The author also thanks Jacqui Cornish, Senior Desk Editor at Ashgate and Jane Read for their copy-editing skills and for seeing the book through to publication. With an author's usual courage, I take responsibility for the published text.

I have already acknowledged my debt to the resources of the Thomas Parry Library and would like to point to some English language sources of information available there that have been of particular value and would help others to update themselves. The online version of *Library and information abstracts* (LISA) has been very useful, particularly for information about non-UK library buildings. The 'architecture and building' heading (usefully subdivided by topic and country) in *Library literature & information science* index and the *Current awareness abstracts of library and information management literature* (also available online), which includes a building/ equipment/furniture heading when appropriate in the printed numbers, have also been rewardingly consulted.

Printed bibliographies by Stevenson and Swartzburg[1] are helpful sources for older material, which is often still of value and which I have not been afraid to make use of for this book when necessary and appropriate. Other publications, especially volumes of library building descriptions, are listed in the chapter notes and where appropriate in the select bibliography at the end of this work, which confines itself to book material.

Of particular importance to my research has been the *Library buildings* series (the title varies slightly), edited initially by J.D. Reynolds, then Herbert Ward, followed by K.C. Harrison, and Dean Harrison, the latter as editor of the last volume (1990–1994). Published by the Library Association and later by the Library Services Trust, it is doubtful whether any other country has such a full published record of its public library buildings. It is a pity that nothing more has been published since the last volume. However, the Council for Museums, Libraries and Archives (MLA) has funded a website (www.designinglibraries.org.uk) that includes a library buildings database, based in the Thomas Parry Library, Aberystwyth, and launched in 2005. This is helping to make good this publication deficiency and is not subject to the delays of the printed volumes.[2] I have also had access to the substantial library planning collection held at the Thomas Parry Library, which includes the former Library Association collection, as well as the material for the biennial Public Library Building Awards nominations, 1995–2003. This augmented planning collection held in Aberystwyth is an archive of national importance to the library and information profession.

As the chapter notes show, particular English language periodicals have proved especially helpful to me in writing this book. In addition to the UK's *Library +*

information update and *Public library journal*, the sources of many informative articles were the *Irish library news*, *Scandinavian public library quarterly*, *Library journal* and *American libraries*; the December and April issues respectively of the last two periodicals include coverage of new American library buildings. From down under the two professional journals *Australasian public libraries and information services* and *New Zealand libraries* have yielded some interesting articles.

The Internet provides access to the web pages of most library services throughout the world. Information about particular library service points varies, but each library building is often illustrated by one or more images. Sometimes a virtual tour of the library may be on offer. With this in mind, I have not peppered chapter notes with web addresses unless substantial information about a building is provided.

Every author's wife deserves special thanks and mine is no exception. Thanks Kathy, this really is the last one – for now anyway.

NOTES

1 Stephenson, M.S. (1990), *Planning library facilities: a selected annotated bibliography*, Metuchen, New Jersey: Scarecrow; Swartzburg, S.G. and Bussey, H. (1991), *Libraries and archives: design and renovation with a preservation perspective*, Metuchen, New Jersey: Scarecrow.

2 Dewe, M. (2005), 'Building on experience', *Public library journal* **20** (3), 18–19.

Introduction

Each new public library building represents a unique amalgam of the possibilities for library service and of architectural and construction practice. While some elements may be innovative and groundbreaking, especially in a period of change, many fundamental planning and design issues have to be considered time and time again from project to project. This book does not purport to cover everything, or to offer instant solutions but sets out and reviews those concepts, issues, topics and options about which the librarian must be concerned and which will need to be fully explored in the planning and design process.

Many of these topics (such as public library purpose, siting, building size, the use of converted buildings, the deployment of information technology, the preservation of library materials, dual-use buildings and the working environment) often have a substantial literature in their own right, which the reader may wish to consult.

The content of this book, therefore, can be seen as part of the investigative, information-gathering process that precedes a firm idea of what is wanted and expected of a proposed library building. Its aim is to save the librarian's time, perhaps stop the re-invention of the wheel on occasions, and to guide and enlighten the librarian's thought processes in the belief that a better public library building will result.

While the librarian will plan on the basis of past and current experiences, it is in the nature of the task to look to the future and, where possible and appropriate, to experiment and offer something new. The danger in doing so (and wanting to be different) is that librarians can become dismissive of the library building achievements of earlier times, and that dishonest descriptions of and unjust comparisons with the past can occur including an avoidance of the 'L' (library) word. In part this is to justify the contents, style and ambience of some modern public library building, and there are those who believe that this is very necessary and entirely justified.

There is also the danger of succumbing to the new millennium notion of describing all new buildings as those 'for the twenty-first century' or 'for the future'. Clearly librarians should be creating buildings for the present – the early part of the twenty-first century – because, while we may glimpse the future, it is largely unknowable. And public libraries and their buildings will change over time as they did in the nineteenth and twentieth centuries. It might also be argued that in the world of the Internet and access to electronic information and virtual library collections, the public library building will become an anachronism. But this is to anticipate the discussion in the final chapter of this book.

CHAPTER SUMMARIES

In Chapter 1, the mission and roles of public libraries are discussed against the background of social, economic and other changes in the UK, and there is review of how these factors have influenced the development of public libraries. This discussion is centred round *The public library service: IFLA/UNESCO guidelines for development* (2001) and the UK's *Framework for the future* (2003); the latter plans the development of public libraries up to 2013. Particular attention is given to the social role of the public library; its concern for the socially excluded and its function as meeting place for the community.

The main thrust of this opening chapter is that planning a library building must be based on decisions as to a library service's mission and roles, which must take into account local needs. The chapter concludes by looking at some of the issues and conflicts that surround public library provision in the UK and the implications of these for library buildings.

Chapter 2 places the public library building in the broader context, principally in the UK, of the role played by modern cultural buildings. Such buildings may be seen as national and civic symbols, playing a role in inter-city rivalry, contributing to the regeneration of communities, increasing employment, stimulating the provision of public art, and as tourist attractions. Where old buildings are put to new uses, perhaps as a public library, then they play a vital role in building conservation.

Whether cultural icon or, for example, a force for regeneration, library buildings need to fulfil three basic requirements: they must be well built, be suited to their purpose, and display aesthetic qualities.

Chapter 3 reviews the range of static service points used in the UK for public library service, from the central or main library to branch libraries of varying scale. It touches on various debates, such as the role of central libraries, the arguments for their decentralization, and the over-provision of branches.

The question of library size and its calculation is discussed, followed by an outline of the range of services, facilities and amenities that might be offered to children, young people and adults in the public library building. The implications these have for space requirements are looked at in a simplified fashion at this juncture in the book.

A final section explores the pros and cons of different library plan shapes, and the significance of the location of the entrance for traffic routes through the library and the organization of its interior.

Chapter 4 acknowledges the role of the librarian in deciding upon the location of the library building, and the importance of the brief in such decision-making; it also looks at the factors involved in placing the library in its community. This is done from two points of view: the selection of a location from a number of possibilities and the factors that will influence library design once a particular site has been chosen. One of these factors is whether the library is to be an independent building, constructed in association with another building, or as part of another building.

Chapter 5 examines solutions to library provision other than a new building: the pros and cons of a range of alternatives are considered, such as refurbishment, extension, and the use of converted premises. A number of case studies and examples from the UK and elsewhere illustrate these various solutions. Part of the argument for employing such alternatives relates to the preservation of older buildings, including library buildings, some of which are now listed.

Chapter 6 looks at what can be done to give the library building 'green' credentials and so avoid health risks to its occupants (by creating a good working environment), as well as provide for energy efficiency. In addition to the safety of the staff, consideration is given to the collection, its security and preservation management, and the need to design buildings that help minimize the effects of a disaster, such as fire or flood. The chapter concludes by considering various library materials handling systems, such as automated storage and retrieval and robotic sorting.

Depending upon the nature and size of a public library building, many of the issues of the previous chapters are likely to be reflected in the architect's brief for the library. In Chapter 7 we look at the brief, which describes the librarian's requirements for the building in philosophical, quantitative and qualitative terms, providing the information for the architect's design solution. Writing the brief requires a great deal of preparatory work by the librarian, involving a needs assessment using such techniques as community consultation and market research.

The chapter goes on to consider the later stages of creating a building, including construction and moving in and making the building operational. It also examines the role of the participants in this creative process, such as the architect (and their selection), the interior designer, and the work of the design team.

In Chapter 8 we look at how library buildings, both large and small, are designed to exemplify a number of qualities that will have been identified in the architect's brief. These include flexibility, offering choice, and being hospitable to information and communications technology. The librarian should be aware also of any potentially undesirable qualities, for example complex building maintenance and 'signature' architecture.

By stipulating these key ingredients for the success of the library building in the brief, and being wary of undesirable ones, the librarian has in part prepared the means for evaluating the building on its completion (post-occupancy evaluation). Evaluation, however, occurs at a number of points in the planning and design process – evaluating sites and architect's drawings, for instance.

Chapter 9 looks at how the public library building can be identified as such and the image it communicates both externally and internally to would-be users. Design concepts, such as the library as a marketplace, living room or bookshop, further define that library image and intentions, as well as being ways of shaping and organizing the building. External features of the structure, such as views into the interior, free-standing statuary and public spaces, also contribute to the library's appeal. Internally, gardens and courtyards, colour and guiding, for instance, go to create a comfortable, helpful and attractive ambience, as do structural and other features, like atriums and lighting.

Chapter 10 leaves aside the physical character of the library building, and looks at how its overall organization and interior layout are influenced first by whatever general principles are applied to determine the spatial relationships of library spaces and to their interior arrangement. The second influence is the series of decisions as to how the public areas are to be organized, for instance by function, subject or user group. Finally, resolution of the way in which library materials are to be arranged in the public departments and areas will also have an effect.

The chapter continues by considering other elements of the library layout and concludes by noting the relationship between library organization and layout and good communication between staff and users.

In Chapter 11, we conclude by examining the debate about the end of the book and the demise of libraries. It reviews the accusations made about UK public library buildings, such as their poor location and outmoded design, and argues that better space provision and funding are equally important issues for their survival.

In resolving some of the conflicts that can arise in serving different user groups, the provision of separate accommodation for children, young people, and local and family historians is discussed. A final section looks at potential library building role models in the UK and abroad and concludes that public libraries have historically demonstrated an ability to adapt to changing circumstances, thus helping to ensure their survival.

1 Mission and roles

The three most important documents a free society gives are a birth certificate, a passport, and a library card.

E.L. Doctorow, 1994 [1]

At the start of the twenty-first century the public library is a worldwide phenomenon. Beginning as a mid-nineteenth-century Anglo-American concept, the idea of publicly funded local libraries, offering a range of services and facilities of broad appeal and freely available to all, is now widely accepted, if not universally implemented to the same standard. Much of this international development has taken place in the period after the Second World War, stemming from the influence of America in Germany and Japan, the UK in the Commonwealth countries (Australia and Ghana, for instance) and in Europe following the creation of the European Union. Scandinavian countries adopted the Anglo-American public library concept earlier than other European countries and their library design ideas were particularly influential in the early post-war years in the UK.

As many UK surveys have shown, the public library and its staff are valued and appreciated by their users, particularly where a modern, well-equipped facility is provided.[2] But in today's world the public library has to meet the challenge of whether to be regarded as

> ... a pleasant but scarcely vital, additional factor in people's quality of life? Or ... to be a serious force for social justice, one of the few uncontrolled routes to personal growth we have?[3]

Answering such questions demands that public libraries actively demonstrate their relevance and promote their value to the individual and society at large.

International organizations have helped promote the public library idea. UNESCO's *Public library manifesto*, first issued in 1949, briefly makes the case for the value of public libraries in a democracy through 'free and unlimited access to knowledge, thought, culture and information', and outlines, for example, their mission, funding and management.[4]

The International Federation of Library Associations and Institutions (IFLA) has also played an important role, not only in promoting libraries generally, but public libraries in particular. Its *Standards for public libraries* (replaced by its 1986 *Guidelines*), have been influential in the UK, for example, as regards the size of public library buildings. The latest version at the time of writing, *The public library service: IFLA/UNESCO guidelines for development* (2001), provides an up-to-date account of the purpose, resources and management of public libraries.[5]

THE PUBLIC LIBRARY: A DEFINITION

This worldwide public library movement can be characterized normally as providing a service which:

- is established, supported and funded by the community through some form of local taxation
- provides access to knowledge, information, works of imagination and cultural experiences
- is based on local needs and reflects cultural diversity
- is available equally to all members of the community
- is in principle free of charge
- is free of censorship.[6]

In many countries public libraries are underpinned by specific legislation. This should state the level of government responsibility, how they are to be funded, and place public libraries in a nation's network of libraries and related organizations. Ideally public libraries should have a clear position in a national library and information plan that recognizes their continuing contribution to culture, information provision, literacy and education.[7]

As recommended in the *IFLA/UNESCO Guidelines*, public libraries in England and Wales are supported by specific legislation, the Public Libraries and Museums Act 1964. The legislation introduced ministerial responsibility for public libraries and placed a rather open-ended duty on library authorities 'to provide a comprehensive and efficient library service for all persons desiring to make use thereof'.[8] This duty now also applies to both Scotland and Northern Ireland. Although the legislation mentions certain services, it does not state what the 'duty' of public libraries in the UK might be in terms of purpose and roles. For some, an important feature of the Act is precisely that 'powers and duties are laid down in general terms which allow more freedom to local authorities'.[9] With the phrase 'desiring to make use thereof', the Act places the emphasis on individual motivation to use the library service rather than the expectation that all, or many, will want to do so.

Whatever the possible drawbacks of the 1964 Act, the public library review of 1995 did not recommend new legislation.[10] Later it was said that the public library standards for

England, which came into force in April 2001 with targets to be achieved by March 2004,[11] would demonstrate what constitutes a 'comprehensive and efficient' service.[12] In reality the standards were about access, the range and scope of library services and how they would be measured. It did not tackle the public library 'duty' in terms of its purpose and roles:

> Standards should be more than a mere measurement ... They need to be based on a set of beliefs about the role of libraries in a democratic society. There is a very great danger that we'll miss what is important about the public library service.[13]

A new version of the standards for England was produced in 2004. New Welsh ones have now been published to supersede those introduced in 2002; it is anticipated that these will be achieved by March 2005. Their relevance as regards library buildings is discussed in Chapters 3 and 4.

ROLES, RESOURCES AND COMMUNITIES

To fulfil satisfactorily the IFLA/UNESCO roles of providing access to knowledge, information, works of imagination and cultural experiences, the public library must have satisfactory resources:

- material in all formats
- adequate levels of staffing
- sufficient funds[14] and, it might be added,
- satisfactory information and communications technology – hardware and infrastructure
- a suitable building, although not all library provision is necessarily provided from a static service point.

As well as having adequate resources, the public library will need to be informed about, and consult with, the community it is to serve. In other words it should involve local citizens in the development of the library service.[15] This is especially true as regards the library and information needs of particular community groups, if resources are to be deployed satisfactorily. Consultation is particularly important when a new building or improved accommodation is being planned, because of the opportunities such projects offer for change and development. Both community needs analysis and public consultation are dealt with in Chapter 7.

In addition to a knowledge of the community to be served, the librarian must also be aware of general social and other trends that might affect local provision, such as:

- demographic change
- change in employment patterns
- political change
- educational change

- technological change
- economic change.[16]

Such changes are characterized in the UK by alterations in population structure; increasing demand for a 'flexible' workforce; an emphasis on choice in public services; the need for better educated and skilled employees; the change towards lifelong learning and skills training; and the range of electronic formats that nowadays co-exist with the book. Other factors include changing family structures, the 24-hour society, and increased leisure time. Also, as noted in Chapter 2 and later in this chapter, cultural institutions, including public libraries, are expected to contribute to the government's wider social, economic and political objectives.

People places, an Australian guide to planning public library buildings in New South Wales, spells out the need to identify trends likely to affect their function and design in the coming years. It recognizes that some trends are peculiar to New South Wales, while others are also found overseas. Those affecting Western societies, including the UK, can be listed thus:

- an ageing population, of whom a significant number may have physical and other disabilities
- the speed of developments in information and communications technology, giving rise to the problem of the information-rich and information-poor in society
- the multicultural nature of society, due to immigration, economic migration and the arrival of asylum seekers
- the existence of indigenous cultures, as in Wales and other parts of the UK
- competition from other providers of information, education and entertainment
- the changing nature of rural and urban communities.[17]

For the UK, further 'drivers for change', such as increasing population mobility and new forms of democracy (which includes electronic voting), and their possible implications for public libraries are discussed in *21st century libraries*.[18]

INFLUENCES FOR CHANGE AND DEVELOPMENT

The purpose and roles of public libraries in the UK, the identity of their intended users, and the ways in which they should serve their communities, have been the results of a variety of national as well as international influences. The significance of the Public Library and Museums Act 1964, which made public library provision mandatory in England and Wales for the first time, has already been noted. After the Act, the subsequent development of public libraries owed much to the various research reports produced under the auspices of, for example, the then Department of Education and Science (the Library and Information Series) and the British Library.

The late 1980s to the present day have seen a plethora of further reports from, or sponsored by, such bodies as the Audit Commission, the Department of Culture, Media and Sport (or its predecessor, the Department of National Heritage) or from think tanks and foundations like Demos and Laser. Often repetitive of earlier work, and with laboured titles, they say what's right and what's wrong with public libraries and generally advocate a great deal of change, development and innovation – even moneymaking through income generation or fees for services. They often, however, make interesting comments about the location, design and quality of public library buildings and these are summarized towards the end of this chapter. Through its publications on planning and design, including those on library buildings, CABE (the Commission for Architecture and the Built Environment) is of particular importance to the subject matter of this book. Funded by central government, it aims to promote quality in the built environment in England.[19]

In noting these influences, a number of which will be referred to in this and subsequent chapters, the work of the Library Association (now the Chartered Institute of Library and Information Professionals or CILIP) should not be overlooked. Its reports and statements have been used widely to inform and assist change and the further development of public library work. Of particular importance have been the professional guidelines produced by CILIP's groups for work in specialist fields, such as those for local studies, and children and young people.[20] Both of the latter include guidance on the kind of accommodation required for these important aspects of the public library service.

Internationally the work of IFLA and its sections has been important for the formulation of specialist standards and guidelines which cover library services to (amongst other user groups) hospital patients and disabled people in the community, and multicultural populations.[21] The Library Buildings and Equipment Section of IFLA is concerned with the design and construction of libraries of all kinds all over the world. It holds seminars, arranges study tours and publishes a newsletter and seminar proceedings.[22]

Change and innovation, however, is not derived solely from reports, research, statements, standards and guidelines. Individual library services pioneer change and good practice, reflecting excellent leadership, better resources (if sometimes of only a temporary nature), and ideas that reflect community needs. Research publications of the kind mentioned earlier usually draw on such library services as models and examples for others and today there is great emphasis on learning from best practice. Generally speaking, there is nothing new in this approach, as it was through the pioneering work of individual UK public library systems in the last 150 years that overall service development took place.

LOCAL GOVERNMENT REORGANIZATION

Like other public services, libraries have been much affected by the state of the economy and by local government reorganizations of the 1970s (the 1960s in London) and the 1990s. That of the 1970s created larger local authorities serving larger populations. These enjoyed the benefits of greater resources, leading to improved library provision and the employment of specialist staff.[23] It was suggested this reorganization would bring about:

• the dual use of library buildings by school and community populations
• the use of buildings outside library hours as local centres
• an increased cultural role for librarians, leading to more cultural and social complexes.[24]

Further local government reorganization of the 1990s undid some of the 1970s structure in that a number of unitary authorities (with responsibility for libraries) were created in England alongside existing authorities. Many of these unitaries, such as Portsmouth and Southampton, had been previously independent library authorities. In Wales and Scotland public libraries are the responsibility of their respective 22 and 32 single-tier councils,[25] while in Northern Ireland they continue to be under the five area education and library boards.

In spite of the benefits for libraries conferred by local government reorganization, the reality by the late 1990s was one of continuing financial cuts leading to reduced opening hours and branch closure, coupled with fewer book issues and reduced usage,[26] although there have been improvements more recently, as regards opening hours and library use, for instance. In 1997 library buildings were found to be in a state of disrepair with a 'need to spend £600m on building refurbishment to bring library buildings up to acceptable standards'.[27] A figure of £650 million for repairs and refurbishment in England alone had been estimated earlier, and it is this figure that is repeated in parliament's 2005 Select Committee on Public Libraries report.[28] Whatever the figure, it is likely to have risen due to inflation and further building deterioration. In Wales in 2002, it was noted that

> Many of the library buildings in Wales date from the early 20th century and are in need of some regeneration themselves to meet the needs of today's users.[29]

The Audit Commission's *Building better library services* (2002) reiterated these problems, noting also the poor location as well as the poor condition of buildings. The publication urged librarians to:

• have a clear vision as why and how services are provided
• be accountable for the use of resources
• think about services from the user's point of view
• provide the services people wanted

- improve access, including physical access to buildings
- make services easy to use
- develop non-user awareness
- learn from bookshops.[30]

Both library managers and councils can be held accountable for delivering an improved service through local plans, best value review, comprehensive performance assessment, and by meeting library standards.

As with *Who's in charge?*, discussed in Chapter 2, Charles Leadbeater's *Overdue: how to create a modern public library service* claimed that, without change, public libraries could fade away by the end of the decade. Libraries were asked to build on their traditional strengths while making themselves more appealing to people as 'curiosity satisfaction centres'. *Overdue* recommended the creation of library 'hubs' in shopping centres, drawing lessons from the retail environment and mixing leisure and learning. It also recommended the creation of a national library development agency (NLDA) which would develop a public library network and 'turn libraries around in the next decade'.[31] The NLDA idea has not been generally well received by librarians, nor the negativity of the report, although the author argued that overstatement was necessary to ensure that action would result.[32]

Librarians do not necessarily find change difficult nor are all their libraries in terminal decline. Essex Library Service's work with reader development activities and its provision of Sunday opening, computer workstations, and a web-based interactive citizen's information service all suggest that public libraries are becoming 'more firmly established with the majority of people as the places to find support for learning, reading and creative leisure'.[33] Indeed, while many countries around the world face similar challenges and difficulties to the UK, there does not appear to be a feeling that their public library systems are in decline, terminally or otherwise. In Australia, which has some similar problems to the UK, including poorly located, crowded and unattractive buildings, there is recognition of the need to improve public libraries in a variety of ways. They are, however, a heavily used and appreciated community provision, and research demonstrates the value of libraries and 'their potential as the focus for learning cities or communities'.[34] In Denmark, Slagelse County Library has demonstrated how it will meet the demands for change in the twenty-first century through, amongst other things, a remodelling of its library premises.[35]

CHOICES FOR THE PUBLIC LIBRARY

Given the wide range of roles that the public library can serve – education, recreation, information and culture – and the many groups that will make up a community, librarians have some hard choices to make as to:

- the public library's overall mission
- which of the above roles to adopt and what emphasis to give to them
- which particular groups to target for library service, without ignoring the 'general' library user.

With these decisions in place, the librarian can then decide what services and facilities to offer (in general and to particular groups) and what the implications of these decisions might be for a library building. Before considering this latter issue, however, the public library mission, its potential roles, and its service to the community at large and to particular groups, need to be considered. Guidance in this area of decision-making is offered by a number of American Library Association publications, including the seminal *Planning and role setting for public libraries*, which, for example, looks at the role of the public library in the community it is to serve.[36]

TARGETING USERS: INDIVIDUALS AND GROUPS

'Libraries are for all' has long been part of the public library's philosophy and this is certainly true in terms of its accessibility to anyone wishing to make use of it.

However, public libraries have traditionally targeted particular groups in their community. In the beginning this was largely the general adult and child reader but now services are being provided more specifically, for example, to business people, local and family historians, the housebound, those in hospital or prison, teenagers, the visually and hearing impaired, ethnic minority groups, the unemployed, local organizations and the local authority. People can often fall into more than one of these categories.

Potential public library users are categorized by the *IFLA/UNESCO Guidelines* as being:

- people of all ages and at all stages of life
- individuals and groups of people with special needs
- institutions within the wider community.

The *Guidelines* recognize that 'it is not always possible to serve all users to the same level' and that priorities must be established.[37] Priorities will be based on the social trends and developments (as noted above) and on local needs, as well as the requirements of government. In the latter case funding may be available to implement and support service provision, although usually for a limited period.

Children and young people are a priority for public library service and the Irish *Standards*, for example, state that one of the function of a public library 'must be [as] a resource for children and young people'. The library acts as their 'gateway to the world of knowledge' and as a centre for literacy, information skills and culture.[38] And 'children's services growing in importance' was one of the ten trends pointed out in *Better public libraries*.[39]

In the UK, and in the light of cultural, demographic and technological changes, *Start with the child* (2002) looked at the fundamental questions posed by the earlier report, *Investing in children*.[40] It examined the needs of children under four headings, one of which was: 'appropriate environments and services', spelt out as:

- a safe and welcoming environment with spaces which support diverse activities and provide a haven for users of different ages; the needs of older children for their own space, including study space and casual seating, were noted
- technology to support and develop reading and access to information
- impressive and interactive displays, activities and exhibitions
- libraries that are more like shops, encouraging a visit and providing a place to 'hang out'
- a welcome for groups, and the need to treat children with respect as individuals.[41]

New and refurbished library buildings provide the opportunity to rethink provision and accommodation for children and young people, who are all too often given an inadequate space allowance, and with insufficient attention paid to the needs of young adults. The National Library Board of Singapore has remedied this latter criticism by opening a community public library in a shopping mall for young adults from 18–35. It aims through its design to create a place that young people like to visit, with popular bands playing in its performance space and users singing and dancing to them.[42] Such 'lifestyle libraries' for young people are attracting increased notice in the public library worlds of Germany, Spain and elsewhere.[43]

Attention must also be given as to how the library will meet the needs of adults, community groups and those users unable to visit the library or requiring special provision of one sort or another. Much of the targeting is currently concerned with making libraries more socially inclusive, as discussed later in this chapter, the argument being that of the two models for service delivery – a focus on the individual or on the group. A shift from the former to the latter should take place: 'Library services would be more targeted and positive action would be taken to meet the needs of particular groups'.[44] In reality the two 'models' have to some extent always existed side by side and 'particular groups' in the context of the quotations are those believed to be socially excluded from public library service.

MISSION AND ROLES

The overall mission, purpose or vision for the public library, and the precise roles that it is to serve, is only partially answered by the four functions noted earlier: education, information, recreation and culture. The *UNESCO/IFLA Guidelines* offer the following statement of public library purpose:

The primary purposes of the public library are to provide resources and services in a variety of media to meet the needs of individuals and groups for education, information, personal development, including recreation and leisure. They have an important role in the development and maintenance of a democratic society by giving the individual access to a wide and varied range of knowledge, ideas and opinions.[45]

Individual countries may have formulated a national statement for their own public libraries which individual library systems can then adapt. Or library systems can formulate their own statement to reflect their local circumstances. A UK national mission statement for the public library service was formulated and approved in 1991 as an authoritative statement which individual library services could adapt to their own situations. This is shown as Figure 1.1.

The public library is a major community facility whose purpose is to enable and encourage individuals or groups of individuals to gain unbiased access to books, information, knowledge and works of creative imagination which will:

* encourage their active participation in cultural, democratic and economic activities;
* enable them to participate in educational development through formal or informal programmes;
* assist them to make positive use of leisure time;
* promote reading and literacy as basic skills necessary for active involvement in these activities;
* encourage the use of information and an awareness of its value.

The local and community nature of the service requires special emphasis to be placed on the needs and aspirations of the local community, and on the provision of services to particular groups within it, while also providing access to wider resources through regional and national networks.

Figure 1.1   UK Public Library Service Mission Statement[46]

The 1991 UK mission statement has many similarities to that in the 2001 IFLA/UNESCO *Guidelines*, although it is 'book'-, rather than 'media'- oriented. Additionally it draws attention to the library as a major community facility and shows a concern for its value in encouraging economic activities and 'the use of information and an awareness of its value'.

Perhaps reflecting 'the needs and aspirations of the local community' part of the mission statement, the 1995 *Public library review* suggested that the then Department of National Heritage (DNH) 'should set a new comprehensive framework for public library services that will allow considerable flexibility in local choice'.[47] This objective, it was believed, could be achieved without new legislation, or the amendment of the existing 1964 act. At the same time, however, the *Review* said that the DNH should issue *Public library policy and planning guidance* notes that would:

- be persuasive, not coercive
- assist in the formulation of a broad strategic local plan, stating priorities and emphases
- explain the four principal library purposes (or roles) and 13 core functions.

The four purposes were described as follows:

- meeting the demands of future generations
- creating a community asset
- operating a beneficial service
- meeting the needs of occasional users.

The purposes and the unstructured list of 13 core functions, that included services such as the loaning of books and other material, and information and local studies provision, appear an odd mixture.

The core list's relationship to the four purposes is not explained and includes a number of 'core functions' that relate to library buildings: for example, the public library as a familiar, relaxing place (safe, warm and well lit).[48]

The framework envisaged in the *Review* eventually appeared in 2003 as the Department of Culture, Media and Sport report, *Framework for the future*, which plans the development of public libraries in the constituent countries of the UK up to 2013. This *Framework* is a 'long-term strategic vision ... to encourage imaginative innovation and greater operational effectiveness and efficiency, adapted to local need and circumstances'.[49] This, like earlier reports, is about the necessity for change and development in public libraries to meet the needs of a modern world.

The report says that libraries need a modern mission based on evolution, public value, distinctiveness and the local interpretation of national programmes. It proposes as central to the modern mission of the public library that its current focus should be on its roles in developing reading and informal learning, access to digital skills and services (including e-government) and building community cohesion and civic values. These are not really new roles but the means of achieving desired outcomes from the existing roles such as education, and emphasizing the social role of the public library.

When planning a new or improved library building, the librarian must be clear which roles the building is to fulfil and how these will be reflected in the services and facilities that will be accommodated. The librarian has the choice of following the services highlighted in *Framework for the future*, including potential new ones (such as hosting and managing websites for local community groups) or incorporating *Framework's* service ideas – in whole or in part – into its own response to community needs. Such a response might include services in the cultural and arts fields, largely ignored by *Framework* and *Better public libraries.*

ROLE IN EDUCATION

The educational purpose of the public library, its earliest role and continuing strength, is seen as:

- supporting formal and informal education
- facilitating lifelong learning
- supporting literacy, considered the 'key to education and knowledge'[50]
- supporting the acquisition of new proficiencies; computer and information skills and visual literacy, for example.

Today, the term 'learning' is preferred to the more passive, formal 'education'. 'Learning' is seen as an active process and covers the 'work libraries do with the education sector and with individuals and communities outside it'.[51] Education and learning are both high political priorities, as demonstrated by changes to the school curriculum (with emphases on literacy and numeracy), the expansion of further and higher education and the emergence of different ways of learning, such as e-learning and distance learning, through the Open University and other universities, for example. Politicians are keen to remedy the situation in the adult population where many lack formal qualifications and one in five adults has poor literacy skills.

There is also a desire to create a Learning Age culture that sees learning as a lifelong process; where

> ... individuals and communities take charge of their own learning and recognize its importance both in meeting their own goals and in building a strong economy and an inclusive society.[52]

The Learning and Skills Councils and 'Learndirect' are outcomes of this approach. The Museums, Libraries and Archives Council (MLA) is working on a strategy, which will include the establishment of regional learning and support units, to improve and advance the learning role of libraries (and museums and archives) and attract new users.

Activities in support of the varied educational role of the public library include work with schools, homework clubs, reading programmes, holiday language classes, study circles, ICT classes to assist learning, finding information and reader development,[53] adult literacy, and providing study space for those unable to study elsewhere. Even the most basic (and not particularly attractive) study space will be well used if there is a need for it.

Public libraries are urged to cooperate with educational institutions – schools and colleges – in teaching the use of information resources. The educational role of the public library also allows people to develop personal, independent learning, as well as assisting those engaged more formally in the educational process. The Stockholm Public

Library Visitor Pathways project had amongst its objectives helping users to act more independently and providing a virtual service in an easy and accessible way.[54]

ROLE IN INFORMATION

The *UNESCO/IFLA Guidelines* consider information to be a basic human right and that public libraries should, therefore:

- collect, organize and exploit information, including business, local or community information
- provide access to information sources, including the Internet
- act as a community memory – through the provision of a local studies, local history or heritage service, possibly in conjunction with museum and archive services
- act as an electronic gateway to the information world.[55]

The Scottish public library standards endorse the importance of reference and information services for communities and also suggest that:

- consideration should be given to the public library providing an information service to the local authority
- service points should offer material on welfare rights, employment, law, job and career information, and so on.[56]

Public libraries in the UK are encouraged to cooperate with other agencies and often provide accommodation for one-stop shops (local authority help centres), the Citizens' Advice Bureau, careers offices and tourist information centres. The People's Network, initially funded by the National Lottery, offers free access to information sources, including the Internet at public libraries throughout the UK. In spite of being an innovative and successful service, the People's Network has been described as

> ... capital-rich and revenue-poor, conforming to the popular Whitehall notion that buildings and equipment, once built and bought, run themselves and in time become services to the public.[57]

Such electronic gateways may not necessarily be accessed from a library building but from a village hall, for example: Newport Library Service in Wales plan an information point at a local supermarket.[58] The availability of such facilities can help create 'e-government' – the electronic interaction between citizens and the state. Telecentres – providing access to computers primarily for business purposes – are to be found in library and non-library settings. For example, Birmingham Central Library is developing and sustaining the city's creative industries with its business information service – 'Business insight'. It also opened its first business branch in a converted custard factory.[59]

As part of their reference and information provision, public libraries are responsible for a local studies service. This collects, organizes and makes available (nowadays often electronically) printed and other information about a locality. Use of this 'community memory' has increased considerably in the UK in recent years due to an upsurge of interest in local and family history and the desire to establish a 'community identity'. This local studies provision may take place in separate premises from the usual library service point, and this development will be discussed in Chapter 11.

ROLE IN RECREATION AND PERSONAL DEVELOPMENT

The library's role in recreation and leisure is covered in the IFLA/UNESCO *Guidelines* by the concept of personal development, which includes:

- personal creativity and the pursuit of new interests
- access to knowledge and works of imagination
- basic education, awareness and life skills, relating to such matters as health, literacy and jobs[60]
- user education.

As *A manifesto for London's libraries* puts it:

> Libraries feed the human spirit, fuelling the desire to create something beautiful or meaningful. They satisfy the need to share in an uplifting experience through a novel, poetry, video or piece of music. As well as such permanent sources of inspiration, libraries also promote a wealth of fulfilling experiences.[61]

This personal development role clearly overlaps with those concerned with education and information provision as well as the social role of the library. In the late 1970s it was said that

> The social role of librarians is in its infancy but an increasing number of the profession believe that involvement in literacy campaigns, for example, or the provision of information to help people to understand an increasingly complex society, is a vitally important part of a librarian's work.[62]

People undoubtedly use the public library to support their hobbies, sport and other leisure interests, for help with personal issues, to acquire new skills, and to read imaginative literature:

> I believe that libraries should promote equality of opportunity in a society in which knowledge, ideas and information are increasingly important in work and hobbies, as a source of individual identity and a focus for a sense of community.[63]

But the library service stands accused of being one that 'largely supplies fiction to those who could well afford to pay for it'.[64] The public library emphasis in its personal development role is seen often as being on the loan of books, a large percentage of which is fiction – not only fiction but often 'light' fiction and even comics and teenage pop magazines. This 'dumbing down' (or 'widening access', depending on the point of view) would appear to be confirmed to some extent by the fact that contemporary modern authors (those appearing in the Man Booker and other prize shortlists, for example) do not figure in the top 20 authors for adults in the Public Lending Right's lists. But then public libraries have long given up the idea of restricting their stock to worthy and classic literature, or their music provision to classical and folk music, for example.

Recent reports have taken public libraries further down this road by encouraging them to make more copies of best-sellers available more quickly to readers. With this view of the supposed leisure emphasis of public libraries in mind, the Institute of Leisure and Amenity Management argued in 1995 that libraries are 'essentially a community leisure service and should be managed as such'. Therefore 'they are best served as part of strategically planned integrated leisure services'.[65]

Given the pressure on resources, lack of investment (except for specific projects), and financial cuts, libraries should make a decision as to which business they are in – broadly represented by the education/leisure divide – and 'pursue their chosen route'.[66]

There is great interest at present in promoting reading development amongst children, young people and adults through, for example, high-quality contemporary black fiction, special collections for older men, poetry and local autobiography.[67] A feature of this development has been book-based television publicity, reading schemes for children, and the formation of readers' groups or circles in libraries to discuss contemporary books and for other literary activity. The IFLA/UNESCO *Manifesto* argues for the imagination and creativity of children and young people to be stimulated and for 'creating and strengthening the reading habits in children from an early age'.[68]

This emphasis on reading reflects the part that libraries can play in combating illiteracy; this is estimated at around seven million people in the UK. It is suggested that public libraries should form part of a national strategy for literacy.[69]

ROLE IN CULTURE AND THE ARTS

The cultural purpose of the public library is achieved by:

- providing a focus for cultural and artistic development in the community
- helping to shape and support its cultural identity
- reflecting the cultural variety in the community, such as languages spoken and read and cultural traditions:[70] in Wales, for example, libraries are seen as 'vital to the growth of a bilingual culture'.[71]

This cultural function will be reflected in the range of library materials provided, the establishment of partnerships with local organizations, the provision of space for cultural activities, and the organization of cultural programmes which reflect local culture or cultures. The content of its collection and work of the local studies service should also reflect this local cultural focus.

Since the days of the lecture room, which might be used for a talk, film show, concert or exhibition, public libraries in the UK have been involved in cultural activity and supported the arts. Whether as 'animateur', or as a library professional with responsibility for a gallery, museum or theatre, or because of the provision of sound recordings, videos, works of art (including pictures), sheet music and play sets, librarians continue to demonstrate their commitment to culture and the arts.

After the Second World War, the term 'extension activities' was used to describe some of this cultural function, which 'perhaps implies an optional extra to the core of public library provision, and there are many in librarianship who still take this view'.[72] Encouraged by the provisions of the 1964 legislation, many newly built libraries of the 1960s and 1970s included features such as a meeting room, a gallery, exhibition and performance space.

Further encouragement came from the 1975 report, *Public libraries and cultural activities*.[73] The Central Library and Arts Centre at Rotherham (1976), Leighton Buzzard Library and Arts Centre (1979) and Hexham Queen's Hall Library and Arts Centre (1981) all provided a variety of non-library spaces, including a café (in Hexham's case, a restaurant), and are notable examples from the period. More recent libraries, such as those in Worcestershire at Evesham (1990) and Kidderminster (1997), Sunderland City Library and Arts Centre (1995) and Cootehill Public Library and Arts Centre (Cavan County, Eire, 2001) also provide performance or other spaces for the arts. In Wales in 2002, libraries were being asked to ensure 'that new buildings have adequate exhibition space and meeting/activity space'.[74]

This relationship between libraries, culture and the arts has continued to develop due to:

- departmental responsibilities of librarians, that include the arts, especially following local government reorganization in the 1970s
- community librarianship – seen as indistinguishable from community arts
- the relevance of multicultural arts
- the fact that 'libraries took the opportunity provided by local authority equal opportunities to contribute towards the support and understanding of different cultures'.[75]

Further influences came from the requirement to create Local Cultural Strategies, the seeking of partnerships between libraries and arts organizations (both within and outside the local authority), and because cultural and arts activity could be seen to contribute to local authority objectives, such as social inclusion. Librarians needed to demonstrate that 'there was a role for libraries to play in strengthening the support infrastructure for the arts at local, regional and national level'.[76]

What libraries do for the arts can be put into four broad categories:

- the use of library premises for arts activities on behalf of the community or to promote libraries
- developing audiences for reading, literature and other arts

- providing collections and resources to support the arts community
- providing information and publicity for arts events and opportunities.[77]

The IFLA/UNESCO *Guidelines* state that

> The public library should be a key agency in the local community for the collection, preservation and promotion of local culture in all its diversity.[78]

Many of the activities noted above will help promote local culture, while local studies collections should be concerned with the collection and preservation of its records. The public library as part of an arts or cultural complex is considered further in Chapter 4, where the Norfolk and Norwich Millenium Library (Figure 1.2) is reviewed.

SOCIAL ROLE

The public library has always been a place of both formal and informal resort and its value in this regard, especially for some sections of society, is being increasingly recognized.[79] The public library's social role is reflected in:

- its importance as a public space and meeting place
- the opportunities it provides for informal contact
- providing a positive social experience that can contribute to an individual's feeling of well-being[80]
- its contribution to social inclusion.

The library as a meeting place

Much is now made of the role of the library as a meeting place, both in the outside setting of the library and within the building itself, especially those libraries serving communities with few 'people places'. The public library, however, has always been a place of resort – a place to be with others, yet alone; to fill in time purposively or not; to reflect, relax or react. It is a place that is different from other kinds of place, with its own conventions of public behaviour.

As a place of resort, people enter a familiar and friendly environment, make informal contact and can engage in library-based activities. More used than almost any other town centre facility (public, commercial or retail), the public library is seen as a 'safe' and 'neutral' environment. It is a place that crosses 'the boundaries between learning and leisure, enlightenment and entertainment, casual use and dedicated study':[81] for all and open to all. Libraries have also been described as 'hangouts' or 'third places' – neither home nor work, where 'visitors are not encumbered by the role either of host or of guest'.[82]

Increasingly libraries are being persuaded to be more than places of resort and to be meeting places – people-friendly communal spaces – places to hang out, to get away from the solitude of computer use, to enjoy a cup of coffee with others, a place for a

Figure 1.2   Norfolk and Norwich Millennium Library, the Forum, Norwich (2001)
Source: The author

family outing, to check and send e-mails, and to make new friends. In order to create this ambience and increase general library use, libraries have been encouraged to turn their backs on past conventions. Rules about eating and drinking have been relaxed and noise disregarded, and libraries have been urged to be less bureaucratic in their dealings with users. Public space is allowed to become private space, with the conflicts that can arise over behaviour and noise in what might be a largely open plan, one-room library. It is commented that

> the library has become a popular meeting place, with noise rather than quiet a prevalent feature at entry and exit points, at counters, and in most parts of the library other than those clearly designated for study and research.[83]

This relaxed attitude to behaviour, and the changes implemented by libraries as regards stock provision for example, have not been universally welcomed and form part of the criticism that libraries (along with other public institutions like the BBC and the universities) are lowering their standards: 'confusing excellence with elitism'[84] and 'polluting the culture of serious reading'. Public libraries stand charged with being

> ... sad, confusing places for older users ... Libraries have not so much changed as progressed into a chaotic compromise between cut-price high-tech and buying and, indeed, selling.[85]

It is easy to dismiss this as an 'oldie' rant but efforts should be made to meet these criticisms rather than seeking to favour a new audience over the old.

Social inclusion

But it is in the matter of social inclusion that librarians and their libraries are being challenged currently. Some would argue that social inclusion has long been part, both directly and indirectly, of the public library's purpose. Indirectly, it has provided refuge to the out-of-work and homeless in the now old-fashioned, spacious and warm newsroom. Directly, its service agenda includes the provision of books and other materials to those who are housebound, in hospital or in prison. Such services have a social, even welfare, dimension, providing social contact, relieving loneliness, assisting rehabilitation, and alleviating a distressful experience. 'Outreach' took this concern for those unable (or unlikely) to visit the library a stage further by

> ... taking stock and staff into the community to read stories to children in parks or manning book collections and information points in local markets or other strategic locations.[86]

People may be excluded from participation in many aspects of everyday life, such as using libraries, because of unemployment, discrimination, bad health or family breakdown. *Mapping social inclusion in publicly-funded libraries in Wales* sees the disadvantaged as falling into four groups: the disadvantage being classed as physical, mental, economic or locational. It recognizes there may be some overlap between the four groups and that social inclusion is also an issue for libraries in the higher and further education sectors.[87]

Set up in 1997, the Social Exclusion Unit tries to combat this problem in England and liaises with home country administrations. For example, Merton Library and Heritage Service have addressed inequalities by changes to the staffing structure and by adopting appropriate policies to create a service based on principles of social justice and equality.[88]

Government guidance for English local authorities on social inclusion suggested in 1999 that library and information services should 'develop their role as community resource centres providing access to communication as well as information'. Action plan challenges included sustainability and long-term resource issues; community ownership and community partnership; integrating the library's role within a wider geographical framework; and demonstrating benefits and outcomes.[89] The guidance document provides examples of buildings-based social inclusion:

- in a deprived area of Eastbourne, the library service was reorganized and offered at five locations close to an under-used library and aimed at different target markets
- in the Moss Side area of Manchester, the Powerhouse has developed as a youth centre, with library and information centre, ICT suite, music and arts studios, fitness centre, sports hall, performance area, café, crèche and residential wing
- Trafford has integrated three of its small libraries into existing well-used facilities, a school and two leisure centres
- at Peacehaven, the library has developed into a local resource centre.[90]

> Public libraries are especially powerful agents for inclusiveness. They are open to all, non-threatening and non-judgmental. They are frequently the only point of access to information and learning that is available to the deprived, the excluded or the disaffected.[91]

Open to all?, a report about social inclusion and public libraries, includes a review of the libraries' record in this area and concludes that 'UK libraries have adopted only weak, voluntary and "take it or leave it" approaches' and that services for the excluded 'remain patchy, uneven and often time-limited'. This results in under-utilization of the public library by excluded groups, insufficient information about their 'needs and views' and the creation of barriers that 'exclude many disadvantaged people'.[92]

There has been little discussion of the problems that might arise from libraries becoming more inclusive towards the seriously disadvantaged, such as the homeless. In the mid-1990s, the Enoch Pratt Free Library in Baltimore installed railings on window sills to prevent homeless people sleeping on them and children from climbing on them and coming to harm. Homeless people also used the washroom for prolonged periods and to bathe and wash their clothes, necessitating the installation of a buzzer system. Opposition to the railings resulted in a demonstration by homeless people and others.[93]

Public libraries, according to *Open to all?*, will 'in order to make a real difference ... need to undergo rapid transformation and change'.[94] Among the report's recommendations for change is

> ... a recasting of the image and identity of the public library to link it more closely with the cultures of the excluded communities and social groups.[95]

The public library, it is argued, needs to be rebranded, 'so that the new image is one of a proactive, friendly, relevant and easily accessible environment.'[96] In general, no one would disagree with these comments but voices are raised against the social inclusion approach in the professional press, seeing the library being hijacked for social work.[97] Questions of branding and image are discussed in Chapter 9.

AN EVER-EXPANDING FOCUS

The nature of a public library service within a particular community will depend on the extent to which a local interpretation of the above roles reflect community needs and circumstances. A public library building should be designed with a clear understanding of the purpose and roles of that particular building. But the roles a library plays may alter over time – roles may be upgraded or downgraded or new dimensions introduced. New roles may appear to materialize, as in *Framework for the future*, but can probably be accommodated within existing ones. Public libraries were founded in the UK largely from educational motives, but the priority assigned to this or to the other main public library roles of information, recreation and culture, have never been formalized in the UK. *Framework for the future* emphasizes the provision of particular services and facilities reflecting particular roles, although the cultural role is largely ignored.

The public's and politicians' view of the public library is likely to be that of a leisure-oriented service, while acknowledging the good work and achievements done in respect of the other library roles. The lack of a firm legal description of public libraries' roles, as opposed to the political directions suggested in the *Framework* document, has both advantages and disadvantages for the provision of library service and the buildings that house them. The disadvantage is that the library becomes an ever-expanding focus for new services, facilities and amenities, such as 'family space'.[98]

A 1998 social audit of public libraries divides this 'expanding' range of functions into:

- established roles – education, information, and so on
- social and caring roles – personal development, social cohesion (by fostering connections between groups and communities), community empowerment and self-determination, local image and identity, and health and well-being
- economic issues – business information, supporting job-seeking and training opportunities, regeneration (due to the physical presence of the library) and tourism.[99]

The social and caring roles acknowledge the additional benefits that flow from the presence of a building and the library services it houses. Economic issues emphasize (with the exception perhaps of training) long-standing library service activities, reflecting established roles which have been reconsidered in this 'economic' light. 'The data suggest that public libraries enrich the lives of many people. The social audit technique makes that enriching process visible.'[100]

Making decisions as to the nature of that enrichment still seems to demand an agreed 'core' and 'a prioritized list of other activities', if the public library is not to be overwhelmed.[101] Perhaps *Framework for the future* offers this, responding also in part to the UNISON view that what is needed is a national strategy for public libraries, within which it would be possible 'to operate with clear and achievable aims'.[102]

PROBLEMS AND UNRESOLVED ISSUES

The worth of the public library may be universally recognized and promoted nowadays but this is not to say that its existence is an untroubled one. Inadequate and dated legislation, underfunding, lack of specialist staff, the (sometimes conflicting) needs of different community members and groups, and the differing demands of changing political masters can make delivery of a satisfactory library service a difficult challenge for librarians. Certainly in the UK the purpose, roles and priorities of the public library are not clearly defined in law. Who are public libraries for? In a democratic, egalitarian and socially inclusive society the answer will no doubt be 'everybody'. This only exacerbates the great British problem, identified by Comedia, of libraries 'never able to say no' and leads to the dissatisfaction expressed by this newspaper letter writer:

> The old-fashioned silent reference libraries – a life-saver in the past for disadvantaged people who through no fault of their own had missed out on education – have largely disappeared in favour of people-friendly communal spaces, where children scream, mobile phones are used and conversations held without any attempt to lower voices.[103]

Public libraries are often urged to market themselves. Marketing means that an organization or public service must ask: What business are we in? Who do we serve? What products and services should we provide? This implies making choices about roles, services and target audiences. In other words attempting to be 'all things to all people' is a recipe for disaster rather than success.

The UK Audit Commission concluded in 2002 – largely reiterating its 1986 performance review statement – that 'Councils ... need to fundamentally challenge why and how they provide library services ... explicitly outlining the services that people can expect'.[104] There can be no real quarrel with such a statement, whose implementation would reflect local needs and priorities, a point reiterated in *Better public libraries*: 'Each library will develop its own bespoke programme and service priorities'.[105] Such decisions, however, could not be made without taking into account any formal national concept of the role of public libraries as might be enshrined in legislation or a national library and information plan.

LIBRARY BUILDING ISSUES

In summary, planning public library buildings and the services and facilities they seek to provide are beset by the following range of issues:

- the lack of clarity in the library legislation – this means libraries are subject to changing views of changing governments and there is a reluctance to enforce existing legislation
- the range of potential roles or functions – raising questions of:
  - the relative importance of education and recreation – it has been suggested that because of the Internet public librarians should promote entertainment as the overall public library mission.[106] Others argue that the 'traditional mission of the public library: supporting the self-education of the citizenry ... has been devalued of late in favour of popularizing the library to attract more users'.[107]
  - the relative importance of information and recreation
  - whether libraries exist primarily to serve the individual or groups
  - whether to emphasize personal development or group education
  - taking on the functions of other institutions or businesses (gallery, shop, restaurant, café, and so on)
  - inadequate funding – the reliance on one-off funding for development[108]
  - the commercialization of culture – private interest encroachment on public libraries with its potential to modify 'the basic premise of a library's cultural mission to the detriment of the public and the institution itself'.[109]

SOME POSSIBLE REMEDIES

A summary of the building-related issues brought out in this chapter that will need to be taken into account during planning and design include:

- the need to adapt and change for the early twenty-first century – public libraries can no longer be sustained by the view that they are 'a good thing'
- creating public libraries that will be landmarks in their community
- finding better locations: 'the feasibility of placing libraries in village shops, and developing kiosks or micro-libraries in diverse locations ... [these outlets] could include shopping centres, railway, bus and motorway service stations, and other places that attract sustained flows of people'[110]
- considering co-location and sharing of premises with other local authority services
- building and running one or two regional library centres or 'hyperlibraries' as models for future development of such centres[111]
- considering partnership funding for capital and other projects, as described in Chapter 2
- improving the appeal and signage of library buildings – adopting the ethos of the bookstore, supermarket and other retail outlets
- responding to the information and communications technology environment (perhaps electronic links to the home) and developing public libraries as communications centres for a mobile population

- remedying the physical neglect of existing libraries, to include better cleaning and maintenance
- providing better amenities and facilities (toilets, café and crèche, for example)
- encouraging use by young people (by providing games consoles, for example) and other infrequent or non-user groups
- offering longer and more convenient opening hours to include evening and Sunday opening
- resolving the conflicts arising from multi-use space
  - meeting places for social interaction that clash with isolated spaces for thinking, reading, and quiet study or relaxation
  - good acoustics for live performances and muffling voices during library transactions
  - a visually stimulating environment versus non-distracting surroundings.[112]

The planning and design of public library buildings takes place against a background of a changing society, competing library roles and the requirement for service points to make a wider contribution to their local community as, for example, agencies for regeneration and social inclusion. Planning has to bear in mind also the demands for economy, efficiency and effectiveness, quality and accountability. The various stages of this planning process are discussed later, in Chapter 7.

NOTES

1   Doctorow, E.L. (1994), *New York Times* 27 March, 20.
2   General Consumer Council for Northern Ireland (1995), *Turning over a new leaf*, 2 vols, Belfast: GCC for NI.
3   Matarasso, F. (2000), 'The meaning of leadership in a cultural democracy: rethinking library values', *Logos* **11** (1), 38–44: 42.
4   The latest version is from 1994 and is now prepared in cooperation with IFLA. It is available in over 20 languages on its website: www.ifla.org/VII/s8/unesco/manif.htm.
5   *The public library service: IFLA/UNESCO guidelines for development* (2001), Munich: Saur.
6   *The public library service: IFLA/UNESCO guidelines for development* (2001), 1–2, 8, 9, 19.
7   *The public library service: IFLA/UNESCO guidelines for development* (2001), 14, 15.
8   *Public library and museums act 1964*, London: HMSO.
9   Phillips, B.J., Beck, T. and Maltby, A. (1977), *Public libraries: legislation, administration and finance*, London: Library Association and Chartered Institute of Public Finance and Accountancy, para 51(e).
10 *Review of the public library service in England and Wales* (1995), London: Aslib, 173.
11 Department of Culture, Media and Sport (2001), *Comprehensive, efficient and modern public libraries – standards and assessment*, London: DCMS.
12 Goulding, A. (2001), 'Setting the standard for comprehensive and efficient public library services', *Journal of librarianship and information science* **33** (2), 55–8.
13 Bob Usherwood, quoted in Rickett, J. (2000), 'Setting standards – at last', *Bookseller* (4923) 12 May, 30–31: 31.
14 *The public library service: IFLA/UNESCO guidelines for development* (2001), 11–12.
15 *The public library service: IFLA/UNESCO guidelines for development* (2001), 20–21.

16   *National network – local service: standards for the public library service in the Republic of Ireland* (1999), Dublin: Library Association of Ireland, 5–7.

17   Nesbitt, H. and Nield, B.V. (2000), *People places: a guide for public library buildings in New South Wales*, Sydney: Library Council of New South Wales, 11–17.

18   Worpole, K. (2004), *21st century libraries: changing forms, changing futures*, London: CABE and RIBA, 9–11.

19   www.cabe.org.uk.

20   Martin, D. (ed.) (2002), *Local studies libraries: Library Association guidelines for local studies in public libraries*, 2nd edn, London: Library Association; Blanchard, C. (ed.) (1997), *Children and young people: Library Association guidelines for public library services*, London: Library Association.

21   For a full listing, see *The public library service: IFLA/UNESCO guidelines for development* (2001), 110–11.

22   www.ifla.org/VII/s20/slbe.htm.

23   Department of Education and Science (1973*), Public library service: reorganization and after*, London: HMSO.

24   Phillips, B.J., Beck, T. and Maltby, A. (1977), paras 230, 232.

25   For a description of improvements, particularly as regards library buildings, in the Highlands Region of Scotland since local government reorganization, see Brownlee, S. (2001) 'High fliers', *Scottish libraries* **15** (1), 16–17.

26   UNISON (1997), *The future of the public library service*, London: Unison, 6.

27   UNISON (1997), 18.

28   Resource (2001), *Building on success: an action plan for public libraries*, London: Resource, 11. A draft consultation document; House of Commons, Culture, Media and Sport Committee (2005), *Public libraries: 3rd report of session 2004–05*, vol. 1, London: Stationery Office, 31.

29   *Public libraries ... open to all: contributing to a better Wales* [2002], Aberystwyth: Society of Chief Librarians Wales and CILIP Wales, 4.

30   Audit Commission (2002), *Building better library services*, London: Audit Commission, 1.

31   Leadbeater, C. (2003), *Overdue: how to create a modern public library service*, London: Demos, 14; Leadbeater, C. (2003), 'Creating a modern public library service', *Library + information update* **2** (7), 12–13.

32   Hyams, E. (2003), 'Funding the issue, communicating the problem', *Library + information update* **2** (9), 26–7.

33   Kempster, G. and Palmer, M. (2000), 'Re-inventing th public library: a view from the front line', *Logos* **11** (4), 211–14: 211.

34   Bundy, A. (2003), 'Changing lives, making the difference: the 21st century public library', *Australasian public libraries and information services* **16** (1), 38–49: 38.

35   Bjarrum, C. and Cranfield, A. (2004), 'The future is now – library re-engineering in the 21st century', in *Libraries as places: buildings for the 21st century*, edited by M-F. Bisbrouck and others, Munich: Saur, 39–63.

36   McClure, C.R. and others (1987), *Planning and role setting for public libraries*, Chicago: American Library Association. For details of later publications see www.ala.org.

37   *The public library service: IFLA/UNESCO guidelines for development* (2001), 24.

38   *National network – local service: standards for the public library service in the Republic of Ireland* (1999), para 1.2, 2–3.

39   *Better public libraries* (2003), London: CABE and Resource, 8.

40   Library and Information Services Council (England) (1995), *Investing in children*, London: HMSO.

41   *Start with the child: a report of the CILIP working party on library provision for children and young people* (2002), London: CILIP, 11; Douglas, J. and Griffiths, V. (2002), 'Youthful promise', *Public library journal* **17** (4), 97–9.

42   Oder, N. (2004), 'Ambitious meets audacious', *Library journal* **129** (2), 42–5.

43   For further details see www.bertelsmann-stiftung.de.

44   Pateman, J. (2000), 'Social exclusion: putting theory into practice', *Public library journal* **15** (2), 39–41: 39.

45   *The public library service: IFLA/UNESCO guidelines for development* (2001), 2.

46   Library and Information Services Council (1991), *Setting objectives for public library services*, London: HMSO, 12. The mission was restated in Department of National Heritage (1995), *The public library service in the 1990s: guidance for local authorities*, London: DNH, 5.

47   *Review of the public library service in England and Wales* (1995), 23.

48   *Review of the public library service in England and Wales* (1995), 23–4.

49   *Framework for the future* (2003), London: Department of Culture, Sport and Media, 5.

50   *The public library service: IFLA/UNESCO guidelines for development* (2001), 2–3.

51   Resource (2001), *Using museums, archives and libraries to develop a learning community*, London: Resource, 5.

52   Resource (2001), 4.

53   Boughey, A. (2000), 'Implementing the "New Library: the People's Network" and the management of change', *Aslib proceedings* **52** (4), 143–9.

54   Johansson, A. (2002), 'A meeting place for the future', *Scandinavian public library quarterly* **35** (3), 4–7.

55   *The public library service: IFLA/UNESCO guidelines for development* (2001), 4.

56   Convention of Scottish Local Authorities (1995), *Standards for the public library service in Scotland 1995*, Edinburgh: COSLA, 37–41.

57   Heywood, S. (2003), 'Soapbox: [The People's Network]', *Library + information update* **2** (8), 20.

58   'Wales adds £1m to sector budget' (2004), *Library + information update* **3** (11), 8.

59   Blagg, A. (2004), 'Getting creative in Birmingham', *Library + information update* **3** (6), 26–9.

60   *The public library service: IFLA/UNESCO guidelines for development* (2001), 5–6.

61   *A manifesto for London's libraries* [c. 2002], London: London Libraries Development Agency, 13.

62   Phillips, B.J., Beck, T. and Maltby, A. (1977), para 235.

63   Leadbeater, C. (2003), 'Creating a modern public library service', 12.

64   *Ex libris* (1986), London: Adam Smith Institute, 43.

65   Institute of Leisure and Amenity Management (1995), *Public libraries in a leisure context*, Reading: ILAM, [1].

66   Barton, D. (ed.) (1996), *Public libraries: influencing the future*, Bruton, Somerset: Capital Planning Information, 3.

67   See for example, Brumwell, J. and Hodgkins, L. 'Reader development in the East Midlands' (2003), *Library + information update* **2** (7), 42–4.

68   *IFLA/UNESCO public library manifesto* (1994), The Hague: IFLA, 2.

69   McClelland, N. (2003), 'Building a literate nation: the key role of public libraries', *Australasian public libraries and information services* **16** (2), 56–65. This describes the UK situation.

70   *The public library service: IFLA/UNESCO guidelines for development* (2001), 7.

71   National Assembly for Wales (2001), *Library and information matters 1999 and 2000: report by the Minister for Culture, Sport and the Welsh Language*, Cardiff: National Assembly for Wales, 2.

72   Liddle, D., Hicks, D. and Barton, D. (2000), *Public libraries and the arts: pathways to partnership*, Bruton, Somerset: Capital Planning, 11.

73   Department of Education and Science (1975*)*, *Public libraries and cultural activities*, London: HMSO.

74   *Public libraries ... open to all: contributing to a better Wales* [2002], Aberystwyth: Society of Chief Librarians Wales and CILIP Wales, 8.

75   Liddle, D., Hicks, D. and Barton, D. (2000), 13.

76   Liddle, D., Hicks, D. and Barton, D. (2000), vii.

77   Liddle, D., Hicks, D. and Barton, D. (2000), 25–6.

78   *The public library service: IFLA/UNESCO guidelines for development* (2001), 9–10.

79   This and many other issues relating to the roles discussed earlier in this chapter are considered in Kerslake, E. and Kinnel, M. (1997), *The social impact of libraries*, London: British Library.

80   *The public library service: IFLA/UNESCO guidelines for development* (2001), 7.

81   Greenhalgh, L. (1993), *The future of public library services. Working paper 2: The public library as a place*, Bournes Green, Gloucestershire: Comedia, 1.

82   Harris, K. (2003), 'Your third place or mine?', *Public library journal* **18** (2), 26–8.

83   Awcock, F.H. and Dungey, P. (1997), 'Buildings for the new millennium: a study tour of recent library buildings', *LASIE* **28** (3), 34–41: 36.

84   Usherwood, B. (2004), 'Lessons from *Today?*', *Library + information update* **3** (1), 21.

85   Hogan, J. (2000), 'Public library changes and me: a traditional user's perspective', *Assignation* **18** (1), 20–22.

86   Phillips, B.J., Beck, T. and Maltby, A. (1977), para 235.

87   Library and Information Services Council (Wales) (2003), *Mapping social inclusion in publicly-funded libraries in Wales*, London: Artemis Consulting, 8–9.

88   Durrani, S. and Smallwood, E. (2003), 'Mainstreaming equality, meeting needs: the Merton Library approach', *Library management* **24** (6/7), 348–59.

89   *Libraries for all: social inclusion in public libraries: policy guidance for local authorities* (1999), London: Department of Culture, Media and Sport, 5, 6. For the London Borough of Merton's response to this policy, see Pateman, J. (2000), 39–41.

90   *Libraries for all: social inclusion in public libraries: policy guidance for local authorities* (1999), 15–17.

91   Resource (2001), 10.

92   Muddiman, D. and others (2000), *Open to all? The public library and social exclusion, vol. 1: Overview and conclusions*, London: Resource, viii.

93   Kartmann, J. (1994), 'Demonstrators rail against Enoch Pratt railings', *American libraries* **25** (8), 708–9.

94   Muddiman, D. and others (2000), xi.

95   Muddiman, D. and others (2000), x.

96   Muddiman, D. and others (2000), 62.

97   For example, Daniels, F. (2004) 'Hijacked for social work', [letter], *Library + information update* **3** (9), 21.

98   Peoples, A. (2004, 'Public libraries for the future', *Library + information update* **3** (10), 31–3.

99   Linley, R. and Usherwood, B. (1998), *New measures for the new library: a social audit of public libraries*, London: British Library, 18–58.

100   Linley and Usherwood (1998), 97.

101   *Borrowed time? the future of public libraries in the UK*, (1993), Bournes Green, Gloucestershire: Comedia, 58–9.

102   UNISON (1997), see 26, 18.

103   Brady, W. (2003), 'Art galleries and museums should not be forced to dumb down' [letter], *Independent* 18 December, 19.

104   Audit Commission (2002), 1.

105   *Better public libraries* (2003), 6.

106   Vavrek, B. (2001), 'Wanted! Entertainment director', *American libraries* **32** (6), 68–71.

107   Alstad, C. and Curry, A. (2003),'Public space, public discourse, and public libraries', *Libres* **13** (1), no pagination.

108   Hyams, E. (2003), 27.

109   Leckie, G.J. and Hopkins, J. (2002), 'The public place of central libraries: findings from Toronto and Vancouver', *Library quarterly* **72** (3), 326–72: 360.

110   *Review of the public library service in England and Wales ... : summary and schedule of recommendations* (1995), London: Aslib, 31–2.

111   *Review of the public library service in England and Wales ... : summary and schedule of recommendations* (1995), 31.

112   For a fuller discussion of some of these points, see *Better public libraries* (2003), 5–9.

2 Sources of renewal and innovation

Architecture is not fashion design. It's much more important – it's the main legacy that any society leaves behind.

George Ferguson, 2003[1]

Architecture has become very newsworthy in recent years, with completed projects, those in the pipeline and those being proposed all being the subject of considerable media attention and public interest. This is especially true if they are large-scale, expensive and of controversial design. Additionally a hint of scandal, scenes of political infighting, delays in decision-making, building faults and reports of project and financial mismanagement, while regrettable, nevertheless all contribute to an awareness and concern for what is happening to the built environment. In the UK, the Millennium (what's it for?) Dome, Wembley Stadium (the two towers controversy), the long-delayed British Library, the 'wobbly' Millennium Bridge, the British Museum's Great Court (with its saga of the 'wrong' stone), the leaking Bath Spa project, and problems in raising the now much celebrated London Eye ferris wheel, have all attracted attention. At the local level controversy and opposition may surround public library building projects and their design in the UK, as at Brighton, East Sussex, where in the late 1990s a modern design was a cause for concern, mainly from conservation groups,[2] and at Brixworth (Northamptonshire, 1999), where the original design was modified by local opinion because of its 'petrol station' appearance.

Given the apparent building bonanza of recent times in the UK, fuelled by new approaches to funding, such as National Lottery money, and wider community consultation for public buildings, it is not surprising that there has been controversy, as well as significant achievements. Provision for sport, cultural institutions (including public libraries) and the media – all three areas the overall responsibility of one government department, the Department of Culture, Media and Sport (DCMS) – have improved resources and the local environment in many localities.

Sport is benefiting, for example, from the construction of the much-admired Millennium Stadium, Cardiff, and the new Wembley Stadium due to be completed in

2006. And cultural institutions in the UK – theatres, concert halls, art galleries, museums, archives and libraries – all provide recent examples of notable buildings. In the last three categories, these include:

- the Museum of Scotland in Edinburgh, The Lowry at Salford Quays (with its theatres and galleries) and the Jersey Archive
- national library buildings, such as the British Library and the extensions to the National Library of Wales (most recently Y Drwm, a drum-like small auditorium, opened in 2004)
- university library buildings at Lancaster (the Ruskin Library), Coventry, Sheffield and the London School of Economics
- public libraries at Durham, Bournemouth, Peckham (Figure 2.1), Brighton and Norwich.

Better facilities for the media include the striking and prize-winning Lord's cricket ground Media Centre.[3] And new BBC regional facilities are provided within the Birmingham Mailbox and the Norwich Forum, also the home of the public library.

Figure 2.1 Peckham Library, London Borough of Southwark (2000)
Source: Len Cross

By providing better facilities and services to the nation at large as well as local communities, many of these building projects, including public libraries, help to further urban and rural regeneration, improve local employment, and provide tourist and visitor attractions, as well as responding to other government agendas, such as social inclusion and lifelong learning.

Internationally too, architecture – including library architecture – has had a high profile. After 9/11 much world attention was focused on the emotionally charged World Trade Center architectural competition in New York. In February 2003, the design of Daniel Liebeskind, architect of the Jewish Museum in Berlin, was chosen. The race to complete facilities in time for the 2004 Olympic Games in Athens, including the main stadium with its futuristic roof of two movable arches, also put buildings in the news.

In the library world, and beyond, the black granite extension to the Royal Library in Copenhagen (1999), known as the 'Black Diamond', and the circular, tilted building of the Alexandria Library (2002) in Egypt have attracted international attention. The newsworthy Bibliothèque de France (1995), one of Paris's *Grands Projets*, and San Francisco Public Library (1996) have been, however, the subjects of some debate, the former because of the apparent impracticality of its four high rise storage towers, and the latter for its resolve to embrace the electronic future at the expense of a library's more traditional elements.[4] Inhabitants of Seattle, too, were anxious about Rem Koolhaus's all-glass exterior design for its public library, which opened in 2004, but the final result has been considered a triumph.[5]

BUILDINGS AS SYMBOLS

A new dimension to the funding and provision of many such public buildings in the UK is the demand from clients for their projects to be something more than just good architecture. They should be innovative structures, providing so-called landmark, cutting-edge, state-of- the-art or flagship buildings that may, it is hoped, become local or national icons. Great buildings do put places on the map. In Bilbao, Spain, the Guggenheim Museum, as part of an urban renewal effort using the work of many famous architects, has attracted international interest and acclaim, contributing significantly to the growth in visitors to the city. Buildings like this can come to symbolize a city or indeed a nation, as is the case with the Sydney Opera House.

Since the late 1970s France 'has had a deliberate policy in relation to the promotion of modern architecture, resulting in some spectacular and well-publicized schemes' like the Louvre pyramid, the Pompidou Centre, the Bibliothèque de France and Villeurbanne Library, the last-named also one of *Les Grands Projets*. The UK too has come to see the 'benefits of using architectural quality as a way of promoting a city'.[6] Buildings, both old and new, including public libraries, can thus become renowned features of a city's urban landscape: public libraries in New York, Stockholm, Glasgow, Toronto or Shanghai are some examples. The proposed new Library of Birmingham (frontispiece), with concept designs by the Richard Rogers Partnership, is already being talked of as an icon before it is built. In part this may be due to a distinctive design feature: a canopy roof (with sky garden) which covers the building and its surrounding area.[7]

On a smaller scale, the UK town of Braintree in Essex boasts a public library building (1997), with a distinctive dome, that is fast coming to symbolize the town.[8] A similar case might be made for the older Fulwell Cross Branch Library (London, Redbridge, 1967) by the architect of the Roman Catholic Liverpool Cathedral, Sir Frederick Gibberd.

URBAN AND RURAL REGENERATION

The desire today of the UK's towns and cities to acquire symbolic buildings mirrors something of the creative force of the Victorians and their concern for civic pride. But today even more appears to be required of UK public buildings, particularly cultural buildings. For in addition to fulfilling their purpose and being architectural icons, they must help encourage economic regeneration through the visitors they attract, as well as giving a place a competitive edge over others. In Wales, for example, the National Botanic Garden (the Great Glasshouse) near Carmarthen, and the Millennium Stadium and Millennium Centre for the Arts, both in Cardiff, are all modern-day architectural symbols and visitor attractions, as much as local resources. Elsewhere, the Eden Project in Cornwall, among the top ten UK visitor attractions, has been responsible for economic regeneration. It is visited probably as much for its architecture as for the plant life displayed in its large dome-covered biomes.

Public libraries too can contribute towards economic regeneration and the encouragement and support of tourism. Sunderland's library service, for example, has been part of a coordinated approach to the city's regeneration through culture, sport and tourism.[9] Quality library buildings can in themselves attract visitors, as much as the services and facilities on offer, such as temporary loan, archives and local studies provision, a tourist information centre, exhibitions, guided tours, a café or a shop. The Visitors' Centre at the National Library of Wales, albeit in a different library sector, is a major example of this approach and, like the Eden project, also encompasses an educational function.

Abroad, the radical architecture of Singapore's Esplanade Arts Centre (2002), which includes a public library devoted to the performing arts (and described as a 'boutique' library), is designed to contribute to making Singapore a cultural capital with world status. The proposed Barcelona Universal Forum of Culture has been criticized, however, for putting an expensive and tourist attraction over the needs of its citizens.[10] Toronto is set to acquire an international architectural profile through work by world-famous architects (Will Alsop, architect of Peckham Library, Frank Gehry and Daniel Liebeskind).[11]

Framework for the future describes the aims of public libraries as, for instance, the promotion of books and reading. There is also the political requirement for public libraries to have an economic value, to combat social exclusion and to assist in the regeneration of urban and rural communities. Physical urban or rural regeneration is bound up with economic and social issues but attention must be paid also to the built environment so as to give people a pleasant place to live. The UK government has policies for economic and social development that include public/private partnerships, and they support and supplement other schemes, such as Sure Start, the work of the Social Exclusion Unit and the Active Citizenship Centre. The latter is concerned with civil renewal and sees a role for public libraries as agents of change in community-building, with the example of Chicago's libraries in mind.[12]

There are many examples of regeneration in the UK's towns and cities in which buildings are playing a part, including public libraries, as mentioned earlier. As has been stated about our cities and towns: 'urban renaissance is the key not merely to more economic and social success, but to our individual fulfilment as citizens and human beings'.[13]

The need for regeneration is also a rural problem, as there too people are disadvantaged by, for example, the lack of local services and seasonal employment. In England grants for transport, shops and other service needs are administered by the Countryside Agency. Since 2003 a Sustainable Communities Award has been made in England by the Office of the Deputy Prime Minister for the most innovative regeneration schemes. Qualifying criteria include 'creating a good quality built and natural environment'.[14] As in towns and cities, there is potential for the public library to play a part in regenerating village life and this is discussed in Chapter 4. The rural one-stop shop at Waters Upton in Shropshire, and England's first, is an example of what might be done. The centre comprises a post office, village shop, ATM (cash machine), ICT access centre, community office and regular police surgeries.

The regeneration of urban communities has resulted in dockland development in Liverpool, Cardiff, Swansea, London and Glasgow, as well as city centre development in Birmingham, Portsmouth and the City of London. Although dependent on urban development, new commercial buildings and better infrastructure, regeneration (as noted earlier) can be linked also to the provision and improvement of cultural facilities. With the help of lottery money, for example, parts of the South Bank (including the Festival Hall) are to get a makeover.

Public library buildings are often a vital part in urban regeneration, as demonstrated by new public library service points, in Peckham, Stratford (London, Newham),[15] and at Frith Park, Sheffield, part of a shopping centre regeneration project. Chester plans a new library as part of the regeneration of a 1960s area of the city. The Swiss Cottage development is seeing £75 million spent on the surrounding site, including apartment block, park, leisure complex and community centre: the renovated Swiss Cottage public library was completed in 2003.

In 2002 Lord Rogers was complaining about losing the urban planning fight for Britain's larger towns and cities: 'When we look across the water, Britain's [urban areas] are a pale shadow of the best examples on the Continent'.[16] Not all urban development necessarily favours libraries. Whatever the problems of Birmingham Central Library, this 30-year-old building is to be replaced by offices and relocated on another site. Its present site generates 5,000 visitors a day: the existing library 'may not be ... as impressive a design as the new library at Alexandria, but at least it has stood in the very heart of the city that spawned it'.[17] The wish to replace the Birmingham Central Library (1974) with a new building at a different location aroused heated debate. An appeal to list the library as a building of architectural and historical significance was made by the Twentieth Century Society, which regarded it as a fine example of brutalist architecture which should be kept. The Department for Culture, Media and Sport rejected the appeal, so opening the way to its demolition.[18] More positively, however, the new Birmingham Library is to be part of the Eastside Regeneration Initiative, a revitalization of the east side of the city, that includes the creation of a new city park. In Austria, the new Vienna Central Library is expected to help regenerate a declining part of the city.[19] Public libraries in the US, such as those in Nashville and Chicago, are also found to be helping revitalize neighbourhoods or communities through investment in buildings, staff, the needs of their users, and as partners in civic initiatives.[20]

BUILDING CONSERVATION

Regeneration can also be furthered by putting old buildings to new uses or continuing to use existing buildings suitably modernized; an approach which also supports the building conservation agenda in many towns and cities. The wish to conserve old buildings and put them to good use can be seen in the Tate Modern, London (housed in a former power station), and the Tate North, Gateshead (once a large grain store, the Baltic Exchange), as well as in other listed building conservation projects. New public libraries too have been housed in converted buildings: Sunderland Central Library (1995) is accommodated in a former store; Leamington Spa Library (1999) is located in what was once a swimming pool in the Royal Pump Rooms; and Cricklade Library, Wiltshire (2002), occupies a converted glove factory. Irish examples include Buncrana (1999), Donegal, in a converted and extended church, and Macroom, Cork County (2000) in a converted cinema. Older UK public library buildings, which have been refurbished, remodelled and often extended, continue in use as modern service points: for instance, Wavetree Library, Liverpool (2002), Putney, London (1998), Burnley (1994) and Croydon (1993).

As will be seen in Chapter 5, a number of public library buildings, including some from the post-war period are listed buildings. English Heritage, Cadw (in Wales), Historic Scotland, and the Environment and Heritage Service of Northern Ireland advise their respective home governments on the listing of buildings of architectural and historical interest. Generally speaking, buildings have to be 30 years old in England to be listed and by that time they may be no longer fashionable and, for various reasons, in an unsatisfactory condition. They can pose conservation problems because of the modern, and sometimes experimental, materials and construction. Nevertheless, listed buildings can be a positive force in the regeneration of urban areas.[21]

The Brighton example noted earlier illustrates the wider conservation issue in the UK surrounding the placing of modern buildings in 'sensitive' historic urban areas. The UK's more restrictive approach is in contrast to that in France, where

> Genuinely modern [buildings] using the technology, structures, forms and materials of their period give historic areas an appearance of continuing evolution – layering, producing a 'collage of time'.[22]

PUBLIC ART

As will be seen in Chapter 9, public art is also a feature of public library buildings and their immediate environs, both in the UK and elsewhere. Said to be one of the ten best pieces of public art, Janet Cardiff's 'The Missing Voice' (1999) is a sound journey from London's Whitechapel Library to Liverpool Street Station.[23] An Irish example of public art is the seven-metre-high, polished stainless steel external sculpture at Cabra Library (2001) in Dublin, whose design concept is loosely based on Irish standing stones and reflects the relationship between the world of information technology and an older culture.

Two early pieces of library art work were John White's kinetic sculpture of a man reading a book in Cleckheaton Library, West Yorkshire, and Clare Smith's 'Limehouse Reach' in Limehouse Library, portraying a contemporary universal goddess.[24]

PUBLIC BUILDINGS: THE POLITICAL DIMENSION

In comparison with the UK's former Conservative governments (1979–97), 'New' Labour have been more well disposed towards cultural institutions, abolishing museum entry charges for example. The general financing of public libraries, however, has not improved under their stewardship but National Lottery money has been made available to support various building and other projects. One such project, the People's Network – providing public access computers free of charge and funding for associated staff training – has helped change the face of the local public library.

Such additional funding is usually given to deal with a local or national need and also to support the opportunities and challenges resulting from a government agenda concerned with particular political, economic and social outcomes.

DEVOLUTION AND DECENTRALIZATION

Under a Labour administration devolved government has taken place for Scotland, Wales and Northern Ireland, although the latter's assembly is suspended at the time of writing (early 2005). This means that home country governments take over responsibility for many matters, including cultural ones. Public libraries are now part of that devolved responsibility and time will tell how differing approaches (to standards, for instance) will affect public library services and their building provision in the devolved countries. In England the overseeing of public libraries (and museums) is the responsibility of the Department for Culture, Media and Sport (DCMS). The Museums, Libraries and Archives Council (MLA, formerly Resource) advises government on policy and is also the strategic agency for all the three types of institution across the UK. Northern Ireland and Scotland have agencies advising their governments and in Wales there is a new body, CyMAL (Museums, Archives and Libraries Wales), established in 2004 as a policy division of the Welsh Assembly.

Both Scotland and Wales have wished to construct impressive, and expensive, parliament and assembly buildings in Edinburgh (completed 2004) and Cardiff respectively, both of which are many times over their original budget. It is possible to overlook the financial mismanagement of these projects by thinking of their potential iconic value, like the Sydney Opera House, notoriously overbudget. When finished, these buildings will no doubt come to be seen as potent symbols of national identity.

Labour's commitment to regional government and regional assemblies has resulted so far in the formation of the Greater London Authority (GLA), with a City Hall (2002) designed by Foster and Partners, who were asked to create a new landmark for the capital.[25] However, regionalization in the library world has already materialized in the shape of the English regional MLAs (Museums, Libraries and Archives Councils), whose job is to provide strategic leadership in their region: the MLA West Midlands (the Regional Council for Museums, Libraries and Archives) is one example. In London, the London Libraries Development Agency develops and coordinates strategy for library and information services across London.

With their network of main libraries and branches (often designated community or neighbourhood libraries), public library services are decentralized institutions. National museums and galleries, like the Tate Gallery, the Imperial War Museum and the Royal Armoury, also currently demonstrate this desire to decentralize their institutions for the economic, employment and other benefits to local communities.

THE POLITICAL AGENDA

Framework for the future

In 2003 the DCMS published a ten-year plan for public libraries in England called *Framework for the future: libraries, learning and information in the next decade*. This identified three main aims for public libraries: the promotion of books and reading; encouraging access to the digital age; and developing community and civic values. How these aims relate to the generally accepted roles of public libraries – education, information, recreation and culture – were discussed in Chapter 1.

Following the *Framework for the future* report, the DCMS commissioned MLA to prepare a three-year action plan of projects and programmes aimed at the report's three central themes. That for 'community and civic values' saw the need to provide library premises for twenty-first century requirements and promote best practice in the planning and designing of quality library buildings.[26] Working with CILIP and others to further the provision of quality premises, MLA has funded the creation of a library buildings database (www.designinglibraries.org.uk), initially for public libraries, an audit of public library buildings to provide 'an update of a 1999 report which listed an appalling backlog of capital work', and workshops on design.[27]

The *Framework* report has its supporters and critics. Its critics say that it offers no radical new vision for 2013, no really fresh ideas, and that it dodges the issues of sustainability and funding. The latter are particularly important as regards library buildings:

> The scale of the problem [requires them] to address the state of the other 3,000+ buildings [which] is far bigger than the PFI [Private Finance Initiative], and ad hoc capital windfalls or one-off funding projects can accommodate.[28]

The report has been compared unfavourably with a similar document from the Department of Culture, Arts and Leisure in Northern Ireland, called *Tomorrow's library*, which include costed plans for library building improvements.[29]

Better public libraries

Better public libraries complements the *Framework* strategy, outlining what twenty-first century libraries should be like, reinforcing the points it makes through a number of examples. The report says that:

> For many potential users the outmoded design and poor location of some library buildings is a deterrent in itself. We need innovative solutions to make them relevant again.[30]

The reception of the report varied from the generally favourable (with a difference of opinion on some points, and a plea for bigger libraries to cope with the suggested extra features), to one castigating its 'flabby writing and flabby thinking' and its failure to give reasons for its assertions. The latter ends with a worried comment on the characterization of libraries as 'living rooms in the city', saying that most living rooms are spaces without books.[31] A reply from one of the report's authors was happy that the report had stirred up debate and noted that

> Overall use of libraries is rapidly declining; and according to all the examples in *Better public libraries* the impact of radical design of their libraries has seen a large increase in visitor use.[32]

An unexpected editorial in *Country Life* says of *Better public libraries* that it provides 'an unintentionally hilarious list of what makes libraries bad ... and what makes them good'. The writer's advice is to bin the text 'and just look at the pictures, there is a ravishing selection of the best new library buildings, such as Bernard Stilwell's for March in Cambridgeshire'.[33]

The magazine's opinion of the text is somewhat extreme, as *Better public libraries* with its examples will no doubt have an influence on the service provision and design of public libraries in the coming years. The attempt noted by *Country Life*, however, to portray the difference between traditional (old-fashioned or 'bad') and modern ('good') libraries through lists of 'what's in' and 'what's out' in public library design is not only hilarious but shows a lack of knowledge about library history and architecture. Many of the things said to signify a modern library – open access, open-plan design, shared space and cafés – have been in place for years. Others – disabled access and network space – have been responded to when there was the social or technological need to do so. Modern libraries may have domes, galleries, mezzanines and clerestory lighting and no doubt will continue to do so when the design situation calls for it. And libraries can be (and are) stand-alone buildings: it is one option among many, as Chapter 4 demonstrates.

Who's in charge?

The *Who's in charge?* report of 2004 by the bookseller, Tim Coates, and published by the charity Libri, takes its criticism further. It says that the public libraries' death knell is sounding, unless there is change by local councils and the government bodies responsible for monitoring and overseeing them. It was the latest in a series of documents to express negative feelings about public libraries and in particular about their premises. For example, it bemoans the lack of well designed and welcoming buildings:

> Many public libraries throughout the country are drab and dismal. It is as if there were an assumption that any attempt to create an attractive space is a waste of taxpayers' money.

The report urges a more professional approach to planning and designing library buildings and for libraries to learn from the commercial and retail trades. Much of the report's comments on buildings, however, relate to the neglect and poor maintenance of existing buildings,[34] which is considered in a later chapter. It sounds the warning:

> If we do not address the fundamental structural problems of the library service, there may be no libraries to provide these excellent services to readers in ten or twenty years' time.[35]

While not denying there were important issues to be faced, headlines in the professional press like 'Death sentence unfair' and 'MLA is several steps ahead of Libri' show that much was already being achieved by the *Framework for the future* action plan and the work of MLA to deal with matters raised in the report.[36]

The London Borough of Haringey provides an example of a failing library service taking the kind of action advocated by the *Who's in charge?* report. Following an Audit

Commission inspection, the borough asked Instant Library Ltd in 2001 to take over its failing libraries, archives and museum service under a public/private partnership arrangement. Where libraries had been neglected, 'improvements were made to buildings through low cost measures, amongst other solutions'. By 2003 the service was thriving once more and this without the use of unlimited funds or Instant Library subsidies.[37]

LIBRARY BUILDINGS AND CHANGE

As has been seen, there is plenty of pressure for existing public library buildings to be upgraded and for new libraries to be innovative, attractive twenty-first century libraries, and there can be little quarrel with these objectives. *Who's in charge* and other reports have urged public libraries to take lessons from the retail trade, in particular the large, chain bookshops such as Waterstone's. Branding is part of this approach, exemplified in London by Tower Hamlets' Idea Store concept for its new library facilities; as is the invitation to consume coffee and cake and buy from the shop on a library's premises. There may be a danger that, as with museums, the library experience is becoming interchangeable with shopping. The question for debate, considered in Chapter 9, is whether public libraries should be decidedly different from, rather than similar to, bookshops, supermarkets and Internet cafés. One view is that

> Surely libraries should differ from bookshops or Internet cafés? Perhaps a touch of high mindedness symbolised by that despised Classical architecture is still relevant: libraries ... should, after all, be primarily champions of reading.[38]

COMPETITIONS, PRIZES AND AWARDS

The desire to erect prestigious buildings is a major feature of inter-city rivalry. They lend a competitive edge in the bid to become European Capital of Culture (ECofC), for example. Competitions such as ECofC help to celebrate, publicize and promote new architecture, as do national architectural competitions and more specialized contests like the Public Library Building Awards scheme in the UK.

EUROPEAN CAPITAL OF CULTURE

The European Capital (formerly City) of Culture initiative, promoted by the European Union, began with the choice of Athens in 1985. The ECofC competitive process provides the incentive for a city to improve its cultural image and infrastructure, as part of its bid to be nominated. Since the mid-1980s, Berlin, Glasgow, Dublin and Copenhagen, amongst others, have enjoyed the city of culture status. Being designated

ECofC in 1990 helped transform Glasgow from a depressed industrial city into a lively one with remarkable architecture. As soon as the city was awarded the title, it put £32 million into the improvement of art and cultural facilities. Visits to theatres, museums and galleries increased by both locals and visitors and there were big attendances at cinemas and pop concerts. Glasgow became well known for its tourist, conference and shopping facilities.[39]

To mark the year 2000, nine cities were designated ECofC, including Avignon, Cracow, Helsinki and Santiago del Compostela. This group of cities – some with library building projects under way – not only presented their own individual cultural programmes but also collaborated on an author and literature project, promoting reading.[40]

Cork, European Capital of Culture 2005, sees it as an occasion 'for the city to celebrate its heritage, its contemporary culture and to bring artists and events of international calibre to Ireland'.[41] The benefits for its library service include a new library at Tory Top (2005, c.770m^2), the go-ahead to tender on a 1,200m^2 library at Bishoptown, and the preparation of a brief in 2005 for a new central library of about 4,000m^2.

Designation as a Capital of Culture is a coveted title, not only for the status and cultural activity it brings to a city, but because it is an opportunity for a city to improve its urban environment through cultural building projects, which may include public libraries. Thessaloniki in Greece, for example, began work on its new central library building when nominated ECofC for 1997.

Eight British cities put in bids to be considered ECofC in 2008. This was reduced to six cities in 2003 – Cardiff, Birmingham, Liverpool, Oxford, Bristol, and Newcastle jointly with Gateshead. Liverpool, which opened a new arts centre in 2003 (the Foundation for Art and Technology, or FACT), was eventually chosen ECofC for 2008 in mid-2003. On past experience, Liverpool could be richer by 15,000 jobs and £220 million in tourist income. Liverpool's ECofC win was decided by its public architecture, listed buildings, impressive visual arts, a strong sense of civic purpose and the commitment of ordinary people.[42] A year-long festival is promised of art, architecture, ballet, comedy, cinema, food, fashion, literature, music, opera, science and theatre. For the library service, Liverpool's success means it will open new and refurbished libraries, including a major refurbishment of the central library, aimed for completion in 2008.

A number of the UK cities bidding for the title of ECofC 2008 had plans for library buildings. The proposed Library of Birmingham (a replacement building for the current central library) formed part of that city's bid. At a cost of £3 million, Bristol had plans for four new libraries – the first to be built in the city for 20 years – linked to its ECofC bid. Newcastle has acquired the funds for a new central library, and the proposed Newcastle Cultural Quarter at the University of Newcastle (to include a library), and due in 2008, was part of the city's ECofC bid.

The possible danger in competitions of this kind is that a concentration on the emblematic nature of a building (whether library or not) portrays it as being more about its architecture than its *raison d'être*. Purpose too, especially in cultural buildings, may be obscured by a keenness to exploit the potential of an upmarket café, restaurant or shop, which may push other functions to the margins of the building or impinge on much-needed space. The Victoria and Albert Museum was once criticized for advertising itself in 1988 as an 'ace café with museum attached', seemingly placing more emphasis on its non-museum facilities than its museum mission and suggesting, perhaps, a greater concern for image than purpose.

The extension to the National Gallery of Ireland in Dublin, nominated for a 2002 Royal Institute of British Architects (RIBA) Stirling Prize, allocated much of its new space to an atrium, shop and restaurant. The range of gateaux at the Idea Store (the public library in Tower Hamlets), the quality of the sausages in the National Library of Wales and the wines in Tate Modern sometimes seem to attract as much, if not more, media attention than the cultural purpose of the institution.

ARCHITECTURAL PRIZES AND AWARDS

RIBA have their own annual award scheme – the Forum, Norwich, gained an award in the Arts and Leisure group in 2004 – but are also responsible for awarding the RIBA Stirling Prize mentioned above.[43] In 2002 it went to the Gateshead Millennium Bridge but in 2000 it was awarded to Peckham Library. The Jubilee Library, Brighton was nominated in 2005 but the award went to the Scottish Parliament building. Brighton Library was, however, given a RIBA award in 2005, along with The Campus at Weston-super-Mare, which includes a public library and Alton Library, Hampshire. Other national architectural associations may also have award schemes in which public library buildings feature from time to time: the American Institute of Architects (AIA) scheme is described below. The New Zealand Institute of Architects made a local award in 2001 to Manukau City Council's Tupu-Dawson Road Youth Library, pointing out its high IT content and study/homework ethos, and a national award in 2004 to South Christchurch Library in Beckenham, particularly for its environmental sustainability.[44]

OTHER AWARD SCHEMES

In the UK, The Prime Minister's Better Public Building Award encourages and celebrates excellence in design for publicly funded building projects.[45] Past winners were Tate Modern (2001) and the City Learning Centre (2002), but in 2003 Bournemouth Library was given that accolade.[46] This was designed by the Building Design Partnership and replaced a library that had once been called the second worst in England.[47] Two buildings were of interest to librarians in 2005: the Prime Minister's award going to Brighton's Jubilee Library, and one of the finalists, The Sage, Gateshead, which includes Explore Music, a music information service.

The Civic Trust operates a variety of award schemes: special awards (for access, culture and regeneration and sustainability for example), awards, commendations and mentions.[48] Over the years a number of libraries have been recognized by the trust for their contribution to the built environment. In 2002 Peckham Library was given an award, and the refurbishment and extension of the Linen Library, Belfast, received a 'mention'. March Library, Cambridgeshire, gained further recognition in 2003, by winning an award in the trust's Market Towns Award category – it was considered to have given the town a new lease of life.[49] Also in 2003, Bournemouth Library and Calne Millennium Library received the trust's commendations. 2004 saw an award for New Bar Library, Belfast, a commendation for Hamilton Town House, Lanarkshire (in 2005), which includes the public library, and mentions in 2004 for the Idea Store, Bow, Tower Hamlets and Walsall Central Library (new entrance).

LIBRARY BUILDING AWARDS

The UK has separate award schemes for academic and public library buildings. Winning an award, which on one occasion in the past has prevented an intended library closure, clearly generates enormous pride and goodwill and is a cause for justified celebration.[50] The scheme for academic libraries is organized by the Standing Conference of National and University Libraries (SCONUL) and for public libraries by CILIP's Public Libraries Group. Their Public Library Building Awards (PLBA) scheme has operated biennially since 1995. Awards are made in four categories: small and large new building, and small and large converted or refurbished building. The scheme includes libraries in the Republic of Ireland and has several features: library services nominate their building or buildings for consideration; the awards are sponsored by two library furnishing companies; the competition is judged solely by a panel of librarians, who are obliged to take an holistic view of the library rather than being solely concerned with its design. The criteria used to evaluate nominated buildings are discussed briefly in Chapter 8 and a list of winners – in 2003, PLBA honours were divided equally between Irish and UK libraries – is given in Appendix 1.[51]

Although a nominee in the 2001 competition, Rugby Library (Figure 2.2), opened in 2000 as part of an art gallery, museum and library complex, was not given a Public Library Building Award. Readers of *Public library journal*, however, nominated it as their favourite library.[52] A 'makeover' of the PLBA scheme was announced in 2004 for the 2005 event. Size and a building's new or refurbished status were no longer to be the main focus of the award categories. Five new categories were devised: partnership; architect meets practicality; interior design; heart of the community; and accessibility. There will also be a delegates' choice decided by votes at the Public Library Authorities Conference and electronic votes recorded by Public Libraries Group members on its website.[53]

The Library Building Awards Program of the American Institute of Architects (AIA) and the American Library Association (ALA) is different from the British one in that the one scheme covers all types of library and involves architects as well as librarians in the

Figure 2.2   Rugby Library, Warwickshire (2000): the Drum houses the children's library and part of the museum and gallery on the first and second floors
Source: Lynda Carnes

judging process. These biennial awards have been jointly sponsored by the ALA's Library Administration and Management Association and the AIA since 1963. They 'recognise distinguished accomplishment in library architecture by an American architect for any library and without regard to location or type'. Public library buildings attracting awards since 1991 are listed in Appendix 2. In 1991 they were all public libraries. In the spirit of the awards program, 1991 also included recognition of a library building in Berlin.[54]

There are other library building award schemes in North America and elsewhere. The Connecticut Award for Excellence in Public Library Architecture offers two awards every other year (for a library under and a library over $1,672m^2/18,000ft^2$), as well as honourable mentions, and is administered by the Connecticut State Library and two professional associations.[55] Ontario Library Association's Library Building Awards, run every third year since 1996, offer awards for best new building, renovation or restoration. The purpose of the scheme is 'to encourage excellence in architectural design and planning of libraries in Ontario'. The next awards will be made in 2007 to allow a good number of projects to build up. The Japan Library Association's Library Architecture Award has been given since 1985.[56] These award schemes, and the content of this and later chapters, provide evidence of a continuing provision of public library buildings throughout the world.

The position of public library construction in the US has been recorded since 1968 in the December issue of the *Library journal*. In addition to new buildings, arranged by state, there is a list of additions and renovations, and a six-year cost summary for new buildings, which average around over 100 a year. In 2003 a total of 195 public library building projects of all kinds was reported, although together with academic libraries this was the lowest number completed since 1985. In 2004 the number of public library projects rose to 203, with large projects in San José and Seattle accounting for 27 per cent of all expenditure.

A few examples will suffice here to show the increasing provision of public library buildings in mainland Europe in recent years.[57] Following the passing of the Flemish Public Libraries Act in 1976, the Belgian province had constructed 164 new libraries by 1997.[58] France has reported a growth in public library building since 1986, providing new libraries for small communities and replacement buildings in large cities and branch libraries.[59] Examples of its large libraries are the Jean-Pierre Médiathèque (Paris, 1989), and the eight-storey Orléans Médiathèque (1994).[60] Major early twenty-first century public libraries are those at Marseille, Nice (2002),[61] Reims (2003), and Toulouse (2003),[62] amongst others. Since the 1980s, the Netherlands too has been responsible for some impressive large new public libraries at Rotterdam (1983) and The Hague (1995), for instance. The increased investment in good public libraries was marked by a Dutch publication highlighting 15 recent examples.[63] One British writer noted that 'far from being old hat, libraries have never looked more interesting' and recorded further new libraries being planned and built abroad in Amsterdam, Milan and Turin.[64] Figure 2.3 shows an interesting project completed in 1998 in Veria, Greece.

Figure 2.3   Veria Central Public Library, Greece (1998): the library exterior reflects the Macedonian
style of house
Source: Antonis Galitsios

FUNDING

Around the world, the primary source of public library funding, including that for
buildings, is taxation at local, regional or national level, the sources and proportions
varying in each country. In the UK, the money comes from local and national taxation.
Secondary sources can include donations from funding bodies or private individuals;
revenue from commercial activities; revenue from user fees; sponsorship from
external organizations, and National Lottery funds for specific initiatives. Money for
UK library buildings may be acquired by local authorities through loans, but
increasingly funds are obtained through partnership with one or more bodies and
larger buildings are sometimes heavily dependent on National Lottery funding or a
Private Finance Initiative. In their role as a planning body, a local authority may
require a developer to provide new library premises free of charge, except for the cost
of fitting out, as a 'planning gain' for the community. Such financial contributions
towards community infrastructure are secured by Section 106 agreements under the

Town and Country Planning Act 1990 as a way of meeting the needs of residents in new developments.

Although making a block grant to UK local authorities for capital purposes, central government does not require that money be spent specifically on library buildings. Such decisions are made locally. Where appropriate, local authorities can fund capital expenditure for library buildings and associated costs through loans. The Public Works Loan Board considers loan applications from local authorities for capital purposes authorized by government departments and, where granted, collects repayment. Repayment periods are governed by the type of loan, fixed or variable (10 or 30 years).

To help libraries with estimating the cost of public library building projects, as well as layout, computer software emanating from the US called *Libris Design* is freely available from a Californian website administered by the State Librarian, which also includes information on facility planning topics.[65] An American architect warns of the danger of seeing the project budget just as the building budget, forgetting about fitting out and various miscellaneous costs, for example, and the need for a contingency fund of perhaps 10 per cent. In other words, he warns, fewer square metres can be built than the available project budget might suggest.[66]

NATIONAL LOTTERY FUNDING

The UK National Lottery was established in 1994, and much public building for cultural purposes is supported in whole or in part by funds from the various strands of lottery monies.[67] In the early years the emphasis in arts funding was on large capital projects but, since 1998, funds have gone also to small, local projects. Public libraries have received funding from the New Opportunities Fund (NOF) (for the People's Network and digitization projects), the Heritage Lottery Fund, and the Millennium Commission, which supports large-scale regenerative projects. The NOF and the Community Fund were merged in 2004 to create the Big Lottery Fund, which will also manage Millennium Commission funding.[68]

Lottery funding for public library buildings has included:

- the location of the Cornish Local Studies Collection – the Cornwall Centre – in a listed building in Redruth (2001)
- Surrey History Centre (1998)
- the Forum, Norwich, which includes the public library
- Tredegar, Caerphilly (2004) – the library is part of a joint school and community venture funded partly from the lottery and partly from Europe.

Receipt of lottery funding for a project does not guarantee its long-term success. Projects like the Millennium Dome, the Sheffield National Centre for Popular Music, the National Botanic Garden, Wales, and the Baltic Centre have all experienced difficulties.

This is usually due to under-use of their facilities leading to financial problems. Other National Lottery concerns are:

- the unequal distribution of funding: some areas get more than others, London receiving more lottery cash than other regions[69]
- time spent on securing the funding and the need to demonstrate that a new library building will satisfy the government's particular social or educational agendas
- sustainability: the main issue for the future, not just for building but also for the People's Network: where will the funds come from to maintain and develop the library building and its services?

One opinion of the Millennium Commission expenditure to celebrate 2000 was that it was wasted on buildings no one really wanted, leading to 'a new generation of liabilities ... for decades to come'.[70] The Carnegie building inheritance was often seen in a similar light – generously funded buildings without the money to fully support the library service they implied. One way to secure sustainability for a guaranteed period, however, is through buildings funded by the controversial Public Finance Initiative (PFI).

PUBLIC FINANCE INITIATIVE

PFI has been defined as 'the private sector funding or management of capital assets that have traditionally been in the public sector'.[71] Public libraries can use PFI as an alternative method of acquiring facilities and services. Schools are making considerable use of PFI – 650 schools, mostly PFI funded, were scheduled in 2002 – and perhaps public libraries should learn from their experience.[72] 'PFI is a procurement solution ... A consortium undertakes to design, build, finance and operate facilities on behalf of the public sector.'[73] Various opportunities for libraries have been spelt out,[74] and a number of PFI projects are in the pipeline.

In Brighton the new central library (opened in 2005 and not the same building referred to earlier in the chapter) is part of a development with hotel, shops and residential space and is partly PFI-funded. DCMS cash is being used to underpin three PFI library-building projects in Croydon, Liverpool and Rochdale.[75] In Newcastle £27 million of PFI funding is to be used for a new city-centre library project (planned to open in 2007) and to refurbish three branches. At Rhondda Cynon Taf a PFI scheme for a lifelong learning centre is to include a public library.[76]

The prize-winning Bournemouth Library was PFI-funded and is seen as something of a model for the future. The agreement was not only for the design, building and maintenance of the library but also for the provision of ICT and its maintenance.[77] Kent County Council operates a PFI contract, but in this case solely for the council's ICT system that covers the library and a public information network of more than 1,000 terminals. Bournemouth was the first library to combine the two aspects – the building and ICT. The reason for Bournemouth choosing PFI, and the procedure involved, has been explained by its librarian. The benefits are, for example, a fully serviced building for 30 years and value for money. The issues to be dealt with include the amount of staff involvement, building flexibility into the contract, and timescale implications for the design. Tips for a successful PFI procurement run from 'getting the fundamentals right' to 'getting the contract management right'.[78]

Although there are benefits (extra investment in service provision and long-term protection of services), PFI is a controversial approach to providing public facilities and services. It is encouraged by government, which 'considers the private sector to be better equipped to deliver services hitherto the province of local government'. But as has been pointed out, contracts for 20–25 years reduce a local authority's financial flexibility and increase, rather than reduce, its range of rented buildings: 'PFI is designed effectively to make the public sector the tenant of the private sector'.[79]

OTHER FUNDING SOURCES

Some examples are given below of other funding arrangements for library buildings, which (as with other methods) usually influence the outcome, and involving a variety of partnership arrangements, which can include European funding.

- Sources of funding for Lowestoft Library and Record Office (Suffolk, 1975, refurbished 2003) were the European Regional Development fund; Capital Modernization Fund; New Opportunities Fund and Sure Start.[80]
- Funding of Dover's new Discovery Centre (Kent, 2003) came from Kent County Council; District Council; the Kent and Medway Learning Skills Council; the Single Regeneration Budget and the National Lottery.[81]
- Wing Library (Buckinghamshire, 2002) – a partnership between the County Council and Wing Hall Trust provided the capital for the new building.[82]
- Knutsford Library (Cheshire, 2002) and its site were given to a developer who built the new library (at no cost to the local authority) as part of a bigger development.
- Idea Stores (London, Tower Hamlets, 2002 and 2005) were supported by national and European grants, proceeds from building sales and money from three Sainsbury's family trusts.[83]
- Selsdon Library, Croydon (2004) 'has a new library thanks to the council's "creative negotiations" over the building of a new Sainsbury's complex'.[84]
- Staffordshire County Council has signed a £3 million partnership 'deal' to refurbish 19 libraries, which could be a model for other library services, and aims for 40 per cent increase in visits over three years.[85]
- At Bristol a variety of partnerships are being used for its proposed four new libraries: mixed development to include a library; part of supermarket redevelopment plan; a land deal with a primary care trust; and joining forces with community education.[86]
- Cambridgeshire: stylish new libraries have benefited from a number of funding opportunities in partnership with local community initiatives.[87]

- Caerphilly Library Service has used public/private partnerships to relocate its Oakdale Library to a better, leased site, and the new Tredegar Library is to share space in the community wing in a new community school, along with other agencies.[88]

A 2003 library impact study identified partnerships as contributing to the success of library building projects, particularly in the two case studies it examined, at Norwich and Stratford, where they are part of a larger development: 'an array of services under one roof'.[89] As the government's 2004 spending review provides no extra money for the People's Network, or to remedy under-investment in book budgets and buildings,[90] the financial attraction of various partnerships seems even more necessary than before.

Buildings provided and maintained by library authorities are not exempt from rates and will also need to be insured, an important aspect of disaster planning and discussed in Chapter 6. Bylaws will cover the use of library premises by members of the public.

FUNDING IN OTHER COUNTRIES

In a number of countries, Belgium for example, there are state subsidies for library buildings. Under the Finnish Library Act public libraries receive government grants towards the cost of constructing and renovating a library. Masku Public Library, opened in 1996 received a state grant of 45 per cent for the project, as a library service is seen a one of society's basics.[91] In the Irish Republic, the Department of the Environment and Local Government with the advice of the Library Council provides capital grants for libraries to local authorities. The grants cover 75 per cent of building and fitting-out costs and 50 per cent of stock and equipment costs. Grants are given subject to the guidance and approval of a library's plans by the Library Council. Grants of 50 per cent towards the annual rent paid for leasing premises are also paid.

In France, the creation of twelve large regional public libraries (BMVR), to act as a balance to the national library (Bibliothèque de France) in Paris, has benefited from state support of a 40 per cent grant to the local communities concerned, such as Poitiers and Rennes:

> The progam created in 1992 is coming to a close [2003] but it has had an obvious impact on France's library network ... the renewal and diversification of public architecture and [has] also encouraged designers to rethink the document/reader relationship, relaxation spaces, [and so on].[92]

There are examples, however, of countries following similar funding approaches to those in the UK. Following PFI legislation in Japan in 1999, a number of local authorities have made use of this funding method, including Kurara City Libraries, although not without some questioning.[93] Kolding in Denmark proposes to use a public/private partnership to finance a new public library. It would be built together with a hotel, shops and flats but is unlikely to be run by the private company, except in a peripheral way, for example, for income-generating services.[94]

SUSTAINED FUNDING

Funding is required not only when a public library is established but also to allow it to 'be sustained on an assured and regular basis'; for example, to maintain the library building, to pay for new and replacement books and other materials, and to ensure that information and communications technology can be upgraded and replaced. It is the absence of adequate sustained funding that leads to many of the faults and problems associated with public libraries and their buildings that engender the kind of criticisms mentioned in this chapter. As noted above, money is not made available 'to make our buildings attractive, welcoming spaces that are fit for purpose'. Decline in library use may thus in part be due to the neglect of UK library buildings.[95]

'COMMODITY, FIRMNESS AND DELIGHT'

However funded, and whether or not they are recognized as landmark architecture or quickly become cultural icons, buildings, including libraries, should fulfil three fundamental requirements. As expressed by Henry Wotton (1568–1639) after Vitruvius: 'Well building hath three conditions: Commodity, Firmness and Delight'.[96] This means they should be:

- well built ('firmness'); that is, strong and durable
- functional ('commodity'); that is, suited to their purpose
- display aesthetic qualities ('delight').

As the above quotation indicates, these requisites were known in ancient times but their timelessness is demonstrated by their re-statement in 2002 by the Commission for Architecture and the Built Environment (CABE).[97]

'FIRMNESS': STRENGTH AND DURABILITY

Architecture is about building, but a building is not necessarily regarded as architecture if the emphasis has been placed on it just being well built and functional. Such criteria could be used to judge the post-war prefabricated house and branch library (built cheaply and quickly), for example, or the farm, industrial and commercial buildings of today, used for storage, manufacturing, retailing and office space.

Whether just a 'building' or more impressively 'architecture', a well-built structure that offers protection from the elements is obviously essential. Soundness of structure will be affected by a building's design, the skill of those who construct it, and the nature of the building materials used. Modern buildings make much use of concrete, steel, glass, metal and plastic, alongside (or instead of) more traditional building materials. Modern building technology means that libraries can be tall buildings, that they can be built wholly or partially underground, can have wide roof spans, and an artificial environment.

Where appropriate, traditional materials – stone, timber, flint, brick – can be used to reflect the character of particular localities and regions of the UK, and in what may be regarded as architecturally sensitive, and usually historic, locations. Branch libraries, such as those in Cornwall at Penryn and Bude, for example, being smaller in scale often provide the opportunity to use local materials and perhaps to reflect local vernacular styles. Brixworth Library and Community Centre, Northamptonshire, makes use of a mix of traditional materials (timber and stone) and modern ones (steel and large areas of glass). Architecture is not just about big and well known works by distinguished architects, as the three basic characteristics will also be found in small-scale buildings, including public libraries.

Experimentation in design and with materials – the use of non-traditional building methods and materials – can pose unexpected problems in the long term. Their durability and the effect of weather (and weathering), for example, cannot always be foreseen: the leaky flat roofs of post-war buildings and the deterioration of reinforced concrete, for instance, are notorious. Without experimentation, however, there can be no innovation and without innovation there can be no real change. The issue, therefore, is not to reject the new out of hand but to question its implementation and try to anticipate and minimize any difficulties it might bring.

There have been problem library buildings such as Birmingham Central Library – its planned replacement was noted earlier – and the 1964 History Faculty building (which includes a library) at the University of Cambridge by the late, renowned architect, James Stirling. This latter building continues to attract worldwide architectural interest, and has a large glazed section (covering the library area) which fronts an L-shaped interior segment. In spite of its aesthetic qualities, the building developed a number of defects – leaks, falling tiles and bricks, and overheating via its glass roof. These became problems of so serious a nature that the university contemplated its replacement in the 1980s. It was not demolished, but restored, and is now a listed building.

Concrete structures, such as Birmingham Central Library, can pose problems (of stability and therefore of safety) and, like Newcastle Central Library, may not wear well. Where appropriate, appearance can be revitalized through cleaning, cladding and the use of colour, although this might seem like a clumsy attempts to mask a building's defects in order to heighten its visual appeal. In early 2003, it was said that £24 million would be needed to repair and modernize Birmingham Central Library and create conditions to store archival and other collections to meet national standards.[98]

The Pompidou Centre, the distinctive 1977 cultural complex in Paris, includes a major library element. Designed by Renzo Piano and Richard Rogers, it has been described as 'an unfinished structure with the scaffolding left in place'[99] – escalators and service elements are on the exterior of the building – and it exemplifies some of the problems of modern buildings. Soon after opening the centre showed signs of deterioration. This may be put down to heavy use – it caters for 17,500 daily visitors – as much as to the nature of the design and the materials used. Eventually the centre was closed for over two years for maintenance and refurbishment, reopening in 2000. The closure enabled a renovation and a reorganization of the interior space, giving it a fresh look as well as facilitating structural repairs.

Today, however, more is required of a building's structure than protection from the elements and ease of maintenance. Energy efficiency, sustainability and a good internal working environment are also important matters, both in the UK and elsewhere, and are affected by a building's design and materials. These issues are discussed in Chapter 6.

'COMMODITY': SUITABILITY TO PURPOSE

Time will reveal whether a building, such as a public library, is sound and well built. Putting it into use will fairly quickly demonstrate whether or not it is entirely suited to its purpose. If the latter is considered to be the case, then a library can be said to be functional and this is a characteristic that all librarians want to see in their library service points. In planning their buildings librarians may well invoke such mantras as 'form follows function' and 'design from the inside out'. These are ways of articulating their almost overriding concern for functionality – their desire for a building whose form (shape, internal plan, appearance, glazing, for example) reflects its purpose. The belief is that this will result in a good library building. In many ways this approach reflects the functionalism school of architecture which holds that it is the architect's duty to see that above all else the buildings they design function well.

Generally speaking, the librarian sees a functional building as one that accommodates library activities and services satisfactorily and 'works' on a day-to-day basis. The building's design features do not hinder, indeed positively assist, the library's roles and the services that support them, as well as its various operations and staff and user activities associated with them. Such functionality, however, is not achieved without considerable planning input, with attention being paid to such factors as space allocation, spatial relationships and traffic flows. Another aspect of building functionality is whether its services, such as heating, ventilation, lifts and cabling, work properly and are not a constant cause for complaint and concern.

The conundrum that emerges from designing a library suited to its current purpose is that its purpose can change, at the very least in part, over time. In order to cope with this problem, another unfailing requirement of librarians is flexibility. A flexible building, it is believed, will accommodate any future changes that may be demanded of it. For a variety of reasons, too much emphasis on flexibility may be a largely an expensive attempt to prepare for the unknown. This important matter will be looked at again in Chapter 8.

The symbolic implications of buildings have already been aired earlier in this chapter. Although referring to academic libraries, it has been said that

[A] building's *library* functions per se should in no way be compromised to meet any other subordinate function. Regrettably I do not believe that this always occurs.

The library may be required, for example, to be a symbol, or a statement of a new beginning, or a social and communications centre. And architects may have other ideas.[100]

'DELIGHT': THE AESTHETIC APPEAL

For a structure to be considered architecturally significant, rather than just a well built, functional building, it must display aesthetic qualities. While in the past ornament or decoration might be thought to have helped define architectural quality, this is no longer the case, although decorative features, such as colour, mosaic and sculpture, may well be part of what helps turn a building into something of greater value and significance. Other characteristics are required, however, and these might include a building that:

- delights those that see it, evoking a variety of emotions, like admiration, inspiration and pleasure – it may have a 'wow' factor: in other words, 'celebrating that invigorating quality and power that architecture can have, not only to function as shelter, but also to inspire those who encounter and experience it'[101]
- makes a distinctive contribution to the environment
- is a good place to be
- enhances the lives of its users by its imaginative use of space
- adds something to a structure beyond the demands of utility
- contributes to identifying its own purpose.

Assuming that a building will be well built, good architecture is therefore a combination of functional and aesthetic qualities. A library suits its purpose and, through its appearance and the experience of using it, offers something more than just functionality to those who may visit it. Objective evaluation can be made of the soundness and functionality of a library building, as discussed in Chapter 8, but an assessment of its aesthetic qualities is likely to be more subjective and personal.

The eye of the beholder

Differing views, firmly held, about the aesthetic quality of a building, where so much depends upon the eye of the beholder, may result in a building awakening strong and contrasting emotions. People are usually quick to form an opinion about the look of a new building, be it a concert hall, local supermarket or public library. They decide that the building is beautiful or ugly, inspiring or dull, welcoming or forbidding, indentifiable or anonymous. They may feel that being of traditional construction and design the building fits in with the local built environment or, being hi-tech, it strikes a discordant note. Depending upon people's opinion of a building, they may condemn it with a nickname like 'Colditz' or admire it with the sobriquet 'The Expresso Machine' or 'Erotic Gherkin', or call it 'The Bookends' – the affectionate portrayal of one town library – or the 'Big Enchilada', the colourful description of San Antonio Public Library (1995). There are also the voices of the undecided or unconcerned, whose lack of enthusiasm may also imply some kind of opinion about the visual impact of the building.

Those who revere the symmetry, harmonious proportions, building materials and so on of classical and Georgian architecture may find the asymmetrical, discordant, sculptural nature of modern architecture displeasing, describing its architects as 'blobmeisters' or 'fracture- merchants'. Many such judgements, whether passed about a local library, office block or housing, are passed by those who have never seen their interiors, nor used them as visitor, worker or resident. Their approval or disapproval often comes from their personal aesthetic sense of what is visually right and proper for a particular environment or location.

It was this sense that Prince Charles exercised in his criticism of late twentieth-century architecture, which included the condemnation of specific buildings. In his speech to the RIBA in 1984, he condemned the proposed extension of the National Gallery in London, likening it to 'a monstrous carbuncle on the face of a much-loved friend'. In a television programme and accompanying book, two libraries came in for the Prince's disapproval. Birmingham Central Library was said to look like an incinerator for books rather than a place were they were kept, and the British Library in the Euston Road likened to a collection of brick sheds whose reading room compared to an assembly hall of a secret police academy.[102] The Prince suggested that these buildings do not live up to his idea of what a library should look like, although his comments in respect of Birmingham did not to take into consideration the quality of its interior. Bordon Library, Hampshire (1986), by Robert Adam, and described as a 'classical' library making use of brick, seemed to meet the Prince's approval.[103] It begs the question, which will be considered in a later chapter, as to whether a library can and should have a particular appearance. As Nolan Lushington commented in the 1970s, 'the two basic schools of architectural thought make the library into a brick fortress or a floating glass palace'.[104] And, as will be shown in Chapter 11, it is the latter school of thought that is currently influencing library buildings, and especially large public libraries, today.

The plans to replace the 1973 Birmingham building, not just because of its appearance and physical condition, do not detract from its place in the history of library buildings, for the UK had never built a public library on this scale before or since. The British Library, in spite of the governmental, funding and managerial vicissitudes attending its long birth (and resulting in an incomplete library to that originally planned), has on the whole confounded its princely critic:

> The British Library engages with the public – and includes large public exhibition galleries, as well as its inside and outside cafés – in a way that it never did in the old British Museum.[105]

Function v aesthetics

In judging a building, architects, architectural critics and many others will tend to place the emphasis on how a building looks, rather than the way it fulfils its purpose. It is this former quality that is more likely to attract attention and an architectural award. Its functional aspects, so important to the user or inhabitant, may well be less than satisfactory and will have to be put up with – or ameliorated as best as possible – in use. The Sydney Opera House is an example of an iconic structure whose inside spaces (and poor acoustic and lighting) fail to meet entirely the functional needs of its users, or to match the awe-inspiring exterior beauty. The opera house is now being refurbished under the supervision of the Danish architect's son.[106]

Interestingly, the residents of a well regarded housing estate designed by James Stirling loved the interiors of their homes but their external appearance was cause for dissatisfaction. In a phone-in about Birmingham Central Library, following Prince Charles's remarks, a caller mentioned the quality of the library's interior.

Aesthetics and functional requirements can be a source of conflict in the planning and designing of a library building, if what the architect wishes to convey aesthetically and emotionally appears to interfere with a building's functionality. To suggest that a balance of the two qualities is required, and compromise may be necessary, may seem like a betrayal of both librarian and architect: 'function should never be allowed to predominate over form, but rather should go together, function finding fulfilment in form.'[107]

Such conflict can be reduced, however, by a knowledgeable client, an imaginative architect and a team approach to planning and design that includes consultation with users. A knowledgeable client is the librarian who has informed themselves about the stages of the planning and building process and the part they play, and has thus, amongst other things, taken the trouble to assess the needs of the community to be served by the library and prepared a satisfactory brief for the architect: 'the finished building reflects the dedication and sensitivity of the client just as much as the contribution of the architect'.[108] An imaginative architect is one who will design a sound, distinctive and functional building in response to the librarian's brief, and within the limitations imposed by the available site and finance.

The design team approach is a common way of guiding a building project, of monitoring progress and resolving difficulties. As in private sector projects, the architect of a public library is likely to get involved with those who will use the building – members of the general public as well as library staff.

Time and space

Architectural and library history demonstrate that public library buildings are of their time as regards building materials, library purpose and architectural style. The public library service and buildings of the 1890s were different in what they sought to achieve, and how they looked, from those of the present day. While there may well be a general consensus about a given historical period and whether its buildings, including libraries, are good or bad architecture, this can change over time. The belated appreciation of Victorian, Edwardian (and indeed of some twentieth century) architecture shows this. It begs the question as to how the well-regarded library buildings of today will be viewed in 25 or 50 years' time. For buildings can go out of fashion and there is a desire to replace the old with the new, sometimes, perhaps, just for that very reason.

Whatever the visual appeal of a library building, it must be supplemented by structural soundness and functionality. For the architect's design to respond to the functional requirements of a library, he/she must be informed fully of its purpose, roles, aims and objectives. This requires that those commissioning the building have formulated a clear idea as to the building's mission and functions. There is general international agreement as to the overall mission and various functions that a public library can fulfil, as shown in the previous chapter, but individual nations and particular localities will have their own priorities and emphases that will be reflected in the design of specific public library buildings for today.

NOTES

1   Moye, C. (2003), 'The gospel according to George', *Telegraph property* 21 June, 6–7.
2   The plans were to be the subject of a public enquiry but local government reorganization meant the process started anew.
3   Murray, P. (2004), 'The ten best buildings', *Independent review* 16 June, 19.
4   For a brief description of San Francisco Public Library see Freeman, M. (1998), 'The library on the bay', *Public library journal* **13** (6), 95–6.
5   Gumbel, A. (2004), 'The perfect city library', *Independent review* 25 May, 12–13.
6   Loew, S. (1998), *Modern architecture in historic cities: policy, planning, and building in contemporary France*, London: Routledge, 2, 226.
7   'An icon for Birmingham' (2003), *Public library journal* **18** (1), 3.
8   Broadley, R. (2000), 'Shop front for a treasure house', *Public library journal* **15** (3), 72–3.
9   Devine, J. (2002), 'Sunderland shines on', *Public library journal* **17** (1), 11–13.
10   For details of the Forum Barcelona 2004, see www.barcelona2004.org.
11   Merrick, J. (2004), 'Toronto, we have lift-off', *Independent review* 16 June, 12–13.
12   'Civil renewal: £1m for citizenship' (2004), *Library + information update* **3** (2), 12.
13   Rogers, R. and Power, A. (2000), *Cities for a small country*, London: Faber, vii.
14   www.odpm.gov.uk.
15   McMaster, R. (2002), 'Stratford Library – vision of the future', *Assignation* **19** (2), 40–42.
16   Quoted in Merrick, J. (2002), 'The urban guerrilla' *Independent review* 26 July, 4.
17   Glancey, J. (2003), 'Shelf life', *Guardian* 10 March, 13.
18   'Free to demolish' (2003), *Library + information update* **2** (4), 16.
19   Pfoser, A. (2003), 'A library with its own underground station ...' (in German), *Bibliothek* **55** (6), 403–9.
20   Albanese, A.R. and others (2001), 'Libraries as equity building blocks', *Library journal* **126** (9), 40–43.
21   For further information about the problems of conserving post-war buildings, see Macdonald, S. (2001), *Preserving post-war heritage: the care and conservation of mid-twentieth century architecture*, Shaftesbury: Donhead.

22 Loew, S. (1998), 1.

23 Lovell, V. (2004), 'The ten best public art works', *Independent review* 12 January, 6.

24 Miles, M. (1989), *Art for public places: critical essays*, Winchester: Winchester School of Art, 159, 160, 217, 218.

25 The GLA is not responsible for London's public libraries, which rests with the 32 London boroughs and the City of London.

26 A summary of the action plan is given in *Framework for the future: turning vision into action for public libraries* (2003), London: Resource.

27 'Building work begins' (2004), *Library + information update* **3** (2), 5.

28 Unidentified chief librarian quoted in Usherwood, B. (2003), 'A framework with a fragile foundation: thoughts from a critical friend on *Framework for the future*', *Library management* **24** (6/7), 305–9: 308.

29 *Tomorrow's library: views of the public library sector* (2003), Belfast: Department of Culture, Arts and Leisure in Northern Ireland

30 *Better public libraries* (2003), London: CABE and Resource.

31 Crudge, R. (2003), 'Bigger buildings, better services' [letter], *Library + information update* **2** (10), 29; Smelt, M. (2003), 'Flabby writing, flabby thinking in Resource report' [letter], *Library + information update* **2** (11), 29.

32 King, S. (2003), 'CABE bites back' [letter], *Library + information update* **2** (12), 29.

33 Ssshhh!!!!! [editorial] (2003), *Country life*, 21 August, 31.

34 Coates, T. (2004), *Who's in charge? Responsibility for the public library service*, London: Libri Trust and Laser Foundation, 18.

35 Coates, T. (2004), 1.

36 'MLA is several steps ahead of Libri' (2004), *Library + information update* **3** (6), 2.

37 Edmonds, D. (2003), 'Portfolio for success', *Library + information update* **2** (7), 50–51.

38 Ssshhh!!!!! [editorial] (2003), 31.

39 Burrell, I. (2003), 'How Glasgow seized its chance to put unsavoury image behind it', *Independent*, 5 June, 9.

40 Berndtson, M. (1999), 'Cities of Culture 2000 – the libraries' role', *Scandinavian public library quarterly* **32** (4), 23–5; Also www.lib.hel.fi/english.

41 www.corkcorp.ie/facilities_art_city of culture.hmtl.

42 Vallely, P. (2003), 'Liverpool's art and architecture help it to cultural crown', *Independent* 5 June, 9.

43 www.riba.org.

44 www.nzia.co.nz.

45 www.betterpublicbuildings.gov.uk; see also *Better public buildings* (2000), London: Department of Culture, Media and Sport.

46 'PM's best building is ... a library' (2003), *Public library journal* **18** (4), 109; For details of the award scheme and other winners see, www.bciaward.org.uk.

47 Bournemouth Library and others of the same period are described in Bradbury, D. (2003), 'Read all about it', *Telegraph magazine* 15 March, 50–54.

48 www.civictrust.org.uk

49 'Civic plaudits for library buildings' (2003), *Public library journal* **18** (2), 47.

50 'UK/Eire share honours' (2003), *Library + information update* **2** (11), 3; Gowland, J. and Brady, J. (2003) 'How does it feel to be a winner?', *Public library journal* **18** (4), 80–82.

51 See also www.cilip.org.uk/groups/plg/plg.html.

52 'Tackling a new flagship for Rugby' (2000), *Public library journal* **15** (3), 74–5.

53 Knight, T. and Campbell, J. (2004), 'Public Library Building Awards – new categories for 2005', *Public library journal*, winter, 30.

54 An illustrated article featuring the award-winning libraries is usually found in the April issue of *American libraries*. Libraries are also briefly described at: www.ala.org/ala/lamaawards/aiaalalibrarybuildings.hmt.

55 www.cslib.org/awardexcel.htm.

56 For details of winners, etc, see www.accessola.com; www.jla.or.jp.

57 For 36 UK and European libraries, illustrated and annotated, see www.worpole.dircon.co.uk.

58   Storms, M. (1998), 'Building libraries in Flanders: twenty years of public library construction, 1978:1997' (in Dutch), *Bibliotheek-en archiefgids* **74** (4), 136–40.

59   Fayet, S. (1996), 'The construction of public libraries: general tendencies' (in French), *Bulletin des bibliothèques de France* **41** (5), 8–13; For a list of recent French municipal libraries, see Chaintreau, A-M. and Gascuel, J. (2000), *Votre bâtiment de A à Z*, Paris: Éditions du Cercle de la Libraire, 277–84.

60   Agnoli, A. (2001), 'From library to resource centre' (in Italian), *Biblioteche oggi* **19** (8), 88–92.

61   Fenart, P. and Michelizza, F. (2002), 'A town with a regional mission (BMVR) finds a home in Nice' (in French), *Bibliothèque(s)* (4), 58–9.

62   Bernillon, S. and others (2002), 'Behind the scenes at Toulouse's new resource centre' (in French) *Bibliothèque(s)* (3), 64–6.

63   Krol, J. (2003), *New library buildings in the Netherlands*, The Hague: Netherlands Public Library Association.

64   Pearman, H. (2001), 'What a turn-up for the books', *Sunday Times* 2 December, 18.

65   www.librisdesign.org; see also Hall, R.B. (2004), 'Libris DESIGN and financing public library buildings', *Bottom line* **17** (1), 20–27; Campbell, A.L. (2003), 'Magical models', *Library journal* **128** (3), 38–40.

66   McCarthy, R. (2004), 'Understanding project costs and building costs', *Bottom line* **17** (1), 6–9.

67   www.lottery.culture.gov.uk.

68   www.biglotteryfund.org.uk.

69   Peachey, P. (2003), 'London given more lottery cash than any region', *Independent* 5 February, 9.

70   Buchanan, K. (2003) 'London "taste police" slammed', *Western mail* 12 December, 3.

71   Drinkwater, R. (1996), 'PFI opportunities for libraries: a view from the leisure sector', in Barton, D. (ed.), *The Private Finance Initiative: opportunities for libraries?* Bruton, Somerset: Capital Planning Information, 11.

72   Pyke, N. (2002), 'New school or industrial shed: school design best and worst', *Independent education* 17 October, 4.

73   Levett, S. (2003), 'Getting into bed with the private sector ...', *Public library journal* **18** (3), 61–2, 64: 61.

74   Barton, D. (ed.) (1996), *The Private Finance Initiative: opportunities for libraries?* Bruton, Somerset: Capital Planning Information.

75   'DCMS cash for three PFI projects' (2003), *Library + information update* **2** (9), 6.

76   'Two PL schemes on horizon' (2004), *Library + information update* **3** (2), 15.

77   Sibthorpe, R.A. (2001), 'A new path to follow', *Library Association record* **103** (4), 236–7; Levett, S. (2003), 61–2, 64.

78   Sibthorpe, R.A. (2001), 237.

79   Conway, P. (1996), 'A view from local government' in Barton, D. (ed.), 30, 27.

80   'Lowestoft reopens' (2003), *Library + information update* **2** (4), 15.

81   'Dover celebrates its new Centre' (2003), *Public library journal* **18** (4), 108.

82   ['Wing Library'] (2003), *Public library journal* **18** (1), 23.

83   'Funding idea' (2003), *Library + information update* **2** (10), 9.

84   'First come, first served' (2004), *Library + information update* **3** (2), 5.

85   'Staffs £3m boost' (2002), *Library + information update* **1** (6), 8.

86   BBC News 31 January 2003: http://news.bbc.co.uk, 11 April 2003.

87   Hyams, E. (2001), 'Seizing the opportunity in Cambridgeshire', *Library Association record* **103** (7), 420–21.

88   Evans, G. (2004), 'Building on partnerships in Caerphilly', *Y ddolen* (38), 14.

89   Bryson, J., Usherwood, B. and Proctor, R. (2003), *Libraries must also be buildings? New impact study*, London: Resource, 8.

90   'Brown neglects PN' (2004), *Library + information update* **3** (9), 2.

91   Evans, H. (2004), 'Finland 2: better by design', *Y ddolen* (36) 16–17; Schüler, S. (1996), 'Contemporary library planning in Finland', *Scandinavian public library quarterly* **29** (3), 22–4.

92   Rouyer-Gayette, F. (2004), 'Libraries as places: buildings for the 21st century' in *Libraries as places: buildings for the 21st century*, edited by M-F. Bisbrouck and others, Munich: Saur, 183–200: 183–4. In English and French.

93   Yamaguchi, K. (2003), 'Can the future of libraries be entrusted to PFI?' (in Japanese), *Toshokan Zasshi* **97** (8), 518–21.

94   Lerche, A. and Madsen, G. (2004), 'Library in a new way' (in Danish), *Bibliotekspressen* (6). 150–53.

95   Murray, D. (2003), 'Whom do you serve?', *Library + information update* **2** (2), 23.

96   Quoted in Curl, J.S. (1992), *Classical architecture*, London: Batsford, 12.

97   *Design review* (2002), London: CABE, 17.

98   Glancey, J. (2003), 13.

99   Reid, R. (1980), *The book of buildings: a traveller's guide*, London: Joseph, 336.

100   'An interview with David Kaser' (1987), *Library administration and management* **1** (3), 76–7.

101   Mackertich, P (2001), *Architectural expressions: a photographic reassessment of fun in architecture*, Chichester: Wiley-Academy, 9.

102   Charles, Prince of Wales (1989), *A vision of Britain*, London: Doubleday, 32, 65. The book also lists the prince's ten architectural 'principles' (78–97), some more contentious than others.

103   Charles, Prince of Wales (1989), 122.

104   Lushington, N. (1976), 'Flow of function in libraries: some randon notes on functional design', *American libraries* **7** (2), 92–5: 93.

105   Pearman, H. (2001), 18.

106   Marks, K. (2004), 'Sydney invites opera house architect back for an encore and a facelift', *Independent* 10 February, 82.

107   McDonald, J.A. (1967), 'Twenty-five years of public library architecture, 1941–1966', in McDonald, J.A. and Hunt, D.H., *Public library architecture*, Philadelphia, Pennsylvania: Drexel Press, 25.

108   Rogers, R. (1990), *Architecture: a modern view*, London: Thames and Hudson, 22.

3 Service point provision, size and shape

The library should have adequate space to implement the full range of library services that are consistent with the library's strategic plan and that meet local area or national standards/guidelines.

IFLA/UNESCO, 2001[1]

As this chapter demonstrates, not all library buildings occupy the same status in a library system, which may comprise a number of service points spread over a geographic area of some size, whether urban or rural. The fundamental planning questions are therefore what kind of service point is under consideration and where it fits in a library system's building provision strategy. Related to this is the question of what size of building is to be provided and how this can be determined. Associated with its service point role and size is the question of what services, facilities and amenities should be provided in a projected library. Chapter 7 explores how these are largely determined by the specific needs of the community for whom the building is being provided: this chapter describes the main elements of a library building and its service options.

The nature of a service point, its size and component parts can result in library buildings of different plan or shape – rectangular or circular, for example. This chapter concludes by considering some of the likely advantages and disadvantages of varied library plans or shapes.

UK SERVICE POINT PROVISION

In early 2003 there were 4,624 public library service points (including 656 mobile libraries) in the UK provided by just over 200 library authorities.[2] Library numbers have, however, declined since 1993 by 156, when they totalled 4,780. Public libraries are also responsible for library service at nearly 17,000 other locations, in homes, hospitals, prisons, for example, throughout the UK, a significant decline from a figure of 19,277 in

1993. Since that date the total number of service points has dropped from 24,481 to 22,083, a decrease of 10 per cent. The amount spent on premises by public libraries in 2002–2003 was 11.2 per cent of total expenditure, excluding capital charges, a drop from 12 per cent in 1997–98.

In spite of increased expenditure, on acquisitions, for example, and government exhortations for service points to improve their hours of opening, by being accessible at more convenient times, including evenings and Sundays, the statistics reflect a continuing decline in book loans, although an increase in library visits. The introduction of public library standards for England and Wales may encourage a future improvement.

Comparing 1993 with 2003, both service improvement and regression are shown by the numbers of libraries:

- open less than 10 hours weekly fell from 424 to 169 (not included in the service point figure of 4,624 given above)
- open 10–29 hours decreased by 38
- open 30–44 hours dropped by 177
- open 45–59 hours per week jumped from 751 to 845
- open 60 hours and over declined from 46 in 1993 to 39 in 1998, but increased to 54 by 2003.

The busiest libraries in the twelve UK regions in 2001–2002 were (for the whole of England), Liverpool Central (and in the other UK countries), Cardiff Central, Dunfermline and Belfast Central.

TYPES OF LIBRARY SERVICE POINT

Public library service points (1971) described the variety of library buildings serving various sizes of urban and rural population in the UK and the position remains much the same today.[3] At the heart of city-based library services, both large and small, is the central (or main) library, often housing large stocks, specialized departments and the library administration. In counties, library services may be administered from an independently sited headquarters or from offices within a county council building. Depending upon its location and other local circumstances, the headquarters building may include storage facilities, some county-wide services and some public departments.

The next tier of library service is provided by district, divisional, group, regional or area libraries. These are located in major urban centres – possibly called regional headquarters – and may have some responsibility for the oversight of a number of branch libraries (the next level of service point provision) in the surrounding locality.

Branches of various sizes are the most numerous of public library service points. Small communities are usually served by a part-time branch library and those under 1,500 population by a mobile library, or a smaller vehicle in sparsely populated areas.

Public libraries also make personal deliveries to the housebound and are involved with the provision of library service in old people's homes, schools, hospitals and prisons, for example. The separate library accommodation required to facilitate such provision, or to provide mobile or other vehicle-based library service, are not the subject of this book. However, sometimes factors connected to such provision may affect static public service points, because of the need to consider alternatives to a mobile library service, or the requirement to provide an 'outreach' library base, garage or other facilities.

The nomenclature of library buildings is undergoing change in the UK, with smaller libraries in particular being called community, neighbourhood, outreach or hub libraries. Staffordshire has devised a set of terms for libraries serving different population sizes and offering a particular level of library service:

- portal libraries, for populations of over 50,000 and based at busy central locations
- town libraries, for populations of 20,000–50,000
- neighbourhood libraries, for populations of 10,000–20,000, preferably located in dual-use buildings
- community library services – small drop-in service points (for populations of 5,000–10,000); drop-off points (for example, post offices) for populations of under 5,000; mobile library services; services to residential homes, day centres, and so on.[4]

CENTRAL LIBRARIES

Although sometimes applicable to libraries further down the hierarchy, the roles of a central library can be summarized as follows:

- to act as the command headquarters and library service flagship
- to provide resources in depth
- to act as a local branch or community library, offering a popular library service for all age groups
- to reinforce district and branch collections
- to serve those living outside the bounds of the city and beyond
- to act as a channel for accessing information held locally and elsewhere
- to act as a special or academic library for some users, such as students, specialists or citizen scholars
- to house the research collections
- to house the principal non-book material and non-print collections, such as maps, sheet music, sound and moving image recordings
- to organize and offer cultural events.[5]

A central library is not therefore one building and one collection 'but more as a series of libraries, organized in different ways, with varying purposes, and serving people of many levels'. It may be organized into departments or library areas reflecting subject matter, function, reader or interest groups, or by form of material.[6] These and other ways of organizing a library are discussed in Chapter 10.

Librarians and politicians like central libraries as impressively demonstrating to the local community the importance that they, and society, attach to educational and cultural provision.[7] Nevertheless, the idea of such a library leviathan was being questioned from the 1970s onwards in the US, where large (and very large) buildings are more numerous than in the UK, with a view to finding improved and more economic methods of delivering the services they offer.[8] Early in the 1960s, however, Wheeler inveighed against what he called 'the split-personality library' alternative – one which divided up the central library, usually because of site and funding problems, across more than one building.[9] For example, one of the main functions of a central library, to house a large, little-used retrospective collection has been questioned, as it could be stored elsewhere. Also queried is whether the central library should act also as a branch library, or whether separate provision should be made. Following the destruction of Norwich Central Library by fire (see Chapter 6), it was asked in the mid-1990s whether 'we need to replace the Central Library, or should we be bold and go for a distributed virtual service with only a small branch library serving inner city residents'?[10]

One of the planning issues considered in the mid-1970s by Tucson (Arizona) concerned what was to be included in its new main library. Readers, it was recognized, use a main library in a variety of ways but should it provide 'a complete package'? It was suggested for Tucson that a children's room was unnecessary and that the administration, technical services, storage and some support service might be housed elsewhere. Mention was also made of an earlier proposal that Tucson's main library should have one important function – a reference service.[11] Writing about alternative central library models, F.W. Summers comes to a similar view, that 'if the central library is not to have something of everything' it should emphasize information services, assist database searching and provide a 'place for the serendipitous exploration and acquisition of knowledge'.[12] Interestingly there are 29 reference-only libraries in separate buildings in the UK, of which 20 are in England.

From personal experience, one writer would not advocate the decentralization of a library's technical services and offices to another location, as this was felt to lead to lost staff time, transport costs and operational difficulties.[13] Another insists, however, that there is no economic justification, especially given modern electronic networks, for housing technical services in expensive central library space. He also argues that where special collections are made available by a public library 'it does not follow that they can best be provided in the traditional monolithic central library'.[14] This suggests separate libraries for specific subject fields and user groups, such as music, the arts, and local studies, and for business people, children and young people. Such separate facilities, it is argued, should be housed close to those who would make most use of them. Some examples of this approach that have emerged in the UK and elsewhere – particularly in Singapore with its 'lifestyle' and 'boutique' libraries.

In spite of the questioning of the idea of the central library, a number of large new American examples were planned and built during the 1990s and are referred to at various points in this book.[15] An examination of the use of two of Canada's largest central libraries, Toronto and Vancouver, in 2002 showed that they fulfil many of the normative ideals of public spaces and act as important resources, although private market interests threaten their varied role as public places.[16] An earlier examination of Toronto, along with Rotterdam Central, showed that there were similarities (they are both pyramidal structures, for instance) but also differences. Rotterdam was thought to be 'much more extrovert, a social and cultural information centre for Rotterdam and its region'.[17]

Large libraries in some other countries may have a support role for smaller library systems within their region, or have a particular regional mission. For example, the Bibliothèques Municipales à Vocation Régionale (BMVR, or Town Libraries with a Regional Mission) in France. The BMVR in Nice (2002) is one of twelve such libraries and has a striking design – the library's box-like administrative building perches on the Salvador Dali-like chin of a human-shaped sculpture.[18]

COUNTY LIBRARY HEADQUARTERS

As they tend to reflect the history and structure of individual county library services, these buildings vary considerably. County headquarters buildings house support and services for a county's libraries and their users. They may accommodate such elements as offices and workrooms for the library administration, bibliographical, cataloguing and processing activities, staffroom facilities, computer services, special collections, reserve stock storage, the schools library service, display and exhibition preparation, and garaging for library transport and mobiles. They may also act as a local public library service point.

A number of counties in the UK, such as Hampshire, still work from adapted, sprawling premises. Others have the use of council offices, as at Durham, Nottinghamshire and Norfolk, or purpose-built premises, many erected in the 1950s, 1960s and 1970s. West Riding was reputed to have built the largest county headquarters ($4,831m^2$) in 1964, while in the same year Kent unveiled an exciting headquarters consisting of a bookstack tower, administration block and multi-sided students' library building. By contrast, Montgomeryshire's headquarters (1963) was at the other end of the scale at $1,093m^2$.[19] Some headquarters buildings include a local branch, as in West Sussex, or even a town or central library, for example at Northallerton, North Yorkshire (headquarters extension and town library, 1977), Warwick (a 1983 conversion of council offices), and at Dorchester, Dorset. Staffordshire and Somerset both have their own separate headquarters buildings.

Headquarters buildings of the 1980s and 1990s include three Scottish ones at Oldmeldrum, Aberdeenshire (1987, $1,486m^2$), Stirling (1984, $1,350m^2$) and a conversion for Midlothian (1993, 455m²). In Northern Ireland, Armagh (South Eastern Library and Education Board, 1981) and Omagh (Western Library and Education Board, 1991) were also both built to house teachers' centres.

DISTRICT LIBRARIES

District, divisional, area or group libraries are really large branch libraries. They owe their designation in part to the changes wrought by successive local government reorganizations, and to the need to create a tiered library structure for managerial purposes in a library system where there are many service points of differing size and scale. In both urban and rural areas they usually offer a full range of services on a scale appropriate to local circumstances and the number of potential users. In many ways the district library offers a service similar to a central library, and in counties they are often the 'central' libraries because of their location in market and other towns. Similarly, some urban library systems may not have a central library and the district libraries are in effect the local 'central' library. In large urban and county authorities, district libraries may have some administrative or other functions allotted to them. It is suggested that such libraries, preferably associated with a shopping centre, would serve a population of 25,000 or more.[20]

Singapore has no central library but some of its libraries are designated regional libraries, those at Tamine (1994, 6,300m²), Woodlands (2001, 11,000m²) and Jurong (refurbished 2004), for example.[21]

BRANCH LIBRARIES

Prior to the Second World War, municipal library systems, excepting those in major cities and towns, consisted of only a central library, with possibly a few branches. County libraries relied on deposit collections in small community centres to meet their readers' needs and on its library headquarters' postal section to supply books requested by readers. Nevertheless some county branches, in Lancashire and Middlesex for example, had been built. The post-war period, however, saw an enormous growth in the establishment of branch libraries in both urban and rural areas with new functions being taken up by county library headquarters. Ken Stockham notes the family resemblance of 1960s branch libraries: possibly too much glass and a tendency to a 'box-like' appearance.[22]

Branch libraries can vary a great deal in size and scope, depending upon the population served, the services provided and special requirements, such as to hold reserve stock, house a special service, accommodate community facilities, or garage a mobile library. However, many branch libraries will be small, essentially one-room buildings with work and restroom facilities for staff. Today, materials for loan will consist of a variety of formats, there will be a quick reference collection, some reading and study places, computer facilities and Internet access, and special provision for children. Depending on local need there may be a meeting room and refreshment provision.

In a 1968 conference paper, Alan Longworth responded to the question: 'The branch library – is it necessary?'.[23] Longworth suggested that localized communities, in the days before increased mobility, accounted for the opening of branch libraries, which tended to be 'copies of the early central libraries without administrative offices' and provided easy access to books. Longworth questioned branch library provision and travel distance standards, saying that people will travel more than a mile for a good library service and especially if parking is easy: 'mobility tends to favour the larger unit of service'. He then advances the advantages of a centralized system but notes that city size and the transport congestion of today, as well as the likely numbers of users attracted to such a library make such a solution unrealistic: 'but a system based on an over-provision of small service points is also not efficient'. The compromise, he suggests, is a central library and fewer branches. Nevertheless the needs of children, those without personal (or reliable public) transport, for example, must be considered.

Case study: Runcorn and Warrington

A related aspect of the centralized/decentralized issue discussed earlier is whether library service in an urban area is best concentrated in a central library or provided through a dispersed or decentralized pattern of branch library provision. In the UK, as part of the follow-up research arising from the establishment of the Runcorn Shopping City Library (described in Chapter 7), a survey was conducted in the mid-1980s of the community and library members of Runcorn and part of Warrington, both having broadly similar populations. Runcorn was served by its then new 1981 building and its Old Town Library of 1906. Warrington was served by a central library (1857) and eight branches, three coming within the study area, one of which was a dual-use library, serving both a school population and the general public.

The study found that there was little overlap in the catchment areas of the two Runcorn libraries and the three Warrington branches but Warrington Central Library drew users from the entire area. The research found that levels of awareness, of use and of a favourable attitude to libraries were higher in Runcorn than in the Warrington study area. Stronger library consciousness in Runcorn was considered to be probably due to its style of library provision but the report acknowledged the Runcorn 'solution' could not be fully applied to Warrington. The research concluded that

> The centralized provision of Runcorn gave a more effective solution than the dispersed provision of Warrington [but] could not be applied elsewhere without regard to the infrastructure of the area concerned. Runcorn New Town was ideally suited physically to this form of library provision.[24]

OTHER SERVICE POINTS AND STORAGE SOLUTIONS

It can be seen, therefore, that the library system structure of central or county headquarters, district, branch and mobile service point is a well established one. This is not to say that their cost, functions, effectiveness and numbers – with the implications for library building provision – have not been questioned. Centralized or decentralized library systems, the use of prefabricated buildings, popular reading outlets in shopping centres and storage facilities are some of the issues and possible solutions raised by such questioning. Like public libraries themselves, mobile libraries are a successful worldwide phenomenon. Librarians, nevertheless, still look for better ways of bringing both the physical and virtual library to those unable or unlikely to use larger centres, and to those in small communities or sparsely populated areas. Solutions might involve the provision of a prefabricated or transportable library for use in community centres or similar premises.

PREFABRICATED BRANCH LIBRARIES

Even if not always purpose-built, library service points are normally housed in traditionally built structures. Working with limited funds, dealing with uncertainty and change in a community, or wishing to promote library use (perhaps by providing small outlets for popular books), the purpose-built branch library may not always be the best answer. A possible (and cheaper) solution to uncertainty and change, and an alternative to new build, is the prefabricated branch library. Potentially relocatable and reusable, it has other advantages that include the speed of construction, ease of extension by the addition of further units, and comparable maintenance costs to a traditional building. In the past, library suppliers both in the UK and in the US have been able to offer a 'package' library by providing both the prefabricated building, shelving, furniture and furnishings.[25]

In the UK the prefabricated buildings were available in a variety of sizes (74 to 167m²) to serve populations from 1,000–2,000 to 4,000–5,000 and a considerable number of such buildings were erected throughout the country; for example, Hadleigh (Suffolk, 1967, but replaced 20 years later), West Heath and Druids Heath (Birmingham, 1974 and 1976) and Berkeley (Gloucestershire, 1976). Drawbacks to this type of library structure relate to the external design, which may not suit all environments, the stigma attached to mass-produced prefabricated structures and practical issues associated with flat-roofed buildings (where used) and temperature control. There is also a danger that a satisfactory temporary solution becomes a long-term (almost permanent) one. Prefabricated buildings are still available from a number of manufacturers but something more customized and less utilitarian in appearance would be required by those contemplating this kind of solution.

KIOSK LIBRARIES

In the US, Porta-Structure Industries produced three prefabricated library buildings: porta-kiosks (16m^2), porta-boutiques (46m^2) and porta-structures (149m^2). The last named was the largest and could be used as a prefabricated branch library – a porta-branch. The others, also known as storefront or mini-libraries, could be used to promote library use through their location in shopping centres, parks, rapid-transit stations and on city streets.

Much discussed in the US in the 1970s and 1980s, the kiosk concept has some attraction today for the librarian in the UK and elsewhere attempting to reach out to those who generally do not use libraries. Even in the 1970s, the idea was apparently not new in the US but had often been unsuccessful because too much was attempted in too small a rented space (93–139m^2). It was considered a mistake to try to provide a full service branch on the cheap, probably wrongly located in a failing shopping centre.

In revisiting the concept in the 1970s, Baltimore County chose an eight-sided, peaked roof, prefabricated structure (approximately 117m^2), that could be erected in a shopping centre parking area or elsewhere. It created its own shelving system, with books (mainly paperbacks) displayed by category. This so-called storefront library, with issues of 150,000 a year – and here is the contrast to earlier such libraries – contained no reference material, no study tables and was operated by volunteers as a satellite of the nearest branch. The library, open for a minimum of 40 hours a week, served areas too densely populated for a mobile and too small to justify a full service branch.[26] In the same decade the District of Columbia used kiosks and porta-branches as they were flexible and inexpensive and could be removed if a failure or expanded if a success.[27] One Washington D.C. porta-kiosk, used also as a centre for activities, was dubbed 'the kiosk in the park'. The popular reading outlet, symbolized by the kiosk or storefront library, was not without its critics, one considering it efficient but not effective. It was efficient in giving high circulation at low cost but ineffective socially. It provided leisure reading for those who could afford to pay for it, offered no exposure to other library services and removed the educational purpose of libraries: libraries were 'taking inadequate services out to the people'.[28]

In 1979, Cincinnati and Hamilton County embarked on a Books-in-the-Mall project – 'to increase the availability of library services and experiment in their delivery'. Their small kiosk library (46m^2) flourished alongside two bookshops in the urban shopping centre to the mutual advantage of all three. The kiosk was open the same hours as the shopping centre, including Sundays. As in Baltimore, books were arranged by category (see Chapter 10) and consisted of an uncatalogued browsing collection of best-sellers, romances, westerns and how-to-do-it books. On average, items were issued seven times a year, giving the kiosk a greater circulation per square foot than any of the library's other agencies. The project's success was put down to 'combining commercial techniques with traditional library services' – and the kiosk acted as an access point to other library services.[29]

Both small and large portable libraries were used by Fairfax County, Virginia, in the 1980s for new areas – firstly a mini-branch in a shopping mall (27m²) and secondly two outdoor free-standing libraries (149m²) with seats for 32 readers. Once again, library stock consisted of popular paperbacks and high turnover material. As a response to rapidly expanding needs, Fairfax County found portable structures to be highly satisfactory.[30]

A 1993 American survey of portable libraries concluded that '80 percent of the owning systems are satisfied with their portable libraries ... [they] attract new users, increase circulation and maximize system visibility'.[31] The London Borough of Hammersmith and Fulham was said to be looking at ways of serving potential library users coming into the borough each day. The council is proposing that kiosk libraries be located at major bus or tube stations, stocking best-seller and popular titles. In Gosford, Australia, where library loans were falling, it was reported in 2002 that a loan service at the railway station was being offered to commuters from 5.30 a.m. This 'Book Express' service was operating from a minimalist library – a trolley, plastic boxes and a sign – and use and publicity have been greater than expected.[32] While these two examples target commuters, *Public library service points* may have had such popular reading outlets in mind when it talked about 'in-filling' service points for those who need only recreational reading and are unable or unwilling to travel far to a library.[33] For example, Islington has established mini-libraries in convenient places, such as community centres. They contain about 700 books and are open once a week.[34]

LEASED/RENTED PREMISES

By 1979, however, Baltimore had turned its back on the relocatable mini-library in favour (once again) of a leased unit, preferably in a shopping centre. Leasing over five years cost less than a portable building and a shopping centre offered units of 139–279m². Portable buildings were found to be insufficiently spacious and so their cheapness was unsatisfactory if this resulted in inadequate premises. As with portable libraries, the new leased units concentrated on one function and were therefore 'bigger but not better'.[35]

As can be seen from the American experience, leased premises can be a means of providing a service point. This is usually in a shop or shopping centre and in a period of library growth and development can be a useful solution to service point provision. Public libraries in the Republic of Ireland have made considerable use of leased premises with the support of central government funds. However the solution should only be seen as a temporary measure, as the premises and their location are unlikely to be entirely ideal and as expenditure mounts over the years the local authority has no negotiable asset at the end of it.

OTHER SERVICE DELIVERY METHODS

Other ways of providing a public library service have to be considered where a static service cannot be justified, usually in rural or sparsely populated areas. A number of methods may be utilized, such as a mobile library, shared use of non-library premises, and stand alone information terminals,[36] each having a variety of planning and design implications.

Mobile libraries

A mobile library, most often associated with a road vehicle, may be less commonly housed on board a boat (Norway) a train (Sweden) or in a helicopter (the former USSR).[37] Used to provide library service to small rural communities which do not justify a static service point, mobile libraries are able to offer a range of formats for loan, links with the wider library and information world, as well as study and reading space. The urban mobile library provides a similar service in towns and cities. A variety of specialist mobile vehicles may be used for delivering services to children, promoting local history or providing information services. In some sparsely populated areas a small van is used to provide households with a door-to-door service. Mobile library design, although extremely important, is not a topic for the present book and IFLA's *Mobile library guidelines* offer guidance on such matters as vehicle types, interior layout, and furniture and equipment. More significantly for library buildings, it provides recommendations for the garage and work areas that will need to be provided in those libraries from which such vehicles operate.[38]

While the mobile is a worldwide solution to the provision of library service where a static service is not warranted, other methods have been tried. *Library services to small communities* and other publications describe the variety of such solutions, including mail-order or a postal service, which would require appropriately designed library work areas.[39] Two other solutions also require a vehicle for service delivery and have implications for garaging and work space. Once again, vehicle design is an important issue, although not discussed in detail here. More significant here, is to record attempts to offer a service similar to that provided by a static service point.

Container libraries

A fully equipped and stocked movable library building, rather like a commercial container in shape, is transported to a site for two days, and thus can serve up to three sites a week. Pioneered in the UK by Cornwall for communities of 'intermediate' size, the container offered a good size, changing stock, a branch standard of service, and almost level access. A fundamental weakness of the scheme was the failure to find appropriate sites, or of gaining access to sites, where the container service was needed. In addition, although cheap to build, the containers were expensive to maintain.

Derbyshire gave consideration to the Cornwall container and other alternatives but a suitably adapted box trailer that met the library service's requirements was obtained.

Rather than acquire its own prime mover, the semi-trailer container library was moved by a contractor. The container was more expensive than in Cornwall and there were additional cost implications, it was higher off the ground with heavy doors, although potential stock gains were lost to a foyer and excessive staff facilities. Cornwall and Derbyshire's container libraries involved taking the library 'building' to the communities they served.

Transportable libraries

Bradford's transportable or roll-on, roll-off library was concerned with taking the library furniture and book stock to community centres or other accommodation. After providing a library service at one location, a van arrived to transport the library to another. In this way a number of communities were served by the resources. While intended to replace part-time branches it ended up giving service to communities which needed such a library.

In spite of the publicity and interest in the work carried out by Cornwall, Derbyshire and Bradford, their initiatives were regarded as experiments that in the end were not adopted permanently by the authorities concerned.[40]

Fold-away libraries

These experiments brought the library to the people: a more recent development, the 'fold-away' solution, leaves the library in place but moved and stored away. The system was devised by Point Eight for the Keith Axon Centre (London, Redbridge), a single-space but multi-functional community building. Shelving units are mounted on castors and hinged to the wall units which can be folded together with the books secure inside. Reproduced and enlarged local Edwardian photographs on the ends of the shelving bays provide an attractive background when the units are 'folded-way'.[41]

STORAGE LIBRARIES

Until recently, the construction of a building solely for book storage was not common in any library sector in the UK. Public libraries may outhouse materials in adapted buildings when there is a space problem but usually the storage of less-used material (the reserve stock) is accommodated in the library buildings themselves, either centrally or on a distributed basis. Clearly the collection management policy of a public library system as regards the question of the retention of older material (including cooperative obligations) will have an impact on the space requirements for all the buildings within a library system.

One of the driving forces for a new larger library is often the desire to display more open-shelf stock and/or to house more conveniently and economically a large retrospective collection, whose use, as noted earlier, may not justify the space it is accorded. Such general reserve stocks may be duplicated in a number of library systems around a region and the country as a whole. Subject cooperative schemes may seem an answer to such a problem but this usually means a large retrospective collection in a specific subject field has to be housed, the bulk of which, once again, may be little used.

Cooperative storage at regional centres, possibly in conjunction with other types of library, may be the answer. Models come from the UK national and academic library sectors or from abroad; for example, the Harvard Depository[42] or the Danish Repository Library for Danish Public Libraries.[43] The Research Collections and Preservation Consortium (ReCAP), which includes New York Public Library, aims to provide a facility for the long-term provision of off-site shelving and servicing of library collections in appropriate environmental conditions. ReCAP's potential to be also an artefactual repository of digital material has been the subject of investigation.[44]

The Urquhart Building at the British Library provides an example of a major UK storage library and some British university libraries have separate storage buildings, such as the University of Wales, Aberystwyth. One public library example of a large storage facility is that at Liverpool, although it is not in a separate building, but in an extension (8,370m^2) to the Brown Library, and is solely for the city library service. The facility, an eight-storey building opened in 1977, brought together the contents of three repositories formerly in different parts of Liverpool. It includes some public and backroom services, with the stack occupying just under two-thirds of the accommodation (5,255m^2).[45] It has to be said that providing such reserve stacks may be a thing of the past for many UK library systems.

In discussing the basic issues which must be decided early on in establishing a storage facility, Gloria Stockton in the US notes the need to state its function or mission. She goes on to quote the mission statement of the Northern Regional Library facility:

> The facility was developed to store, preserve, and provide access to low-use library material of research value, in cost-effective economical manner for the libraries of the University of California, and, secondarily, for other libraries in California.[46]

In Britain, cooperative storage may be something that can be organized through the regional cooperative systems or the regional agencies for museums, libraries and archives (MLACs), although this does not appear to be high on the agenda. A collaborative storage approach, where libraries agree on collection management policies for stored material, rather than just sharing a facility, would seem a more economic and efficient solution.[47]

THE BEST OPTIONS

Although a central library or county headquarters heading a system of district, branch and mobile libraries is well established in the UK, it is a structure that is open to question. Centralization or decentralization, and fewer branches and more middle-ranking libraries are some of the issues for debate. The purpose-built and mobile library can also be questioned in some circumstances and a case made for prefabricated, portable and transportable (and even drive-through)[48] service points to meet changing needs and demands.

Librarians may have to face survival conditions and in these circumstances one way of reducing expenditure is to use standard plans ('pattern book libraries') and create purely functional libraries, whose structure, operation and maintenance are aimed at reducing costs.[49] First, however, the library size must be estimated.

LIBRARY SIZE

So far, little has been said about the size of library buildings. Terms like small, medium-sized and large are only helpful in conveying library size in the most general way. An examination by the author of UK building projects, both new and conversions, in the UK from 1975 to 1994[50] revealed that British public library building could be usefully grouped by the size ranges listed in Figure 3.1. This provides a framework for deciding, as shown later, what might be considered a 'small' library building and what might be seen as a 'large' one. As might be expected, projects constructed during this period in each category decrease in number (with some exceptions) as building size increases. Some indication of the proportion of libraries in each category will be given later in the chapter.

Category A:	Under 249m²	Small
Category B:	Between 250 and 499m²	
Category C:	Between 500 and 749m²	Medium
Category D:	Between 750 and 999m²	
Category E:	Between 1,000 and 1,999m²	
Category F:	Between 2,000 and 2,999m²	Large
Category G:	Between 3,000 and 4,999m²	
Category H:	Between 5,000 and 6,999m²	
Category I:	Between 7,000 and 9,999m²	
Category J:	Above 10,000m²	Largest

Figure 3.1   Library building size in the UK, 1975–94

Based on Figure 3.1 the terms 'small, medium-sized, large and largest' library could be interpreted in the following way in the UK:

- small library = up to 499m²
- medium-sized library = 500m² to 1,999m²
- large library = 2,000m² to 9,999m²
- largest library = over 10,000m².

Werner Mevissen, however, categorized libraries as 0 to IV – smallest to large – according to bookstock size, the smallest having up to 2,000 volumes, the largest much in excess of 50,000.[51] As demonstrated below, methods for calculating library size suggest a strong relationship between library size and population size, and/or the size of the book and other library materials provided. In reality this relationship in terms of resultant library size does not seem to be a strong one, at least in the UK.

CALCULATING LIBRARY SIZE

There are a number of ways to determine the overall size of the library building.

- Employing a formula that utilizes community and library data, such as the VSC Formula devised by Wheeler and Githens for estimating the size of the public library. In this formula V is the number of volumes, S the number of seats and C the circulation in volumes per annum.[52]
- Through an investigation of the space provision in libraries of communities with similar populations. In this method the space provided per head or per 1,000 head of population in each building under comparison is calculated and an average figure in square metres/feet arrived at for all the buildings. This average can then be multiplied by the population to be served in the new building to give an estimate of its required size. A major criticism of this method is the assumption of the adequacy of those buildings used in making the calculation. The floor space figures given in the UK's *Public library statistics* go some way to allowing the adoption of this comparative approach. The regional averages, however, for net floor space per 1,000 population vary considerably from 42m² (Scotland) to 18m² (Eastern and East Midlands),[53] although the figures for individual library authorities probably permit more useful comparisons.
- The application of recognized national or international standards, which
  - may propose an overall size for a library, usually related to the potential user population, or
  - provide a methodology for calculating overall size by either (1) stating a space allowance per head or thousand head of population, or (2) providing the means of calculating the required size of individual elements of the building. These elements can then be totalled to give an overall library size. This approach can be used in a general way, calculating space needs for the collection, reading and

study spaces, and so on, across all library areas. Alternatively, it can involve making calculations for named library areas, such as the children's section, ICT area or that for reading newspaper and periodicals.

Australia's *People places* provides a methodology and examples for applying the approaches in (1) and (2) above, which it calls population-based benchmark and service-based benchmark methods.[54] A similar approach to the service-based benchmark method is that proposed by Anders Dahlgren,[55] based on calculations for collection, user seating, staff, meeting room and special-use space requirements. He offers a worked example for 'Sampleville Public Library' as part of his description and explanation. A more recent publication, and one that can help with the detail of the service-based benchmark approach, provides space allowance guidance for calculating the individual library areas by using 'building blocks' and for projecting 'total area'.[56] These 'building blocks' are the space requirements, for example, for photocopying, shelving, computer stations, microform equipment and display areas. A factor is also given for the addition of non-assignable space needs, and 33⅓ per cent of the net figure is suggested.

Most of the above methods make use of recognized space allowances, such as the amount of space required to house 1,000 books or to display a certain number of periodicals. Unless obliged to estimate space requirements in a given way (using standards, for example), the librarian may want to calculate the overall size of a proposed library by at least two methods to see what the difference or similarity might be – an average of the two figures might be a way forward. It is thought that the incremental approach is better than the fixed formula one.

The drawback to all these approaches is that they are not library community specific and therefore take no account of local conditions or requirements. In addition they may be slow to accommodate the space needs of new formats and new service provision. They will probably not include non-standard parts of a library building, such as an archive service, theatre or museum, and guidance for these facilities will have to be sought elsewhere.

INTERNATIONAL GUIDELINES AND STANDARDS

There has been a movement away from prescriptive standards to guideline documents where, in respect of library building, examples of current practice may be given rather than universal applicable quantitative standards.[57] This change is reflected in the way IFLA's standards publications have altered over the years. The IFLA *Standards for public libraries* (1977) include quantitative space standards, formulated in 1973. These were only included in IFLA's *Guidelines for public libraries* (1986) as an unrevised appendix. In the absence of a revision and omission from the current guidelines the earlier standards continue to be used by the international community. A number of countries have their own library space standards, some seemingly derived from the IFLA ones.

GUIDELINES AND STANDARDS IN THE UK AND IRELAND

The 2001 standards for England say nothing about quantitative space provision, nor do the earlier Convention of Scottish Local Authorities standards for Scotland.[58] The Welsh standards ask library authorities 'to compare their performance against an indicative Standard as minimum threshold for space allocated to library provision per 1,000 resident population, namely 23 square metres' (revised upwards to 28m² for publicly accessible space in the 2005 standards). The requirements of technological developments and the needs of people with disabilities must be taken into account in the public space provided.[59] This is very basic guidance indeed, as no indication is given as to how the figure was arrived at (possibly best practice) nor as to what the standard is to cover. Does it include non-assignable space for example?

In the Irish Republic, standards for public libraries offer no quantitative space guidance. As regards the number and distribution of service points (and also, one may infer, their size), the standards say that this is best left to library authorities and 'their knowledge of the actual catchment population of each proposed service point, local travel-to-work patterns, and local needs in general'.[60]

As Berriman and Harrison wrote in 1966 in their discussion of standards, 'it is quite clear that few British public libraries reach any of the published recommendations', whether American, German or international.[61] The present author has seen a few older UK libraries planned on generous lines (probably to IFLA standards). Nevertheless, the impression still remains that, in contrast to other countries, UK library buildings are not as spacious as they could be and that too many very small service points are built. There is a feeling that the space provided for public libraries is what can be obtained rather than what is needed. Comparing the spaciousness of most UK academic libraries to that of the country's public library buildings only emphasizes the point, as does comparison with public libraries elsewhere. Viadana Library, Italy, for example, housed in the Palace of Culture (4,000m²), serves a population of 17,000 with a library of 1,700m² (100m² per 1,000 population).[62]

THE SMALL LIBRARY

Using the author's suggested size categorization of UK public libraries (Figure 3.1), small libraries may be seen as those falling in category B (250–499m²), with the smallest being under 250m² (category A). In the years 1975–94, the smallest libraries (category A) accounted for about 40–50 per cent of building projects; those in category B for about another 25 per cent. Together, the smallest and small libraries accounted for the majority of library buildings in the period in question. A number of UK libraries in the smallest category are very small indeed, anything from around 30m² to 90m², with a few in the 20m² class. It is difficult to imagine that anything more than a very basic and cramped library service can be given in accommodation so small, even if newly provided.

Some countries may have a minimum size for a library building. In Ireland this is 93m^2 but in reality only projects of around 186m^2 attract financial support from central government. In New South Wales, Australia, the minimum recommended size is 139m^2 gross, and in Ontario, Canada, not less than 230m^2 for a branch in a multi-branch system, plus 14m^2 for each additional 1,000 volumes over 3,000 volumes in its collection.[63]

Small in US terms has been defined as 'any building with fewer than twenty thousand gross square feet [1,858m^2]' But, as Anders Dahlgren writes, there is a debate as to whether this constitutes 'small' and he suggests that it is not possible to define a 'small' library simply in terms of its square metres but as one that functions 'from just one public service desk' with possibly some behind-the-scenes administrative and other activities taking place.[64]

From the 1930s onwards different authors have written about planning small public libraries. On the whole they tend to be short, general planning manuals with examples of small library buildings but with no great emphasis on the particular needs of such libraries.[65] Dahlgren, however, does note a few design considerations:

- single-storey construction unless the site does not allow it
- a single service desk that should enable staff to serve, supervise and monitor the public area
- interior space that should be square or rectangular, as other shapes may be difficult to use effectively.[66]

The question of the shape of the library, whether small or large, is discussed later in this chapter.

Nottinghamshire's *Design of small branch libraries*,[67] although of a similar vintage to Wheeler, brings out more of the design issues to be faced in small libraries:

- which sizes of population are to be provided with a static library
- size – about 242m^2
- the design should allow for expansion
- site – usually comparatively restricted in area for small libraries
- the need for parking
- easily maintained landscaping
- except for busy periods there will only be one member of staff – the design must assist ease of supervision
- scale of bookstock for populations of different sizes.

The Nottinghamshire pamphlet is in the form of a brief and suggested arrangements are provided for the building as a whole and detailed layouts for particular areas. It should be noted that nowadays there is a trend away from libraries staffed by a single person because of health and safety considerations.

Public library service points recognizes various levels of branch and other library provision relating to small population size:

- communities with about 4,000 population, which usually provide a service (30+ hours) on most weekdays
- communities between 1,500 and 4,000 population, usually provided with a small, part-time library (15–20 hours)
- communities below 1,500 population, served by mobile libraries, with sparsely populated areas served perhaps by a smaller vehicle.[68] A Welsh view is that a library is so central to social, cultural and recreational life and activity in a small community that it justifies a service point (possibly a joint-use facility) for a population under 1,500.[69]

This guidance is generally followed by UK library authorities. Note, however, the Staffordshire approach described earlier (page 67). But what is lacking is advice on appropriate building size to suit the two levels of population to be provided with static library accommodation. Some examples of small UK public library building are listed in Figure 3.2.

Charing Library, Kent (1977, 144m^2)
Bordon Library, Hampshire (1986, 360m^2)
Listowel Library, Co. Kerry (1995, 370m^2)
Bourtreehill Library, North Ayrshire (1996, 300m^2)
Dalgety Bay Library, Fife (1996, 490m^2)
Chipping Ongar Library, Essex (1996, 250m^2)
Somerton Library, Somerset (1997, 200m^2)
Worcester Park Millennium Library, London, Sutton (2000, 262m^2)
Cardonagh Community Library, Co. Donegal (2002, 215m^2)
Cashel Library, Tipperary, (2002, 430m^2)
Littleport Library and Learning Centre, Cambridgeshire (2002, 157m^2)
Magherafelt Library, County Londonderry (2002, 280m^2)
Alderley Edge Library, Cheshire (2004, 200m^2)

Figure 3.2   Small public library buildings (under 500m^2) in the UK and Ireland (Categories A and B)

THE MEDIUM-SIZED LIBRARY

In the UK a medium-sized public library has been seen as one that serves a population in the 15,000–30,000 range.[70] In terms of size this can mean a library in the 500–749m^2 bracket – the category C grouping in Figure 3.1. However, sampling libraries built in the period 1990–94, the sizes of some premises may fall below this category, while others may be above it. The author has suggested that UK libraries of medium size are those of 500–1,999m^2, categories C, D and E. In the period 1975–94, libraries in category E (1,000–1,999m^2) were more than twice the number in category D (750–999m^2). Those in category E were similar in number to those in category C (500–749m^2).

Examples of medium-sized libraries in the UK and Ireland are listed in Figure 3.3.

Conisbrough Library, Doncaster (1985, 603m²)
Newark Library, Nottinghamshire (1988, 879m²)
Letterkenny Library, Co. Donegal, (1995, 962m²)
Braintree Library, Essex (1997, 1,300m²)
Wester Hailes Library, Edinburgh (1997, 1,200m²)
Beckton Globe Library, London, Newham, (1998, 1003m²)
Newbury Library, West Berkshire (1999, 1,400m²)
March Library, Cambridgeshire (1999, 1,000m²)
Berwick-upon-Tweed Library, Northumberland (2000, 797m²)
Rugby Library, Warwickshire (2000, 1,422m²)
Cabra Library & Bibliographical Centre, Dublin (2001, 900m²)
Durham Clayport Library, Durham (2002, 1,100m²)
Knutsford Library, Cheshire (2002, 596m²)
Parklands Library, Liverpool (2002, 750m²)
Alton Library, Hampshire (2004, 740m²)

Figure 3.3   Medium-sized public libraries (500–1,999m²) in the UK and Ireland (Categories C–E)

THE LARGE LIBRARY

As noted earlier, it was suggested that in UK terms large libraries could be seen as those in the size range 2,000–9,999m² (categories F–I). The most numerous group in this size range is the 2,000–2,999m² category and building projects that include refurbished and extended libraries are listed in Figure 3.4.

Morden Library, London, Merton (1990, 2,129m²),
Lewisham Central Library, London (1994, 2,570m²)
Kidderminster, Worcestershire (1997, 2,225m²)
Putney Library, London, Wandsworth (refurbishment and extension 1998, 2,300m²)
Ellesmere Port Library, Cheshire (refurbishment 2000, 2,984m²)
Stratford Library, London, Newham (2000, 2,000m²)
Sutton Central Library, London (1975, refurbished 2005, 2,300m²)

Figure 3.4   Large public libraries (2,000–2,999m²) in the UK (Category F)

Examples of UK public libraries in the size range 3,000–4,999m² are listed in Figure 3.5.

Willesden Green, London, Brent (1989, 4,460^2)
Southampton Central Library (refurbished 1930s building, 1992–93, 3,531m^2)
A.K. Bell Library, Perth (exterior walls and façade of former 1838 infirmary kept, 1994, 4,700m^2)
Lincoln Central Library (refurbishment and extension 1996, 3,335m^2)
Bournemouth Library (2002, 3,850m^2)
Norfolk & Norwich Millennium Library (2001/2, 4,621m^2)

Figure 3.5 Large public libraries (3,000–4,999m^2) in the UK (Category G)

Libraries in the categories above 5,000m^2 and under 10,000m^2, however, are few in number in the UK, and some are listed in Figure 3.6.

Dundee Central Library (refurbished 1996, 9,213m^2)
Ilford Central Library, London, Redbridge (1986, 5,918m^2)
Cardiff Central Library (1988, 8,872m^2)
Croydon Central Library (1993, 6,000m^2)
Sunderland City Library & Arts Centre (1995, 5,022m^2)
Brighton Library, Brighton and Hove (2005, 5,000m^2)

Figure 3.6 Large public libraries (5,000–9,999m^2) in the UK (Categories H and I)

A well documented foreign building in this large library group is Münster Public Library, Germany (1993, 9,751m^2).[71]

METROPOLITAN LIBRARIES

The largest public libraries are represented by the International Association of Metropolitan Libraries (INTAMEL), formed in 1968. INTAMEL (now the Metropolitan Libraries section of IFLA) concerns itself primarily with libraries of cities with a population of 400,000 or more, although exceptions may be made for capital cities or major conurbations with a lesser population, for example. Of the 150 metropolitan public library systems noted in the mid-1970s, however, some were serving populations of 1–2 million, others 2–4 million and the largest in excess of 5 million, sometimes exceeding a population of 10 million. Population figures are derived from the number of metropolitan inhabitants rather than the core city population.[72]

Metropolitan public library systems include overseas cities such as New York, Tokyo, Melbourne, Toronto, Rotterdam and Hamburg and in the UK, London, Birmingham, Edinburgh, Leeds, Glasgow, Sheffield, Cardiff, Bradford, Manchester and Liverpool. It is in UK cities such as these that the largest public library buildings (of varying vintage) will be found, although those over 10,000m^2 – Birmingham Central Library and the Mitchell Library, Glasgow – are rarities.

According to INTAMEL's guidelines, metropolitan city libraries should provide various services from central, branch and district libraries.[73] In this respect they may not seem very different from the library structure and service provision described earlier. What is different is the scale of operations. There are likely to be greater resources, including subject libraries and special collections at the central library, attracting visitors from beyond its boundaries, and a larger number of district and branch libraries. In addition the leadership and influence of the metropolitan library system will be of importance to the wider region.

Detailed published accounts of British metropolitan libraries include those for Birmingham,[74] Glasgow,[75] and of those abroad for Toronto and Malmö (1997, 14,000m²).[76] Information about other larger foreign buildings is given in Chapter 11.

Just because they are very large, it does not mean that Metropolitan libraries in the UK stand still as regards buildings and services. New roles have been devised for the Mitchell Library, Glasgow, and these include 'acting as a visitor and tourist attraction targeted at the citizens of Glasgow, and British and international tourists'.[77]

SERVICES AND FACILITIES

Whether small, medium-sized or large, and depending upon the roles assigned to them, public libraries will offer a variety of services, facilities and amenities to children, young people and adults, as well as accommodation for staff. In summary these are:

- *lending services*: books and other printed material, such as maps, sheet music and play sets; sound and moving image material, for example, talking books, CDs, DVDs; toys; pictures; and interlibrary loans
- *reference and information services*
  - access to special collections and materials: for example, newspapers and magazines; business information; local history and archives collections; basic skills materials; language materials; electronic journals; CD-ROMs, and the Internet
  - access to information: general reference collection; community information; council information point, Citizens Advice Bureau, and Tourist Information Centre
- *library based activities*: exhibitions and displays; musical and other performances; publishing; storytelling; school holiday programmes; homework clubs; parents' and carers' groups; pensioner groups; reader groups; chess and other board games; use of word processing and other software applications; watching television, and equipment for listening to music, and so on
- *external activities*: mobile library services; outreach activities; services to schools, prisons, hospitals, and so on

- *library facilities*: for example, toilets; cafe; photocopying; telephones; buy and sell notice board; shop; and meeting rooms
- *managerial and support services*: administration, workroom, staff, storage and garage facilities to manage and support the library building and services and, if applicable, other service points such as branches, mobiles, schools, prisons and hospitals.[78]

As 'we live in an era of institutional upheaval' where grocery shops sell stamps and videos, and major stores are offering financial services and banking, public libraries, it is suggested, must consider combining the traditional with the new, the free with the money-making.[79]

From the designated purpose and roles assigned to a particular service point, it will be possible to decide which services and facilities it will comprise and offer and their spatial implications. It is vital not to adopt a 'shopping list' approach to determining what a library building will consist of and offer, but to ensure that it reflects a given community's needs and ambitions, as emphasized in Chapter 7. A public library can vary in make-up from what is essentially a single space to more complex accommodation; it may be a stand-alone structure, co-located with other buildings or be part of another building.

SPACE CATEGORIES

Whatever the precise nature of a given public library, and the services, collections and facilities that are to be offered, four basic categories of space will make up the building:

- space for users
- space for staff – increased space for both staff and users is required nowadays because of the need to provide them with ICT equipment
- space for library materials – because of the impact of the People's Network, reference stock has had to be reduced in a number of UK libraries to make space for computer terminals
- non-assignable space – the space additional to the above and required for circulation, such as entrance lobbies, corridors, lifts and stairs, as well as toilets and space for building services.

Although they might also be seen as spaces for users and staff, it has been suggested that two further types of space are needed:

- meeting room space – number, size, furnishing and equipment will be determined by the existence of similar community facilities, and the range of activities – lectures, performances, meetings, children's activities, and so on – envisaged by the library
- special use space – required for furniture and equipment, such as photocopiers, vertical files, self issue terminals, and so on.[80]

It can be useful to look at a library in these simplified terms and, as was seen earlier in this chapter, it can be a useful way of estimating library size. But, as indicated below, a greater variety of spaces may be necessary today if people's expectations as regards facilities and amenities, for example, are to be met. The accommodation requirements of a small public library building are fairly simple. These become more complex with increased size, the provision of non-library facilities (a shop or café, for example), and responsibility for (or an association with) other types of organization such as a theatre or museum. One such successful multi-purpose structure (which is also of striking appearance) is the Beckton Globe Library in the London Borough of Newham. Here, the local service centre, hall, café and crèche share the building (Figure 3.7).

Figure 3.7 Beckton Globe Library, Newham (1998): includes local service centre, multi-purpose hall, café, crèche, etc.
Source: London Borough of Newham

Large or small, simple or complex, a better library building is more likely if the client has a clear idea as to the 'business it is in'.

PLAN SHAPES

STANDARD LIBRARY PLANS

In a situation of development and change in a library system, where a number of new (and particularly small) service points are required fairly quickly, then the use of a standard, but adaptable, library plan may be an acceptable response. Clearly the prefabricated buildings described earlier can be utilized in such a situation but an architect-designed solution, which follows the needs of a specific library authority, is likely to be preferable.

One UK library system which made use of standard plans for many years was Lancashire County Libraries, which opened 73 libraries between 1960 and 1974. At one time it had four designs for library buildings, ranging from 208m² to 435m², to serve populations of 2,000–4,000 to 8,000–12,000. Advantages of the standard plan include the saving of time and expense (lower costs in construction and use) and in the preparation of working drawings. The major challenge was that of rearranging the elements of the standard plan to suit a particular site. In Lancashire there was also a standard furniture schedule and so libraries of the same size had the same amount of shelving and furniture, which helped with costing. When the standard plan was not appropriate, as for the medium-sized library at Morecambe (1967, 1,300m²), then a one-off design was called for and produced interesting results – a building of interlocking hexagons.

In 1980 Lancashire opened two libraries chosen from a new family of standard plans. Size range changed (150m²–470m²), with the largest design catering for a population of 10,000–15,000. The standard design was based on a core space of 100m² to which various levels of band space (additional space) and over space, for a meeting room, for example, were added.[81]

The use of prefabricated buildings and standard library plans are not so prevalent in the UK today, but their time may well come again. They are approaches that could be considered in places where there is a surge in construction activity or in those countries with a developing public library service.

Libraries large and small can individually have a variety of shapes – rectangular, circular or hexagonal, for example. The next section examines these plan shapes, a source of controversy in designing library buildings.

When a library is housed independently in a single structure of a given form or shape, its design may consist of more than one building, linked in some way and perhaps using more than one plan shape. The Lord Louis Library, Newport, Isle of Wight (1981), is a series of pavilions, linked by a central passageway, and with an octagonal-shaped lending library. On a larger scale, Münster City Library (1993) consists of two buildings, one either side of a street, linked by a walkway at first floor level, with an integrated building at basement level. Malmö also consists of two buildings: the renovated old library (1998) and the modern one (1997) linked by the Cylinder, a circular-shaped entrance building.

Whatever the size of a library, its shape or form, if unusual, may arouse controversy. A 1970s survey of American main library building stated that 'occasionally an odd-shaped public library building appears on the horizon, in spite of all that experience has taught us'. It went on to note – with approval – that of the 20 or so public libraries surveyed, all but three were oblong, the exceptions being square or L-shaped.[82] So-called 'odd-shaped libraries', and particularly circular libraries, are disliked by some commentators on library buildings. There are, it must be said, examples of seemingly odd one-off library shapes, such as 10 and 16-sided buildings, a cogwheel solution and a shell-like design, as well as what have been called 'informal plans'.[83] Sometimes library shape may be related to the architect's concept for the library, as at Tampere in Finland, where the bird-like plan of the building represents the wood grouse (see Chapter 9).

It is recognized that the size and shape of the site will be influential factors in determining the library's form. Difficult sites may produce irregularly shaped buildings: Derringham Bank Library (Humberside, 1987) is irregular at all levels inside and out. A triangular site, for example, is likely to give a wedge-shaped library building and the triangular spaces at its corners may be difficult to put to effective use. Examples of triangular buildings in the UK include East Kilbride Central Library (1989), Portchester Library (Hampshire, 1984) and Frome (Somerset, 1990), and, in the US, Flushing Library, New York (1998)[84] and Brooklyn Public Library's Visual and Performing Arts Library. Examples of other non-UK public libraries with varied shapes are listed in Figure 3.8.

Denver Library, Colorado, US (old plus new building, 1995, 37,160m² + 11,6613m²) – octagonal storytelling pavilion dominates a collection of geometric shapes[85]

Almelo Library, Netherlands (1994, 4,780m²) – curved irregular shape

Sandtown Library, Gauteng, South Africa (1995, 4,500m²) – triangular

Penrith, New South Wales, Australia (1995, 3,500m²) – triangular[86]

Enköping Library, Sweden (1995, 1,1930m²) – semi-circular extension[87]

Vuotalo Library, Finland (2000)- semi-circular[88]

Figure 3.8 Non-UK varied public library buildings plans

RECTANGULAR AND SQUARE BUILDINGS

For both large and small libraries, the rectangle, and less frequently the square, is the most common and most preferred shape for a library building, being economical to construct, better acoustically, giving greater visual control, minimizing walking distances, and least wasteful of interior space. The Cohens recommend that

> library areas of heavy traffic and book stack spaces should be square or large rectangles, everything else being equal. Other library areas can take more pleasing shapes.[89]

The ubiquitous rectangular or square library can be made more individual by rounding or 'cutting off' the corners of the building, creating a sawtooth-shaped wall or by placing window bays at regular points in the exterior walls. Hampstead Central Library (Camden, 1964) is essentially a long rectangle but with rounded ends.

An interior feature, such as a gallery, courtyard, atrium or void, may also be included in the design to lend variety to the building and the implications of some of these features are discussed in Chapter 9. For example, Skelmersdale District Central Library (Lancashire, 1978) is a square modular building with a central void.

The combination of more than one rectangular block can create other plan shapes, such as the L-shaped or T-shaped library or more irregular groupings, such as a small rectangle linked to a large one (Tillydrone Library, Aberdeen, 1991). Examples of these rectangle-based plan shapes are listed in Figure 3.9.

E-shaped:	Broadstone Library, Dorset (1983)
L-shaped:	Gateshead Central Library (1976 extension to 1926 building); Warminster Library, Wiltshire (1982); St Neots District Library, Cambridgeshire (1985); Whiterock Library (Belfast Education and Library Board, 1985); Newent Library, Gloucestershire (1987); Liniclate Library, Western Isles (1988); Stirling's Library, Glasgow (1993); Langport, Somerset (1994); Cottingham Library, East Riding of Yorkshire (1998); Glastonbury Library, Somerset (2000); Ardkeen Library, Waterford City (2002)
T-shaped:	Burnham Branch Library, Buckinghamshire (1973, with unequal 'arms'); Farnham Common Branch (Buckinghamshire, 1974); Prestbury Library, (Gloucestershire, 1978)
H-shaped:	Little Chalfont Library, Buckinghamshire (1974, irregular H-shape); Hayle Library, Cornwall (1982, irregular H-shape)
U-shaped:	Seaton Branch Library, Cumbria (1973); Newry Branch and Divisional Library (Southern Education and Library Board, 1987)

Figure 3.9 UK public library buildings with rectangular plans

The plan shapes noted in Figure 3.9 split the library building into a number of linked spaces or wings that may pose supervision problems, although they offer 'infill' expansion possibilities for the future. However, a larger site area is needed, a greater length of wall in relation to floor space is required, and traffic patterns are more complicated and influence the amount of usable space.[90] The location of the entrance may need rethinking in some instances if an extension is contemplated later. Unlike a deep square or deep rectangular library, such 'odd' plan shapes may provide better opportunities for the provision of natural light, without recourse to roof lights or other design elements.

CIRCULAR BUILDINGS

In spite of its use in classic library buildings, such as the reading room of the British Museum Library, Manchester Central Library, Stockholm Central Library and the Library of Congress, some librarians are suspicious of circular plan solutions, especially for small libraries, seeing them as inflexible. The American, Joseph Wheeler, condemns the circular library as one that is 'usually more costly and results in less usable space. This type of design negates the "modular" idea'.[91] Anders Dahlgren says that 'the arc in a circular wall is difficult to use effectively'.[92] Shelving, for example, may need to be custom-made to make a neat fit for such a wall arc. However, in the last 40 years there have been a number of circular public libraries in the UK, mainly small to medium sized buildings (Figure 3.10), although they seem to have gone out of fashion more recently.

Chichester Library, West Sussex (1966)
West Sussex County Library Headquarters (1967)
Jesmond Branch, Newcastle upon Tyne (1963)
Bradmore Green Branch, Croydon (1963)
Bourne Hall Library, Museum & Social Centre, Epsom & Ewell (1969)
Stubbington Library, Hampshire (1974)

Figure 3.10   UK public library buildings with circular plans

Sometimes another plan shape or shapes is supplemented by a major circular element, as at Calne, Wiltshire (2001), where the adult lending library and display facilities are housed in a drum-shaped part of the building (see Figure 3.11). At Rugby (2000, 1,422m^2), a circular area, the 'Drum', which opens off the main library foyer, is the children's library.[93] At the Huntingdon County Library Headquarters (1971), a two-storey gear-wheel shaped building with a gallery is set into a roughly rectangular administration block. At other times the circular element forms a smaller part of the overall plan of a library, perhaps housing a particular department, the children's library, for example, as at Romford Central Library (Haringey, 1965), Crawley Branch (West Sussex, 1963), or at Whitton Branch Library (Richmond, 1973). At Haverfordwest Library (Pembrokeshire, 1969) there is a circular exhibition and lecture hall.

SEMI-CIRCULAR AND SIMILAR BUILDINGS

A library in the form of a half circle is a good shape for a radiating shelves layout, which offers admirable supervision. Like the circular library, however, the semi-circle is not generally considered to be a flexible shape.

The Chandler's Ford Library (Hampshire, 1983) is close to a horseshoe in shape, rather than forming half a circle, and, lacking in depth, seems unlikely to be very flexible and easy to extend, although the interior has recently been refurbished to include a lift.

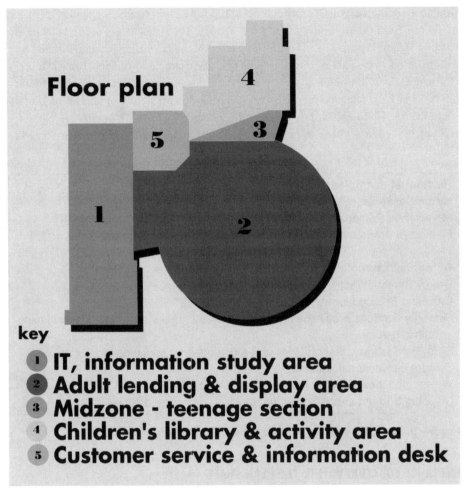

Figure 3.11 Calne Millennium Library, Wiltshire (2001): library plan showing a mix of building shapes
Source: Wiltshire Library Services

A similar-shaped building is Gillingham Library & Museum (Dorset, 1993). Montebelluna Public Library (2002), in northern Italy is a horseshoe-shaped building around an open space which is used as a meeting point. Its windows face adjacent parkland.[94]

HEXAGONAL AND OCTAGONAL BUILDINGS

Related to the circular-shaped public library are those with six or eight sides. As with circular buildings, 'slices' of the whole may be used for different library areas, as at

Greenhills Branch Library (Eastwood D.C., 1982) which is roughly octagonal in shape. At Telford Town Centre Library (Telford & Wrekin, 1988), segments of the building are used for different purposes. As with the circle, the hexagonal or octagonal shape may feature as only one part of the overall design, for example at Shildon Branch Library (Durham C.C., 1981) which has an octagonal entrance area, at Dundee Central Library (1978), which is octagonal in part with galleries on two floors, or at Didcot Library (Oxfordshire, 1992), which has a distinctive octagonal children's section as part of a rectangular building. Other examples of hexagonal and octagonal libraries are listed in Figure 3.12.

Hexagonal examples
Hylton Castle Branch, Sunderland (a large and smaller hexagon, 1967)
Morecambe Regional Library, Lancashire (three linked hexagons, 1967)
Fleetdown Branch, Kent (hexagonal with projecting entrance rectangle, 1972)

Octagonal examples
Selsey Branch, West Sussex (1964)
Crowland Branch Library, Lincolnshire (1974)
Mowbray Gardens, Rotherham (plus shared rectangular entrance with swimming baths, 1973)
Burntwood Library, Staffordshire (three octagons for public departments plus more conventional shapes, 1987)
Weymouth Library, Dorset (half-octagon shape, 1990)
Chipping Barnet Library, Barnet (interlocking octagons, 1991)

Figure 3.12 UK public library buildings with hexagonal and octagonal plans

ENTRANCE LOCATION WITHIN THE PLAN SHAPE

The location of the library entrance, whatever the building shape, is an important factor in ensuring ease of entry and of movement through the building. A square building allows the entrance to be placed centrally on any of its four sides, with the effect of dividing the interior into two main sections – left and right of the entrance. An entrance on the corner of a square building permits the creation of a diagonal 'path' through the library, once again dividing it into two.

An oblong or rectangular library is likely to have its entrance in one of the two longer sides. A site may nevertheless dictate an entrance on a short side, and, if the rectangle is both long and narrow, this can create an interior that is less easy to plan and administer. One solution here is to place the entrance to one side of the short wall, thus creating a route through the length of the library close to the long outer wall. A wider rectangular shape, with a centrally placed entrance on the short side, will permit an access 'corridor' through the length of the building, once again dividing the floor space into two major elements. Other plan shapes stemming from the rectangle, such as the L- or T-shaped library, will usually benefit from a centrally placed entrance, at the right angle in the L-shaped building, or at the junction of the long and short elements of the T-shaped library for example. Much, however, depends on the access route to the L- or T-shaped building and the relationship of the entrance to stairs and lifts or escalators.

Other regular geometric shaped premises, such as the circular or hexagonal library (however much despised by the experts) will generally allow the entrance to be satisfactorily placed on any point of the exterior, site being a determining factor. A triangular-shaped library often has its entrance at one of its angles but a better location is probably in the centre of one of the long sides of the plan shape.

As has been demonstrated, library shapes or plans can be varied, although the rectangle and square are preferred over 'odd' shapes. Nevertheless, the librarian may be fearful of anything out of the ordinary, preferring the luxury shoebox to a more adventurous design. Or the librarian may willingly embrace a more unusual design rather than be thought a stick-in-the-mud who plumps for the shoebox, whether luxurious or not. What the latter part of this chapter demonstrates is that, rather than responding to the appeal of the safe solution or being attracted to the unusual one, the librarian is on surer ground if he or she understands the implications of what is being proposed and makes a judgement based on that understanding – a judgement that positively influences the library design outcome.

The success of a library and its building does not depend solely on its size and shape or the services, facilities and amenities it offers but is particularly related to a satisfactory location. It is this question that is considered in the next chapter along with factors affecting actual siting.

NOTES

1   *The public library service: IFLA/UNESCO guidelines for development* (2001), Munich: Saur, 43.

2   *Public library statistics: 2001–02 actuals* (2003), London: Chartered Institute of Public Finance and Accountancy.

3   Department of Education and Science; Library Advisory Council (England); Library Advisory Council (Wales) (1971), *Public library service points: a report with some notes on staffing*, London: HMSO.

4   Audit Commission (2002), *Building better library services*, London: Audit Commission, 31.

5   Adapted from: Martin, L.A. (1969), *Library response to urban change*, Chicago: American Library Association, 43.

6   Martin (1969), 43.

7   Summers, F.W. (1984), 'Alternatives to the central library', *Public libraries* **23** (1), 4–7: 4.

8   Rawlinson, N.K. (1990), 'The central library – a fatal attraction: why do cities persist in building these dinosaurs?', *Library journal* **115** June 1, 6.

9   Wheeler, J. (1958), *The effective location of public library buildings*, Urbana, Illinois: University of Illinois Library School, 22–4.

10   Hammond, H. (1996), 'Norfolk and Norwich Central Library: the emerging phoenix', *New library world* **97** (1130), 24–31: 28.

11   Anderson J.F. (1978), 'Main libraries: time for mutation', in *Library space planning*, edited by K. Nyren, New York: Bowker, 5–6.

12   Summers (1984), 6.

13   Peterson, H.N. (1972), 'Developments in the planning of main library buildings', *Library trends* **20** (4), 693–741: 705.

14   Summers (1984), 5.

15   Altman, E. (1995), 'We must be doing something right', *Public libraries* **34** (5), 256, 258.

16   Leckie, G.J. and Hopkins, J. (2002), The public place of central libraries: findings from Toronto and Vancouver', *Library quarterly* **72** (3), 326–72.

17   Bowron, A. (1990), 'News from the Low Countries', *Canadian library journal* **47** (5), 307–8: 308.

18   Fenart, P. and Michelizza, F. (2002), A town library with a regional mission (BMVR) finds a home in Nice' (in French), *Bibliothèque(s)* (4), 58–9.

19   For descriptions of Kent, Montgomeryshire and West Riding, see Berriman, S.G. and Harrison, K.C. (1966), *British public library buildings*, London: Deutsch, 85–102.

20   *Public library service points* (1971), 4–6.

21   Preuss, J. (1995), 'Tampines Regional Library, Singapore', *Asian libraries* **4** (3), 8–12.

22   Stockham, K. (ed.) (1969*) British county libraries: 1919–1969*, London: Deutsch, 59.

23   Longworth, A. (1968), 'The branch library – is it necessary?', in *Proceedings, papers and summaries of discussions at the Public Libraries Conference, Brighton, 1968*, London: Library Association, 36–42.

24   Cheshire County Council (1985), *The Cheshire library survey. 3: What kind of library? Comparison of centralised and dispersed library provision*, Chester: Cheshire Libraries and Museums Department, para. 8.5.1.

25   Franks, C. (1978), 'Package up your troubles: an introduction to package libraries', *Assistant librarian* **71** (6), 68–70.

26   Hemphill, B.F. (1976), 'The second generation store front library' in *Library space planning*, edited by K. Nyren, New York: Bowker, 7–8.

27   Byam, M. (1977), 'Kiosks and porta-branches', *Library journal* **102** (2), 162–3.

28   Ballard, T (1985), 'Library buildings: form follows function', *Library journal* **110** (20), 44–6: 45.

29   Singh, S. (1985), 'Happy mall fellows', *American libraries* **16** (2), 154.

30   Paine, A.W. (1985), 'Consideration of portable structures in meeting library needs', *Illinois libraries* **67** (9), 813–15. Article includes plan.

31   Akin, L. and Dowd, F.S. (1993), 'A national survey of portable library structures: what works and why', *Public libraries* **32** (5), 267–9: 269.

32   Flores, A.A. (2002), 'Book Express: a mini library for rail commuters', *New library world* **103** (1178/79), 272–6.

33   *Public library service points* (1971), 6–7.

34   'Simple ideas triumph' (2004), *Library + information update* **3** (11), 8.

35   Hemphill, B.F. (1979), 'Mini-libraries: when bigger isn't better', *Library journal* **104** (21), 2517–18.

36   Capital Planning Information Ltd (1993), *Library and information provision in rural areas in England and Wales*, London: HMSO, 52 ('Alternative patterns of access'); Haggis, S. and Goulding, A. (2003), 'Books to rural users: public library provision for remote communities', *New library world* **104** (1186), 80–93.

37   Wan, T. (1991), *Alternative methods in the provision of mobile library services, with particular reference to Hong Kong*, Thesis, Aberystwyth: Department of Information and Library Studies, University College of Wales.

38   Pestell, R. (1991), *Mobile library guidelines*, The Hague: International Federation of Library Associations, 41–2.

39   Pybus, R. (1981), *Library services to small communities*, Truro: Branch and Mobile Libraries Group of the Library Association; Library Advisory Council (Wales) (1978), *Library services in rural areas [and] Library services to Welsh industry: two reports*. London: HMSO, 2–4; Kim, C.H. (1977), *Books by mail: a handbook for libraries*, Westport, Connecticut: Greenwood. Describes American (and some Canadian) practice and experience.

40 *Container and transportable libraries: experiments in Cornwall, Derbyshire and Bradford* (1978), Sudbury: Branch and Mobile Libraries Group of the Library Association.

41 '"Fold-away" solution for small spaces' (2004), *Library + information gazette* 19 November, 5.

42 Kendrick, C.L. (1999), 'High density storage libraries: the Harvard Depository model', in *Solving collection problems through repository strategies*, edited by P. Connolly, Boston Spa: IFLA Offices for UAP.

43 Henriksen, C.H. (1992), 'The Danish Repository for Public Libraries', *Scandinavian public library quarterly* **25** (2), 21–4.

44 Neal, J.G. (2004), 'The ReCAP artifactual repository planning project', *Library collections, acquisitions, and technical services* **28** (1), 25–8.

45 Harrison, K.C. ed. (1987), *Public library buildings 1975–1983*, London: Library Services, 140–41.

46 Kennedy, J. and Stockton, G. (eds) (1991), *The great divide: challenges in remote storage*, Chicago: American Library Association, 60. See also Part 2: 'The building program', 27–46.

47 O'Connor, S., Wells, A. and Collier, M. (2002), A study of collaborative storage of library resources', *Library hi tech* **20** (3), 258–69.

48 Johnson, C. (1997), 'Drive-through library a first', *Incite* **18** (9), 15.

49 Thompson, G. (1976), 'The planning and design of library buildings in survival conditions', in *Survival '76*, edited by V. Whibley, London: Library Association, 7–17.

50 The projects are listed in three volumes of the 'Library buildings' series for 1975–1983, 1984–1989, and 1990–1994.

51 Mevissen, W. (1958), *Büchereibau/Public library buildings*. Essen: Heyer, 27–8.

52 Wheeler, J.L. and Githens, A.M. (1941), *The American public library building*, Chicago: American Library Association, 41-4. A brief description of the use of this formula is given in Thompson, G. (1989), *Planning and design of library buildings*, 3rd edn, London: Butterworth, 203.

53 *Public library statistics: 2001–02 actuals* (2003), London: Chartered Institute of Public Finance and Accountancy, 19, 55, 81.

54 Nesbitt, H. and Nield, B.V. (2000), *People places: a guide for public library buildings in New South Wales*, Sydney: Library Council of New South Wales, 24–33. This document and supplementary material at www.slnsw.gov.au/plb.

55 Dahlgren, A.C. (1988), *Public library space needs: a planning outline*, Madison, Wisconsin: Wisconsin Department of Public Instruction.

56 *Building blocks for library space: functional guidance* (1995), Chicago: American Library Association; see also Brawner, L.B. and Beck, D.K. (1996), *Determining your public library's future size: a needs assessment and planning models*, Chicago: American Library Association, Chapter 6.

57 *The public library service: IFLA/UNESCO guidelines for development* (2001), Munich: Saur, 102-4. Library building standards from Canada and Spain are listed as an appendix.

58 *Comprehensive, efficient and modern public libraries: standards and assessment* (2001), London: Department for Culture, Media and Sport; Convention of Scottish Local Authorities (1995), *Standards for the public library service in Scotland*, Edinburgh: COSLA.

59 National Assembly for Wales (2001), *Comprehensive, efficient and modern public libraries for Wales: standards and monitoring*, Cardiff: National Assembly for Wales, 16; CyMAL (2005), *Comprehensive, efficient and modern public libraries for Wales: promoting higher service standards 2005–08*, Aberystwyth: CyMAL, 47.

60 *National network – local service: standards for the public library service in the Republic of Ireland* (1999), Dublin: Library Association of Ireland, 56.

61 Berriman and Harrison (1966), 21.

62 Aliani, A. and Bettoni, G. (2003), 'Three levels and five sections' (in Italian), *Biblioteche oggi* **21** (8), 17–19, 21–4.

63 Nesbitt, H. and Nield, B.V. (2000), 24; *The public library service: IFLA/UNESCO guidelines for development* (2001), 103.

64 Dahlgren, A.C. (1996), *Planning the small library facility*, Chicago: American Library Association, 1–2.

65 For example: Myller, R. (1966), *The design of the small public library*, New York: Bowker; Wheeler, J.L. (1963), *The small library building*, Chicago: American Library Association; 'Library architecture', in *Small municipal libraries: a manual of modern method* (1934), 2nd edn, Edinburgh: Library Association and Carnegie United Kingdom Trust.

66   Dahlgren, A.C. (1996), 10–13.
67   *Design of small branch libraries* (1963), [Nottingham]: Nottinghamshire County Council.
68   *Public library service points* (1971), 9–10.
69   Library Advisory Council (Wales) (1978), *Library services in rural areas; library services to Welsh industry*, London: HMSO, 2.
70   Department of Education and Science (1981), *Designing a medium-sized public library*, London: HMSO, 1.
71   Sanin, F. (1994), *Münster City Library*, London: Phaidon.
72   Campbell, H.C. (1967), *Metropolitan public library planning throughout the world*, London: Pergamon, chapters 4–6; Campbell, H.C. (1973), *Public libraries in the urban metropolitan setting*, London: Bingley, 20–26.
73   Campbell, H.C. (1973), 30–33.
74   Library Association. Reference, Special and Information Section (1975), *The new Birmingham Central Libraries: proceedings of the twenty-first annual study group*, edited by A. Mason, London: The Section.
75   Alison, W.A.G. (1980), *The Mitchell Library, Glasgow: the new extension*, Glasgow: Glasgow District Council.
76   *A library for all times* (1997), Stockholm: Swedish National Council for Cultural Affairs.
77   Hyams, E, (2002), 'Bringing glamour to Glasgow', *Library + information update* **1** (8), November, 44–6.
78   For a list of spaces, see also *The public library service: IFLA/UNESCO guidelines for development* (2001), 44.
79   *Future of public library services. Working paper 1: key themes and issues of the study* (1993), Bournes Green, Gloucestershire, 4–5.
80   Dahlgren, A. (1988), *Public library space needs: a planning outline*, Madison, Wisconsin: Wisconsin Department of Public instruction.
81   Dolan, M.J. (1981), 'Long life, low cost, loose fit', *Service point* (23), 25–8; see also Demarest, R.C. and Friedman, R.M. (1989), 'The modular library', *Library journal* **114** (20), 74–6.
82   Peterson, H.N. (1972), 693.
83   Thompson, A. (1963), *Library buildings of Britain and Europe*, London: Butterworth, 16–17.
84   Strong, G.E. (2001), 'Flushing Library: a year of success', in *Library buildings in a changing environment*, edited by M-F. Bisbrouck, Munich: Saur, 125–39.
85   Fialkoff, F. (1994), 'Denver's dream library', *Library journal* **119** (21), 58–9.
86   Pattingale, G. (1995), 'Penrith's new library', *Australasian public libraries and information services* **8** (1), 24–5. Includes a plan.
87   Ehlin, I. (1997), 'Enköping Public Library', *Scandinavian public library quarterly* **30** (1), 8–11.
88   Myllyllä, R. (1999), 'Vuotalo Library and Cultural Centre' (in Finnish), *Kirjastolehti* **92** (1), 6–7.
89   Cohen, A. and Cohen, E. (1979), *Designing and space planning for libraries: a behavioural guide*, New York: Bowker, 64–5.
90   Cohen, A. and Cohen, E. (1979), 63.
91   Wheeler, J.L. (1963), 3.
92   Dahlgren, A.C. (1996), 11.
93   'Tackling a new flagship for Rugby' (2000), *Public library journal* **15** (3), 74–5.
94   Follina, T. (2003), 'A community venue: the architect's viewpoint' (in Italian), *Biblioteche oggi* **21** (3), 30–32.

4   'Location, location, location'

A good location is essential to fulfillment of the library's mission of service to its community.

Gerard McCabe, 2000[1]

Whatever the architectural and functional merits, or demerits, of a newly provided public library facility, its success will be judged by the use made of it: by, for example, the number of its visitors, the level of membership, the volume of loans and enquiries, and the amount of ICT use. Success for the library is principally attributed to the right location having been chosen through the cooperative efforts of planners, librarians and others.

An understanding of the process and methods of determining a library's location is not only important when planning a new building but also if a librarian has to judge whether an existing and serviceable library building should continue in use or be replaced by another located elsewhere in the vicinity. A knowledge of the principles and practice of library service point location will also be important should a service point strategy suggest the closure of one or more libraries or the need for additional ones.[2]

A public library is usually part of a library system that contains a variety of service points as described in the previous chapter. The location of any one library building must therefore be seen as part of a service-wide strategy for service point provision and siting – one that considers such questions as the optimum distance between libraries, bearing in mind the distance that users are prepared to travel to reach a library, the scale of car ownership and the quality of the available public transport. The user's library and information needs are a determining factor for the individual in matters of travel distance.

The most effective location for a public library will be one that takes into account where people are to be found in the community, how they move around, and the character of the surrounding built environment, both existing and planned. Equipped with this information the librarian will also be able to evaluate alternatives to new stand-alone premises – the proposed use of a well located redundant building, for example; occupying shared accommodation; or a building situated in a complex along with cultural, civic, leisure, educational or retail facilities.

Location is concerned with the library's best position in the community to ensure the greatest possible use. The nature of its precise site – its size and shape, for example – will affect the building's appearance, the number of floors and the location of the entrance. All may influence library usage but none as much as the right location.

It may seem hardly worth discussing the principles involved in choosing a site for a public library, as in the UK the long-held American viewpoint seems to hold sway – that it should be 'in the heart of the downtown pedestrian crowd' (although not necessarily in the geographical centre of a place) or suburban shopping centre. In 1973, libraries associated conveniently with shops were endorsed by Taylor and Johnson, although they draw attention to some of the drawbacks such a location might entail.[3] Thirty years later, Charles Leadbeater, the author of *Overdue: how to create a modern public library service*, wrote that

> Attractive modern 'hub' libraries in shopping centres should be at the heart of any attempt to create a modern public library service ... new users are more likely to be attracted by bright, light, retail formats which blend learning and leisure.[4]

There are several of these which work well in Brisbane, Australia, such as Chermside Community Hub, linking the library with an acquatic centre and services club, and featuring an outdoor area, coffee hub and colourful art.

Less accepted, perhaps because of the different legislative and local authority set-up in the UK, is an American view that the public library building should not be shared with or placed with civic or cultural institutions or other buildings. Equally strong is the American belief that the public library should not be placed in or near a school. Adoption of these 'principles' in the US can be put down largely to the influence of Joseph Wheeler who, while having much of importance to say, was dogmatic in his views, both as regards siting and library design. He wrote in 1941, for example: 'Challenge all proposals to house a museum, art gallery, public auditorium, or any other non-library community activity in the library building'.[5] He also felt that visitors to other kinds of institution had different patron habits from library users. This is not to say that American practice continues to hold to this or other notions, as there are, for example, libraries in shopping centres, libraries shared with a medical centre, and school-based public libraries in the US.

As will be seen, a number of public libraries in the UK have been erected in association with other types of institution, building, or building complexes, including schools. The pros and cons of the different locations these arrangements imply will be considered later in this chapter. Location issues relating particularly to the use of refurbished and extended libraries and the conversion of 'alien' buildings to public library premises will be considered largely in the following chapter.

WHO SHOULD SELECT THE LOCATION?

Who should identify and then select a library site? Should it be the librarian, perhaps following the simple rules that have emerged over the years? Or should the decision be left to other experts? The best answer is the librarian, who knows the library's aims and objectives, working together with the town and country planner, the statistician, the computer specialist and the architect, amongst others, and employing the modern methods and tools noted later in this chapter.

Identifying potential locations for a library, especially a major library building, is not a simple task, although the criteria by which identified sites are then evaluated are quite clear. If retail site selection methods (which bridge marketing, economics and geography) are to be used to identify sites, then the librarian will need the help and expertise of others. Statistical modelling and the use of a Geographic Information System (GIS) also demand the knowledge and expertise of others to guide the selection of the most appropriate library location.

LOCATION FOLLOWS BRIEFING

Chapter 7 makes it clear that having decided there is a need for a new library building, the librarian, in consultation with others, has to decide what kind of building is required to fulfil its agreed purpose and roles. Then a location has to be found which will permit the required building to be constructed. Indeed, as more than one expert has indicated, it is impossible to evaluate likely sites without an idea of what it must accommodate.[6] This implies, of course, that the librarian has a choice of site and this may not be the case. In a less than ideal situation the librarian must decide what compromises are acceptable in respect of a given site and what might be done (at the time or in the future) to alleviate particular problems that might arise, perhaps of insufficient space. A location and site acceptable to the librarian may, however, impose constraints on the architect's design solution and offer particular challenges that will have to be overcome; the design requirements of a conservation area, for example. Sometimes such challenges provide opportunities for the architect; for instance a sloping site may usefully allow entry at the middle level of a multi-storeyed building. An appreciation of the influence of an unsatisfactory site on both the use and design of the proposed library will help the librarian argue for a better location should this be necessary.

SITE SELECTION

It is now time to look at the principles and practices that might be used in identifying potential library locations. In summarizing the library profession's view on the location of the public library, Christine Koontz writes that 'retail site selection methods are considered valuable by the majority of librarians'.[7] Arguments can be advanced, however, that public libraries are not shops in that, for example, income generation and profit are not their *raison d'être* and that, unlike shops, they are tied to administrative boundaries, thus affecting their location. As Gulten Wagner writes: 'libraries have little in common with the two chief principles of these establishments: the ideology of profit making and the ideology of consumption'.[8]

William Robinson claimed, however, that the profession's simple statements that the library building should be 'central and accessible' or 'in any healthy shopping centre with public parking nearby' are not very helpful. He believed that libraries should be located according to retail principles, as it would seem, according to Koontz, do many librarians.[9] But whether retail site selection theory and practice is appropriate or not, the kind of simplistic statements that guide librarians are considered questionable and a more sophisticated methodology is argued for.

An early attempt to use a more sophisticated approach to siting was the employment of an adapted version of Reilly's Law (used for estimating the best site for retail use) for library location in Scunthorpe. Its application, however, was not considered

> ... a matter for the amateur enthusiast but for the professional planner ... who should be asked to apply it and produce a plan showing the resulting recommended site or sites[10]

Koontz argues for statistical modelling combined with experience and professional judgement to be used in making library location decisions. The model she proposes will use data, for example, to:

- estimate geographic dispersion of the population and the size of the market areas ...
- forecast use levels at other locations [than the existing one] ...
- estimate potential use levels of targeted markets or sub-groups within the population in order to develop new services and potential new facility locations.[11]

Koontz says that more sophisticated approaches can be employed today using computers and GIS software that relates data to maps. This makes possible the processing of spatial information for market analysis and aids the location of library facilities.[12] In a case study, Koontz demonstrates how GIS data can be used to show graphically, for example, how far most users live from an existing library and the topographical barriers to use, such as busy roads. If GIS data shows where users are coming from to use existing libraries, and then those areas from which few people visit, there should be a good indication of those places where new library buildings might be needed and located.[13] The publication *Modelling use at individual service points* has as one of its aims: 'To create a weighting formula around those elements that will allow individual library authorities to predict the probable use of a particular service point'.[14] This meets part of the objectives of Koontz's proposed statistical model noted above.

Identifying potential sites for a public library should be assisted by the data gathered through market research. The need for such information should be borne in mind when the community needs assessment is carried out. Further market research may be needed subsequently, as indicated later in the chapter, to assist in the evaluation of particular sites and the final selection.

LIBRARY LOCATION MASTERPLAN

In a later chapter there is a discussion of service point evaluation. Such evaluations should be part of a strategy or masterplan for devising or reviewing library building provision and siting within a library system whether serving an urban or county area. As Australian librarian Warwick Dunstan wrote

> For every city, it should be possible to devise a theoretical distribution of library locations which is a maximisation of service standards and a maximisation of costs.[15]

Clearly such a strategy for library locations will need to take into account patterns of growth and change in town and country and relate them to a local authority's development plan. Like most such schemes it will need to be reviewed from time to time and may suggest the closure and relocation of some service points and the addition of others. An example of such a review, and one which offers alternative scenarios for the future, was that prepared by San Diego Public Library. Although carried out in 1977, it still provides a helpful model of how to examine a library service's buildings against its mission, aims and objectives and the local communities where they were located. It documented libraries' strengths and weaknesses, both as service points and buildings, and made recommendations about future projects, such as the site for the proposed new central library and the relocation, expansion or combination of branches, as well as new construction.[16]

In the UK, a 1996 strategic review of public library provision in London, which it calls 'Library City', comments that

> Little research has been done on the distribution of libraries throughout London in the context of changing fortunes of town centres and other social and economic factors.

It notes also that 'borough library services operate as a series of separate *cul de sacs* rather than as part of an ever-widening network' and that 'there is no hierarchy of provision' (the city has no major reference facility, such as New York or provincial large cities in the UK). Amongst the report's recommendations was that each London library service should review the role and location of its libraries, both locally and in a London-wide context.[17] This would be a step in the right direction towards a library location masterplan for London.

SITE EVALUATION

What principles and practices might be used in evaluating potential library locations? In Chapter 7 there is a brief account of choosing a site for Runcorn Library: the library's location in Shopping City had already been decided upon and pedestrian counts were used to help finalize the selection of one of the two proposed sites. The following Canadian case study of the influential Metropolitan Toronto Library is a more complex site selection situation, but reflects many of the factors discussed more fully later, and is based on information prepared for the Metropolitan Toronto Library Board by the architect and other consultants in 1971.[18] At that time there were six area boards in Toronto responsible for library service. The Metropolitan Toronto Library Board and its central library (dispersed over a number of buildings) provided certain city-wide services and facilities, such as centralized acquisition and processing and a major reference collection. The library needed a new home and the process of choosing its site and a description of the building are given below. In 1998 the seven library boards were united to form Toronto Public Library, operating from 98 locations that included the Metropolitan Toronto Library, now known as the Toronto Reference Library.

Case study in site selection: Metropolitan Toronto Library

Following the compilation of a preliminary programme or brief, ten sites were considered as potential locations for the proposed new Metropolitan Toronto Library. All were in the central area of Metropolitan Toronto and in close proximity to the subway (underground railway). Fifty-eight criteria, divided into two levels, were drawn up for the evaluation of the ten sites, although cost of land was not amongst them.

First-level criteria (six categories) were factual, objective matters and independent variables. The five second-level criteria were interdependent or co-acting and more subjective. The two criteria levels, their categories (with an indication of their implications) and the weightings for the first-level criteria are listed in Figure 4.1.

Each first-level criterion was assigned its weighting according to its relative importance as a factor in locating and planning the new library. With a weighting of 6, 'Metro-wide access' was considered the strongest factor. A perfect score for all criteria was expressed as a power of 3: for 'Metro-wide access' a score of up to 18 was therefore possible for each site under consideration. 'Development potential' and 'Availability' were the next strongest factors and were both weighted 5. For site analysis purposes, 'Development potential' was further sub-divided into (a) buildable area – whether the site could meet the phase 1 building space requirement; (b) parking – the ability to accommodate 50 cars; (c) expansion – ability to accommodate phase 2; and (d) open space.

Following the first-level evaluation, four of the ten sites were eliminated. Only those with scores of over 40 were evaluated at the second level. The four sites were eliminated because of inadequate size, poor access, the need for extensive demolition and

(Weighting factors in brackets are explained in the text)

First-level criteria

Metro-wide access (6): by public and private transport
Development potential (5): see text
Absence of established community (2): disruption considered undesirable
Absence of site constraints (3): for example, natural or man-made
obstructions
Adequacy of present zoning (2)
Availability (5): whether questionable or of uncertain timing

Second-level criteria

Potential of project area: for example, ability to encourage other
development
Human participation: such as ability to contribute positively to life in the
area
Amenities: for example, proximity to other public and special libraries
Architectural design potential: such as ability to meet image requirements
Moral & legal problems: for example, expropriation of property

Figure 4.1   Metropolitan Toronto Library: site evaluation categories

disruption to existing communities, or a combination of these factors. After the second-level evaluation, also using a scoring procedure, the assessment recognized that three sites would make good locations for the new central library. That at Yonge/Asquith was preferred and is where the library is now sited.

In late 1973 the site and design concept for the library was approved. There had been some opposition to both the scale of the building and its design which resulted in a reduction in size and its redesign. Construction began in 1974 and the library was completed in 1977. The building (33,816m²), provides accommodation for over 1.2 million volumes and seats for more than 1,300 people. It is distributed over five library levels with a lower floor for administration, technical services and compact storage area. The five floors and their mezzanines project from the perimeter, leaving a large central atrium topped by a skylight. Two glass side-hung lifts within the atrium and close to the entrance provide one means of getting to the upper floors. Of open-plan design, the public areas are located to the front of each floor with staff workroom areas and closed stack area behind. On the ground floor an internal street links two entrances at opposite corners of the building and these can be used without coming into the library itself. The library is separated from the street by pools of water which are also used as security barriers.[19] Outside, the library is adjoined by a small park and amphitheatre.

The idea of using site-rating charts to compare site options in an objective fashion, as for Metropolitan Toronto Library, is endorsed by other library planning experts. As in the Toronto example, criteria scores are weighted.[20] Also in Canada, the Ontario library buildings guidelines bring together suggested site evaluation criteria under four headings: access; site development and availability; library use considerations (such as proximity to other daily activities); and architectural design. The guidelines also say that the same criteria should be used to evaluate shared buildings or locations. In such situations access criteria may be met but design considerations may be compromised. It is important therefore that the librarian be involved in site selection.[21]

LOCATIONAL FACTORS

The choice of a satisfactory library site is usually the most important decision to be made in ensuring a library's success in terms of use. Its selection, however, may arouse controversy due to cost, or nostalgic attachment to an existing library location, for example. Obtaining the best site can be a lengthy process not just because of the time needed for evaluation but due to possible political infighting, disagreement or delay. And politicians may be the final arbiters of where the library is to be located.[22]

In addition to being able to meet the demands of the architect's brief, choice of a library's location is determined also by the factors listed in Figure 4.2.

- Cost of the site
- User accessibility
- Travel distance and service point distribution
- Site size and shape
- Relationship to other buildings
- Physical suitability of the site[23]
- Desire to group the library with other buildings

Figure 4.2   Site locational factors

COST OF THE SITE

This will be an important consideration in the selection of the site. The best sites are likely to be the most expensive because of their retail or commercial potential. A cheap but poorer site is likely to be uneconomical in the long run, however, because of lower levels of use. Wheeler was particularly concerned that per circulation cost would then be too high. He felt also that it was better to save on building costs than site costs and opposed the decentralization of a main library (as discussed in the previous chapter) as not being a practical alternative to the necessity of paying for a strategic central library site.[24] Other site costs might include those for the demolition of existing structures and site preparation.

Site cost may be avoided where the new building is to be constructed on the existing library site or on other land in possession of the funding authority, where required site criteria can be met, or by the exchange of sites owned by, for example in the UK, a district council.

Related to the question of cost is the question of the proposed life of the planned building, which it is suggested should be an investment for at least 50 years. As will be seen in the next chapter, upgrading old buildings, whether from the 1890s or 1930s, which are still in a good location, can be a sound undertaking.

USER ACCESSIBILITY

As level of use will be a key factor in determining the success of a library, the ease of user access, whether as pedestrian, cyclist or motorist, is perhaps the most important factor in ensuring that success. This requires an assessment of the way people move around the community on foot and by public and private transport. This usually means that certain locations will be preferred. Others, such as quiet streets or parks, it is argued, should be avoided, although these too may have a good proximity to main traffic routes or other busy areas.[25] A related factor is whether parking can be provided on the site or is available close by. Some libraries do provide on-site parking for users but in other instances it is solely for library transport, and the vehicles of staff and disabled visitors. Generally speaking, parking is a community issue rather than one for the library alone.

The question of access into the library building for the disabled, the elderly, young children and mothers with children is considered in Chapter 6. Here it is worth noting that physical barriers, such as a busy road, even where tunnels, bridges and crossings are provided, may deter users from visiting the library. The basic requirement is that the site 'should be accessible to the greatest number of users'.[26]

TRAVEL DISTANCE AND SERVICE POINT DISTRIBUTION

The professional consensus is that library success is bound up with the nature of its location, in a shopping centre, for example. One American survey suggests, however, that 'distance from home was the decidedly predominant reason for approval or disapproval of location'. Distance from school and parking was ranked second by children and adults respectively, with shopping coming third.[27]

Gulten Wagner notes that, since the public library is free,

> The major real cost to the consumer is travel cost, including time and inconvenience. Thus distance is a signifier of dysfunction in using these institutions.[28]

She goes on to point out that public transport as a signifier of accessibility should not just take into account its availability but also its timing and frequency.[29]

Discussing travel distance in respect of branch library siting in the US, it was noted that there was a plethora of criteria used in New York and elsewhere: a half-mile radius (the maximum distance a child is expected to walk); 15 minutes by bus; 30 minutes by car, or in shopping centres where, it is assumed, everyone goes.[30] For the UK, the position stated in 1962 was that

> In urban areas no person should normally have to travel more than a mile to a library ... [and that] the distance should be less in heavily built-up areas where natural centres of population are closer together and the density of population justifies the provision of more branch libraries.[31]

It was argued a few years later, however, that it was not unreasonable, even in an urban area, for some readers to travel more than a mile in order to have the advantage of a full range of library services and that modern public and personal transport and parking facilities made this possible.[32] Although recognizing a variety of service point provision and the need for a flexible approach to travel distance, these comments reinforce the one-mile standard as regards travel distance and that continues to be used today in England for some contexts.

The public library standards for England support the objective that 'library authorities must enable convenient and suitable access for users of libraries'. This objective is measured by 'the proportion of households living within a fixed distance of a static library', and convenient opening hours, including the time service points were not available, for example, due to emergency closure. The travel distance measurement target varies according to the type of local authority. Generally speaking this is within one mile, for 100 per cent of inner London borough households, for example, and within two miles for 85 per cent of households in county councils.[33]

Welsh standards require library authorities to ensure that 85 per cent of the proportion of its households are either within two miles of a static library, or that they are within 30 minutes by public or private transport.[34] Scottish standards state that 'the number and distribution of library service points will depend largely on the objectives and priorities of the local authority', and 'they should be located where the public come together to use a range of services'.[35]

Distribution of branch libraries is clearly related to population density, natural and man-made barriers, and so on. Service point use, however, may be more related to travel distance, particularly from the home, and questions the shopping centre location (discussed later in this chapter) much-championed by librarians. It is generally recognized that people will contemplate longer travel distances to visit a central or district library in order to make use of greater, more varied and specialized resources.

In locating library service points, the librarian will want to map out the market or catchment area of each library. This is often defined by size of population and administrative boundaries, rather than the distance travelled by users or with regard to the distance between different service points. As indicated earlier, distance may be a major factor affecting library use, in particular where distance is combined with other socio-economic factors, such as age, education and people's means of transport. Physical, social and cultural barriers, the quality and the nature of library provision combined with inappropriate opening hours are also likely to affect use. Notional and actual catchment areas for individual libraries can be much the same in some instances and in others less so because, as indicated above, different factors affect a reader's choice of library. As noted in a Berkshire-wide survey,

> This is not very helpful ... if investigating the library needs of an area where a new library is proposed or defining the community served by a library for a community profile.[36]

Reporting on research into the effects of distance on library effectiveness and the indicators that were most important and relevant to the groups surveyed, Koontz concludes:

> convenience of location ranked in the top ten of all indicators for four of the seven surveyed groups ... interestingly enough, the groups not ranking location in the top ten were library managers, trustees, and service librarians.[37]

While access to a library is a significant issue, convenience of its location (that is, the distance people are willing to travel to a service point) is equally or possibly more important. Guidelines – as factors to be considered – rather than travel distance standards may be more helpful to librarians in determining library locations.

SITE SIZE AND SHAPE

A site should be large enough to meet the demands of the architect's brief. One that is larger than present requirements, however, will provide space for the future extension of the library, whether as part of a phased library development or in anticipation of possible future needs. Space around the building will help give a quieter environment, better natural light, eliminate the risk from fire in adjacent structures and permit landscaping. A site that is too small can mean more (smaller) floors, limit what can be built, or provide problems of access. A generous site might encourage the library to be set off by, or set back in, landscaped grounds, which Wheeler sees as conflicting with accessibility.[38] Not only accessibility but visibility, which is also considered important, may be reduced by landscaping and the setting back of the library premises. As was discussed in the previous chapter, the shape of the site will help determine the shape or plan of the building, and also the orientation of the building on the site.

RELATIONSHIP TO OTHER BUILDINGS

The relationship of a library to other buildings may affect its design in a number of ways. The first of these will be its appearance: the need to blend in with other dominant buildings or to fit into a conservation area may dictate, for example, the choice and colour of building materials. Even where no such constraints apply a building of modern design may not be welcomed. The second is likely to be its scale: the need to observe a particular roof line or height may mean a certain amount of the library building having to be placed below ground. The British Library is the most famous large-scale library example of this issue, as its building had to reflect the scale and feel of the nearby St Pancras station and hotel.

A site close to noisy activities or transport routes may require the library to have design and sound insulation treatments to combat noise. Some large libraries have been built beside busy roads in recent years, such as those at Durham, Kidderminster and Ilford.

PHYSICAL SUITABILITY OF THE SITE

Although today virtually anything is constructionally possible – witness 'the largest basement in London' for the British Library – the cost may be considerable. The unsatisfactory nature of the ground may disbar a favoured library site because of contamination or the limited load capabilities of the land, for example. If such an unfavoured site is chosen, however, it is likely to involve extra building and other costs, or adversely affect the size of the structural grid. The discovery of archaeological remains may delay work on a site and, if of particular significance, may require amendment to the design of the library to permit display and access. Such a discovery, and its incorporation into the building, can give an added visual dimension to its appeal and also attract visitors to the library. More dramatically, important archaeological remains may necessitate a change of site. In Barcelona, the site agreed in 1997 for the state public library was changed in 2002 for that reason and plans made for it to be located near the Estacion de Franca in 2006–07 rather than the old Born Market.[39] The ideal site may escape the librarian and so it is even more important that he/she understands the pros and cons of various locations as revealed though a site evaluation study.

FREE-STANDING, SHARED, CO-LOCATION OR INTEGRATED?

If a library is not to be erected as an independent building on its own site, but is to be a shared building or grouped with other buildings, then choice of the library's location will be linked with that of the other building or buildings. In such a grouping, it may be the library which is the dominant institution and whose siting needs will be most influential. The association, co-location or sharing of the public library with other types of building or building complexes (civic, cultural, community or educational) opens up a wide variety of possibilities as regards location. Bournemouth Library, for example, occupies the upper storeys of a striking new building in the town centre, above shops at street level (see Figure 4.3). Such approaches may offer pragmatic solutions to local circumstances rather than carefully thought out philosophies and far-sighted community plans.

Figure 4.3   Bournemouth Library (2002)
Source: David Barbour/Building Design Partnership

An independent, free-standing location is a preferred solution for many libraries both large and small. It gives greater visibility, offers a better sense of identity and provides space for expansion or for building in phases, as at Bexley (phase I, 1980, phase II, 1989 and further phases contemplated) or Kidderminster, for example. However, public library buildings in the UK have neither in the past nor today always had the benefit of an independent, free-standing location. They may be co-located or linked with other public buildings, may share a local authority building, or be integrated with (for example) a school library, or integrated (in part) when archive and other heritage services are brought together in accommodation with the local studies department. Taylor and Johnson identified this range of possibilities as long ago as 1973, noting the potential of dual-use buildings, libraries built in association with community and health centres and the use of village halls or similar buildings for library purposes. The authors thought, however, that 'a library with civic centres containing public offices, police stations, magistrates courts, etc, is not compatible with the evidence of library use'.[40]

SHARED PREMISES

Sharing premises can be looked at in two ways. Two disparate services may occupy the same building and perhaps share a common entrance but otherwise have no other relationship; a public library branch alongside a health centre or swimming pool, for example. On the other hand, there may be a certain degree of convergence, and some sharing of physical resources. Both approaches will, it is hoped, encourage library use from users of the non-library part of the building. *Building better library services* asks whether there are 'opportunities to make services more accessible by sharing buildings with other organisations?'[41] This section demonstrates that such opportunities do exist and have been taken up by librarians both now and in the past. Whether this makes library services more accessible in the desired way, and thus better used, is a matter for debate.

Sharing premises can make financial sense in that one site and one structure are needed, with some saving over two buildings because of common elements. Where a building is shared more fully, leading to better use of what could be under-used facilities, such as meeting and staff rooms, then an even more efficient and effective use of resources is achieved. A needs assessment should be made of proposed tenants of shared buildings so that those with similar needs and non-conflicting patrons can be identified, studied and sharing accepted or rejected.

Conflict can arise over the appropriateness of the site for all parties: parking needs, design issues (such as future expansion), the location of the entrance, and the security of common areas, for example. Whether services co-exist side by side or some building elements are shared, a written agreement is required. This would cover such issues as signs, building security, cleaning and repairs, and scheduling of room use.

> With the proper amount of caution, planning, and written agreements, a shared library facility can be the best possible environment for both parties, and a strong, healthy association can evolve.[42]

A different view, and largely concerned with situations where library buildings are shared with social agencies, perhaps with a view of attracting the disadvantaged non-user, is less encouraging. It is suggested that the social agencies will get more space than the library, and the disadvantaged (other than 'problem patrons') will not use it. One commentator summarized the position thus: 'the shared-facility concept of a building is simplistic, inefficient, and wasteful, but laden down with concern and good intentions'.[43]

The linking of libraries with some unlikely companions has been noted earlier and this has continued in the last 50 years or so, with libraries – usually branch libraries – built in conjunction with, for example, sports facilities, a swimming pool, health centres or clinic, old people's homes, or under flats on a housing estate (Figure 4.4). It has been suggested that a library and a bookshop could share premises as a way of dealing with some of their overlapping functions and sharing resources.[44] In one Netherlands town a library shares its premises with a bank, providing a useful centre for the community.

More appropriate, because of the information service they provide, is the hosting of tourist information centres, citizens' advice bureaux and local authority one-stop shops in many public libraries of all sizes. Less frequently, space is provided for the careers service and other council facilities such as a rent office or registrar of births, deaths and marriages. New and converted buildings continue to be shared with museums, record offices or art galleries.

John Harvard Branch Library, Southwark (ground floor of office block, 1977)
Selby Library, North Yorkshire (ground floor of housing development, 1984)
Gourock Library, Inverclyde (ground floor of housing development, 1988)
Barnstaple Library, Devon (includes record office, 1988)
Mildmay Library, Islington (adjoins day nursery, 1987)
Kinlochleven Visitors' Centre/Library, Highland Region (1989)
Tillydrone Library, Aberdeen (adjacent to council nursery and site for health clinic, 1991)
Wavelengths Library, Lewisham (with swimming pool, 1991)
Didcot Library, Oxfordshire (career service, registrar of births, deaths and marriages, 1992)
Banchory Library, Aberdeenshire (flats above and below, 1993)
Dulverton Library and Porlock Library, Somerset (both include a visitor centre and Porlock a parish room, 1994 and 1996)
Downham Market, Norfolk (shared with district council and local college, 2000)
East End Pool and Library, Newcastle upon Tyne (2000)
Outer West Customer Service Centre, Pool and Library, West Denton, Newcastle upon Tyne (2003)
Anniesland Library & Learning Centre, Glasgow (ground floor of tower block, 2002)
The Campus Library, Weston-super-Mare, North Somerset (part of a multi-use building, 2004)
Shirley Library and Housing Office, Southampton (2005)

Figure 4.4 Shared library buildings in the UK

CO-LOCATION

Joseph Wheeler was against locating the library with civic, cultural and other buildings, saying the library did not belong. Cultural activities for group involvement, for instance, require 'totally different attitudes and procedures' and 'schools are almost always away from the ... center of things'.[45]

Co-locating the library with other cultural and information services, such as a museum or tourist information centre, and with a shopping precinct can, it is thought, have benefits for the level of use. Desirable proximity to other kinds of building has been ranked by one Canadian state in the following order: shopping; community space such as a square or mall; business/offices, cultural/educational.[46] The Australian librarian Warwick Dunstan devised a five-part locational classification in the 1970s showing 'the major elements towards which [Australian] public library locations appear to be oriented'. Categories one to three cover three levels of shopping centre (regional, community and neighbourhood), fourth is civic or community centres (including schools and other locations), and finally transportation corridors (sub-divided into major and minor corridors).[47]

Another view is that 'public libraries do not have very strong links with any particular activity' but that 'their strongest affinities after the shops' are with education and civic accommodation. It is suggested that cluster analysis can be used to examine the relationship between libraries and other town facilities.[48]

INTEGRATION

Dual-use libraries are an example of integration. Papworth Everard Library (200m²) in Cambridgeshire, and opened in 2000, serves two communities – the local residents and the organizations on site serving the disabled. People with disabilities can use the library with ease because of suitable signage and assistive technology. Outside the library is a sensory garden shared with other local organizations and agencies for people with disabilities.

A number of public libraries house both the local studies department and an archives department or record office. One development, that will be considered more fully in Chapter 11, takes the major local studies collection or department for a town or county out of the public library building and into other premises. This either provides for a shared building or a fully integrated service with a record office, as at the Surrey History Centre, and occasionally with related services, such as a museum.

The following sections and examples, that group libraries with education, cultural, leisure and other service provision, demonstrate the varied range of shared, co-located and integrated building situations that have occurred in the past and exist today.

LIBRARIES AND EDUCATION

The relationship between public libraries and schools goes back to the nineteenth century where, in some instances, school libraries were made available to local children and residents, as well as pupils. This concept of dual or joint use by community and school continues in modern times both in the UK and elsewhere. Another public library link with education is demonstrated by the inclusion of 'learning centre' in the title of many new branch libraries, emphasizing the provision of ICT facilities for independent learning (Figure 4.5).

Scotswood Family Learning Centre, Newcastle upon Tyne (1993)
Huyton Library, Knowsley (includes learning resource centre and art gallery, 1997)
Epsom Library, Epsom & Ewell (includes a learning centre, 2001)
Tavistock Library & Learning Centre, Devon (2001)
Anniesland Library & Learning Centre, Glasgow (2002)
Burnbank Library, South Lanarkshire (includes a learning centre, 2002)
Clifton Library, Nottingham (includes a learning centre, 2002)
Littlepoint Library & Learning Centre, Cambridgeshire (2002)
Britwell Library & Play & Learning Library, Slough (2003)
Tiverton Library & Learning Centre, Devon (2004)
Bell Green Community Library & Learning Centre, Coventry (2004)

Figure 4.5   Libraries and learning centres in the UK

The Idea Store brand being adopted by Tower Hamlets seeks to create a retail image in contrast to the library stereotype. The accommodation (1,125m²), opened in 2002 at Bow, makes use of the original Passmore Edwards Library and converted adjacent council offices. The emphasis is on the library's educational role.[49] There are 49 public access PCs, access to computer-based training with tutor support at key times, and a range of computing courses, from basic to advanced. In addition to a full programme of adult learning, there is a wide range of events and activities. Three areas of the Idea Store are identified as Learning Labs.

Tavistock Library and Learning Centre, Devon, was opened in 2001 and occupies premises (515m²) on The Quay, that runs along Tavistock Canal. Associated with the library is accommodation for other organizations and council offices. A bridge and a pedestrian walkway link The Quay with the Wharf Arts Centre. The library includes 23 public access computers – 11 in a meeting room/ICT suite – and a total of 40 computer points are provided to cater for future expansion.

A recent concept (but one tried before) is that of the 'extended school' which is seen as a means of joining up family and community – the library as part of a large leisure and learning facility. A related approach is the discovery centre; that at Dover, for example, brings together the library, adult education service, museum, UK Online, as well as café, theatre and nursery.[50]

Libraries can also feature as part of a complex of facilities that may contain educational institutions, such as the 1970s Abraham Moss Centre in Manchester or the more recent 'discovery centres' or 'extended schools'. In addition to that at Dover, the county of Hampshire is proposing to see all its libraries, big and small, as 'discovery centres', although it will not necessarily give them all that name.[51] The library service will work closely with archives, museums and adult education, as is locally appropriate. An example of an extended school is that for Parklands High School, Liverpool, which is part of a £25 million PFI development that will include a library, day nursery, one-stop council shop and learning and leisure facilities.

Libraries that serve both a school and the local community are usually known as dual-use libraries in Britain. Such an arrangement is not a recent phenomenon, nor peculiar to the UK, and joint-use or school-housed public libraries are to be found in the US,[52] Canada, Australia, Sweden (where almost 40 per cent of public libraries are integrated with a school library),[53] Germany and elsewhere. The discussion of the dual-purpose concept below has many lessons for those who are contemplating sharing their accommodation with others.

Dual-use libraries

A joint-use [or dual-use] library is one in which two or more distinct groups of users are served with equal priority in the same premises, the governance of which is cooperatively arranged between two or more separate authorities.[54]

Secondary schools are the most frequent location but they may also be established in association with a tertiary institution or be part of a community facility or centre that includes both school and library. Examples of the less frequent association with a tertiary institution include Blyth Community College and Cowpen Library (2002) in the UK, Härnösand public library and college of higher education (2000) in Sweden, the public and university library in Valence in France,[55] and those in the US at San José, for example, where the public library integrates with a university library on a campus location.[56] It is suggested that such links are developing because the boundary between library users and students is blurred by lifelong learning ambitions. This section can only provide a brief description of this integrated service provision, noting its pros and cons, and planning and design implications. Factors that appear to encourage success or militate against it will also be considered.

On the face of it, dual-use libraries have much to recommend them: one set of premises, staff, library materials and equipment serving two groups of users who are usually provided for separately. Better library provision will result from a joint service than from a single service, with interaction between school pupils and the general public. And yet opinions about their efficacy can be highly polarized – usually because of good or bad experiences – and have generated a substantial professional literature. Problems may relate to a site that is not central and thus a drawback for some, such as the elderly;[57] there must be misunderstandings as regards the roles of the joint service, mixed perceptions of whom the library is 'for', and unwillingness on the part of some people to go to a school.

An Australian study of school/community libraries examined what factors seem to make for their success or militate against it, as well as listing building design requirements that would appear to need particular attention. Factors that seem to militate against success fall into five categories and these are identified in Figure 4.6.

- Planning problems: such as inadequate assessment of user needs
- Governance problems: for example, absence of a formal agreement and of firm commitment to the concept
- Physical problems: such as difficulties of public access due to the location in the community and/or school
- Usage problems: for example, dual systems of acquisition, etc., and use of the library as a classroom
- Staffing problems: such as inadequate staffing levels and inflexible and territorial attitudes

Figure 4.6   Factors militating against dual-use success[58]

Fourteen keys to likely success were identified as important for those planning such an arrangement and some are listed in Figure 4.7.

- A firm commitment by the two partners to the project
- A clear understanding by all concerned of the philosophical and operational aspects involved
- A single staffing structure
- A formal signed agreement before the joint service begins
- A building of adequate size for the two groups, designed to facilitate both group and individual use
- Effective channels of communication

Figure 4.7   Keys to dual-use success[59]

Australian experience would suggest that dual-use library success is higher in small rural communities 'and/or where there is a strong sense of community identity'.[60] But there are examples of successful dual-purpose libraries in urban areas. Factors for success stipulate a building of adequate size for both school and public library requirements and the Australian study goes on to suggest (Figure 4.8) that there are particular design issues that require attention.

There is also the question of whether the library should be an independent, purpose-built building or linked to the school premises. One view is that ideally a purpose-built library is preferable but experience shows that in small rural towns expanded school facilities can make satisfactory public provision. The library design should reject the 'hard' (the institutional) in favour of the 'soft'. 'A community/school library needs to say: "relax, don't be frightened, use this space".'[61]

Separate library areas for pupils and adults are not required in joint-use libraries, except for group work and where there is specific public library provision for particular age groups, such as the under-fives and children under 11.

- On-site location – 'good visibility from and proximity to a major public thoroughfare and adjacent parking are needed'
- Access and entry – a common entrance is preferred and the public should not have a complicated route via playground or buildings to the library
- External lighting and signposting – to ensure safe access at night and readily identify the library building and the route to it
- Internal design and furnishing; for example, separate accommodation for a class size group, adequate staff and storage areas, sufficient and suitable shelving and seating, bearing in mind different age groups

Figure 4.8 Design issues for dual-use libraries

Recent research shows that the number of dual-use libraries has increased in recent years and, as Figure 4.9 shows, they are found in both rural (Cornwall and Scottish Highlands) and in urban locations (Liverpool, Hillingdon, Bolton and Trafford). The research has found that, in the right circumstances, dual-use libraries can be an extremely effective form of library provision, enabling a 'better standard of library service to be provided than would otherwise be possible'.[62] As indicated in Figure 4.7, the most successful dual-use libraries are those whose design takes into account both clienteles and are at the heart of the community rather than on the periphery, for example at South Woodham Ferrers, in a new town.

Callington Library, Cornwall (1972)
Padgate Library, Cheshire (1982)[63]
Werrington District Library, Cambridgeshire (1982)
South Woodham Ferrers Library, Essex (1983)
Harraby Library, Cumbria (1990)
Aston Community Library, Rotherham (1990)
Bovingdon Library, Hertfordshire (1991)
Shawbost School/Community Library, Western Isles (1992)
Tarbert School/Community Library, Western Isles (1992)
Hunts Cross Library, Liverpool (1993)
Harlington Library, Hillingdon (1994)
Papworth Everard Library, Cambridgeshire (2000)
Winnersh Library, Wokingham, Berkshire (2003)

Figure 4.9 Dual-use libraries in the UK

Both in Britain and the US the nature of school life has been altered by shootings and other events caused by either pupils or outsiders. Security becomes an issue, with a greater chance that this can be compromised by a dual-use library. It is suggested that appropriate policies and procedures and good design can help with this issue, and in particular by locating the library at the outer edge of the school building rather than in the centre.[64]

Case study: Abraham Moss Centre, Manchester

A very ambitious link between education and libraries is exemplified by the Abraham Moss Centre in Manchester, opened in 1974.[65] The centre contained a secondary school, a college, community sports and social facilities and a public library to meet both the needs of the complex and the local community. There was adequate parking but the main shopping area was half a mile away. The centre replaced Crumpsall District Library which was situated in a busy shopping centre and on a main transport route. Parking was difficult there and the library was not built in association 'with any other focal point for community and cultural activities'.

It was hoped that library use would benefit from all those who visited the Abraham Moss Centre for educational, sporting and social reasons and by a large part of the community. It was expected that this change in library location would affect the identity of users and the demands placed on the library service.

An investigation into the change of location came up with fairly predictable results, bearing in mind the nature of the complex and its distance from the shopping centre; for example:

* an increase in adult and child membership
* increased use by the under-40 age group
* a decline in use by the over-40 age group.

The investigation confirmed 'certain expectations about the effects of moving a public library from a shopping centre to an educational and recreational complex'.[66]

LIBRARIES WITH CIVIC BUILDING AND OFFICES

Elsewhere, at Oxford (1897), for example, a Victorian library can find itself part of a large local authority building and neighbour to facilities such as council offices, a public hall and police station. Occasionally a library may be built in conjunction with probably less appropriate neighbours; the public baths and wash-houses at Shoreditch (1898) is one example. In modern times this grouping approach to public buildings that includes a library can be seen in the concepts of the civic, leisure or cultural centre.

As noted above, libraries located with other civic facilities are ranked above cultural institutions in order of preference, although, as has been seen, opinion differs. There are numerous examples of libraries co-located with, or forming part of, civic buildings, or accommodating council offices or a one-stop shop within the library building (Figure 4.10). An interesting development in County Donegal is the construction of public service centres, such as those at Cardonagh (2002) and Milford, which also house the public library. Similarly, Achill Library (2003), County Mayo, on Ireland's largest island, is located in a new integrated services centre.[67]

Worthing Library, West Sussex (part of civic centre, adjacent to former library now museum, 1975)

East Grinstead Library, West Sussex (includes branch of Social Services, 1984)

St Neots District Library, Cambridgeshire (forms part of civic centre area, 1985)

Chelmsford Central Library, Essex (ground floor of county hall complex, 1988)

Waterthorpe Community Library, Sheffield (arts space and accommodation for three council departments, 1989)

Maldon Library, Essex (shares with other council departments, 1993)

Beckton Globe Library, Newham (includes local service centre, as well as youth, adult education and community facilities, 1998)

Chard Library, Somerset (includes district council offices in converted mill, 1998)

Wavetree Library, Liverpool (plus one-stop shop in renovated 1903 building, 2002)

Upminster Library, Advice and Service Centre, Havering, London (2005)

Figure 4.10 Libraries with civic buildings and offices

LIBRARIES WITH CULTURAL AND ARTS FACILITIES

Although the major public library buildings between the two world wars increased the variety of the accommodation they provided (to include local history and business departments, for example), Manchester Central Library (1934) was particularly notable for having a theatre in its basement. In more recent times the library and theatre combination has been repeated at St Pancras Library, Camden with its Shaw Theatre, and at Thurrock, where the building contains both the Thameside Theatre and local history museum.

As discussed in Chapter 2, public libraries are seen as having a cultural role that can go beyond the provision and promotion of books and other library materials. This role can be fulfilled in part by its association or co-location with cultural provision, such as a theatre, heritage centre or art gallery in a cultural complex or district, or by providing such facilities within an ambitious multi-functional library and arts building.

The Wythenshawe Forum (Manchester 1971) was built as the cultural part of the civic centre and includes library, theatre, public hall, swimming pool, sports hall, restaurant, coffee bar and licensed bar. Its importance stems, apparently, from the Forum as a social experiment rather than from the dullish quality of its library building.[68] The Forum, including the library, has, however, undergone a recent major remodelling and upgrading of this cultural and community hub.

Case study: Norfolk and Norwich Millennium Library

A modern, if somewhat different example, is the Norfolk and Norwich Millennium Library, which is part of the city's Forum building. Whatever the architectural merits of the Forum building – and it has been highly praised – the library component appears to get a poor deal. Taken as a whole, no one can doubt that the Forum is an impressive building in terms of its scale and its enormous glass entrance façade. From outside the building the glass frontage provides a view of the interior, especially attractive when lit up at night. From the inside it frames the medieval church standing opposite.

There is a large public or civic space outside the building and also inside, both of which can only have seasonal or irregular use. In addition to the library, the Forum, partly funded by the National Lottery, contains a heritage visitor centre, learning centre, restaurant, café and BBC facilities. Its special features are said to be its semi-circular, atrium-based library, the use of daylight, reducing energy use, and naturally ventilated atrium.[69]

The library lies beyond the full-height interior public space, 'shelved' on three glass-fronted public floors, with staff offices above, to the rear of the building. The D-shaped first floor is the largest, with a radial shelving layout that already seems cramped. The views out from the library floors may be arresting, but the floors themselves are not particularly distinctive in design terms. Given all the discussion about creating 'technopolis' that followed the fire that destroyed the 1960s building, this does not seem a good exchange. The library's spatial needs and identity seem to have been subsumed by the need to create an imposing building with an enclosed public space and to provide a view out. Although welcoming the Forum's green credentials, is 'the blurring of functionality and the blending of civic and environmental concerns [as] precursors for future library design' the best mix for public library and information service provision?

Other libraries with cultural and arts facilities

Comparable examples are shown in Figure 4.11. In Ireland, Cavan County's Cootehill Public Library and Arts Centre (311m^2) was opened in 2001. A varied façade with bilingual signs, a clock and large windows invites users into the building. A mezzanine houses the arts centre, meeting room and staff rooms. County policy requires the incorporation of arts spaces in its new library buildings to make the best use of limited capital resources.

Elsewhere in the world libraries may also be part of a cultural grouping, as at the Sahara West Library and Fine Arts Museum (1997) in Las Vegas, US, or the Palace of Culture in Viadana, Italy. The latter houses the public library, two museums, a gallery of modern art, a historical archive, a youth information service, conference room and other services. The multimedia library (1,700m²) serves a population of 17,000: at 100m² per 1,000 population that is worth remarking upon.[70]

Bourne Hall Library, Epsom & Ewell (museum and social centre, 1969)
Wythenshawe Forum, Manchester (cultural part of civic centre, 1971)
Halesowen Central Library, Dudley (theatre and hall, 1971)
St Pancras Library, Camden (plus Shaw Theatre, 1971)
Thurrock Library (phase 2: Thameside Theatre and local history museum, 1972)
Solihull Central Library (plus theatre, 1976)
Rotherham Central Library & Arts Centre (halls, rooms, galleries, café, etc., 1976)
Bromley Central Library (adjacent to theatre, 1977)
Hexham Library & Arts Centre, Northumberland (theatre, restaurant, etc., 1981)
Barbican Library, City of London (in Barbican Centre that includes concert hall, art gallery and other facilities, 1982)
Rhyl Library, Museum & Arts Centre, Denbighshire (1986)
Folkestone Library, Museum & Art Gallery, Kent (art gallery added to original building of 1888)
Bellshill Cultural Centre, Lanarkshire (exhibition area, hall, coffee bar, multi-purpose room, 1989)
Denbigh Library & Museum, Denbighshire (1989)
Bradford-on-Avon Library, Wiltshire (museum, exhibition and meeting space, 1990)
Peterbrough Central Library (with John Clare Theatre, 1990)
Weymouth Library, Dorset (designed to link with arts centre, 1990)
Southampton Central Library (shared with City Art Gallery, 1993)
Sunderland City Library & Arts Centre (1995)
Letterkenny Library & Arts Centre, Donegal (1995)
Rugby Library, Warwickshire (plus museum and art gallery, 2000)
Cootehill Public Library & Arts Centre, Cavan (2001)
Lydd Community Library, Kent (includes craft centre, 2002)
Blanchardstown Library, Fingal (linked to Arts Centre, 2002)
Durham Clayport Library (part of cultural, advice and information services in Millennium City Centre, 2002)

Figure 4.11   Libraries with cultural and arts facilities in the UK and Ireland

Libraries in association with cultural and leisure facilities are one thing, but libraries acting as general leisure and cultural institutions have their American critics. The contribution 'to general culture through non-book activities is of trivial proportions ...

[and] libraries as entertainment centres have formidable competition'.[71] Nevertheless, in UK communities where leisure and cultural facilities are poorly represented, the library's existence, location and facilities are often a local asset in these important fields. The library building and its interior decoration (including works of art) as a contribution to culture in itself is considered in the next chapter.

LIBRARIES WITH LEISURE FACILITIES

An example of the library as part of a centre with leisure and other facilities, is the Lifestyle Centre at Epsom, Surrey, which has restaurants, cafés and a wine bar on the ground floor. On the first floor are the library and learning centre (2001, 1,394m²), doctor's surgery, crèche, children's play area, gym, resource centre for older people, café, display and exhibition areas and some multi-purpose community rooms. The building also houses a private leisure and fitness club and residential units. Access to the library is from a spacious central concourse and is served from the entrance by lifts, stairs and escalator. There is a central enquiry and reception point next to the library entrance.[72] Springburn Library, Glasgow, was relocated in the Springburn Leisure Centre at the head of the main shopping centre. The refurbished leisure centre also houses the Springburn Museum and a new fitness suite.[73] Epsom, Springburn and others in the UK are listed in Figure 4.12, and Figure 4.13 shows another example, from Newcastle upon Tyne.

West Swindon Library, Swindon (part of leisure centre, the Links Centre, 1985)
Chester Lane Centre, St Helens (activity centre with library, 1990)
Marcus Garvey Library, Haringey (within leisure centre, 1991)
Bradley Stoke, South Gloucestershire (part of leisure centre, 1999)
Epsom Library, Epsom & Ewell (part of Lifestyle Centre, 2001)
Springburn Library, Glasgow (in Springburn Leisure Centre, 2003)
Library @ the Phoenix Centre, Sutton, London (part of leisure and community facility, 2004)

Figure 4.12   UK libraries with leisure facilities

LIBRARIES AS COMMUNITY FACILITIES

In the mid-1960s J.D. Reynolds was arguing for the library as a busy centre of village life and talked about cooperation with other public services – not just a clinic next door.[74] Many libraries of all sizes have community facilities such as exhibition space and meeting rooms, of particular importance in small communities. Reynolds seemed to be arguing for more than this; for the library as part of a hub that is an important centre of community life, providing facilities and services to both young and old. (Figure 4.14 gives some examples.)

Figure 4.13 East End Pool and Library, Newcastle upon Tyne (2000): a shared building for leisure and library facilities
Source: Newcastle upon Tyne Libraries and Information Service

---

Brandon Library, Suffolk (integral part of youth, community and library centre, 1972)

Liniclate School/Community Library, Western Isles (school, theatre, museum, swimming pool, etc., 1988)

Laisterdyke Centre, Bradford (library, youth and community centre, 1985)

Stanley Library and Community Centre, Wakefield (hall, playgroup, kitchen, etc., 1991)

Betws Centre, Bridgend (village centre, 1994)

Brixworth Library and Community Centre, Northamptonshire (includes a community hall and café, 1999)

Bilborough Library and Community Centre, Nottingham (meeting room, café, crèche and outdoor play space, 2002)

Brynaman Community Library, Neath Port Talbot (in community centre, 2003)

Llanfyllin, Powys (on ground floor of youth and community centre, 2003)

White Rose Information Resource Centre, New Tredegar (the library is part of a community wing, shared with a variety of parties, 2004)

Figure 4.14 Community centre libraries in the UK

In small communities today, where school, shop, post office and pub may well have disappeared, the library has this potential to be the community centre: the library building becomes the focus for a range of community facilities. The 1995 review of the public library service also suggested that

> A public-private sector working party should be set up to examine the feasibility of placing libraries in village shops [since 2004 South Gloucestershire have had a very small one in the back room of Severn Beach post office] and developing kiosks or micro-libraries in diverse locations.[75]

This reflects to some extent the discussion about portable, kiosk and mini-libraries in the previous chapter.

SHOPPING CENTRE LIBRARIES

Leytonstone Branch Library (1934) signalled another departure in that the library is accommodated above shops with an entrance at street level and steps to the library on the first floor. This solution has been utilized in a number of late twentieth-century public libraries, such as Bedford, Mansfield and Cardiff, and continues into the twenty-first with Bournemouth, for example. It is a design solution that is dictated by the commercial value of ground floor space and one made more acceptable to users today through the provision of lifts and escalators. A more recent but related development has been the inclusion of the library in the ubiquitous modern shopping centre, as at Havant, Llandudno, Bath and Ardkeen (Waterford), or its location just outside, as at Telford. Figure 4.15 shows these and other UK examples.

An article by L. Johnstone on public libraries in shopping centres considered the benefits of such a location to users, the library and the shopping centre itself. For users there are, for example, the advantages of one-stop shopping and library visit, adequate parking, and the proximity to other facilities such as cafés, childcare facilities and toilets. Benefits for the library include the potential for increased library use, and partnership with shop owners, such as a bookshop. Maintenance, cleaning, security and so on become the responsibility of the centre, and the library may experience favourable financial arrangements because of the benefits it brings to the shopping centre. Such benefits include increased use of the shopping centre, encouraging use of other centre facilities, stability of tenancy, and the provision of business information services to the centre. Johnstone identified the link between book borrowing, shopping and utilizing the car, and sums up by saying

> Coupled with trends of growing consumerism and the increasingly recognised values of libraries, [this link] will ensure that the mutually beneficial juxtaposition of libraries and shopping centres will continue into the future.[76]

However, the shopping centre is unlikely to be an appropriate location for a central and main library. Where branch libraries are located within shopping centres, the librarian

Andover Central Library, Hampshire (above shops, 1972)
Bedford Central Library, Bedfordshire (above shops 1972)
Oxford Central Library, Oxfordshire (above shops, 1973)
Portsmouth Central Library (near old Guildhall, civic offices, linked to main
    shopping area and transport services, 1976)
Dundee Central Library (with shopping centre and theatre, 1978)
Hemlington Community Library, Middlesbrough (within an estate of modern
    housing; free-standing building in a shopping precinct, 1982)
Runcorn District Library, Halton (shopping centre location, 1981)
Ealing Central Library (first floor of shopping centre, 1984)
Chesterfield Library, Derbyshire (on a corner of major shopping development,
    1985)
Shipley Library, Bradford (part of shopping complex, 1985)
Ilford Central Library, Redbridge (close to pedestrianized shopping centre,
    theatre and town hall, 1986)
Redhill Library, Surrey (first floor of shopping centre, 1986)
Uxbridge Central Library, Hillingdon (in middle of pedestrianized shopping
    precinct and close to civic centre, 1987)
Cardiff Central Library (over shops, 1988)
Telford Town Centre Library, Telford & Wrekin (outside shopping precinct,
    1988)
Fleetwood Central Library, Lancashire (on main tram and bus route, and close
    to market, 1988)
Hounslow Area Library (within shopping centre, 1988)
Fordingbridge Library, Hampshire (adjacent to car parking and supermarket,
    1989)
Bath Central Library, Bath & North East Somerset (above supermarket, 1990)
Wootton Bassett Library, Wiltshire (in small shopping precinct; between two
    storeys, 1991)
Penrith Library, Cumbria (part of arcade of small shops, 1992)
Leominster Library, Herefordshire (above retail development and bank, 1993)
Somerton Library, Somerset (adjacent to shopping precinct, 1997)
Muirhouse Library, Edinburgh (in shopping centre, 2000)
Idea Store, London, Tower Hamlets (adjacent to shops and market, 2002)
Bournemouth Library (above shops, 2002)
Arena Park Library, Coventry (shared site in retail park, 2005)

Figure 4.15 UK libraries associated with shops and shopping centres

should be as concerned with accessibility within the shopping centre as much as with the shopping centre as a desirable location in itself.

Libraries adjacent to or in shopping centres seem set to become a worldwide solution to location. Singapore, for example, opened shopping centre libraries in 1996 and 1997.[77] However, libraries in supermarkets themselves are a much rarer animal and seemingly occupy an exclusively American habitat. The earliest known supermarket-based public library branch in the US, dating from the late 1980s, is Comotara Branch (74m²) operated by Wichita (Kansas) Public Library, which signed another ten year agreement with the store in 1996.[78] Comotara is one of Wichita's three busiest branches and majority of use comes from new readers. As patrons are allowed to return library materials to any service point it often deals with more returns than loans:

> People are willing to drive to our central facility to do research but they are less likely to make the trip back just to return materials.[79]

In 1996 the Adams Memorial Library, Latrobe, Pennsylvania, placed its newest facility, Unity Branch (60m²), inside the Davis Supermarket in a shopping plaza. In the store, the library's rented space is near the video rentals outlet. The supermarket provides electrical outlets and phone lines and the library provides the shelving, furniture, equipment, and so on. The library offers high use items, such as picture books and best-sellers, a small reference collection, audio tapes and magazines and newspapers for browsing. Library hours are not the same as the supermarket but a bookdrop is provided for returned material. 'Unity library will effectively use the Internet ... [and] use public/private partnerships in a cost-effective manner'.[80]

The literature about shopping centre libraries emphasizes the benefits to the public library, but rarely the disadvantages, which often relate to the quality of the library premises. The disadvantages of such a location are those connected with library image and visibility, upper floor positions, compromised space requirements, and an all-purpose commercial interior of little distinction. Telford Library, Shropshire, which is located outside the shopping centre seems to have none of these disadvantages and may be a much better model to follow. Recent recommendations for shopping centre locations, based on case studies of Edmonton Green, Mansfield, Chesterfield, Weston Favell (Northampton) and Bath, conclude by saying that 'the library should be visually attractive, provide a quality service and enhance the overall image of the centre'.[81]

The public library building can, therefore, contain or be part of cultural, leisure, civic and educational services of various kinds and may also take its place amongst local shops and stores. The 1995 review of the public library service suggested that suitable locations for new public library 'outlets', as it called them, 'could include shopping centres, railway, bus and motorway service stations, and other places that attract sustained flows of people'.[82]

SHARED LOCATIONS ABROAD

In Australia and Canada, library service points have already been located in railway stations. Montreal Municipal Library opened a new branch on the pedestrian overpass in the McGill Metro Station in 1981.[83] The main library in Vienna (2004, 8,885m²) is designed to bestride a railway station.

The library and cultural centre in Vuotalo, Finland (2000) houses a library, workers' college, cultural information centre, a multi-purpose hall, a comprehensive school and a sixth form. Designed as a half-circle and situated in the centre of Vuosaari, the building is ecological in design.[84] Another cultural centre, in Ludwigsburg, Germany, and opened in 2002, comprises an adult education centre, museum and central library.[85] Reykjavik Main Library moved in 2000 to new premises which it shares with the City Archives and the Museum of Photography.[86]

A Danish example of dual use is to be found at Holmsland. In 2001 the library moved into a building connected to a school, having previously been located inside the school itself. The floor area increased from 350 to 1,100m² and computers with Internet access have been placed in the area between the school and the library.[87] Hvide Sands, another dual-use library, also in Denmark, and where school and library relations were strained, solved its problems with a library extension providing separate counters for school children and adults.[88]

As host, neighbour, tenant or joint provider, the public library building and its location often accommodates and offers more than might be expected. It has the ability to be the major focus or major contributor to community life. Selecting the location for a public library, however, can be a time-consuming and complex task in which financial and political influences may loom large. Choosing an alternative to a new library building (as discussed in the next chapter) such as an existing non-purpose built structure, should also be guided by the issues discussed in this one. A major additional factor, however, will be a community's desire for building preservation and conservation.

NOTES

1   McCabe, G.B. (2000), *Planning for a new generation of public library buildings*, Westport, Connecticut: Greenwood, 27.

2   Garrison, G. (1966), 'Some recent public library branch location studies by city planners', *Library quarterly* **36** (4), 151–5. Deals with the 'controversial question of closing or relocating obsolescent branches' in urban areas. The use of a branch survey by planners is described.

3   Taylor, J.N. and Johnson, I.M. (1973), *Public libraries and their use*, London: HMSO, 61.

4   Leadbeater, C. (2003), 'Creating a modern public library service', *Library and information update* **2** (7), 12–13: 12.

5   Wheeler, J.L. and Githens, A.M. (1941), *The American public library building*, Chicago: American Library Association, 14. This was one of the authors' 33 'Generally accepted principles of library planning'.

6   Chitwood, J.R. (1972), 'Elementary notes on site selection', in *Library buildings: innovation for changing needs: proceedings*, edited by A.F. Trezza, Chicago: American Library Association, 151–4: 152.

7   Koontz, C.M. (1997), *Library facility siting and location handbook*, Westport, Connecticut: Greenwood, 25.

8   Wagner, G. (1992), *Public libraries as agents of communication: a semiotic analysis*, London: Scarecrow, 30.

9   Robinson, W.C. (1976), *The utility of retail site selection for the public library*, Champaign, Illinois: Graduate School of Library Science, University of Illinois, 7.

10   Roberts, R.G. (1966), 'Reilly's Law: the law of retail gravitation', *Library Association record* **68** (11), 390–91.

11   Koontz, C.M. (1997), xv–xvi.

12   Koontz, C.M. (1997), xvi, 109–61. For an example of the use of GIS, see, 'Essex: GIS catchment survey and statistics', in England, L. and Sumsion, J. (1995), *Perspectives of public library use: a compendium of survey information*, Loughborough: Library & Information Statistics Unit, Department of Information and Library Studies, Loughborough University of Technology and London: Book Marketing Ltd, 189–94.

13   Koontz, C. and Jue, D.K. (2001), 'The location of your library building: why it is important and how to do it using GIS (Geographic Information System Software)', in *Library buildings in a changing environment*, edited by M-F. Bisbrouck, Munich: Saur, 144–53.

14   Creaser, C. (1998), *Modelling use at individual service points*, Loughborough: Library & Information Statistics Unit, Department of Information and Library Studies, University of Loughborough, 2.

15   Dunstan, W. (1977), 'How and why the urban public library usually end up in the wrong place', *Australian library journal* **26** (15), 265–9: 266.

16   San Diego Library Department (1977), *A master plan for the San Diego Public Library*, San Diego, California: San Diego Library Department

17   Burton, C., Greenhalgh, L. and Worpole, K. (1996), *London: library city. The public library service in London: a strategic review*, Stroud: Comedia, 1996, 44, 66, 71.

18   Moriyama, R., Bowron, A. and Ellis, J.B. (1971), *Metropolitan Toronto Central Library: programme and site selection study*, Toronto: Metropolitan Toronto Library Board.

19   For an illustrated, brief description of the library see Bushman, A.G. (1977), 'Design concepts to "complete your mind"', *American libraries* **8** (8), 426–8.

20   Rohlf, R.H. and Smith, D.R. (1985), 'Public library site selection', *Public libraries* **24** (2), 47–9.

21   *Building libraries: guidelines for the planning and design of public libraries* (1986), Ontario: Ministry of Citizenship and Culture, 31–3; Appendix D, 52.

22   For the story of Chicago Public Library's search for 'shelter' and the political process, see Nelson, M. (1987), 'Trouble in second city', *Wilson library bulletin* **61** (5), 18–21.

23   Thompson, A. (1963), *Library buildings of Britain and Europe*, London: Butterworth, 9–10; Rohlf, R.H. and Smith, D.R. (1985), 47–9.

24   Wheeler, J. (1958), *The effective location of public library buildings*, Urbana, Illinois: University of Illinois Library School, 2, 24.

25   McCabe, G. (2000), *Planning for a new generation of public library buildings*, Westport, Connecticut: Greenwood, 30–31. Rehearses the arguments against putting a library in a

public park. There are examples, however, of Scandinavian public libraries in parks at Hillerød, Denmark, and Malmö, Sweden.

26 Rohlf, R.H. and Smith, D.R. (1985), 47.

27 Hill, T.S. (1972), 'On the location of library buildings', in *Library buildings: innovation for changing needs: proceedings*, edited by A.F. Trezza, Chicago: American Library Association, 155–9: 157–8.

28 Wagner, G. (1992), 30.

29 Wagner, G. (1992), 32–4.

30 Byam, M. (1977), 'Kiosks and porta-branches', *Library journal*, **102** (2), 162–3: 162.

31 Ministry of Education (1962), *Standards of public library service in England and Wales*, London: HMSO, 33.

32 Department of Education and Science; Library Advisory Council (England); Library Advisory Council (Wales) (1971), *Public library service points: a report with some notes on staffing*, London: HMSO, 1–2.

33 *Comprehensive, efficient and modern public libraries: standards and assessment* (2001), London: Department for Culture, Media and Sport, 10.

34 National Assembly for Wales (2001), *Comprehensive, efficient and modern public libraries for Wales: standards and monitoring*, Cardiff: National Assembly for Wales, 6–7.

35 *Standards for the public library service in Scotland* (1995), Edinburgh: COSLA, 66.

36 Stevens, A. (1990), *Getting to know our customers*, Reading: Berkshire Library and Information Service, 20.

37 Koontz, C.M. (1997), 38.

38 Wheeler, J.L. (1967*), A reconsideration of the strategic location for public library buildings*, Urbana, Illinois: University of Illinois Graduate School of Library Science, 31.

39 Pavesi, A. (2003), 'The library has yet to appear' (in Italian), *Biblioteche oggi* **21** (4), 39–42.

40 Taylor, J.N. and Johnson, I.M. (1973), 62.

41 Audit Commission (2002), *Building better library services*, London: Audit Commission, 26.

42 Adams, M.L. (1986), 'A shared housing primer', *Library journal* **111** (20), 65–6: 66.

43 Ballard, T.H. (1985), 'Library buildings: form follows function', *Library journal* **110** (20), 44–6: 45.

44 Line, M. (2003), 'A joint library and bookshop experiment' [letter], *Library + information update* **2** (10), 28.

45 Wheeler, J.L. (1967), 28.

46 *Building libraries: guidelines for the planning and design of public libraries* (1986), 32.

47 Dunstan, W. (1977), 26–7.

48 Osborn, E. (1971), 'The location of public libraries in urban areas', *Journal of librarianship* **3** (4), 237–44.

49 Godowski, S. (1999), 'Selling the idea of learning', *Architect's journal* 9 September, 50–51.

50 'Dover Discovery Centre' (2003), *Library + information update* **2** (12), 10.

51 Ward, R. (2003), 'Turning vision into reality', *Public library journal* **18** (3) 51–2.

52 For Oak Park (dual-use) Library, Ventura, California, see Boyden, L. and Weiner, J. (2000), 'Sustainable libraries: teaching environmental responsibility to communities', *Bottom line* **13** (2), 74–82.

53 Hansson, J. (2001), 'Is it a good thing to integrate libraries?', *Scandinavian public libraries quarterly* **34** (4), 17.

54 Browne, M. (ed.) (1981), *Joint-use libraries in the Australian community*, Canberra: National Library of Australia, 72.

55   Heranz. E. (2001), 'Displaying the resources of a public and university library: the experience of Valence', (in French), *Bulletin des Bibliothèques de France* **46** (1), 84–8.

56   Modigh, B. (2000), 'Härnösand', *Scandinavian public library quarterly* **33** (2), 19; 'Three plans for shared-use libraries in the works' (1999), *American libraries* **30** (1), 21–3.

57   For access to a joint-use facility, resources and services, see Browne, M. (ed.) (1981), *Joint-use libraries in the Australian community*, Canberra: National Library of Australia, 83.

58   Commonwealth Schools Commission (1983), *School/community libraries in Australia*, Canberra: The Commission, 104.

59   Commonwealth Schools Commission (1983), 100–101. Other reasons for success are given in Browne, M. (ed.) (1981), *Joint-use libraries in the Australian community*, 21–2.

60   Commonwealth Schools Commission (1983), 105. A population smaller than 3,000 is suggested. Overseas, a figure of 10,000 is considered a reasonable upper limit, but this can be quite arbitrary, see Browne, M. (ed.) (1981), 4.

61   Browne, M. (ed.) (1981), 50.

62   McNicol, S. (2003), 'Dual-use libraries: do they work?' *Library and information update* **2** (10), 52–3: 53. The author also maintains a dual-use library website that includes a database of dual-use libraries and bibliography: www.ebase.uce.ac.uk/dual-use/index.htm.

63   Jones, A. (1977) 'Dual purpose libraries: some experience in England', *School librarian* **25** (4), 311–18. Describes examples from the 1960s and 1970s and illustrates various plan solutions.

64   'Changing perspectives: joint use of facilities by schools and public libraries', *Public libraries* **38** (6), 355–9: 355, 356, 359.

65   Department of Education and Science (1973), *Abraham Moss Centre*, London: HMSO.

66   Jones, A. and King, M.B. (1979), 'The effect of re-siting a library', *Journal of librarianship* **11** (3), 229–31: 230.

67   For other Irish examples at Ashbourne and Castlepollard, see *Irish library news* (240), [1] and (242), [2].

68   Ward, Herbert (ed.) (1974), *New library buildings: 1974 issue,* London: Library Association, 10.

69   Edwards, B and Fisher, B. (2002), *Libraries and learning resource centres*, Oxford: Architectural Press, 143–7.

70   Aliani, A. and Bettoni, G. (2003), 'Three levels and five sections' (in Italian), *Biblioteche oggi* **21** (8) 17–19, 21–4.

71   Davies, D.W. (1974), *Public libraries as culture and social centers: the origin of the concept*, Metuchen, New Jersey: Scarecrow, 96.

72   Combe, G. (2002), 'Take your partner', *Library + information update* **1** (2), 39–41.

73   'Fit for the future' (2003), *Information Scotland* **1** (3), 17.

74   Reynolds, J.D. (ed.) (1967), *Library buildings 1966*, London: Library Association, [3].

75   *Review of the public library service in England and Wales ... : summary and schedule of recommendations* (1995), London: Aslib, 31.

76   Johnstone, L. (1999), 'Public libraries and shopping centres', *Australasian public libraries and information services*, **12** (1), 25–30.

77   Mohamed, N.S. (1999), 'New libraries and new innovations', *Herald of library science* **38** (3–4), 245–6.

78   'First library-supermarket mix pleases grocery shoppers' (1987), *American libraries* **18** (1), 8–9.

79   Commings, K. (1996), 'New library locations: go where the patrons are', *Computers in libraries* **16** (10), 24–6: 26.

80   Commings, K. (1996), 25.

81   Morris, A. and Brown, A. (2004), 'Siting of public libraries in retail centres: benefits and effects', *Library management* **25** (3), 127–37: 136–7.

82   *Review of the public library service in England and Wales ... : summary and schedule of recommendations* (1995), 31.

83   Lavigne, N. (1984), 'A library in the Metro station', *Public library quarterly* **5** (2), 47–57.

84   Myllyla, R. (1999), 'Library and cultural centre Vuotalo, a twentieth century meeting place where sparks fly' (in Finnish), *Kijastoleheti* (11–12), 6–7.

85   Stierle, T. (2003), 'Spatial wonder with artistic qualities' (in German), *Buch und bibliothek* **55** (1), 34–8.

86   Jonasdottir, E.K. and Rognvasldsdottir, I. (2001), 'Moving a mountain' (in Icelandic), *Bokasafnid* (25), 2–5.

87   Nyeng, P. (2001), 'Joyous library effort in Holmsland' (in Danish), *Biblioteksspressen* (4), 116–18.

88   Lange, M. (2002), 'Two counters – no popes' (in Danish), *Biblioteksspressen* (6), 171–2.

5 Alternatives to new buildings

Careful planning, skillful design, and community support can transform our historic library building resources into ever valuable twenty-first century centers of learning.

Elisabeth Martin, 2002 [1]

The emphasis in this book is on new, purpose-built libraries. Sometimes this has taken the form of a prefabricated or portable structure or accommodation in a shared building or of co-location in a civic or cultural complex. For a variety of reasons, a new purpose-built building to replace an old one, or to offer a public service for the first time at a new location, may not be possible. Alternatives to a new building will then have to be considered, following the usual needs assessment (described in Chapter 7), and a decision made as to whether:

- to re-utilize the existing library, using the maximum initiative and minimum expenditure
- to refurbish the existing library – at its simplest a redecoration, repair and probably a refurnishing of the premises
- to refurbish and remodel the existing building – a modernization that includes reorganization of internal space; this may require structural alterations
- to extend the existing building – adding to the total area available for library service purposes
- to refurbish, remodel and extend the existing building – this contains all the elements of the three previous alternatives
- to convert a building not originally designed for library purposes – it may be necessary to add to the building to be converted, if more space is needed and the site permits it.

COMPROMISING IDENTITY AND IMAGE?

It would be wrong to pretend that, in adopting one of the alternatives to a new building, one can or should follow most or all of the idealistic principles relating to library identity and image (see Chapter 9). In cases where an existing library is to be refurbished (and perhaps remodelled and extended), or a building is to be converted to library use, then clearly the existing structure imposes constraints on what can be achieved in physical and aesthetic terms. Nevertheless, given the importance of the issues associated with identity and image, they should be taken into account for any older building to be reused or converted.

Accepting one of these alternatives may therefore mean accepting some degree of compromise over the portrayal of library identity and image. A Carnegie library will always be a building of its period, although, as will be seen, much can be done externally and internally to attract and retain users by creating an agreeable contrast between the age of the building and the modernity of the library environment and its services. Using a converted building, especially a listed one (and some public library buildings are also listed), will probably place constraints on what changes or additional features, such as external signage, are permitted. In spite of such limitations, however, the recycling of existing buildings has become a significant feature of public library service point provision.

RUNNING OUT OF SPACE

The main impetus for better and larger accommodation is usually functional – lack of space. Because of the need to provide more by way of stock and services, and where the cost of any kind of alternative premises cannot be afforded, then a more limited objective of making the best use of existing space can be considered. The 'shrinking' library's space problem can be fought through purposive weeding of the library stock, the use of spinners, integrating some sections of the collection (adult and children's non-fiction for example), different furniture configurations and changing space allocations.[2] These potential solutions are summarized in Figure 5.1 and imply a need to recognize that the library may be attempting to do too much in the available space.

Re-utilization of existing space, without major structural alterations, can only be a temporary solution if the space problem is a major one and is not susceptible to real improvement in the ways suggested. It can give breathing space, however, and revitalize the library while other options are considered. Where appropriate, and funds permit, other aspects of the building can also be tackled in a review of existing space, such as lighting, signage and colour schemes, to improve the library's appearance and appeal.

MAINTENANCE OR NEGLECT?

The problems that necessitate the 'makeover' described above will not have arisen overnight. A proper space or facilities management regime might have anticipated the

Review the provision and scale of library services and materials – delete, combine or relocate a service or facility; review stock provision policy

Make use of modern technology – microforms and ICT, such as WiFi hotspots

Look for poorly used or under-used space – the entrance area, an upper floor, for example

Create flexible space – for example, make use of movable shelving units and stackable seating

Create a more appropriate mix of larger and smaller spaces – remove or add partitions, incorporate corridor or other 'dead' space (such as basement or storage areas) into 'live' areas; consider the worth (and cost) of altering interior structural walls

Utilize more economic storage methods – higher shelving (where appropriate); use of spinners; review the space allowances between furniture, shelving and equipment but avoid overcrowding; use mobile shelving in public and in storage areas

Figure 5.1   Reviewing existing space

results of library change and development and adapted and altered the building accordingly, as far as resources would allow. Even if a proactive space management approach is not embarked upon, there seems little excuse for the lack of basic building maintenance and neglect that can mar the public image of library service points, as well as pose health and safety concerns.[3] The fire at Norwich Central Library (see Chapter 6) was in part caused by inadequate inspection and maintenance.[4]

Dirty windows, badly worn carpet, guiding (where complete) whose wording bears little relationship to the contents of the shelves, soiled keyboards and terminals, crude notices, trolleys of unwanted books for sale, furniture dumps under stairs, neglected upkeep of works of art: these are all symptoms of uncaring neglect and lack of maintenance. Without proper maintenance, libraries that were once heralded as the 'latest and the greatest' can go easily downhill in appearance and attractiveness as the years go by. The challenge for the librarian is both to create a library image and then to maintain it.

As with educational buildings, it is possible to put such neglect of the physical environment down to the need for capital investment. As noted in Chapter 1, it is thought that something like £600–650 million is needed to bring library buildings up to acceptable standards,[5] and that this nineties estimate would have increased due to inflation and further building deterioration.[6]

It has been suggested that there are ways through public/private partnership that local authorities can release some of the latent funds tied up in their library buildings. These could be used to develop new services and improve the quality and maintenance of library premises.[7]

REFURBISHMENT AND REMODELLING

Library refurbishment – redecoration, repair and refurnishing – can be seen as a better-financed 'makeover' that allows much more to be achieved than the more basic approach of reviewing and improving existing space. Refurbishment usually goes hand-in-hand with a remodelling or modernization of the library interior. This often has as objectives, for example, the creation of a more open-plan interior, a rationalization of the number of service desks and the introduction of new services and facilities. But, it has been suggested, objectives should include 'the idea ... that when you walk into a renovated library, your reaction should not be "how nice" or "what an improvement" but "WOW!" '.[8]

Remodelling assumes that the library being reorganized is still well sited, both now and for the foreseeable future, and meets required space needs: indeed, if this is not the case, remodelling is not likely to be worthwhile. As with the simpler approach, remodelling will endeavour to make better use of redundant or little used spaces and, structural features permitting, will combine or divide existing spaces to create new library departments or areas.

These and other issues for evaluating a remodelling proposal are listed in Figure 5.2.[9] Sometimes only part of the library may be remodelled, the ground floor for example, or, as at Folkestone (2002), the reception area. This now incorporates a transparent screen by Chris Ofili with motifs typical of the artist's work.

Is the site suitable for the present and immediate future?
Is there sufficient usable space for the present and immediate future? Some of the space-saving methods noted above might be used to ensure this
Are there opportunities to take over space in a shared building?
How adaptable is the building? Are there structural problems to combining spaces?
Will it be staff-intensive to operate?
What will be the problems and costs of making the building more accessible to the disabled, the elderly and others?
What is its structural condition?

Figure 5.2   Evaluating a remodelling proposal

Considerable attention should be paid to the physical condition of the building:

> All of these elements of structure, electrical, mechanical and plumbing concerns should be carefully analyzed and reviewed with a person who is knowledgeable in building maintenance.[10]

In the UK, Glasgow began a modernization programme for its numerous Carnegie libraries in the 1960s.[11] This continued with the refurbishment of the 1925 Shettleston Library and of the Edwardian Rutherglen Library in the late 1980s and early 1990s.[12] As the Shettleston example shows, refurbishment is not just concerned with Victorian and Edwardian libraries. At Burnley, for example, a refurbishment and small extension of a listed 1930 library building was completed in 1994, with attention being given externally to better access and to improving the library setting through decorative ironwork, a frieze, seating and a paved area. On a seemingly larger scale was the refurbishment of Camden's Swiss Cottage Library (also a listed building), by the architect Basil Spence, that originally opened in 1964. The refurbishment, which cost £7.86 million, plus expenditure on new stock, and took two years to complete, saw the library fully open again in 2003.[13] A cleaned exterior and a sensitive interior renewal has brought the building into the electronic library world.[14]

On a smaller scale, Nottingham's Bilborough Library and Community Centre ($327m^2$) is a 1960s building refurbished and extended in 2002. It now includes a variety of community facilities – meeting room, café, crèche, community display area and with potential for an outdoor play space. The centre is used for councillors' surgeries, by playgroups, and by after-school and youth clubs. Other examples of refurbished libraries are listed in Figure 5.3, in addition to four case studies.

SUCCESSFUL REFURBISHMENT

Case study: Dundee Central Library

Completed in 1978 and part of a complex that now includes a theatre, café, conference hall, meeting rooms and exhibition area, Dundee Central Library at $9,135m^2$ is one of the largest public libraries in the UK. A programme of improvement, costing £2 million, took place in the late 1990s, remedying the effects of heavy use, introducing more natural light to a rather enclosed interior and renewing heating, lighting and ventilation systems. This improved the appearance and accessibility to public areas, particularly the featureless entrance, now transformed into an urban garden.

The library occupies two floors: a lending floor that includes the children's library, and a reference floor that houses, for example, the Internet café, local studies and staff facilities. All public departments have been upgraded and all lending departments are open plan and have newly constructed counters. The lending services floor can now be approached by a new staircase which projects into the shopping mall. 'All now have a building in which the environment is light, bright and attractive ... adapted and improved to keep pace with technological advances.'[15]

Case study: Lowestoft Library and Record Office

Lowestoft Library (1975, $2,910m^2$) is a three-storey building plus basement that over the years has also accommodated a schools library service and record office. Although well used, by 2000 the building began to show its age and mechanical and electrical services, especially the lifts, were reaching the end of their life.

Roscommon County HQ & Branch Library (1990)
Ipswich Library (Suffolk, 1994, plus extension; also 2004)
Daniel Hay Library, Whitehaven (Cumbria, 1996)
Page Moss Library (Knowsley, 1997)
Kirkby Library, plus new entrance (Knowsley, 1998)
Tulleycarnet Library (South Eastern Education & Library Board, Northern
    Ireland, 1998)
Cheam Library (London, Sutton, 1999)
Ellesmere Port Library, plus replacement link block (Cheshire, 2000)
West Norwood Library (Lambeth, London, 2000)
Marsh Farm Library (Luton, 2001)
Kinson Library (Bournemouth, 2002)
Folkestone Library, Museum & Art Gallery (Kent, 2002)
Kerry Library County HQ & Tralee Library (Co. Kerry, 2002)
Blackburn Library (Blackburn with Darwen, 2003)
Ealing Library (London, Brent, 2004)
East Park Library (Wolverhampton, 2004)
Upper Norwood Library (London, 2004)
Baldoyle Library, refurbished and extended (Fingal, Dublin, 2004)
Waterford Central Library, refurbishment & extension of 1905 building
    (2004)
Bristol Central Library (2004)
Widnes District Library (Halton, 2004)
Hendon Library (London, Barnet, 2004)
Sutton Central Library (London, 2005)

Figure 5.3   Refurbished libraries in the UK and Ireland

The refurbishment, completed in 2003, aimed for colour, movement, retail features and a sense of fun: colour and design were used to define spaces, and projected images, light, graphics and lettering were all employed. On the exterior, coloured panels replaced some of the glazing, brightening the library's face and helping to reduce solar gain (see Figure 5.4). The colours were repeated inside the building: bright red and dark blue feature walls provide backgrounds for text in various fonts and colours.

Refurbishment included a reorganization of the internal space, providing a coffee shop and local service centre on the ground floor in addition to the children's and lending libraries. The first floor, extended by filling in the mezzanine, includes the learning centre, further lending space and the record office. Recabling this 1970s building to the latest standards to accommodate a large number of terminals does not seem to have posed a major problem. Data points have been installed in the coffee shop so that later it can become a cybercafe.[16]

Figure 5.4 Lowestoft Library and Record Office, Suffolk (refurbished 2003): an imaginative makeover of the 1970's façade
Source: Suffolk County Council, Libraries and Heritage

Case study: Wavetree Library and One-stop Shop, Liverpool

Built in 1903, this Edwardian listed public library (491m²) had fallen into disrepair due to unsatisfactory maintenance. The 2002 refurbishment of the library, to also provide a one-stop shop, included cleaning and repairing the exterior, installing external lighting and signage, landscaping, and improving access to Disability Discrimination Act standards.

The interior has been decorated to a high standard, enhancing the Edwardian plasterwork, and lighting is now in excess of IEE (Institution of Electrical Engineers) and CIBSE (Chartered Institute of Building Services Engineers) standards. A corporate colour scheme, used also for reception desks, seating and other furniture, has been employed to brand the facility and harmonize with the one-stop shop. Other services and facilities include an ICT suite, a 'quick choice' area and an interview room.

Case study: Slaglese County Library, Denmark

Accepting that change is forcing a rethink of its library concept and design, Slagelse County Library worked with its architects to develop two to three models for a redesign of its premises. In particular, the brief mentioned 'a new sense of library aesthetics; a more modern design with an appeal to a younger generation'. The library is currently

139

housed in two separate buildings on either side of a narrow street, joined by a pergola and linked at basement level by an underground tunnel. The library service was fairly traditional as regards design and organization and a management consultancy was employed to advise on necessary change.

Options for the redesign of the library include: (1) reducing the main library collection by 30 per cent to make room for a coffee shop, more study facilities and recreational areas; (2) bringing all the public facilities together in the newer building and locating the administration and technical services in the older one; or (3) extending the new building, the most costly alternative. The library's philosophy is for a service with depth of purpose:

> We are no longer book museums collecting and keeping books and other printed materials for generations to come but vibrant institutions with services to meet immediate needs.[17]

Judging by the 2004 report of a Liber Architecture Group seminar in Bolzano, Italy, the refurbishment of existing libraries that may seem out-of-date and inadequate to meet current needs, as demonstrated by the above case studies, is now of wide, international concern.[18]

LIBRARY EXTENSIONS

Where site and structure permit, space limitations can be overcome by an extension to the existing library building and this often involves changes also to the original structure. There are numerous UK examples of library extensions both large and small, such as the central libraries at Islington (1976) and Southampton (1992/3), Putney Library (1998) and Lincoln Central Library (1996), the last named being described in the case study below. Extensions to smaller libraries include Bicester (Oxfordshire, 1996), Clifton and Bilborough (both Nottingham, 2002), and Middleton Circle (Sutton, London, 2002). The 1981 extension to Glasgow's 1911 Mitchell Library building created the largest public reference library in the UK (50,000m²).[19] Dublin City Library and Archive now occupy a refurbished and extended 1909 building opened in 2003.[20]

Four types of extension have been identified:

- a wing extension, perhaps creating an L-shaped building
- a full-length extension – one that runs the complete length of one wall of the library and so extending the original rectangular shape by another rectangle alongside it
- an infill extension, filling in those open areas which are part of a different library plan shape – an L- or U-shaped building, for example – or a plan with a courtyard or with an irregular elevation
- a wrap-around extension – one that encases the library on three sides.[21] Islington's first new public library since the 1980s, the 'N4' Library and City & Islington

College Centre for Lifelong Learning, is described as a new exterior wrapped around a Victorian structure.[22]

With the exception of the wing extension, such extensions usually create an infilled or larger rectangular library plan.

Extending a library usually involves such challenges as:

- linking the old with the new; creating a feeling of unity rather than of separateness
- deciding whether the new part is to blend in with the original building, or to be strikingly different, as at Putney in London
- making the best possible use of the newly combined spaces.

An extension may involve creating a new entrance to the combined old and new elements, or require a link building which becomes the new entrance to the joined structures. Resolving these and other challenges, as at Falkirk and Aberdeen for instance, is critical for a successful library extension.[23] At Falkirk, the 1993 library extension is linked to the old 1902 listed building by a glass atrium. The extension was designed to harmonize with the original accommodation rather than trying to copy it and has led to a significant increase in available space: 55 per cent and 62 per cent respectively in the lending and reference departments.[24] In Ireland, the 2004 extension to the 1905 Waterford Public Library made good use of local stone.[25] In Aberdeen the 1892 library was extended in 1905 and again in 1982, the exterior being upgraded in 1984. Because of the restricted site, an increase in space was gained in 1982 by the addition of a seven-floor tower unit and by adding a mezzanine floor to the adult library.

Where libraries are planned in phases, or with a view to a later addition, then any future expansion should be anticipated in the original design. At Kidderminster Library (1997), for example, a blank wall shows where an arts or museum building could link with the library. Internally this potential link is signalled by an entrance atrium, which would provide access to any extension that might be constructed.

North American experience spells out what it is like to be involved in a library refurbishment and extension project. One project manager has described her experience of an expansion (1,208m²) and refurbishment of the rest of the building in Homewood, Alabama, that opened in 1997. Her tribulations included unexpected structural and roof insulation deficiencies that had implications for costs.[26]

Writing about alterations and additions to pre-1960s buildings, a Canadian architect offers guidance on some of the opportunities and constraints – conforming to current building regulations, for example. He concludes that problems

> ... may make renovation inadvisable, but in other cases splendid renovations of older buildings can be achieved and functional adequacy obtained by enhancing design to meet new requirements.[27]

Case study: Lincoln Central Library

The decision to redevelop Lincoln Central Library and its site in 1993 marks the start of a project that illustrates many of the points made about library refurbishments and extensions in this chapter. It also contributes to the discussion about the place of public artworks (see Chapter 9), although with some minor allowances, there was no commitment to a Per Cent for Art Scheme by Lincolnshire County Council at the start of the project.

This large-scale project involved keeping the original front wing of the much-loved 1914 Carnegie library building and creating a large two-storey extension, roughly four times the size of the original library behind it. Although the site continued to be a good one, its redevelopment, given the city's long history and range of historic buildings, provided archaeological and design challenges. After public and interest group consultation and the granting of planning permission, the library moved to temporary accommodation in November 1993 and demolition and archaeological work began.

In January 1995, applications were made to the National Lottery and to the Eastern Arts Board; the latter being a request for assistance with the cost of setting up a proposed public artworks scheme. With a subsequent grant of £61,300 from the lottery and some matched funding, there was a total of £77,000 for the scheme. Seven categories of public artwork were commissioned:

- a tapestry (main hall)
- stained glass panels (courtyard lobby)
- glass screen (first floor)
- benches (in courtyard)
- external railings, gates and grilles
- mobiles (children's library)
- glass screen (children's library).

The development manager has described the selection of artists, the detailed design stage, the commission stage, community participation (by local schools) and the installation of the artworks in time for the opening of the central library in June 1996.[28] He concludes that 'the artworks have "humanised" the rather stark feeling of a new building' and that community involvement has 'been instrumental in making the new library feel an integral part of the city'. He finishes by dismissing the idea of public artworks as add-ons and considers that their integration into this project meant that the building and the new service had a far greater impact.

The central library that was created by blending old and new buildings has all its public services on a large open plan ground floor. From here there is access to a public courtyard enhanced by the artworks described above. The first floor houses bookstack, staff accommodation and mechanical plant. The Carnegie element of the building mainly houses the children's library, linked to the teenage section in the extension, and a community room.

CONVERSION OF NON-LIBRARY BUILDINGS

Adapting a non-library building to create a successful public library seems to go against the theory that the library must be purpose-built to be successful. But such a solution has significant advantages, similar to the refurbishing, remodelling and possible extension of an existing library and has been used extensively in the UK and elsewhere, the Netherlands and the US, for instance. The public library at Eindhoven in the Netherlands, for example, has been housed since 1998 in the extended former Philips light bulb factory.[29]

This is a change of heart from the post-war years, when previous experiences of making do with converted buildings meant that librarians were unwilling to accept what was considered second best. This willingness to look more sympathetically on the use of the converted buildings option was reflected in the title of the 1985 IFLA Budapest seminar on library buildings: 'Adaptation of buildings to library use'. A Hungarian librarian posed the question: 'Can a librarian accept an old building?' and answered: '"Oh, he may", or even "Oh, he must".'[30]

Although the conversion of non-library buildings is more likely to be considered positively in times of financial difficulty, such a solution has always been a feature of public library service point provision. This is even more so today, perhaps, with the concern for the conservation and re-use of buildings rather than their destruction. Certain types of structure, for example warehouses, cinemas, factories, department stores, chapels and corn exchanges, lend themselves to conversion because of features like large internal spaces and strong, load-bearing floors.

Sunderland City Library and Arts Centre (5,022m²), opened in 1995, is housed in a former department store. It provides commercial accommodation on the ground and first floors with the library on the second floor and art gallery and administration occupying the third floor. The redevelopment of the Royal Pump Room at Leamington Spa saw its former swimming pool converted to an award-winning public library (1,300m²) in 1999.[31] Lydd Community Library, Kent (225m²), in a converted school building, was refurbished in 2002. There is a mediaeval theme in the children's library and the premises include the Romney Marsh Craft Centre, the regional showcase for professional artists and craft workers. Presentation in the latter area has been improved during refurbishment through new lighting and display cases and the craft centre is separated from the main library section by an artist-designed screen. Forest Gate Library (Newham, London, 2003) was created by the conversion of the lower floor of a 1960s office block at a cost of £1.5 million.[32] In Ireland a number of churches have been converted to public libraries such as Kilfinaghty (Clare County, 2001), Dunshaughlin (Meath County, 1996) and Oranmore (Galway County, 2001); at Buncrana, Donegal (1999) there has been an extension of similar size to the original church building. Even buildings of domestic scale, however, such as a large house or shop, have been converted to branch libraries. Figure 5.5 lists examples of buildings converted to libraries and two case studies follow.

Bishop Auckland Library, Durham, 1993 (listed town hall)
Macclesfield Library, Cheshire, 1994 (listed bank building on part of site)
Port Glasgow Library, Inverclyde, 1996 (municipal buildings)
Sunderland City Library & Art Centre, 1995 (1930s store)
Taunton Library, Somerset, 1996 (supermarket)
Urlingford Library, Kilkenny County, 1996 (court house)
Waterside Library, Derry City, 1997 (workhouse)
Currie Library, Edinburgh, 1998 (primary school)
Tolworth Community Library & IT Learning Centre, Kingston Upon Thames,
    1998 (shop)
Anniesland Library & Learning Centre, Glasgow, 2002 (ground floor of tower block)
Cricklade Library, Wiltshire, 2002 (glove factory)
Littleport Library & Learning Centre, Cambridgeshire, 2002 (town hall)
Ardkeen, Waterford, 2002 (restaurant)
Lydd Community Library, Kent, 2002 (school)
Minster Library & Neighbourhood Centre, Kent, 2002 (supermarket)
Llanbradach Community Library, Caerphilly, 2003 (football changing rooms)
Chatham Library, Medway, 2005 (bowling alley, formerly dockyard building)
Datchet Library, Windsor and Maidenhead, 2005 (house)

Figure 5.5 Library conversions in the UK and Ireland

SOME NOTABLE CONVERSION PROJECTS

Case study: Castle Gates Library, Shrewsbury, Shropshire

An interesting example of a conversion is Castle Gates Library (1,560m²), Shrewsbury, opened in 1983. Here, a group of historic buildings, originally erected for Shrewsbury School, were extensively (and expensively) renovated and remodelled.[33] A significant part of the design solution for the conversion was a small modern structure linking the historic buildings and which also provided a new library entrance. Although medieval and sixteenth-century buildings have been saved by their conversion to library use, space limitations mean that satellite buildings are necessary. The reference service is housed also in a converted building (a furniture repository), and the local studies collection is now part of the Shropshire Records and Research Centre, a new building and briefly described in Chapter 11. By a mixture of luck and good fortune all three buildings are sited very close to one another.

Case study: Chard Library, Somerset

Opened in 1998, Chard Library (600m²) is located in the Holywood Lace Mill, a listed five-storey building constructed in the 1820s (Figure 5.6). The district and county council jointly (and successfully) bid for Capital Challenge Funding for the project and

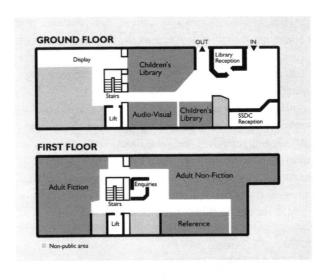

Figure 5.6   Chard Library, Somerset (converted mill, 1998): floor plans and exterior
Source: Somerset Library Service

145

the building is shared with local authority offices and voluntary organizations. The premises posed a number of challenges, such as the building's shape, the large number of structural columns through both floors, the creation of a joint-use entrance and restrictions on external signage. Nevertheless, a potentially derelict site has been brought to life again for community use.

The library occupies part of the ground and first floors. This arrangement places the entrance, children's library and audio-visual collection on the ground floor with adult fiction and non-fiction and reference facilities above. Access is provided to the upper floors by stairs and lift.

Internally finishes are generally the existing, repaired surfaces, although the recovery of an attractive, plastered-up original brick barrel-vaulted ceiling at ground level was not repeated on the first floor because of its condition.

ASSESSING ALTERNATIVES

The pros and cons of the various alternatives to a new building can be usefully discussed under four headings: siting, cost and time, preservation and conservation, and the limitations and opportunities that these options provide. Where a choice of alternatives is to be made, a systematic approach to their appraisal and evaluation should be put in place.

SITING

Siting is the most crucial factor in terms of library success and that for any proposed alternative to a new building should be rigorously assessed. Is the library to be recycled or the proposed conversion well sited for the present and foreseeable future, bearing in mind likely shifts in population and area focus? Where the site is a good one and the existing building can be satisfactorily reorganized, or the site has land available for an extension – and older buildings often do, even on urban sites – then this may be a strong argument for refurbishment, remodelling and/or an extension. A building for potential conversion to a library might offer a significantly better site than an existing building: Nottingham moved out of its nineteenth-century central library building in 1977 into a converted furniture store in the town centre, with a second phase in 1983. At Chester the conversion of a motor car works in 1984 also provides a central location, as well as space for a small modern extension to accommodate offices and meeting rooms.

COST AND TIME

Other advantages claimed for these alternatives to the new library building are that there are savings in time and money. Remodelling and refurbishment, extension and conversion can be carried out in perhaps a third of the time of that required for a new

146

building. Obviously savings in money are made where the choice of alternative avoids the need to purchase a site or to construct a completely new building. Alternatives to new build are thus usually cheaper and quicker to bring about. This is not to say that some conversions, especially of large or historic buildings, will be cheap exercises – they may be very expensive indeed.

K.C. Harrison suggested in the 1980s that the cost of conversion compared to a new building was in the range of 50–60 per cent – a considerable saving, particularly in times of financial difficulty.[34] An American consultant, on the other hand, writing about earlier American experiences, warned that remodelling and expansion costs were no longer 50 per cent of new build and that the cost of an extension, for example, could be 25 per cent more than new construction for the same amount of space.[35] In assessing any alternative, the future costs arising from operating the service, in addition to those of building modernization, will also need consideration.

PRESERVATION AND CONSERVATION

The alternatives explored in this chapter, as the examples show, make a contribution to preserving and conserving the built environment. Older buildings in the community are often worth retaining because of their historical associations or architectural worth; also because there may be few such buildings of the period or of similar scale in the vicinity.

The preservation, restoration and conservation of old, often Carnegie, library buildings has attracted interest, particularly in the US.[36] It was found in a 1990 survey that fewer than half of Carnegie's buildings remain as libraries, while others had been demolished and a significant number converted to other uses. Interestingly, at that date, around 250 'Carnegies' remained basically unchanged out of the 1,300 libraries that responded to a survey.[37] Another American welcomed the

> strong movement... to save Carnegie buildings, not to 'museumize' them but to restore and expand them into functional, modern facilities – without dropped ceilings ... lopping off ornamentation and trying to make them into something they are not.[38]

A later study describes 'Carnegie libraries one hundred years later' giving examples of their remodelling, extension and preservation. An accompanying gazetteer shows the current status of Carnegie buildings in the mid-1990s, indicating library or other use and whether 'razed'.[39]

In 1990 in Mexico, Missouri, an abandoned Carnegie library was brought back into use by moving the building four blocks from its original site and placing it next to the existing public library, itself a former federal post office. Moving and bringing into use again the old library, integrated with the existing one, was about one third the cost of a new structure. The wedded premises provided much-needed extra space, proved functional and could be made disabilities-compliant. A building was recycled and community pride and commitment to the library service demonstrated.[40]

Writing in 2002, the director of planning, design and facilities at Brooklyn Public Library, New York, enthuses over the value of preserving historic libraries generally and believes that 'restoration of these grand and evocative civic buildings can preserve and transform their awe-inspiring spaces to serve generations to come'. She also feels that 'the flexibility of these buildings is often overlooked' and indicates what might be done to successfully re-use them. This includes improving the 'entry sequence'; integrating the new and historic elements of the library interior; installing new climate systems integrated into the building's structure; improving the lighting, both natural and artificial; integrating technology (considered easier in pre-1960s buildings), and taking the opportunity to integrate new services and facilities, such as a reading garden, meeting rooms, youth library or a café.[41]

An account of the restoration of the early twentieth-century Ray Memorial Public Library, Franklin, Massachusetts, in the late 1980s describes how the mahogany and murals were made to shine again. The library director was adamant, however, that the budget for such major work should include the cost of moving to temporary premises.[42]

There is concern in Britain too, over the preservation of historic libraries and a number of libraries are listed buildings, such as Aberdeen Central Library, Motherwell Library, Gateshead Central Library (1926) and Hendon Library (1929 and modernized in 2004). Hendon's new style is shown in Figure 5.7. This listing now includes some post-

Figure 5.7   Hendon Library, Barnet (refurbished 2004): the upper level 'learning zone'
   Source: London Borough of Barnet Libraries

war library buildings, both large and small: Swiss Cottage Library (London, Camden), Kensington Central Library (London), Westcliff Library (Southend) Jesmond Branch (Newcastle) and St Austell Library, Cornwall.[43]

Re-using older library buildings poses the question, recognized both in the US and the UK, of whether to remove or refurbish period decoration and furniture or to refurbish and redecorate the interior in a contemporary fashion. It is controversial as to which approach to take and therefore the two might be combined. The solution of mixing the best of the old with the new was taken during the modernization of Ipswich in 1994. Through renovation, refurbishment and expansion, the 1924 'building has been transformed into a light and airy space with up-to-date facilities ... [but] important historic features have been retained'. The reference library has its original carved bookcases and refurbished ceiling mouldings.[44]

A smaller-scale example of the difficulties of reconciling past and present is the Saltash Branch Library, Cornwall, designed in 1961, and considered England's most Le Corbusier-like building. The library was refurbished and extended by 150m^2 in 1992 and 'demonstrates how a unique building can be successfully extended, faults remedied (as far as possible), and refurbishment carried out to update the interior' – the latter not without some controversy.[45]

The mixing of old and new can be accomplished in various ways: at Shrewsbury good-quality chairs and tables were designed to fit the ambience of the building; at Burnley furniture with a 1930s period feel was acquired, and at Southampton the original (but repainted) radial shelving layout was retained, blending with the extended library area beyond it. On a grander scale the Victorian façade at the front of Croydon Central Library is paired with an admirable modern facade at the rear, which regrettably few will see.

Another aspect of conservation is the incorporation of historic buildings (or parts of them) into libraries. The 1992 Penrith Library, for instance, incorporates the listed old Queen Elizabeth Grammar School building. In Norway two public libraries of the early 1990s integrated the remains of medieval structures – monastery ruins – into new library buildings.[46] Sometimes there is a requirement to save at least the façade of a distinguished building, whatever its original function, and a library is constructed behind it. Salisbury Library (1975) is an example of this, as the library was constructed behind the stone façade and ornamental gates of the Victorian Market House. Hadleigh Library (1987), Suffolk, is situated in an old police station, although as at Salisbury, the library is to all intents a new building constructed using three outer walls of the listed façade.

In weighing alternatives, as discussed at the end of this chapter, it may be better in some instances for the library building to be put to a different use, as a museum for example. A listed 1887 public library in Poole, Dorset, became a Wetherspoon pub in 2002.

Non-UK approaches

As was seen earlier, other countries such as the US, Canada and the Netherlands have made use of alternatives to new library buildings. Zwolle Library, in the Netherlands, is located in the town's shopping centre in two refurbished converted historic buildings.[47] In Sweden, Uppsala City and County Library (1986, 6,600m²) incorporates two old houses into its new structure, and Vadstena Library (1987, 954m²) is housed in a building that was originally a factory and later an asylum.[48] In Italy, the public library in Lissone moved from its small old building to a four-storey reconstructed former elementary school (2002);[49] an elementary school is also used to accommodate the library in Viadana (1,700m²), which is part of a cultural building.

Denmark in the 1990s saw a Japanese-style makeover of the library at Rødekro (1993), the conversion of a power station at Brønderslev (1994), and an extension to the library at Holbaek (1995). Other such 're-use' projects included those at Copenhagen Main Library (1993) and Odense Central Library (1995).[50]

In Spain's Barcelona region, a number of historic buildings have been converted to library use. They include such building types as the Catalan farmhouse, the town house or civil building, and industrial buildings, as well as an old hospital and convent. Some buildings pose problems of inflexibility, a lack of natural light and pose managerial problem. Industrial buildings were seen as not usually having these disadvantages but there are difficulties in differentiating individual spaces in such large, open areas. The Barcelona region's experience suggests that each heritage building's suitability must be separately evaluated. Thus, in addition to assessing the site, accessibility and available usable space, a detailed study of the building should include an historical and heritage analysis, an exploration of the architectural possibilities and whether it will meet functional requirements.[51]

In the US, the renovated and extended 1940 Art Deco Toledo Main Library was linked by a glass wintergarden. The library includes the McMaster Family Center for Lifelong Learning.[52] In Washington, D.C., the Martin Luther King Jr Memorial Library, the only library designed by Mies van der Rohe, but one that is expensive to maintain, could be demolished and replaced by a new building because of redevelopment plans. Preservationists and planners are at loggerheads over what to do with this famous architect's building, with proposals being made for its overhaul, securing historic landmark status to protect it from demolition, or its re-use for another purpose being suggested.[53]

LIMITATIONS AND OPPORTUNITIES

The arguments against alternatives to a new library are often the opposite to those given as advantages: the building for use is poorly sited, unsuitable for a variety of reasons – too many floors, spaces of the wrong size, for example – and may not offer all the expected savings in time and money. Refurbishment, remodelling or conversion may reveal challenges and problems, such as providing disabled access (both as regards cost and the aesthetic effect on the building), the replacement of mechanical and electrical equipment and unexpected structural deficiencies. There are hidden costs to these often unexpected but necessary structural and mechanical improvements.

Limitations on change may be posed by the structure of the building and thus impose design constraints. This may lead to compromises over the layout and workflow in the library. This in turn might give rise to higher operating costs, with more staff needed, for example, than in buildings of a comparable size elsewhere. Also there may be insufficient space both now and for future developments, particularly if a higher staff level has to be accommodated.

Conversely, the characteristics of the building, such as a high ceiling, may permit the construction of a gallery or mezzanine and create additional space. A large internal volume would also allow the insertion of a steel multi-tier structural system, increasing the number of levels and thus usable space in the building.[54]

Difficulties can occur, however, when trying to keep the library open for business during building work.[55] In some instances, following a destructive case of arson, for example, a move to other quarters may be necessary. Costs will be involved in such a move, although in the case of arson, insurance money may well cover this. Enduring noise, dirt, dust, even water and fire is, according to one writer, 'worth it in the long run. Even if the results are not quite perfect'.[56]

WEIGHING THE ALTERNATIVES

Librarians should not be dragooned into accepting a building as a library because some use must be found for it. The best course is to apply the kind of criteria noted earlier and weigh the advantages and disadvantages in order to demonstrate its suitability or otherwise as a public library, bearing in mind the need to minimize, as far as possible, any necessary compromises that may have to be made over identity and image because of the physical limitations of a reused or converted building. The following points should therefore be borne in mind:

- Have the building thoroughly surveyed and checked out before making a commitment.
- For larger projects add a second contingency amount of 15 to 20 per cent to cover unknown factors.
- For larger projects add a time contingency.[57]

An architect suggests that when comparing two or more building alternatives (whether to opt for new build or a conversion, for example), then information should be assembled listing the advantages and disadvantages of each. 'A fundamental requirement is a reasoned case for space requirements for now and a projected future period.' He advises that the assembled information be tabulated for each alternative under such headings as site and location, future expansion and estimated costs. He adds that 'the effort to analyze each alternative thoroughly will be repaid many times'.[58]

Given a careful examination of the circumstances, an alternative to a new building can become a successful library. Such a solution may well be welcomed by a community whose members hold a particular building – Carnegie library or market hall – dear in their affections and would like to see it continue in use. Alternatives can also be worthwhile to a public library system because of the variety of buildings in use that can result. It might be argued that this is no bad thing and that it gives an agreeable diversity to service point provision. But whether new, refurbished or converted, questions of sustainability, safety and security and associated issues will arise in the planning and design of library buildings and these matters are considered in the following chapter.

NOTES

1   Martin, E. (2002), 'Historic libraries and their enduring value', *New Library world* **103** (1178/1179), 259–66: 266.

2   Davis, M.C. (1987), 'Reutilizing existing library space', *Library trends* **36** (2), 411–21; see also 'The space crunch: alternatives', in Fraley, R.A. and Anderson, C.L. (1990), *Library space planning: a how-to-do-it manual for assessing, allocating and reorganizing collections, resources and facilities*, 2nd edn, New York: Neal-Schuman, 53–73.

3   A full discussion of this topic is given in Lueder, A.C. and Webb, S. (1992), *An administrator's guide to library building maintenance*, Chicago: American Library Association.

4   Swaffield, L. (1995), 'Lack of cash a root cause of Norwich fire', *Library Association record* **97** (6), 299.

5   UNISON (1997), *Future of the public library service*, London: Unison, 18.

6   Resource (2001), *Using museums, archives and libraries to develop a learning community*, London: Resource, 11.

7   Russell, P. (2004), 'Free your assets', *Public library journal* Spring, 16–17.

8   Peterman, H. (2001), 'The Free Library of Philadelphia: the library of the past to the library of the future', *Journal of youth services in libraries* **14** (2), 3–8: 5.

9   Adapted from Holt, R.M. (1990), *Wisconsin library building project handbook*, Madison, Wisconsin: Wisconsin Department of Public Instruction, 33–6.

10 Rohlf, R.H. (1980), 'Essential decisions needed in planning for the remodelling of libraries', *Catholic library world* **51** (7), 280–82: 281.

11 Alison, W.A.G. (1978), 'Public library building renewal in Glasgow', *Assistant librarian* **71** (6), 72–5.

12 Miller, A. (1989), ['The refurbishment of Shettleston Library'], *Scottish libraries* (18), 14; 'Backwards into the future: the re-opening of Glasgow's Rutherglen Library', (1992), *Scottish libraries* (32), 9.

13 ['All in a whirl'](2003), *Library + information update* **2** (7), 6,

14 Stungo, N (2003), 'Tome capsule', *RIBA journal* **110** (8), 24–30, 32.

15 Ferguson, C. (1997), 'A centre for discovery in the city of discovery', *Scottish libraries* (65), 14–16: 16.

16 Jenkins, G. (2004), 'Winning by design', *Public library journal* Spring, 10–12.

17 Bjarrum, C. and Cranfield, A (2004), 'The future is now – library re-engineering in the 21st century', in *Libraries as places: buildings for the 21st century*, edited by M-F. Bisbrouck and others, Munich: Saur, 39–63.

18 'The renaissance of the library – adaptable library buildings' (2004) (in German), *ABI-technik* **24** (3), 212–19.

19   Alison, W.A.G. (1977), *The Mitchell Library: the old and the new*, Glasgow: Glasgow District Libraries; Alison, W.A.G. (1980), *The Mitchell Library, Glasgow: the new extension*, Glasgow: Glasgow District Council.

20   *Irish library news* (2003), (232), [5].

21   Holt, R.M (1990), 38–9.

22   'N4 unveiled' (2004), *Library + information update* **3** (9), 15.

23   Scherer, J.A. (1990), 'Function vs. beauty', *American libraries* **21** (4), 312–14, 316.

24   Cameron, M. (1994), 'Falkirk library extension', *Scottish libraries* (43), 12.

25   Slessor, C. (2004), 'Layers of meaning', *Architectural review* **215** (1283), 42–7.

26   Fout, D. (1999), 'Diary of a hard hat librarian', *Public libraries* **38** (5), 306–13. For other views see Ramos, T. (comp.) (2001), 'From the inside out: library renovations from the perspectives of a project manager, an architect/designer and a technology consultant', *Journal of youth services in libraries* **14** (2), 9–13.

27   Mathers, A.S. (1982), 'Designing to meet new requirements of differing services', *Canadian library journal* **39** (4), 210–12: 212.

28   Elgar, G. (1996), 'Culture ain't arts', *Public library journal* **11** (6), 159–63.

29   Krol, J. (2003), *New library buildings in the Netherlands*, The Hague: Netherlands Public Library Association, 24–6.

30   Papp, I. (1987), ' Can a librarian accept an old building?', in *Adaptation of buildings for library use*, edited by M. Dewe, Munich: Saur, 58–71: 70.

31   Astill, M. (2000), 'From public baths to public library – or "how to save a historic building"', *New library world* **101** (1159), 303–8.

32   ['Forest Gate Library'] (2003), *Library + information update* **2** (9), 6.

33   Carr, A.M. and Fullman, T. (1983), *Shrewsbury Library: its history and restoration*, Shrewsbury: Shropshire Libraries.

34   Harrison, K.C. (ed.) (1987), *Public library buildings 1975–1983*, London: Library Services, x.

35   Rohlf, R.H. (1980), 282.

36   Arbogast, D. (1982), 'Architectural conservation and the public library', *Show-me-libraries* **37** (12), 20–25.

37   Bobinski, G.S. (1990), 'Carnegies', *American libraries* **21** (4), 296–301.

38   Kniffel, L. (1990), 'Inviting places', *American libraries* **21** (4), 295.

39   Jones, T. (1997), *Carnegie libraries across America: a public legacy*, New York: Wiley, 105–25, 131–66.

40   Shields, G.R. (1994), 'Recycling buildings for libraries: a moving account', *Public libraries* **33** (2), 93–5.

41   Martin, E. (2002), 259–66.

42   De Baggis, P. (1990), 'Restoring splendour', *American libraries* **21** (4), 308–10.

43   Raven, D. (1998), 'Getting on the special list', *Library Association record* **100** (7), 350–51.

44   'Ipswich mixes best of old and new' (1994), *Library Association record* **96** (10), 537.

45   Dewe, M. and Williams, R. (1992), 'Public library buildings 1992: 1'. *Public library journal* **7** (6), 152–5: 154.

46   Byberg, L. (1993), 'Public library – in a monastery ruin', *Scandinavian public library quarterly* **26** (1), 24–30; Tonsberg Library (1992, 4,900m²) is also described in *Library builders* (1997), London: Academy, 116–19.

47   de Graaff, W. (2003), 'Zwolle public library: an aging collection in a fairly modern coat' (in Dutch), *BibliotheeksBlad* **7** (1), 14–17.

48   *The library of the '80s: Swedish public library buildings 1980-89* (1990), Stockholm: Swedish National Council for Cultural Affairs, 45–54.

49   Rivolta, C. (2003), 'The library at Lissone grows five times larger' (in Italian), *Biblioteche oggi* **21** (2), 39–45.

50   Lauridsen, J. (1997), 'Recent Danish library buildings', *Scandinavian public library quarterly* **30** (2), 8–12.

51   Bonet, I. (2004), 'The public library in heritage building: types and examples', in *Libraries as places: buildings for the 21st century*, edited by M-F. Bisbrouck and others, Munich: Saur, 123–33.

52   Danziger, M.C. (2002), 'Updating a classic', *Library journal* **127** (3), 43–4.

53   Gillette, F. (2003), 'Read 'em and weep', *Bottom line* **16** (4), 135–42.

54   Pettman, B. (1978), 'Alternatives to new public library buildings', *Assistant librarian* **71** (6), 65–6.

55   Holt, R.M. (1990), 37–8.

56   Parks, G.R. (1985), 'A funny thing happened on the way to the addition', *Library journal* **110** (20), 41–3.

57   MacDonald, G. (1996), 'Building reuse: right for the times', *Public libraries,* **25** (5), 288–91: 291.

58   Holt, R.M. (1990), 45. See also the table on 46–8.

6 Sustainability, safety, security and systems

... the library, an institution built on the premise of resource sharing (and hence conservation), has a natural role to play in a reasoned effort to preserve the environment.

Steven Smith (1991)[1]

Although an outline of the matters covered in the architect's brief is provided in Chapter 7, that chapter is mainly concerned with the *process* of creating a public library building. In this chapter the opportunity is taken to look at some of the regulations, legislation, standards and codes of practice that affect the library building and in particular the internal working environment.

The issues raised by legislative, regulatory and other documents concern the librarian because they influence the choices that may be made as regards the conservation of fuel and power, for example, and determine how access and facilities for disabled people can be provided in a library setting. Secondly, they encourage the librarian to think beyond the immediate planning, design and construction of a building to a time when it is in use. The prevention of sick building syndrome – people's well-being adversely affected by a building's environment – and ensuring that the new building reflects the demands of a preservation management scheme will both require attention in the architect's brief, along with other issues, depending on the role of the proposed library.

The Building Regulations, described below, endeavour to ensure a building's fundamental soundness, as discussed earlier, and highlight design issues, such as safety. They are principally concerned with the general welfare and safety of the occupants and visitors to a building, with the emphasis on domestic structures.

But the librarian's brief must also take into account the possibility of the library and its staff becoming targets for vandalism or violence, as well as considering the security of the contents of the library. The library building may also be threatened by calamity, whether during construction (or refurbishment and remodelling) or at some later date. Consequently some attention must be paid to disaster planning and recovery as part of the planning process, and certainly by the time a building is in use. Materials in a variety

155

of formats, especially items which are rare or irreplaceable, as well as equipment and library records, will need to be safeguarded in the event of a disaster, whether of minor or major proportions.

Information technology and communication and other technologies have affected the way libraries operate and how staff and users carry out their various library-related activities. Some consideration therefore needs to be given to the self-service, ergonomic and other issues that surround these new departures to improve library operations, and to the way they affect the welfare of the individuals involved.

This chapter, however, is not a technical discussion of such matters as heating, ventilation and air conditioning (HVAC) or fire safety but draws attention to some of the issues surrounding these and other topics, such as the use of solar energy and the idea of 'green' or sustainable library buildings, and library security. Related to this concept of the sustainable library is that of the intelligent or smart building: 'a building that maximizes the efficiency of its occupants while at the same time allowing effective management of resources with minimum lifetime costs.'[2] This implies a library building that, amongst other things, utilizes computerized controls to monitor and regulate its services, such as air conditioning, lighting and access to the premises, and makes full use of ICT in the provision and facilitation of library services.[3] A new library planned for Prince Rupert, British Columbia, amalgamating the city library and archives, will be a smart building. Electricity, for example, will be generated by rainfall or harbour tides.[4]

MAIN ELEMENTS OF THE REGULATORY FRAMEWORK

THE BUILDING REGULATIONS

These regulations, made under powers in the Building Act 1984, apply in England and Wales: a separate system of building control exists in Scotland and Northern Ireland. Constantly updated, the regulations have been described as

> ... national standards which apply to all types of building ... They cover all aspects of construction, including foundations, damp-proofing, the overall stability of the building, insulation, energy conservation, ventilation, heating, fire protection and means of escape in case of fire. They also ensure that adequate access and facilities for people with disabilities are provided to buildings.[5]

Practical guidance as to how the technical requirements of the Act can be complied with is provided through Approved Documents; the relevant main headings of the regulations (parts A–N) are given in Figure 6.1.

The implications of the building regulations, and of other related legislation, standards, specifications and codes of practice, for the library building are principally the concern of the architect and (in a large, complex building) of specialist consultants for such matters as the library's structure, heating, ventilation and air conditioning. The police, the fire service and the Health and Safety Executive staff may also be consulted where necessary. The main responsibility for complying with the regulations, however, is the company carrying out the construction work. Compliance with the building regulations is achieved through the local authority's building control service or an approved inspector from the private sector.

A: Structure (structural stability)

B: Fire safety (means of escape, fire spread, access and facilities for the fire service)

C: Site preparation and resistance to moisture (deleterious substances in the subsoil, fitness of materials and workmanship)

D: Toxic substances (cavity insulation)

E: Resistance to the passage of sound (airborne and impact sound; walls and floors of dwellings)

F: Ventilation

G: Hygiene (hot water storage, sanitary conveniences, washing facilities, and so on)

H: Drainage and waste disposal

J: Combustion appliances and fuel storage systems (heating)

K: Protection from falling, collision and impact (stairs, ramps, loading bays, and so on)

L: Conservation of fuel and power (reasonable provision for the conservation of fuel and power; insulation, controls to prevent loss and wastage)

M: Access and facilities for disabled people (provision, access, sanitary conveniences and audience seating)

N: Glazing – safety in relation to impact, opening, closing and cleaning

---

Figure 6.1 Building Regulations: Parts A–N

HEALTH AND SAFETY AT WORK ACT 1974

Under this act, employers have a duty of care for all who enter the library building. The Act contains general principles, with regulations enshrining the detail. The Act is enforced by the Health and Safety Executive, whose publications offer much useful guidance, but many duties are carried out by local authorities. As regards personnel, there is a legal duty on employers to ensure 'as far as is reasonably practicable the health, safety and welfare of their employees'. Work places should include provision for:

- environmental measures, such as ventilation, temperature control, lighting levels and adequacy of room dimensions
- general welfare, including cleanliness, sanitary conveniences and washing facilities
- safety measures, such as the use of windows, automatic doors, stairs, ladders, ramps, and so on.[6]

Employers also have a legal duty to make a sufficient and suitable assessment of the risks to health and safety to which their employees are exposed while at work, so that appropriate preventative and protective measures can be taken. There is also a duty to protect employees from assaults, aggression, bullying and other stressful situations.[7]

DISABILITY DISCRIMINATION ACT 1995

This Act (sometimes abbreviated to DDA), has come into force progressively since 1995: from 2004 it requires the removal of all physical barriers to access to libraries and their services, in order to ensure that they are available to those with impairments to their sight, hearing, mobility or learning abilities. New buildings need to be designed to be DDA compliant and older buildings altered. In the latter case, where this poses insurmountable problems (in a listed building, for example), services must be offered in other ways. As regards building and equipment, it will be largely questions of accessibility and the provision of assistive technology, with special attention being given to the wheelchair user. The following matters are amongst those needing consideration in a disability audit relating to physical accessibility:

- parking
- approach to building (for example, dropped curbs)
- entrance accessibility (for example, ramps, steps and handrails)
- doors (exterior and interior) – designed for dignified access; automatic doors
- accessible route(s)
- stairs
- lifts and stair lifts
- floor surfaces and coverings – colour contrasts
- windows – low enough for wheelchair users to see out
- toilets – for the disabled
- lighting – task lighting to assist the disabled
- switches and controls
- signs (for example, Braille signs and shelf marks)
- telephones
- critical distances (for example, width of corridors, aisle width between bays of shelving, width of security sensors)
- furniture height (for example, shelving, tables and counters, computer workstations)
- equipment (for example, photocopiers low enough for wheelchair access)
- meeting rooms
- emergency facilities – alarms, visual as well as audible.

Also, consideration must be given to information access:

- assistive technology (for example, speech OPACs (online public access catalogues), Reading Edge machines)

158

- computer access – hardware enhancement
- reading aids – magnification facilities
- alternative formats (for example, large print and audio books).[8]

The above issues, and many others, in respect of visually impaired people, are covered in Resource's manual of best practice issued in 2000.[9] A new service aimed at giving the visually impaired better access to information and learning opportunities was launched by Powys in 2004. Special computer software in the county libraries aid blind and partially sighted users by magnifying the computer screen and reading and spelling out text.[10]

In Ireland, Donegal County Council have issued an access strategy for their library service called *Libraries for all*. The strategy, which is more wide-ranging than access and services for those with disabilities, includes matters such as the approach to libraries, internal layout, aids to users, lighting, and the use of ICT. In developing the library's design to cater for disabled people, advice and guidance is usually sought from national and local organizations concerned with access and facilities for people with disabilities. At a national level in Ireland, the Equality Authority and Library Council have issued *Library access*, encouraging libraries to develop a planned and systematic approach to helping users with disabilities. The publication includes a consideration of the 'physical environment'.[11]

STANDARDS AND CODES OF PRACTICE

Alongside professional standards, there are various other standards, such as those issued by the British Standards Institution, that affect buildings. Librarians may be familiar with, for example, BS5454 for the storage and exhibition of archival material, discussed later in the chapter. Other British Standards offer, for example, guidance on lighting, fire alarms, ergonomics and workstations.

SUSTAINABILITY

GREEN BUILDINGS

Green library buildings are part of broader professional and social concerns that manifested themselves in the early 1990s as green librarianship – a concern that continues today. The librarian in the workplace is 'buying recycled paper products; promoting energy efficiency in library buildings; developing awareness of workplace pollutants'.[12] Green librarians are against the supermarket and its consumer approach to library provision, and also aim to recycle unwanted library materials on scientific and environmental issues to 'green libraries' in countries in need of them.

This section deals with issues that form part of the green philosophy, such as energy efficient library buildings and its concern for the pollutants said to cause sick building syndrome.

Green, or sustainable, library buildings are part of a green architecture philosophy for which six principles have been proposed.

1. Conserving energy: minimizing the use of fossil fuels
2. Working with the climate: designing buildings to work with the climate and natural energy sources
3. Minimizing use of new resources: and at the end of a building's useful life to form the resources for other structures
4. Respect for users: user consultation and non-use of polluting and dangerous materials
5. Respect for the site: a building that will not destroy or disturb the site
6. Holism: 'all the green principles need to be embodied in a holistic approach to the built environment'.[13]

ENERGY EFFICIENCY

In America in the late 1970s and the 1980s a number of energy-efficient libraries were built. In many instances they used passive solar energy to heat and light their buildings, possibly with little or no mechanical assistance. Library buildings were designed, situated and oriented to store solar heat in the winter and to keep sunlight out in the summer, so keeping the interior cool.[14] One library system built up a network of energy efficient libraries, demonstrating that they go hand-in-hand with improved natural lighting and lower electricity consumption.[15] 'Careful design can produce comfortable levels of even interior lighting' by using perimeter daylighting (windows and clerestories) and core lighting (roof apertures, light wells and atriums) that bring light to the interior.[16]

Some American libraries have made use of active systems which relied on solar collecting panels,[17] but this is seen as inappropriate for non-domestic buildings in the UK.

Buildings in the northern hemisphere employing a passive solar system for heating and cooling are characterized by:

- extensive areas of insulating glass on the south wall of the building and a roof overhang to admit sunlight in winter and to keep it out in the summer
- less glass on the east and west sides
- little or no glass on the north side.

These requirements are seen as a contribution to the minimum components of a successful passive solar library design. Other characteristics include:

> ... interior surfaces with enough mass to capture the heat of the sun during the day and retain it overnight; air locks or vestibules to minimize changes in temperature when doors are open to the outside.[18]

Energy-efficient buildings should give good air quality and balanced natural light and pay attention to ergonomic needs. They offer savings in operational costs which include the control of the power needs of computers and other equipment, as well as lighting and water consumption.[19]

Other passive approaches include the underground library building, usually with a south-facing glass front, and the use of a thermal envelope.

Under the Building Regulations, the energy use method for buildings, other than dwellings, permits complete freedom of design, allowing the use of any valid energy conservation measure. This may be 'gains from solar radiation ... artificial lighting and any other form of heat gain to which the building is subject'.[20] The heat gain from office equipment and computers is one such heat source, as well as posing a problem for the working environment.

Case studies: California and Arkansas

Energy saving continues to be a matter for concern in creating American library premises and is also seen as a way of teaching environmental responsibility to local communities, as in the planning of the dual-use Oak Park Library, Ventura, California. The library's design considered such matters as energy efficiency, air pollution, daylight use, thermal performance, the recycling of construction materials, and the use of environmentally sound construction materials. Modelling tools were used to test the building's sustainability requirements.[21]

An energy-efficient 'green' building was also a design requirement for the Carmel Mountain Ranch Library (1,208m²), San Diego, California. The resultant distinctive building makes use of natural light, natural ventilation and outdoor spaces. This has produced a heavily glazed library, surmounted and protected by an overhanging V-shaped roof, surrounded by attractive landscaping.[22]

Following public consultation, Fayetteville Public Library, Arkansas, committed itself to build a green library to open in late 2004. The building will be registered with the Leadership in Energy and Environmental Design (LEED) scheme, a rating system developed by the US Green Building Council to certify buildings using less energy and natural resources as green buildings.[23]

Improving energy efficiency should also be considered when refurbishing and remodelling libraries. An energy audit can be used to identify and cost appropriate energy efficiency measures: lighting, HVAC, water use, and building insulation (windows, walls and ceilings).[24]

BREEAM ASSESSMENT

The UK equivalent of the LEED scheme is the Building Research Establishment Environmental Assessment Method (BREEAM) which aims to assist in minimizing the

161

adverse effects of buildings on the environment at the design stage. Buildings are judged by criteria for a number of environmental matters, from energy and water use to health, materials and land use, and credits awarded when criteria are met. Buildings are rated on a scale ranging from pass through to excellent; Glastonbury Library, Somerset (2000) achieved an 'excellent', as has Brighton Central Library (2005). The former is shown in Figure 6.2. The latter building allows natural light and heat to permeate the building through glass panels. There is a low energy release ventilation and heating system: shafts in the roof draw out heat and allow the circulation of fresh air. Other examples of UK public libraries with energy-efficient design features include South Benfleet Library (Essex, 1995, 314m²), Bournemouth Library and Tavistock Library and Learning Centre. Naturally ventilated buildings in the UK should follow the CIBSE Building Energy Code (1981).[25]

Figure 6.2 Glastonbury Library, Somerset (2000): achieved an 'excellent' BREEAM
Source: Somerset Library Service

HEALTH AND SAFETY

SICK BUILDING SYNDROME

With energy conservation in mind, the 1970s saw the construction of hermetically sealed buildings serviced by sophisticated HVAC systems. Although energy bills decreased, sickness amongst occupants increased, as the artificial environment seemed to allow workplace pollutants – the chemicals used in carpet manufacture, for example – to adversely affect people's health. Symptoms associated with the problem include headaches, lethargy, irritability and poor concentration and this became known as sick building syndrome (SBS). This is seen not as a disease but as an unhealthy reaction to an unsatisfactory working environment. Among other things, it usually leads to reduced staff efficiency and increased absenteeism.

The cause of SBS is unknown but is probably due to a combination of physical, environmental and job factors. Identified factors include:

- building and office design, such as new furniture, carpets and painted surfaces
- building services and maintenance, such as low level of user control over ventilation, heating and lighting
- indoor environment and air quality, for example, dust particles and fibres in the atmosphere
- job factors, for example, work with display screen equipment.[26]

A German study has suggested that the handling of books and archives may in itself constitute a so far unrecognized pathogenic factor contributing to SBS.[27]

Case studies: Washington and Florida

In 1994, the 45-year-old Kelso (Washington) Public Library was closed as SBS had apparently affected four clerical workers, although cases of the syndrome had been documented as far back as 1986. A significant sum of money was spent on investigating the cause of the syndrome and an examination of heating and cooling ducts revealed 'humongous dust bunnies'. Air samples also revealed a small quantity of fibreglass that could have caused eye irritation and coughing. The air ducts were cleaned, the building's carpeting replaced (as carpet fibres are seen as a cause of SBS), and asbestos tiles beneath it removed, although air samples revealed no airborne asbestos dust.[28]

Northwest Regional Library, Tampa, Florida, had a number of air quality and environmental problems in 1998. This manifested itself in a musty smell, mould on light fittings, and algae and mould in the building's air conditioning system, although this was not considered a health risk to library staff and readers. Following an environmental report, it was recommended (at considerable cost) that the roof be resealed, 'carpeting cleaned or replaced, walls and ceilings cleaned and the air conditioning system and the ducts replaced, and a vigorous house-cleaning regime enforced'.[29]

CREATING A GOOD WORK ENVIRONMENT

Noting that later attempts to remedy SBS can be difficult and expensive, the Health and Safety Executive suggests that its prevention needs to be 'tackled at an early stage during the planning of new building work, refurbishment or change of use'. This can be assisted by compliance with published standards and the creation of the best possible working environment that pays attention to:

- air quality, including ventilation, outdoor air supply and air movement
- temperature
- humidity
- lighting
- noise
- office equipment and furnishings
- maintenance of the building and building services systems
- cleaning operations, including office furnishings
- management systems – good communications and a good relationship between management and staff that enable the discussion of staff concerns
- work organization, including display screen equipment work.[30]

As SBS is linked in many cases to poor ventilation, it is important to have the HVAC system checked regularly. Other changes that might help in existing or planned buildings include:

- alternative cleaning supplies
- provision of opening windows
- use of plants that are effective in cleaning air
- creation of low maintenance landscaping that avoids the use of chemicals.[31]

A 1995 survey of British academic libraries and a sample of public libraries suggested that SBS existed in libraries and that air-conditioned libraries were more likely to be affected than those that are naturally ventilated. Naturally ventilated buildings can have unsatisfactory environments also but these may be caused by other factors.[32] Carpet, for example, seems to be considered a major contributor to SBS. One American university library with the SBS problem reviewed all types of flooring, resulting in most public and stack areas being covered with a carpet-like new generation nylon floor covering, resulting in no ill side effects. Other factors were also considered, such as air quality.[33]

ERGONOMICS

Since the widespread use of computers in the 1980s, concern has been expressed about possible health and safety problems linked to their use in the workplace, including libraries. A number of alleged hazards have been associated with working with a terminal, known as a visual display unit (VDU). Hazards include backache, work-related upper limb disorders (WRULDs) – more popularly known as repetitive strain injury (RSI) – and eye and vision problems. A number of measures have been suggested to deal with difficulties associated with, for example, WRULDs:

- ergonomic improvement to workstations
- improvement of equipment design; also replacement or modification of old or poorly designed equipment
- improvement of organizational work factors, such as limiting time spent at the VDU
- improvement in managerial aspects; for example, warnings of risk, training, encouraging problem reporting
- proper risk assessment and planning – adoption of a WRULDs policy.[34]

All of the above matters are important in overcoming WRULDs and helping to create a risk-free workplace. Some of these points will be looked at in the context of two important themes: environmental factors and workstation design.

ENVIRONMENTAL FACTORS

These have already been mentioned in respect of sick building syndrome, especially in terms of HVAC. In addition to temperature and humidity, however, additional problems for those working with VDUs in the library, whether adult or child, will be noise and light, both discussed also in Chapter 9. Illumination levels, types of lighting, surface colours and finishes, glare and shadow, for instance, can all affect working at a VDU. 'What we may not consider as we move computers into our own libraries is the physical comfort of those using the computers.'[35]

The most common mistake seen in libraries is the poor positioning of terminals in relation to the source of natural light: workstations – often on a run of benching – face the natural light source, rather than being placed at right angles to it. Even when the latter is the case, the terminal should not be close to a window to avoid problems of visual comfort. The most frequent complaint from computer users is said to be eyestrain, caused by glare, excessive lighting, improper ergonomics, poor quality or inappropriately adjusted VDUs, uncorrected or improperly corrected vision and insufficient or non-existent eyecare. Proposed remedies include blinds, non-reflective surfaces, re-location of the computer, a check that it is functioning according to the manufacturer's specifications, changes to the work area, regular sight checks, resting and eye care.[36]

In an electronic environment noise from computer hardware can become an issue, although the use of VDUs causes little noise. 'The best solution, if possible, is to reduce the noise where it is generated' by:

- regular checking and maintenance

- investigation of noise level when buying new equipment, such as computer printers
- isolation of noisy equipment, for example putting a printer in a separate room.[37]

WORKSTATION DESIGN

VDUs are employed in libraries in a variety of situations: at issue counters, when carrying out cataloguing, serials control or online searching, and when undertaking clerical, administrative and managerial work. Library users make use of OPACs, a variety of software applications (such as word processing) and online searching. One terminal may be used at different times for a variety of purposes by different staff and different users.

Workstations are comprised of a number of elements: chair, desk, document holder, VDU and associated hardware, such as keyboard and printer. Key features for ergonomic working are:

- adjustability – of workstation furniture and VDU
- adequate desk space to use the VDU comfortably and, where appropriate, accommodate documents
- provision of additional equipment, such as footrests, forearm rests and anti-static mats
- wire management facilities
- an appropriate workstation layout, including the location of the copyholder.[38]

Common faults that ignore these points result in inadequate desk space, use of inappropriate furniture (usually in older libraries), unsightly and dangerous cabling, and dusty and dirty equipment, particularly keyboards.

Dissatisfaction with existing workstation design may lead to the employment of an interior designer, as at Delft Public Library, to design a new layout and computer workstations. There it resulted in workstations that allowed people to work together rather than alone and the creation of scaled-down versions for children.[39]

PRESERVATION MANAGEMENT

Preservation management is described as

> The managerial, financial and technical issues involved in preserving library materials in all formats – and/or their information content – so as to maximize their useful life.[40]

Eleven key issues for preservation management have been identified and the following are particularly important for library buildings:

- environment and storage
- disaster management
- security.[41]

The first two of these topics are dealt with below, and security is considered in a wider context than that of preservation later in the chapter. As regards disaster management, librarians must also take precautions against the 'quiet' threats to the preservation of library materials, such as poor handling[42] and insect infestation, as well as the major threats, such as fire and flood, discussed later.

ENVIRONMENT AND STORAGE FOR PRESERVATION

Public library materials requiring above-average attention to their long-term preservation will be rare and unique items. This usually means the material found in archival, local studies and other special collections that have been built up over a considerable period of time, the contents of which will be largely irreplaceable.

While it is important that all library materials are properly cared for, rare, unique items and special collections require particular consideration. On a day-to-day basis this means providing the right environmental and storage conditions for the various formats comprising such collections. Proper concern for the housing of such material will also help in its protection in the event of fire and flood.

The British Standard, *Recommendations for storage and exhibition of archival documents* (BS5454), makes a number of recommendations for the environmental conditions (temperature and humidity) necessary for the long-term storage of paper, parchment and other materials, such as film, microfilm, gramophone records, and magnetic and electronic media. The standard also provides guidance on static and mobile shelving, mechanical handling devices (such as hoists, lifts and trolleys) and protective containers.[43] Originally conceived for archives, its recommendations also apply to unique, rare and archival material held in libraries.

Nowadays digital preservation attracts considerable attention and it has been defined as 'the series of managed activities necessary to ensure access to digital materials for as long as is necessary'.[44] The difficulties surrounding this requirement are exemplified by the Domesday Project. In the 1980s the BBC decided to compile a twentieth-century Domesday Book, celebrating the original's 900th anniversary. The contributed content, recorded on two interactive videodiscs (accessed by a special computer system), came from, amongst others, journalists, map makers, statisticians and school pupils. The system was bought by a number of public libraries, often because of the local content, but by the beginning of the twenty-first century the project discs were inaccessible. Early in 2002, however, the BBC announced that software had been developed to emulate the obsolete BBC computer and videodisc player and make much of the information accessible again.

In addition to acquiring digital resources, the library may also create digitized surrogates for material held in other formats, such as photographs, and will be concerned with their preservation, as well as of its own working records. In addition to technology emulation, as used in the Domesday Project, two other routes to digital preservation have been suggested: a technology preservation strategy (preservation of the original software and possibly hardware), or a digital migration strategy (re-encoding digital information in new formats before the old is obsolete).[45]

Institutions will have to decide on a suitable appropriate strategy but where data migration is chosen, it 'entails the creation and maintenance of archive data files'. A number of preservation practices are needed in respect of archive files, such as the archival media used, on- and off-site copies, and checking the integrity of data files. However, 'proper preservation is expensive ... and may be most cost-effectively outsourced to a specialist computing service, data bank, or other organisation'.[46]

For the kind of special and local collection digital material acquired by public libraries, long-term preservation for continuing access to the material will be required and

> ... libraries ... need to be involved in applying their professional skills and expertise to the long-term preservation of digital materials, just as they have taken a role in the preservation of traditional materials.[47]

Environmental conditions for data storage media are those recommended by BS4783, and include the similar requirements for other formats, such as protection from dust pollutants and sunlight, the use of enclosures, and secure storage facilities.[48]

Both BS5454 and the Irish archival standards[49] have much useful advice on housing such important collections, including matters considered in this chapter, such as fire prevention (including acceptance of the use of water sprinklers) and security.

A case has been made in Australia, however, arguing for less reliance on HVAC systems and encouraging the use of passive environmental control in smaller cultural institutions, including public libraries: 'much can be achieved which will be just as effective, cheaper to install and operate, and will use less energy'. It suggests 'using both traditional and modern techniques which do not rely on air conditioning'.[50] Thus, the active environmental control task of an institution is determined by the required indoor conditions, allowing for what can be achieved through passive controls.

DISASTER MANAGEMENT

Depending upon geographic location, public libraries can be damaged by a range of natural occurrences, such as earthquakes,[51] fire and floods. Other damage may be caused by structural failure, poor building maintenance, unstable shelving,[52] deliberate acts of arson, vandalism and threats (such as bomb incidents) that target the building and its occupants. In the UK the principal library disasters in recent years have been those caused by fire and flood. High-profile examples of such library catastrophes were those at Norwich Central Library (fire in 1994) and Lewes, University of Sussex (flood in 2000).[53]

Whether described as disaster planning, disaster preparedness planning, or disaster management, the aim is the creation of a scheme to handle an emergency, whether large- or small-scale, that may affect a library and its holdings. The objectives of such a plan are:

- to prevent a disaster, whatever its magnitude
- to protect library materials in the event of a disaster
- in its aftermath to remove and stabilize library materials prior to repair and conservation.

These objectives can be summarized as anticipation, reaction and damage repair. It is the first objective, 'anticipation', that will be mainly discussed in this chapter.

LIBRARY FIRES

The fire at Norwich Central Library in 1994, discussed in the case study below, was considered to be the worst library fire in recent times. Other UK library fires include that at Birmingham Children's Library (1991), Newtown, Powys (1986), Guisborough Library, Redcar and Cleveland (1996, rebuilt 1999), Grant Lodge Local Heritage Centre, Moray Council (2003), and Ramsgate, Kent (2004), which left a burnt-out shell. Abroad, major library fires include those at Leningrad and Los Angeles[54] (both 1986) and Linköping, Sweden (1996):[55] a replacement building opening in Linköping in 2000.[56] In 2004 the Anna Amalia Library, a UNESCO World Heritage Site in Weimar, Germany, was destroyed by fire and unique material was lost. A new library to house the collection was due to open in Weimar early in 2005 and work had begun on moving books to the new site. Faulty electrical equipment was blamed for the fire.[57] Although there are other reasons for library fires, building works and electrical faults, for example, arson is often the known or suspected cause, and this emphasizes the link between disaster prevention and building security.

A number of alternatives have been identified to protect the library from the risk of fire, with the level of protection being decided by the significance of the library, available funds, an informed judgement as to the degree of protection needed,[58] and by regulatory requirements. For public libraries, it is once again the special collections containing rare and unique material, wherever located in the building, that require a higher standard of protection than the rest of the library's collection.

Case study: Norwich Central Library (1994)

The Norwich fire not only resulted in the loss of one of the first major public library buildings to be constructed after the Second World War, but also in the loss of much unique and rare library material. In addition to the loss of 170,000 reference and lending stock, about 30,000 volumes of the Norfolk Studies Collection were destroyed, along with unique photographs, postcards and maps. Loss was also incurred by the 2nd Air Division Memorial Library and the music section. The County Record Office collection, housed in the basement was badly water-damaged. 'One of the most important issues

169

raised is whether sprinkler systems should be used in libraries and other heritage buildings'. But as one member of staff said at the time: 'I would rather work with wet material than no material at all'.[59]

The source of the fire was old secondary electric wiring in bookcase strip-lighting and the fire spread so quickly because of flammable materials and the design of the building. A report on the fire made 11 recommendations, which resolved the sprinkler issue, as it included a recommendation that 'all major new library buildings should have sprinkler, mist or fog systems installed to limit the spread of fire and its resulting damage'.[60]

The causes of the Norwich fire, however, were seen as being more than just building defects and were summarized as a 'combination of lack of knowledge, poor communications' and 'inadequate inspection and maintenance systems' in the past.[61]

Lessons from the Norwich fire include the need to:

- update the disaster planning manual
- find out where the wiring goes
- use metal cabinets – the wooden card catalogue and its contents were completely destroyed
- provide secure housing for copies of rare local studies material
- rethink levels of fire protection and insurance.[62]

Libraries have learned many lessons from the Norwich fire. Because heat broke upper storey windows at Norwich and allowed fire to enter, metal fire shutters were installed in the Somerset Studies Library on the first floor of Taunton Library. These are linked to the fire alarm system and fall in the event of a fire.

FLOOD AND WATER DAMAGE

The 1966 flood in Florence, Italy, while resulting in the loss and damage of cultural treasures, brought home to the curatorial professions the need for disaster planning. At the same time it provided an opportunity to gain experience from, and improve techniques for dealing with salvaged library and archival materials. Floods in the UK, following the heavy rainfall of 2000, led to the flooding of the University of Sussex bookstore, with material submerged under four metres of dirty polluted water. Flooding in libraries not only occurs because of high water and heavy storms but also from leaks and the water used to extinguish fires. As with fire prevention, building design and maintenance are major factors in preventing disasters, as well as the location of valuable material in the building, and the installation of water detection alarm systems.[63]

Case study: Morgan Library, Colorado State University (1997)

The *Library disaster planning and recovery handbook* is centred around Colorado State University's experience of flooding in 1997. The Morgan Library's newly renovated lower level was entirely submerged under water up to 15 cm above the ceiling tiles. A portion of wall collapsed and the strong force of the water that entered toppled rows of shelving over into the contaminated water. The *Handbook* aims to provide 'details, advice, and recommendations on all aspects of library-disaster recovery based on lessons learned from the experience of Morgan Library'.[64] Some of the points concerning the library building and associated matters in this wide-ranging publication and elsewhere are noted below:

- stabilizing the building – assessing structural stability
- providing temporary library services, possibly in different, temporary premises, and determining the cost of such services
- ensuring proper ergonomic practices at alternative locations
- re-entering the building – being aware of electrical dangers and other hazards and of the environmental concerns of staff
- technology recovery.[65]

To head off the possibility of a disaster, it is recommended that a building survey be carried out to check conditions in and around a library for matters that might lead to problems big or small. A survey to uncover areas of risk would examine such matters as the site, roof, windows, fire safety, security, the environment, storage and staff routines.[66] Construction and renovation projects in the building can (and have) triggered disasters, as the library and its contents are vulnerable to damage at such times.

Much of the disaster planning literature concentrates on how to prevent or cope with an emergency in an existing building. It recognizes, however, that much may be done in the planning and design of new buildings to prevent or minimize the damage caused by disasters of one kind or another, whether small- or large-scale. Desirable building design features include alarm and suppression systems, a pitched roof, no water or drainage pipes over storage areas and the highest standard of fire resistance in building and furnishing materials and structures.[67] Other points include:

- store rooms for inflammable liquids
- prescribed areas for smoking, if permitted at all
- storage – valuable library materials should not be stored in a basement nor on a top floor
- shelving should be non-inflammable; compact shelving is often sealed and provides added protection
- openings in the building for air and light should be vandal-resistant
- provision of external and emergency lighting
- use of fire-retardant materials
- compartmentalization of the building, as this prevents fire spreading.[68]

INSURANCE

Local authorities insure their libraries against a variety of risks, such as business interruption, theft, liabilities (employer, public and products), and 'material damage', covering buildings, equipment (including computer cover), stock and services (such as a crèche or café). Librarians and their authorities should take professional advice over their insurance and regularly review their cover. Buildings are normally insured for their replacement as new but 'the sum insured must also be sufficient to cater for site clearance, architects' fees and public authority requirements' – and inflation.[69]

A library flood or fire will have, therefore, considerable financial implications because of the loss or damage to the building, to equipment and library material and because of service interruption – the cost of providing temporary premises, for example. The fire at Norwich led to an enormous local authority insurance claim at the time, and neither the local authority nor the loss adjusters had any precedent to go by. Insurance cover was for the repair or replacement of the building and its contents, and for temporary services up to three years after the fire.

Identifying the elements of the claim took nearly a year, a cost not met by the insurance company. The library's database was able to demonstrate what ordinary library materials had been lost but the Norfolk Studies collection was more problematical. Given the loss of the collection's catalogue, it took six months to compile a list of desiderata and five months to value it. The total insurance claim was about £14 million, the building plus fees and demolition accounted for 25 per cent; the cost of replacing stock and the re-creation of catalogues largely accounted for the rest.[70]

Similarly, the librarian of the University of Sussex has described the amount of time devoted to working with the insurer's loss adjusters over the library's flooded bookstore. About a year was spent in preparing a very detailed claim and, although there was great difficulty in valuing some material, the insurers agreed to informed estimates. After discussion, it was considered not worthwhile to try to restore the wide range of water-damaged material and the library chose 'to restore what we had lost in broad terms, but not title by title'. This resulted in a smaller settlement (£2.6 million) and a decision to 'use a considerable proportion of the money to help finance a creative e-strategy for the library'. Experience of the catastrophe emphasized the need to keep a detailed record of negotiations and the efforts required to minimize the effects of the flood on library services during the lengthy claims process.[71]

The flood led the librarian to the conclusion that although a disaster plan is essential, and was important on this occasion, it could not be completely helpful in a major disaster such as this.

Lessons learned from the flood are similar to those of the Norwich fire:

- the need to assess the dangers of flooding when locating a library building
- the need for adequate insurance cover

- the value of a written disaster plan
- the need to keep accurate records and statistics, to have copies in a separate building, and to keep records of the action taken during the disaster, including photographs and videos
- the need to learn how to deal with other professions and their jargon, such as the difference between a loss adjuster and a loss assessor.[72]

On a smaller scale, the fire at the 1963 Newtown Library, Powys, in 1986, which damaged all but the non-public areas at the rear, provided an opportunity to build a modern library on the old site using the insurance money. The new building incorporated the refurbished older part which included staff facilities destroyed in the original library.

SECURITY

Security is concerned with the safety and welfare of staff and library users, the prevention of theft and the mutilation of library materials, and the protection of the library building from unauthorized entry and damage.[73] Crime can be 'designed out' in the ways suggested below, but it is acknowledged, however, that factors, like loan restrictions and busy and unreliable photocopying facilities, may encourage the theft and mutilation of stock.[74]

Depending upon the scale of the security problem and the resources available, the range of solutions can involve ID checks, staff training and vigilance, ownership marks on library property and the employment of security staff.

In order to tackle crime, libraries should have a crime prevention strategy that would involve, for instance, prompt attention to repairs and maintenance, and due attention to the library's perimeter and grounds, the building shell and interior. A checklist approach to assist in auditing problems and determining a strategy and tactics, would also involve the procedural aspects of security, like handling cash and keys and locking up, as well as those associated with the physical facility itself.[75]

Various checklists for library building security are given in the library literature and one offers a lengthy list arranged under eight headings:

- property line protection – such as exterior lighting, low profile landscaping
- entry point control – such as doors, windows, secure fire escapes
- interior space control – for example, visibility, controlled access to lifts, toilets and staff areas, mirrors
- management of materials and contents – for example, smoke and fire alarms, secure storage, storage for cash
- protecting personnel (see below)
- protection from personnel – employee crime, access to keys.[76]

Other solutions that have implications for library design and layout include:

- closed access for some items/collections
- providing lockers for bags and coats outside the library proper
- electronic security systems
- closed circuit television (CCTV)
- use of turnstiles.[77]

STAFF SECURITY: ABUSE AND VIOLENCE

Library staff may be verbally abused, sexually harassed, threatened and even robbed or assaulted by what the Americans call 'problem patrons'. These are usually individuals but can sometimes be rowdy youngsters who have found their way into the library and are 'looking for a laugh'. Library staff should be trained to deal with such individuals, whether angry reader, noisy youngster, suspected thief or sexual exhibitionist, according to the nature of their behaviour and within the requirements of the law. Large libraries may have security personnel who can anticipate difficulties and deal with such 'problem patrons' and, where necessary, the police can be called to assist in particular situations.[78]

As far as the library building and its equipment is concerned, emphasis is once again on a layout that is easily supervised, avoiding a 'takeover' of the library toilets or secluded spots in the library for inappropriate or disruptive behaviour. A variety of measures have been suggested to deal with the violence problem, although serious incidents involving assault are rare in the UK: such measures include:

- adequate lighting inside and outside the building
- deterrents, such as security cameras
- adequate queue management, with clear signs and easy access
- policing/patrols
- panic alarms
- secure provision for staff's personal possessions.[79]

In a mid-1990s survey of four public libraries that considered the above measures and other issues, the provision of training received the biggest endorsement from staff, and it was concluded that 'staff can be supported and helped to feel safer through adequate training and sympathetic and appreciative management attitudes'.[80] A 2001 survey 'found that violence is still prevalent in public libraries today across England and Wales', is mainly verbal abuse and coming to be considered as 'part of the job'. Training is still seen as the best response but remains to be implemented systematically. Regrettably, only a serious widely publicized incident is likely to ensure change.[81] In older buildings it is suggested that 'before ... management undertakes an expensive redesign of the library ... [they should] make sure it is appropriate to the risk and relevant needs'.[82]

STOCK SECURITY: LOSS AND DAMAGE MANAGEMENT

The theft of books and other materials is a fairly common occurrence in libraries, as they fall victims to professional or amateur thieves, including members of staff. A 1992 survey report of all types of library concluded 'that losses of books alone exceed £150 million each year. Book mutilation, too, is widespread'. While losses vary from one type of library to another, 'the average loss rate for public libraries alone was 5.3 per cent', although the scale of their loss varied amongst public libraries.[83] In order to minimize the mutilation and loss of library materials, the usual safeguards of visible staff desks and better layouts are advanced.

The deployment of electronic book theft detection systems is not considered foolproof: 'they can be evaded by determined thieves ... and they are inadequate to the task of protecting rare books and manuscripts'.[84] Library departments with rare books and archives, such as a local studies department, can make use of a range of security devices, like CCTV and electronic detection systems. But staff surveillance, restricted access and stricter rules and procedures for requesting, using and returning material are important preventative measures.

Although reporting significant losses, the 1992 report recognized 'the very substantial investment the library service has already made in the prevention of theft and mutilation, and towards minimising the consequences of those acts'.[85]

Stock theft is both a financial and service issue as it results, for example, in replacement costs, loss of income (where a fee is charged for the loan of some formats), the unavailability of wanted items for users, and damage to the library's image and staff morale. A 2001 study of theft of all types of library material, equipment and property in English public libraries found that:

- equipment loss was diverse in character but included loss of computers and related equipment
- there was an increase in theft, resulting in a 10 per cent loss compared with 5.3 per cent in 1992
- the most vulnerable materials were new books, videos, CDs, playstation games and DVDs
- while 'it is possible to "forecast" areas of stock that are vulnerable to theft, it is very difficult to second guess which libraries are most at risk – a fact that makes security management a far from simple issue'.[86]

Case study: theft in a new library

A case study of a new library opening with a stock of 20,000 items demonstrates the amount of theft than can take place. A full stocktake was carried out after six months showing that the percentage loss of book stock across the categories ranged from 5 per cent to 48 per cent. The overall loss averages were 14.4 per cent for fiction and 13.4 per cent for non-fiction; within six months of opening the library had lost 14% of its bookstock. The case study underlines the need for security to be seen as a major challenge and priority for librarians:

> Library security has to be put at the forefront of planning strategy. It is a pointless exercise to spend thousands of pounds on new stock if it is there for the taking (and not returning).[87]

Security factors for library materials include the following:

- electronic security systems have been found to reduce the amount of theft but not put an end to it completely: RFID (radio frequency identification) technology (discussed later in this chapter) could improve future stock monitoring and library security
- CCTV can lead to a reduction in theft-related incidents
- library layout should not be thief-friendly
- those categories of stock prone to be stolen must be identified and protected.

A series of ideal (but user-unfriendly) measures, such as photo ID for admission, have been proposed by one writer on library security and safety and this would put a high degree of security in place in a library. While surveillance cameras are already in use in many libraries, an ideal system is probably not financially realistic (and rather intimidating) for general use in most public libraries,[88] although not perhaps in departments housing rare and valuable material. A less demanding version of these ideal measures designed to stop crime might be enshrined in a set of library rules and regulations. These would require, for example, coats, briefcases and other personal belongings to be placed in a locker outside a room or department that needs to be particularly secure.[89]

A major security discussion point is that librarians wish to encourage the use of the library rather than police the library's collection. Librarians are prepared, it would seem, to absorb the stock losses, or fail to acknowledge them, in preference to a zero tolerance policy that is time-consuming and intimidatory rather than helpful and friendly. Nevertheless, theft is an unsocial act and a more proactive approach to theft is needed; particularly one that protects rare and valuable material: 'Librarians must accept much of the blame for losses to theft, due to their indifference, innocence, ignorance, and complacency.'[90]

ELECTRONIC SECURITY: DATA AND EQUIPMENT

Electronic security issues are concerned with computer misuse; that is, the unauthorized obtaining, removal, alteration or destruction of stored information. While 'good security is imperative; really good security is really expensive' but a number of defensive strategies and tactics have been suggested for keeping data secure, such as firewalls and encryption, although these are not the focus of attention here.[91]

In addition to data misuse, there is also the theft, wilful damage or destruction of computer equipment. The management response to this problem will be to once again ensure that the library site, building features and interior layout offer no help to thieves and intruders by easing access or screening the wrongdoer from observation – equipment should be placed where it can be seen. ICT areas and rooms need to be adequately secure when the building is closed, although such protection is more difficult when public workstations are distributed round the library. Vulnerable hardware can be locked in place, disabled and security marked. Audits and spot checks of security measures, satisfactory inventories, adequate insurance and a plan which anticipates a partial or total failure of IT security, including the kind of disasters described earlier, can all help prevent or mitigate security problems.[92]

VANDALISM

Book damage can be seen as vandalism, but the latter is usually thought of as destructive acts like the daubing of the library exterior, the breaking of windows or the vandalizing of staff and readers' cars. The entry of vandals into the library after closing time can result in damage to library materials and equipment, the spray-painting of walls, and the smashing of furniture and fittings. Vandalism sometimes climaxes in arson, which has the potential to destroy the library and its contents completely.

Vandalism is usually the work of young people and is carried out in pursuit of theft, to publicize a cause, to seek revenge or to engage in 'play' or group vandalizing activity.[93] The prevention of vandalism is tied up with general security of the library building and its contents, as considered earlier, and with such procedures as dealing with cash and locking up.

Damage to buildings and graffiti, it is recognized, encourage further vandalism and so prompt repair of the damage is essential. Whether outside or inside the library, graffiti – messages, names and symbols etched into table tops, glass and plastic surfaces, for example – should be swiftly removed. If it persists, 'consider treating all masonry surfaces with a protective coating to make cleaning easier'.[94] Bournemouth Library uses graffiti-resistant bricks for its exterior walls that can be easily cleaned. Libraries that suffer continually from damage from vandals may need to resort to a fortress mentality and employ grills or shutters over windows and doors. Although unlikely to be a complete cure, greater community involvement that stimulates the positive use of the library by disaffected youngsters, perhaps through games clubs, can be a way forward.[95]

'But of all the precautionary measures libraries can take against such crimes [vandalism, theft and arson], none is more basic than that of securing the building itself.'[96] Basic building protection includes door and window security and installing a burglar alarm system. Other weapons include CCTV; electronically accessed entryways; alarms on exit doors; access authorization cards; and sign-in sheets.[97]

The future of library security and its improvement is bound up with advances in technology, such as biometric smart cards, and of the virtual library, where more and more material is available in digitized or electronic form. Nevertheless it seems there will still be a security task to

> ... preserve our materials ... while at the same time ... protect the library building's occupants ... To lose such a battle, after all, would be to concede defeat in an extremely important war for access to the cultural record of mankind.[98]

Cornwall's libraries have begun issuing and using smart cards for library and other local services, although not specifically as a security device. It is recognized that the smart card presents many opportunities for payment of fines and so on, and even as a loyalty card. The cards are expensive items and their use requires investment in new equipment, such as a smart card reader and digital camera for processing applications – a costly exercise for existing and new library buildings.[99]

LIBRARY HANDLING SYSTEMS

Although principally concerned with books, three problems have been identified concerning the handling of library materials that must receive attention in the architect's brief: distribution, replacement and retrieval.[100] Increasingly there is the potential in libraries for these processes to be mechanized or automated and 'replacement' (returning materials to the shelves) has become more complex with the advent of self-issue systems linked to the robotic sorting of books prior to shelving. With the exception of self-issue systems, sophisticated methods of distribution and so on are principally matters for the operation of large libraries or book storage facilities. Library handling systems are discussed under the following headings:

- materials circulation
- automated storage and retrieval
- self-issue systems
- robotic sorting.

MATERIALS CIRCULATION

This involves:

- the distribution of books and other materials on arrival in the building
- the movement of books to and from the closed access stacks.

For a large and busy public library both of these matters are likely to be of importance, and consideration will be given as to how they might be resolved in structural and spatial terms. In addition to book lifts and hoists, thought might be given to horizontal methods of conveying material such as conveyor belts, with or without the use of containers.

The retrieval of books from the stacks involves three main stages:

- notification of the requested item
- fulfilment of the request – retrieval of the item from its location
- the despatch of the requested item to a service desk.

The retrieval of books from the stacks is often carried out manually, although requesting material often involves a computerized ordering system conveying messages directly to staff. A number of methods for the notification of requests and their subsequent despatch have been devised over the years.

Los Angeles Public Library installed the Translogic book conveyance system featuring 17 delivery stations and initially 100 electrically driven carts. Half the books in each subject department are in closed stacks.[101] The Telelift system is a tried and tested European materials circulation method, now also used in the Shanghai Library:[102]

> In this system a carrier engages in a track which travels from stack to service point and back again on the endless belt system electrically controlled. The striking feature is that the belt, complete with carrier, can climb up and down walls, the books in the carrier being suspended in an inner container which pivots with gravity.[103]

AUTOMATED STORAGE AND RETRIEVAL

In the 1980s a few American librarians wrote about applying industrial storage technology to the needs of libraries, in particular retiring little-used material into automated storage and retrieval units.[104] The difference from what is described above is that staff are not needed to select items from the shelves: they are retrieved mechanically. The Lied Library installed an automated storage and retrieval system in its 2001 building, and Minneapolis Central Library (2006, 32,980m²) is planning to install automated book and materials handling equipment.[105] The space-saving Randtriever, requiring no staff access, where items in boxes are stacked closely up to height of around 7.3 metres and retrieved by machine, is similar to that in the large 1991 Bordeaux Municipal Library (26,000m²). There the library installed a robot adapted for handling the most consulted books. The reader's request is transmitted automatically to a mobile arm which selects the box in which the requested work is found from a stack of containers. The movable arm then puts it down delicately in a cart which is transported up to the reading room.[106]

SELF-ISSUE SYSTEMS

In line with retailing and banking, libraries are turning more and more to self-service operations. Much of this, such as open access to library materials and OPACs (online

179

public access catalogues), with their capacity for reservation and renewal of material, and so on, is now taken for granted. Librarians expect self-service to grow even more in the coming years with advances in the technology.

Most of the attention in this area has been focused on the use of self-service issue systems which 'require a specially designed piece of hardware which has a physical presence in the library'; the design of the station should prevent fraudulent issuing of library material.[107] By the mid-1990s, self-service issue systems were to be found in Cologne Public Library, Toensberg Public Library, Norway, and in Sweden. In the UK, Maidenhead was the first public library to introduce the 3M self-issue terminal in 1995–96.[108]

Of the many issues surrounding the use of self-service issue systems – managerial, consumer, staff and systems issues – only design and security matters, likely to affect the library building, are considered here. Library design may need to be rethought to deal with self-service security issues, especially as regards counters (see Chapter 10), exits and entrances. Also, as in retailing, valuable items should not be the subject of self-service. Swipe cards may be used to prevent non-members or members with defined blocks from entering. As has been found elsewhere, many users may regret the lack of human contact inherent in self-issue systems: 'customers sometimes want personal service, and some might want it all the time'.[109]

In 1999 3M announced a digital identification system using RFID (radio frequency identification) technology to create a method to track and secure library materials. The system eliminates barcode positioning, thus speeding up the issue process, and allows the retention of Tattle-Tape security strips.[110] Books and other resources are 'tagged with tiny microchips activated by a radio query and respond by transmitting a unique identification code'. Singapore prototyped this method in one of its libraries in 1998, a RF sensor automatically cancelling loans returned through the book-drop. The RF sensor and computer screen displayed number are also used by staff to determine to which shelves books should be returned – shelves are numbered.[111] It was reported in 2003 that Antwerp and Utrecht public libraries had installed RFID systems in order to reduce waiting time at counters, reduce bookstock theft and release staff from repetitive tasks.[112]

In spite of the system's advantages, it was said that cost would mean it was unlikely to be widely adopted in libraries in the immediate future.[113] However, the refurbishment of Sutton Central Library, completed in 2005, has created what is believed to be the UK's first self-service public library, employing the latest RFID system: 'This ensures maximum circulation throughput, a simplified checkout/check-in process, multiple item processing, and enhanced workplace efficiency and ergonomics'.[114]

ROBOTIC SORTING

For many public libraries, the main handling problem will be that of quickly clearing books and other materials away from the returns desk. Returned book shelves or trolleys are one way of dealing with this problem, and, although popular with readers, may not suit all situations. Another method of handling returned books is with a conveyor belt at the returns desk or self-return point, like that at the supermarket, removing items to elsewhere in the library (probably a sorting room located behind the counter) for sorting and then shelving, as at the Barbican Library (1982). Alternatively, gravity may be used to send books down a shute at the return desk to a workroom below, as at the Gütersloh Library (1984). Of late, however robotic sorting of returned material has begun to be used.

Silkeborg Library, Denmark, acquired a robot, Tor, for sorting returned books. In 2003 microchips replaced barcodes in books and were also added to CDs, videos and other formats, providing self-service for users, improved stock security and relieving staff of routine work.[115] Another return and sorting system, called Library Mate, was launched by a Danish company in 2003.[116] The Netherlands has announced the development of an automated system to process library loans and sort returned items, and compete with the Swedish Tor-In system. A prototype using barcodes and RFID technology, installed at Leidschendam Public Library, is capable of dealing with 750 items an hour, including non-book material.[117] In Malmö's new public library returned books are transported by conveyor belt to the basement. There they are sorted robotically by bar code into categorized book trucks, which are then taken to appropriate places in the building for shelving or to other destinations, such as reserved books, books for the branches and so on.[118] By comparison with the Dutch system, this is said to feel dated already.

This chapter has highlighted the role of the legislation, rules, regulations and so on that define the minimum standards and desirable qualities of a large, new public building. Dovetailing into this process must be the active consideration and promotion of the concept of sustainability – erecting and running a building that is open to all, that can be used without health hazards, that does not damage the natural environment, and that uses natural features to the benefit of the building and its community.

The openness and inclusiveness of this concept contrasts with the need for preservation management and for prevention of disasters, major or minor. Early planning is essential for the security of staff, users and library stock, as well as the structure. If disasters do occur, whatever their scale, strategies need to have been built into management practice. Balancing openness with security will be greatly assisted by use of some of the sophisticated handling systems now available: again the implications of such items must be considered very early in the planning process.

NOTES

1 Smith, S. (1991), 'The library as an environmental alternative (among other things)', *Wilson library bulletin* **65** (6), 85, 156: 156.

2   Mol, J. (1999), 'Intelligent buildings, a designer's point of view', in *Intelligent library buildings*, edited by M-F. Bisbrouck and M. Chauveinc, Munich: Saur, 83.

3   Jones, D. (1993), 'Staying smart: challenges of library design in the 1990s', *Australian library journal* **42** (3), 214–27: 215.

4   Weatherbe, S. (2003), 'A vision returns to Prince Rupert', *American libraries* **34** (4), 69–71.

5   Office of the Deputy Prime Minister (2002), *Building regulations: explanatory booklet*, London: ODPM, 6.

6   Powell-Smith, V. and Billington, M.S. (1999), *The building regulations explained & illustrated*, 11th edn, Oxford: Blackwell, 5.8.

7   Pantry, S. (1996), *Dealing with aggression and violence in your workplace*, London: Library Association, 12.

8   Brading, J. and Curtis, J. (2000), *Disability discrimination: a practical guide to the new law*, 2nd edn, London: Kogan Page, 200–202; Fisher, B. (2001), 'Best practice in disability access', *Library Association record* **103** (8), 481–3; McCaskill, K. and Goulding, A. (2001), 'English public library services and Disability Discrimination Act', *New library world* **102** (1165), 192–206; Thomason, G. (2000), 'The Disability Discrimination Act (1995): a checklist for libraries', *Brio* **37** (1), 17–21; Mace, S. (2004), 'Enabling technologies', *Y ddolen* (38), 11.

9   Hopkins, L. (ed.) (2000), *Library services for visually impaired people: a manual of best practice*, London: Resource. Section 12, 'Design and adaptation of libraries and services'; 13, 'Aids and assistive technology'.

10   'Free taster sessions for visually impaired' (2004), *Newyddion* (69), [4].

11   www. library-council.ie.

12   Atton, C. (1993), 'Green librarianship: a revolt against change', *Assistant librarian* **86** (11), 166–7: 166; Ephraim, P.E. (2003), 'The greening of libraries', *Library management* **24** (3), 160–63.

13   Vale, B. and Vale, R. (1996), *Green architecture*, London: Thames & Hudson, 69, 70, 84, 107, 128, 141, 150.

14   Brandehoff, S.E. (1981), Libraries catch the sun', *American libraries* **12** (9), 562–3.

15   Walach, M. and Coleman, F. (1983), Solar oriented system', *Library journal* **108** (21), 2205–8.

16   Department of Energy (c. 1988), *Using energy from the sun*, [London: DOE], [4].

17   Paul, J. (1982), 'An experiment in solar design at San José State University', *College & research libraries news* **43** (11), 379–80; Shearer, K. (1981), 'Solar power in the public library', *Public libraries* **20** (2), 35–6.

18   Wendt Cedarholm Tippens Inc. (1985), 'Lake Villa Public Library: district and passive solar energy', *Illinois libraries* **67** (9), 810–12: 810.

19   For further details about sustainability, lighting, ventilation, etc., see Edwards, B. and Fisher, B. (2002), *Libraries and learning resources centres*, Oxford: Architectural Press, Chapter 6: 'Technical factors and engineering design'.

20   Powell-Smith, V. and Billington, M.S. (1999), 116.44.

21   Boyden, L. and Weiner J. (2000), 'Sustainable libraries: teaching environmental responsibility to communities', *Bottom line* **12** (2), 78–82.

22   Steele, M.W. (2002), 'Carmel Mountain Ranch community library', *New library world* **102** (1172), 17–20.

23   Schaper, L.L. (2003), 'Public input yields green library design', *Library journal* **128** (20), 62–4; Brown, B. (2003), 'The new green standard', *Library journal* **128** (20), 61–3; Scherer, J.A. (2004), 'Designing the sustainable library', in *Libraries as places: buildings for the 21st century*, edited by M-F. Bisbrouck and others, Munich: Saur, 161–81.

24   Lewis, E.J., Weltman, E. and Kleinman, J. (1993), 'Energy efficiency in libraries', *Library administration and management* **7** (3), 153–8.

25   Powell-Smith, V. and Billington, M.S. (1999), 16.44.

26   For fuller details, see *How to deal with SBS, sick building syndrome: guidance for employers, building owners and building managers* (1995), Sheffield: Health and Safety Executive, 4–7.

27   Vogel, A. and Stein, W.H. (1994), 'Sick building syndrome in archives and libraries' (in German), *Archivar* **47** (2), 289–98.

28 Kartman, J. (1994), '"Sick building syndrome" shutters library', *American libraries* **25** (11), 979–80.

29 Kartman, J. (1998), 'Officials mull options for sick library building', *American libraries* **29** (2), 19;

30 For fuller information, see 'Creating a good environment' in *How to deal with SBS, sick building syndrome: guidance for employers, building owners and building managers* (1995), 20–29.

31 La Rue, J. and La Rue, S. (1991), 'The green librarian', *Wilson library bulletin* **65** (6), 27–33: 32–3.

32 Morris, A. and Dennison, P. (1995), 'Sick building syndrome: survey findings of libraries in Great Britain', *Library management* **16** (3), 34–42: 42.

33 Steinhagen, E.N. and Kay, M.H. (1999), 'Floor covering options for "sick buildings": a collaborative study', *Journal of library administration* **29** (2) 109–22.

34 Morris, A. and Dyer, H. (1998), *Human aspects of library automation*, 2nd edn, Aldershot: Gower, 46–7.

35 Balas, J. (1997), 'Making libraries comfortable', *Computers in libraries* **17** (8), 49–50: 49.

36 Atencio, R. (1996), 'Eyestrain: the number one complaint of computer users', *Computers in libraries* **16** (8), 40–43.

37 Morris, A. and Dyer, H. (1998), 162.

38 Morris, A. and Dyer, H. (1998), 175–203.

39 van Zeijl, F. (1998), 'The equipment was unsuitable for its use ...' (in Dutch), *BibliotheekBlad* **2** (9), 10–11.

40 Feather, J., Matthews, G. and Eden, P. (1996), *Preservation management: policies and practices in British libraries*, Aldershot: Gower, 40.

41 Matthews, G. (1997), *Preservation management*, London: South Bank University, 5.

42 See 'Preservation education in public libraries' (1997), in *Promoting preservation awareness in libraries*, edited by J.M. Drewes and J.A. Page, Westport: Connecticut: Greenwood, 171–213.

43 British Standards Institution (2000), *Recommendations for storage and exhibition of archival documents*, London: BSI.

44 Jones, M. and Beagrie, N. (2001), *Preservation management of digital materials: a handbook*, London: British Library, 10.

45 Feeney, M. (ed.) (1999), *Digital culture: maximising the nation's investment*, London: National Preservation Office, 41.

46 Feeney, M. (ed.) (1999), 76–7.

47 Jones, M. and Beagrie, N. (2001), 21.

48 Jones, M. and Beagrie, N. (2001), 96–102, 133.

49 Society of Archivists Irish Region (1997), *Standards for the development of archive services in Ireland*, Dublin: Society of Archivists.

50 Pearson, C. and King, S. (2000), 'Passive environmental control for small cultural institutions in Australia', *Australian academic and research libraries* **31** (2), 69–78: 78, 71.

51 Cox, A.M. (1990), 'Three faults, no flaws', *American libraries* **21** (4), 29, 304, 306.

52 Robertson, G. (1996), 'Shelving and safety: an overview', *Felicter* **42** (2), 33–6.

53 Shorley, Deborah (2003), 'Disaster planning: in the end you just cope', *Library + information update* **2** (3), 46–7.

54 The 1993 reopening is described in Reagan, R.G. and Fialkoff, F. (1993), 'Rising from the ashes', *Library journal* **118** (16), 38–40.

55 Culhead, P. (2003), 'The Linköping Library fire', *International Preservation News* (31), 4–9. In English and French.

56 Modigh, B. (200), 'Looking to the future – new libraries in Linköping and Härnösand', *Scandinavian public library quarterly* **33** (2) 17–19.

57 Connolly, K. (2004), 'Weimar's priceless library devastated by fire', *Daily Telegraph* 4 September, 17.

58 Morris, J. (1979), *Managing the library fire risk*, 2nd edn, Berkeley, California: University of California, 33. It includes a list of UK library fires, 1969–78.

59 'Fire rekindles debate' (1994), *Library Association record* **96** (9), 469.

60 Hammond, H. (1996), Norfolk and Norwich Central Library: the emerging phoenix', *New library world* **97** (1130), 24–31: 25.

61 Swaffield, L. (1995), 'Lack of cash a root cause of Norwich fire', *Library Association record* **97** (6), 299.

62 'Faulty cabling caused fire' (1994), *Library Association record* **96** (11), 585.

63   DePew, J.N. (1991), *A library, media, and archival preservation handbook,* Santa Barbara, California: Abc-Clio, 269.

64   Alire, C. (2000), *Library disaster planning and recovery handbook,* New York: Neal-Schuman, xix, xx.

65   Alire, C. (2000), 20–23, 37–8, 49–50, 52, 53–5, 67–9, 108–10, 305–6; Silverman, R. (2004), 'A litany of "terrible, no good, very bad" things that can happen *after* a disaster', *International preservation news* (33), 8–15. In English and French.

66   DePew, J.N. (1991), 236–8; Kahn, M. (1998), *Disaster response and planning for libraries,* Chicago: American Library Association, 21–32; Society of Archivists: Scottish Region (1990), *Disaster preparedness: guidelines for archives and libraries,* London: Society of Archivists, 4–11.

67   Anderson, H. and McIntyre, J. (1985), *Planning manual for disaster control in Scottish libraries and record offices,* Edinburgh: National Library of Scotland, 65.

68   Ashman, J. (1995), *Disaster planning for library and information services,* London: Aslib, 4–10; Morris, J. (1986), *The library disaster: preparedness handbook,* Chicago: American Library Association, 71–5, 78–9; Banks, P.N. and Pilette, R. (eds) (2000), *Preservation: issues and planning,* Chicago: American Library Association, 114–44.

69   Parsons, J. (1992), 'Insurance implications of crime and security', in *Security and crime prevention in libraries,* edited by M. Chaney and A.F. MacDougall, Aldershot: Ashgate, 203–16: 204.

70   Hammond, H. (1996), 27–8.

71   Shorley, D (2003), 47.

72   Howes, R. (2003), 'After a disaster: drawing up the insurance claim', *Aslib proceedings* **55** (3), 181–7: 185–7.

73   For an overview of crime in libraries, see Chaney, M. and MacDougall, A.F. (eds) (1992), Chapters 1 and 2.

74   Matthews, G. (1997), 9.

75   Houlgate, J. and Chaney, M. (1992), 'Planning and management of a crime prevention strategy', in Chaney, M. and MacDougall, A.F. (eds) (1992), 46–69. See also *Security guidelines* (1989), London: National Preservation Office.

76   Lincoln, A.J. and Lincoln, C.Z. (1988), 'Library crime and security: an international perspective', *Library and archival security* **8** (1/2), 1–154: 147–52; a checklist based on that of the Lincolns is given in DePew, J.N. (1991), 99–102; see also Shuman, B. (1999), *Library security and safety handbook: prevention, policies, and procedures,* Chicago: American Library Association, 117–24.

77   McDonald, A. (1992), 'Security policy formulation', in Chaney, M. and MacDougall, A.F. (eds) (1992), 267–88; McDonald, A. (1992), 'Book detection systems', in Chaney, M. and MacDougall, A.F. (eds), 289–97; Matthews, G. (1997), 9.

78   Morris, J. (1986), [see 68], 7–16.

79   See also 'Physical considerations' in *Violence in libraries: preventing aggressive and unacceptable behaviour in libraries* (1987), London: Library Association, [4].

80   McGrath, H. and Goulding, A. (1996), 'Part of the job: violence in public libraries', *New library world* **97** (1127), 4–13: 12.

81   Farrugia, S. (2002), 'A dangerous occupation? Violence in public libraries', *New library world* **103** (1180), 309–19; Killen, C. (2004), 'Being prepared for aggressive behaviour', *Library + information gazette* 5 November, 1–2.

82   Pantry, S.A. (1996), 34.

83   Burrows, J. and Cooper, D. (1992), *Theft and loss from UK libraries: a national survey,* London: Home Office Police Department, iii, 45.

84   Morris, J. (1986), 22.

85   Burrows, J. and Cooper, D. (1992), 43.

86   McCree, Mark (2001), 'Theft: ignorance is bliss?' *Public library journal* **16** (2) , 47–8, 50.

87   McCree, Mark (2001), 50.

88   Shuman, B. (1999), 60.

89   Shuman, B, (1999), 63. See also the collection security checklist in DePew, J.N. (1991), 99–102.

90   Morris, J. (1986), 18.

91   Shuman, B, (1999), 208–50.

92   Davies, J.E. (1992), 'Computer misuse', in Chaney, M. and MacDougall, A.F. (eds) (1992), 182–202.

93   Lacey, S. (1979), *Library vandalism and textual mutilation*, Birmingham: Birmingham Library School Cooperative, 5–19.

94   Morris, J. (1986), 14.

95   Hinks, J. (1992), 'The community approach to crime and security' in Chaney, M. and MacDougall, A.F. (eds) (1992), 231–47; 'Games club cuts crime' (2004), *Library + information update* **3** (2) 17; Barker, M. and Bridgeman, C. (1994), *Preventing vandalism: what works?* London: Home Office Police Department. Full text on WWW; long bibliography includes references to libraries and graffiti.

96   Morris, J. (1986), 1.

97   Shuman, B.A. (1999), 23.

98   See Shuman (1999), 251–64.

99   Jenkins, S. (2004), 'Cornwall unlocks smartcard potential', *Public library journal*, Summer, 2–4.

100   Thompson, G. (1989), *Planning and design of library buildings*, 3rd edn, London: Butterworth, 53–7.

101   Reagan, R.G. and Fialkoff, F. (1993), 40.

102   Wang, R. and Wu, J. (1998), 'A palace for knowledge: the new building of the Shanghai Library', *Asian libraries* **7** (cumulative issue), 196–9.

103   Thompson, G. (1989), 55.

104   Tanis, N. and Ventuleth, C. (1987), 'Making space: automated storage and retrieval', *Wilson library bulletin* **61** (10), 25–7; Kauntz, J. (1987), 'Robots in the library: automated storage and retrieval systems', *Library journal* **112** (20), 67–70.

105   Haslam, M. and others (2002), 'The automated storage and retrieval system (ASRS) in Lied Library', *Library hi tech* **20** (1), 71–89; www.mplib.org/newcentrallib.asp.

106   Melot, M. (1996), *Nouvelles Alexandries: les grands chantiers de bibliothèques dans le monde*, Paris: Cercle de la Libraire.

107   Brophy, P. and others (1997), *Self-service systems in libraries: user requirements and implications*, Preston: CERLIM, University of Central Lancashire, 2.

108   Cookman, N. and Burgess, H. (1996), '3M self issue terminal at Maidenhead', *Vine* (105), 20–23.

109   Brophy, P. and others (1997), 61, 62, 26.

110   '3M introduces Digital Information System' ... (1999), *Information today* **16** (8), 47, 49; Brown-Syed, C. (2001), 'Robots, radio, and patron self-service', *Library & archival security* **17** (2), 65–8.

111   Ngian, L.C. (2001), 'Designing library interiors in a changing environment: the Singapore experience', in *Library buildings in a changing environment*, edited by M-F. Bisbrouck, Munich: Saur, 155–62: 158.

112   Hoflack, M. and Van den Broeck, P. (2003), 'Radio frequency identification systems in Flemish libraries' (in Flemish), *Bibliotheek-en archiefgids* **79** (3), 48–53.

113   Richardson, L. (2003), 'Self services: the present state of play', *SCONUL newsletter* (28) Spring, 18–21: 20.

114   'Sirsi/3M: London Borough of Sutton first to self-service' (2004), *Library + information gazette* 21 May, 3.

115   Jensen, K.B. (2003), 'The future? It is only a few millimetres each way' (in Danish), *Bibliotekspressen* (7), 8 April, 226–8.

116   'Self-service' (2003), *Library + information update* **2** (9), 10.

117   Wieldraaijer, E. (2002), 'The NBD/Biblion company unveils Cor-Lector in competition with Tor In' (in Dutch), *BibliotheekBlad* **6** (9/10), 13.

118   *A library for all times* (1997), Stockholm: Swedish National Council for Cultural Affairs, 87–93.

7 Planning, design and construction

> The building should be planned and designed to be appropriate and adequate for the special type of library work to be done and the community to be served.
>
> *Wheeler and Githens, 1941*[1]

While a building project can be a daunting affair, especially the first time round, it provides the librarian with the opportunity (in consultation with others) to rethink the library's purpose in the community it is to serve, as well as the services it is to offer, and how they might be organized and operated. The results of this consultation and re-evaluation will be reflected in the librarian's brief to the architect, perhaps the librarian's greatest intellectual challenge.

In taking a building project forward, the librarian's role is essentially that of a planner, while that of the architect is as a designer, providing a design solution to the problems posed by the librarian's requirements, as set out in the brief for the library. This is not to say that the librarian should not be interested in or knowledgeable about design – otherwise how can constructive comment be made on the architect's proposals for the building? It is likely, however – and this is another challenge for the librarian – that he/she will not be used to making judgements on matters of design, both in general terms – the architectural quality of the proposed building, for example – or on specific matters, such as colour schemes for the interior. These are matters that cannot be entirely decided by personal taste.

CHALLENGES, PROBLEMS AND DISAPPOINTMENTS

Whatever worries the librarian may have about involvement in a library building project, there are often other problems, disappointments and challenges which may have to be faced in the process.

- Finding and retaining a suitable site – plans for a new central library at Waltham Forest, London, were abandoned after four years because the site was to be sold to the highest commercial bidder.[2]

- Securing and controlling capital costs – a considerable sum of money is required and has to be argued for, much in excess of what might be spent on other library capital projects, and expenditure must be kept within the agreed budget.
- Timescale – the timescale from the inception of the project to its completion may be very drawn out: anything from two to three years for a small building and ten years or more for a large public library.
- Aborted, delayed and reduced-in-scale projects[3] – such disappointments usually stem from financial and siting difficulties. In such an uncertain environment plans can become outdated (although regrettably sometimes still used), and the librarian's commitment to providing new or improved accommodation sorely tried.
- The range of people involved – the team nature of the modern building project is both a comfort and a challenge, in that the librarian has to learn to work with an architect and a range of other specialists from both within and outside the library world, and be prepared to consult widely with staff, library users and local groups. For large structures a senior librarian may act as the library's project officer with the responsibility, for example, for the day-to-day overseeing of the progress of the building.
- The permanency of the results – unlike other projects where change may be possible at an acceptable cost, major mistakes of planning and design may have to be lived with long into the future. This places a great deal of pressure on all those concerned to 'get it right'.

PLANNING, DESIGN AND CONSTRUCTION: AN OVERVIEW

At its most basic, creating a new library building is about planning, design and construction. Information-gathering and decision-making, however, must precede planning, and so there is an earlier, pre-planning stage. Nor is construction the final step in the creative process, as it will be followed by preparing the library for occupancy and use. This creative process outlined below is applicable to other types of building projects, such as library extensions or conversions, although some aspects of those tasks are likely to be different. A remodelling, refurbishment and extension of existing premises, for example, may pose problems of maintaining library service during construction work in and around the building.[4] The conversion of a building to a library may entail physical and structural constraints as to what can be created at the design and construction stages. As will be seen, each of these stages can be broken down into a number of components. CABE has issued detailed information on these various stages, which it labels prepare, design, construct and use, as part of a general guide to ensure successful and quality building projects.[5]

However, if the often-neglected post-occupancy evaluation exercise (discussed in the next chapter) is included in the process, then one can define six stages. These stages, and the main players at each stage, can be summarized as follows:

1. Pre-planning stage – making the case and assessing need; evaluating building alternatives; securing the budget and preparing for participation (the librarian)
2. Planning stage – writing and developing the architect's brief; the selection of the architect and other specialists; site selection (the librarian and architect)
3. Design stage – concept to working drawings (the architect and librarian)
4. Construction stage – the erection of the library building (the builder, the architect and the librarian)
5. Occupancy – moving in and making the building operational (the librarian; furniture, equipment and systems suppliers; removers)
6. Post-occupancy evaluation (the librarian, architect, builder and users).[6]

In reality the individual stages may not be so clear cut and matters might not occur in the order suggested. Some aspects of the pre-planning stage, visits to other libraries, for example, may also take place during the planning and design stages. The development of the architect's brief, especially for a large building, may continue from the planning to the design stage. The fine detail of the library's interior layout may be finalized during the period of relative respite for the architect and librarian provided by construction. Preparations for moving in and making the library ready for use cannot be left until the building is finished but must be made at a much earlier stage in the process.

Although post-occupancy evaluation features as a final stage in this creative process, other forms of evaluation, assessment and review will take place along the way. These might include an evaluation of the existing building but will certainly include a review of the architect's design proposals. All forms of such evaluation are dealt with in the following chapter.

The whole creative process may not follow exactly the sequence suggested by this chapter. In some situations work may proceed as far as the design stage without full briefing (especially in an architectural competition), before local authority or other funding is approved and the project is able to go ahead. Also the site may be pre-determined, especially where the library is part of a developer's or other scheme. A feasibility study, based on an outline brief, may be required for financial, technical or other reasons 'to test reality against aspirations and the vision behind the project'.[7]

Changes can occur along the way in a project, usually because of a reduced budget. This may mean a reduction in its scale, inferior finishes, the re-use of old furniture from the previous building, and changes to design elements of the building where feasible.

In addition to the key players noted at each stage of the process, many other people will be involved. At various times they will include local authority members and staff, library staff and users, library and information consultants, and structural and mechanical and computing specialists.

Similarly, political decision-making by the local authority may override the approach suggested by this outline. It will probably influence the funding, choice of site, architect selection, the design solution and the pace of the project.

Before looking at the stages of the building process in more detail and describing the contribution made by some of the key players, it is worth briefly considering what is meant by planning and design.

In the building context, planning has to be looked at from two perspectives. For the librarian, who is the expert on public library purpose, services and operations, it means assessing what must be done to achieve their aim in successfully creating new or improved library premises. This *modus operandi* is largely the thrust of this chapter. The architect brings to the project a creative imagination and a knowledge of how buildings operate and are constructed. And so for the architect, planning involves the production of increasingly detailed scale drawings of their design for the library, the design being 'the graphical solution of a project or programme – economically, structurally, and aesthetically'.[8] Working together in this planning, design, construction and occupancy process, the librarian and architect employ all their management skills. This means, especially, leading and motivating others to ensure that an attractive and functional library building is delivered on time and within the allotted budget and other constraints. For small public library buildings the planning and design process will be much simpler, with fewer people involved.

PRE-PLANNING OR CONCEPTUAL STAGE

This stage[9] will begin with the recognition and acceptance by librarian and the responsible local authority that new or improved library accommodation is essential. Lack of space, comfort and convenience, changing roles and need, and the unacceptable fragmentation of the library service over a number of sites, might all be part of the librarian's case.

MAKING THE CASE AND ASSESSING NEED

This aspect of the pre-planning stage cannot be confined to summarizing the inadequacies of the physical structure and the necessity for new accommodation. It should also examine the current library provision by profiling the service point and how it is used – whether there is increased or declining use, for example, or under-use (and non-use) by certain groups. This might involve surveys, questionnaires and a charting of library statistics over an appropriate period, thus helping to indicate significant changes and trends. Comparison with similar libraries, national averages, and with trends and developments in modern public librarianship is also often productive. Analysis of this library profile in the light of a community profile, described below, provides the librarian with information for planning and decision-making for the development of the library service in its proposed new or improved building.

A community profile for the area served by the library will identify community issues, changes, developments and social trends (as discussed in Chapter 1) to which the library service may wish to respond in the proposed new or improved accommodation. This requires the public librarian to gather a range of information on such topics as population, education, and recreational and cultural facilities. Analysis of this information provides the librarian with some indication of latent or hidden library and information needs. For example, lack of a community meeting space, cinema or theatre could have implications for the library service, especially if a new building is contemplated.

A service point may well have such library and community studies on file and will only need to bring them up to date. The likely subject matter for the two profiles is indicated in Figures 7.1 and 7.2. Some of the information, statistics for example, will be readily available for the library profile but the community profile will probably require more research. The IFLA/UNESCO *Guidelines* consider community needs analysis as an important management planning tool and offers further guidance on its use and information (including target groups) to be acquired.[10] As shown in Chapter 1, such an assessment in the UK today would take into account the matter of social exclusion and 'barriers to library usage and how to overcome them'.[11]

Membership
Issues
Requests
Library materials: bookstock, videos, CDs, and so on
Resources, such as ICT provision
Use of the library
Non-use of the library
Presentation of the library

Figure 7.1   Library profile: some areas of study

MARKET RESEARCH

More ambitious and more costly than profiling, which may include user surveys, is the use of market research to determine the needs of potential users. This research can help answer some of the basic questions to be solved at this pre-planning stage:

- number of potential users and likely user patterns
- facilities required in the new building
- location of the library, if there is a choice, although there may be a separate site evaluation exercise, as discussed in Chapter 4.

An important example of published market research in connection with a library building project was that carried out for the proposed Runcorn District Library in the 1970s. This study will be contrasted with the market research carried out more recently in Tower Hamlets for its Idea Store strategy.

191

Physical characteristics – geographical features
Population – make-up by age, gender, ethnic groups
Employment
Local government
Education – schools, colleges, university
Recreational and cultural facilities
Information services provided by other agencies
Social services
Housing
Religion
Local organizations
Transport and communications

Figure 7.2   Community profile: some areas of study

Case study: Runcorn District Library

Runcorn New Town was designated in 1964 but there was already an established community with its own library. Runcorn Shopping City, part of the new town development, was constructed as a major concentration of shops, offices, social and cultural facilities. Professional knowledge and judgement helped in the decision to build a new library of 2,230m^2 within easy reach of everyone in Shopping City. The market research was carried out to determine exactly where the library should be sited and what should be provided for potential users: few 'public libraries are built with the benefit of a full-scale market research study'.[12] And, as will be seen in the next chapter, the research and its implications for the resulting library building was subsequently evaluated, further adding value to the project as a case study.

A team was assembled from Cheshire's Research and Intelligence Unit, members of the library staff and the Department of Architecture to carry out the study of the needs of the potential users of a proposed new district library.[13] Patrick Gee, the county librarian at the time, wrote:

> There were ... political, professional and practical reasons why a market research study would be of benefit. It would, we hoped, raise political awareness, arouse public expectations and provide invaluable information to librarian, architect and interior designer on location and content of the library. Those expectations were realised.[14]

As the location, but not exact site, of the library had been agreed upon, the market research examined what locational factors within Shopping City would probably maximize its use, in addition to the likely number and characteristics of future users, and what should be provided by way of services and facilities. Surveys, discussions and pedestrian flow counts were used to collect the research data and the main elements are listed in Figure 7.3.

Runcorn Community Facilities Survey – a survey of residents
Survey of present library use at Runcorn old library and mobiles
Survey of organizations in Runcorn
Discussions with selected groups of potential users
Pedestrian flow counts

Figure 7.3   Runcorn District Library: basic market research data

Much of the research data collected mirrored what might be gathered in profiling a library and its community. However, this market research was expertly carried out and made both direct and indirect contact with many local residents. The study's enquiries (see Figure 7.4) also went much further than the usual user survey, looking at book ownership, readership of magazines, time spent listening to sound recordings, participation in part-time or adult education, as well as reasons for ceasing to use the library. Important for planning were the estimates of usage of the new library, the estimated number of weekly visits, and the likelihood of residents using particular facilities in the library.

People of Runcorn – the make-up of the community; reading and other leisure
    pursuits
Present library usage, non-usage and attitudes to libraries
The new library – number of potential users; facilities required; patterns of use,
    suggestions as to layout, and so on
Siting of the library – pedestrian flow counts, and so on

Figure 7.4   Runcorn District Library: in-depth market research areas

It is not possible to give a detailed account of the findings of the Runcorn District Library market research study here, but the main conclusions were:

- there was a considerable demand for library service – 74 per cent of residents supported a new library
- the level of library use would increase from one third to one half of residents, new users coming mainly from the new town area
- current facilities would continue in use for existing town residents
- it was necessary to identify those services which would be in greatest demand, those which would attract limited use, and those for which there would be little demand at all
- neither of the two library sites was better than the other but the greenfield site was preferred to the limitations and constraints of a mall location
- the study did not provide a precise prediction of future use but gave a strong indication; the library would have to be equipped for that level of use

- there would be a need to monitor use
  - to test the accuracy of predictions
  - to measure the effectiveness of new services against possible demands.

Runcorn District Library opened in 1981 and proved to be one of the most successful libraries in Cheshire. The predictions were tested seven years after the original study when another investigation was commissioned;[15] this is discussed in the following chapter. Taken together, the two investigations – the before and after of a public library building – are probably unique and an important contribution to the library buildings literature.

Case study: Idea Stores

The UK's most socially deprived borough, the London Borough of Tower Hamlets, faced a large bill to bring its public library buildings up to scratch as regards repair and accessibility. Given the under-use of its libraries, the local authority commissioned a major market research exercise 'designed to find out what, if anything, the Council had to do to encourage people to use its libraries'.[16] The research showed that people would use a quality library service with investment in books and ICT and open at convenient times. It also demonstrated that the existing library buildings could not accommodate the proposed combined library and learning centres, that they were wrongly located and would be better placed in shopping areas.

The research thus suggested a different kind of library building, differently located, that would change people's view of public libraries and adult learning. Consequently Tower Hamlets engaged a company to develop a brand strategy for a new style of library – the Idea Store – involving input from focus groups and publicity to promote the Idea Store brand concept. This resulted in

> ... a model of service, and set of values, which the buildings when they are designed will embody. The buildings are vehicles for that service, not dictators of it.[17]

The key principles used in developing the first Idea Store, a refurbishment of an existing building linked to an old library building and near a supermarket, and the later versions, for which it was a prototype, were:

- barrier-free access
- access for people with disabilities
- seamless provision of library and learning activities
- 'retail' rather than 'library' feel to the store
- flexibility and adaptability
- to support self-help as much as possible
- floorwalking staff
- unobtrusive security.

The Idea Store Programme Director argues that

> in Idea Stores, we have created a customer-oriented, flexible facility that enables us to deliver a variety of relevant services to local people ... we have demonstrated to the people of Tower Hamlets that libraries and learning are fun, cool and worthwhile.[18]

Writing in 1985, and reviewing the initial and later Runcorn studies, Norman Roberts commended their timeliness, excellence and value, noting there was much 'for library managers to analyse and discuss'. More critically, Roberts felt that the evidence of the surveys indicated that 'members of the community will expect from their libraries what librarians teach them to expect ... [and] that they are of little use for predictive purposes'. He ends, however, by saying that the survey 'is an indication of the path that must be followed to secure a better understanding of our actual and potential users'.[19] The Idea Store concept, based on market research, and other examples noted in this chapter indicate the seriousness with which needs assessment, as part of the library building planning process, is taken today.

People places summarizes these approaches to needs assessment as:

- identified need – assessing the needs of all stakeholders (service providers, practitioners and consumers) using a range of consultation techniques, such as phone surveys, interviews, focus groups and interactive television game-show technology[20] (market research)
- normative need – collecting socio-demographic information about the community to be served and statistical and other information about the library service (community and library profiles)
- comparative need – comparison with library services in communities with similar characteristics; visits to recently built libraries, discussed earlier as part of the librarian's preparation
- benchmark-based need – methods for determining library size, as discussed in Chapter 3.[21]

COMMUNITY CONSULTATION

A major feature of needs assessment is community consultation which is concerned not only with gathering information but with allowing members of the community to influence the design and other aspects of the proposed building. Following the Norwich fire, discussed in the previous chapter, and as preparation for a new library building, research was carried out into library use. In addition, information was gathered about the changing community to be served. Public consultation was also carried out as to whether more money should be spent on the proposed new library (and record office), although other capital projects would be deferred. An eight-page leaflet was widely distributed in Norfolk with more than 5,000 individuals responding: overwhelming support was given to spending more than the insurance money that would be received.[22]

Two Australian examples of consultation are those undertaken by Camden Council Library Service, New South Wales,[23] and Cambridge Library, Western Australia. In the latter case a group of library stakeholders was established to ensure consultation at critical stages of the project – the brief, the design, and the furniture and fitting proposals. Members were expected to communicate the needs of the group in the community that they represented. In brief, the findings indicated that libraries should be more about books and for human contact, so as to share interests, whether business, recreation or cultural.[24] (The practical results of Cambridge's consultation process can be seen in Figure 7.5.) Hikawa Library, Japan, opened a new library in 2003. There too the community were closely involved in the design process and a webpage chronicling progress was developed.[25]

Figure 7.5   Cambridge Library, Western Australia (2002)
Source: Town of Cambridge

Case study: Library of Birmingham

A consultation steering group was convened in Birmingham to coordinate public consultation for the new library project[26] and a full-time consultation and involvement officer appointed for one year. Consultation involved staff across the library service, organizations which might follow the library to the city's Learning Quarter at Eastside, and the public. To ensure excluded groups were included in the consultation process, target groups were defined.

The consultation would be in two stages: the first stage would feed into the architect's design concept, the second would allow the concept to be appraised. The first stage asked people:

- what they liked or did not like about the existing building
- what they would like the new building to look like
- what kind of materials should be used in its construction
- what the library should feel like and 'do'.

In focusing on the design at the second stage, many of the same questions were asked.

The consultation exercise used a variety of methods, such as postcard and website questionnaires, public presentations and discussions, and discussion groups in schools and youth clubs. Over 1,400 people were consulted between July and November 2002, of which roughly one third were children. The six most common requirements were:

- an accessible building
- an attractive and welcoming building
- a wide range of facilities and spaces
- computers to support both learning and entertainment
- quiet study spaces to support learning
- a wide range of accessible resources.

The consultation programme continued to concentrate on seeking people's views from March to May 2003. The Library of Birmingham is planned to open in early 2008 (but see page 319 for subsequent developments) and the consultation will continue until then and will be followed by evaluation of the new library.[27]

It could be argued that such open-ended consultation raises people's expectations unrealistically, as their wishes can only be taken into account where possible and may be inappropriate to a city centre public library. However, the general conclusions reached by the exercise as to what people expected of the building seem uncontroversial and could be anticipated in a major modern building housing a library. The real value of the exercise seems to lie in the opportunities to publicize and promote the project and the library service generally. Nevertheless a 2003 study concluded that successful planning, including consultation, determines the strengths and weaknesses of a new public library building.[28]

EVALUATING ALTERNATIVES

A major issue in the pre-planning stage might be whether a new building, usually on a new site, is the answer to a library's space and other needs. The advantages and disadvantages of alternatives to a new building have been dealt with in Chapter 5. An associated question is whether the public library is to be built as part of a school, or shopping or other complex, or in conjunction with other local services such as a museum or health clinic. These questions of independence, co-location, convergence and integration were discussed in Chapter 4.

PREPARING FOR PARTICIPATION

For the librarian, this means acquiring a satisfactory knowledge of library planning and design. The extent of this preparation will depend on existing knowledge, interest and experience, and the nature of the building project. In some library systems there may be one or more members of staff who have built up considerable knowledge and experience in this area through involvement in a number of library building projects. The task of preparation could involve some or all of the following:

- visits to library buildings, including those abroad, either by personal arrangement or by joining organized study tours
- exploring the professional and architectural literature about library buildings
- contact with professional associations and other relevant bodies
- attendance at exhibitions, courses and seminars
- investigations into building costs (in order to plan realistically), regulations, codes, standards and legal requirements
- finding out how architects work and the kind of relationship they have with their clients
- familiarization with architects' drawings, symbols and scales
- identifying libraries of particular relevance to the proposed building project.

The last task, identifying appropriate libraries to visit and for study, is made that much easier if there is a single source of past and current buildings information. This need was met in the UK from 1962 until 1994 by the 'Library buildings' series, although later volumes were somewhat tardily published. Other countries, such as Sweden, Finland and the Netherlands, have produced similar volumes but on an irregular basis and some works have been produced from time to time with worldwide coverage. Many of these publications are listed in the Bibliography of this book.

The documentation of library building activity provides an important source of information for those involved in such projects and every country should endeavour to produce an annual (or periodic) comprehensive listing of new library public buildings, such as that which appears in the December issue of *Library journal* each year. This basic phase would be enhanced by a further step, the publication of critical assessments, or building studies, of selected significant libraries, identifying trends and developments. It would help enormously if the documentation of buildings information was collected and held at an agreed national centre and accessible to some degree via a website,[29] as in the UK's library buildings database available via the Designing Libraries website.[30]

END OF THE PRE-PLANNING STAGE

At the end of the pre-planning stage, it is likely that decisions will have been reached as to:

- which alternative is to be used – new build or conversion, for example
- where the library will be located and actually sited, assuming that there is a choice in the matter and that the librarian's outline proposal is sufficient to permit a site evaluation exercise
- the size of the building
- user groups, their library and information needs and probable levels of use
- what might be provided by way of services and facilities
- how much it will cost.

In spite of thorough, exemplary preparation, and a clear outline proposal and recommendations by the librarian, the final decisions (as noted earlier), about the choice of site, the chosen building solution (whether new or conversion, for example), and library size are in the hands of the local authority. The outcomes may not be what the librarian would wish, usually for reasons of cost. These decisions will affect what can be offered by way of services and facilities in the new accommodation. With the local authority's permission to proceed, depending on the way that the politicians decide, the librarian's ambitions may have to be modified and priorities adjusted. The librarian's outline proposals will now have to be turned into a brief for the building and an architect appointed. The real work of planning and designing now begins.

PLANNING STAGE

The temptation to move too quickly to this stage should be avoided, as lack of pre-planning (including the lack of consultation, profiling or market research) and self-preparation can affect the successful outcome of the building project.

PREPARATION OF THE ARCHITECT'S BRIEF

The architect's brief is known in the US and elsewhere as the program and its preparation will make use of the information and decisions taken at the pre-planning stage. The brief or program can be described as a document which:

- confirms the need for a new library related to the projected needs of the community
- sets out the basic philosophy and principles of the library service on which the library is to be planned
- describes the requirements of the client for the building in quantitative and qualitative terms.[31]

The librarian should write the brief with appropriate input from the staff and others (possibly using focus groups[32]) and may, if necessary, be helped in this task by a library consultant. During its formulation, the brief is likely to go through a number of drafts. Should it not meet all the architect's information needs, then a period of consultation to develop the brief more fully will be needed. For large library projects briefing may be a two-part process. A primary or initial brief will state principles rather than excessive detail, concentrating on library purpose, operational factors (how the library is to be run and organized), and quality and design factors. This can then be followed by a secondary or final briefing, allowing detail to be developed within the design team.[33]

THE BRIEF: OUTLINE OF CONTENTS[34]

1. Introduction to the brief
   - short statements on the need for the proposed new library building
   - summary of the size, estimated cost, anticipated opening date, and so on of the new building.
2. The community to be served by the library
   - size of population, distribution, and so on
   - growth and future development
   - library and information needs.
3. The present library building
   - description and size of the building
   - services and facilities provided
   - statistics of membership, stock, seating and equipment provision
   - inadequacies and good features of the present library building.
4. The need for the new building
   - information provided in sections 2 and 3 can be used to outline the case for the new building
   - statutory requirements and funding details, standards, the growth and development of the community, and the inadequacies of the present building will all form part of the case for the new building.
5. The library service within proposed building
   - functions: mission, roles, place in the library system, etc
   - services and facilities
   - organization of the library
   - staff structure
   - stock organization
   - ICT provision
   - operational methods
   - level of expected use.

6. The structure
   - the site
   - design qualities required of the building
   - explanation of standards or other methods of calculating space requirements
   - description of individual library departments, sections, areas and rooms together with the size of each. These should be summarized at the end of this section to show the total required floor space and those of individual areas.
7. Appendices
   - detailed description of library areas using facility sheets, sometimes known as room data or activity data sheets
   - relationship diagrams
   - traffic flow diagrams – users, staff, materials.
8. Tables and charts
   Some information can be provided usefully in the form of tables or charts, some of which may be placed in the main body of the brief, others in the appendices. Examples include:
   - library organization chart
   - statistics relating to the community to be served
   - statistics relating to size of the stock, rate of acquisition, etc.[35]

Another version of the brief suggests six elements:

1. Concise history of the library.
2. The philosophy of the library service as a purpose statement.
3. Library goals, objectives and strategies – now and in the future.
4. The proposed building – a list of every area, answering questions such as its required size, what takes place in the area and how it relates to other areas.
5. Project budget – funds and sources; estimated project budget (indicating fees) and costs for site preparation, construction, furniture and equipment and contingencies.
6. General statement – covering such issues as ease of maintenance, multipurpose spaces and expansion: these are issues which are discussed in the next chapter.[36]

ICT PLAN: PRESENT AND FUTURE

In order to feed its information and communications technology provision requirements into the architect's brief, a library should have an ICT plan. Libraries often have service plans and collection development plans but fewer seem to have comprehensive technology plans

> developed to ensure that the library's technology decisions are made in the context of the library's service priorities as established in the overall library plan.

Wired for the future, from which this quotation is taken, provides a systematic approach to preparing such a plan (and its implementation) using the following outline:

- review library service goals, objectives and activities
- determine which activities require technology-based solutions
- assess current situation
- discover options
- select a technology infrastructure and identify products and services
- develop and manage the implementation process.[37]

A fundamental requirement in planning a library building is for attention to be given to future-proofing. In the past this usually meant general adaptability and flexibility, and the possibility of a future extension. But, as the next chapter demonstrates, there is now also a requirement for the library to be suitable, both now and in the future, for IT developments, permitting flexible provision for users and for staff. Chris Batt asks, 'how can we design the building to be future proof against the changing and increasing demands of information technology?' and lists some fundamental points to be considered:

- the number of power outlets – more than is thought necessary at first
- a network that can meet future demands of diversity and capacity
- storage and work space for the repair and housing of equipment in transit
- dispersed or clustered terminals
- a building that permits the flexible installation, moving and adding of ICT systems (raised floors and ceilings at Batt's Croydon Library)
- cable/wire management.[38]

The rate at which IT develops is evidenced in the need for libraries to now provide WiFi (wire-free Internet) access. In addition to a library's ICT and Internet services it will need to offer WiFi points or hotspots to allow users with WiFi-enabled laptops and personal digital assistants (PDAs) to access the Internet without cables. Lewisham, for example, has installed hotspots in all eleven of its public libraries.[39] It remains to be seen whether this and other developments will invalidate much of the effort that has gone into ICT future-proofing.

PRESENTATION OF THE BRIEF

The librarian should aim to make the brief a concise presentation of the needed information, free from jargon and easy to use through the inclusion of a contents page, index, bibliography, and so on. Tables, diagrams and charts should be provided where they would be helpful, as well as references to other library buildings, if thought appropriate. What is not normally required in the brief are specifications as to:

- the exterior visual requirements (unless, for example, harmonization or contrast with existing buildings is an essential demand of the client)
- the use of materials

- designation of colour
- technical and mechanical details.[40]

WHAT DOES THE ARCHITECT DO?

According to the Royal Institute of British Architects (RIBA), architects solve problems creatively, save clients time and money, and help promote business. They will also manage a building project from site selection to completion. In detail this can mean:

- advising on planning and design options
- visualizing and conveying to the client an acceptable solution
- designing an appropriate building that is fit for its purpose, a pleasure to use and makes a contribution to the environment, as discussed in Chapter 2
- ensuring the client gets value for money
- handling paperwork
- controlling costs[41]
- leading and coordinating the design team.

Selecting the architect

In many instances public libraries, both past and present, will have been designed by the local authority's architect. There are instances, however, where well-known (and even famous) architects, such as Will Alsop, Norman Foster and Richard Rogers, have been responsible for public library buildings and this is increasingly the case for large, prestigious projects. For many a project, 'architect' will usually mean more than one member of the chosen firm – its design team, in fact – although one individual will act as the project architect.

Architectural competitions

Because of the prestige attached to large public libraries, and for various other reasons, a building may be the subject of an architectural competition. The source of public funding may dictate also that architects from the European Community have an opportunity to compete. In Britain, the RIBA will advise on and, if required, manage an architectural competition. In the latter case it becomes an RIBA-approved competition and is managed by the institute's Competition Office,[42] as was the 2003 competition for Crawley Library. There are two forms of competition. The first aims 'to find the right architect or design team for a project', usually achieved through competitive interview. This route is particularly appropriate where time is a factor, funds are not available for a design competition, and there is a need for the architect to help develop the brief. A call for expressions of interest from registered architects is advertised and from the respondents a shortlist of architects is drawn up for interview, the project being awarded to one of them. This approach requires the

203

client to formulate only a broad project brief but to have made a commitment to build.

The second type of competition is 'to find the most appropriate design solution for a project' and the participating architects will be given a comprehensive brief. It is a process that might be said to select the right architect as well as the best design. Such competitions are either 'open' (to all architects) or 'closed' (restricted to invited or selected architects) and demand a detailed brief and a commitment to build. These competitions may also include a competitive interview. The open project competition is likely to be a two-stage affair because of the large number of initial entrants.

Another contest-type approach is the 'open ideas' competition, although this is somewhat different in that its aim is 'to identify a range of possible design solutions against a broad conceptual brief' but here there is no commitment to build.

The pros and cons of an architectural competition are noted in Figure 7.6. Their particular value lies in the range of choice that it produces 'drawings [that] are radical, romantic, ridiculous and rational' and 'submissions [that] can range from phantasy to functional'.[43] An architectural competition can sometimes be the triumph of hope over experience. For although the aim of the competition is the selection of the best design for the building, the controversy and disagreements that can be raised during (and after) the selection process may mean a less than successful outcome. The worst of this is that the library may never be built, at least not in the immediate future nor even to the prize-winning design. More positively, and allowing for the hard and time-consuming work involved, a competition attracts media attention and 'increases interest in and awareness of public libraries'.[44]

Pros
- Objectivity of choice and advice
- Demands a clear and extensive brief
- Rigour of selection criteria
- Public relations value, if the popular choice wins
- Results in high-quality designs
- Chance to compare competing designs
- Increased standing of winning architectural practice

Cons
- Slows the design procurement process
- Adds minor costs
- Extra work for the client's staff
- Modification needed to winning design because of restrictions on communications with the competing architects
- Negative public relations if there is a risk of the winning design not being accepted as an appropriate solution[45]

Figure 7.6   Architectural competitions: pros and cons

Published accounts of public library building competitions include those for Brighton (UK), Oslo (Norway) and Jacksonville (US). In Brighton the competition was won by the local authority's own architects (but not built to their design, as described in Chapter 2), and in Oslo, where competitors included Norman Foster, by a Dutch practice, OMA.[46] In Jacksonville, the central library was built following a competition involving four architectural firms.[47]

David Jones, the Australian library consultant, emphasizes the need for the librarian to be involved in the process of selecting an architect or design team, as the librarian will brief and work with them once selected. He describes what to look for in the selection interview and any subsequent follow-up work, such as discussions with former clients or building visits:

- appropriate professional qualifications – of the architectural and other staff
- an ability to understand the client's needs – by showing they are in tune with the project aims
- good communication and personal skills – orally, graphically and in writing, and in working with others
- a readiness to learn, with no desire to impose their own ideas
- ability to cope with complexity – able to see both the micro and the macro dimensions to the project
- creativity and imagination – showing originality in the creation of a functional building that will attract and inspire visitors
- competence and relevant experience – previous experience of public library building work is not necessarily a guarantee of future success (demonstrated competence in public building projects of a similar scale might be a better test); due recognition should be given to less experienced architects who may give a good interview but do not have an impressive catalogue of past achievements
- the architectural practice – are there frequent changes of personnel? Are specialist professionals, including IT specialists, available? What is the practice workload and are there adequate staff for the project? Is the practice well organized and well equipped? Is the fee reasonable and what does it cover?
- ability to produce value for money
- quality assurance.[48]

Jones recognizes that some criteria are objective and readily quantifiable, such as qualifications. Evaluating others, like communication and personal skills and creativity, is more subjective as they do not lend themselves to quantifiable measurement: 'The wrong choice may result in a monument to missed opportunities. The right team will leave a living testament to a productive partnership'.[49]

In any working partnership, however, problems may arise from time to time. Their resolution will be helped by the design team approach, which encourages cooperation and helps avoid clashes, careful documentation, visits and interviews, and the objectivity gained through the employment of a library buildings consultant. There will be a temptation later for a building's success (or failings) to be laid entirely at the architect's door. But, in a partnership, responsibility for success (and failings) is shared equally by the architect and client.

Case study: roles of architect and librarian

A study of 'the experiences and perceived roles of librarians and architects in the library-design processes of [three] recently completed branch libraries ... in the Greater Vancouver area of British Columbia' reveals some interesting information.[50] In the planning of one library of 1,394m^2 and two of 557m^2, the following factors were observed.

- Librarians spoke more 'about the need for personal flexibility, compromise and diplomacy', and that there were different agendas amongst planning participants.
- 'Architects emphasised the need for a strong, singular vision ... [and] rarely spoke about team dynamics'.
- 'The librarians' lack of knowledge about the building planning process lessened their ability to assume a strong role in the process ... but they were very aware of the importance of participating.'
- There was a difference over the value of library visits; architects saw the dangers in a 'wish list' approach and preferred 'creating fresh, innovative interpretations ... that would make a personal statement'.
- Architects concentrated on form (the 'look') and the exterior, while librarians tended to focus on 'use', the library's place in society, and the interior. If librarians neglected the design of the exterior and architects the interior, because the furniture and its layout were largely the province of a supplier, such neglect could be to the building's overall disadvantage.

The case study reveals two crucial similarities – both professions shared the excitement of the creative process 'and a mutual appreciation of each other's skills and commitment'.[51] Nevertheless the case study is also disheartening in that it reflects almost stereotypical attitudes of the architect/librarian dialogue, as well as revealing a lack of preparation on the part of librarians, and a library building 'by wish list' or 'by numbers' approach.

THE LIBRARY BUILDINGS CONSULTANT

Although customary in the US, the employment of a library buildings consultant for public library buildings is not usual in the UK. Consultants are usually librarians who have had personal experience of library building projects and can be formally hired in that capacity. The arguments in their favour are that they can be objective, give the necessary time, bring a wide experience to the project, have a good knowledge of what information the architect requires, and can understand and evaluate architects' proposals and plans. Of particular value is their ability to act as an expert interpreter between the library and architectural professions.[52]

There are, therefore, considerable benefits to employing a consultant throughout a project, but he/she can also be engaged to carry out one or more of the following tasks:

- evaluate an existing library building and recommend changes
- participate in the pre-planning stage
- assist in writing the architect's brief
- assist in the selection of the site
- review the architect's design proposals – from concept to floor plans
- advise on the selection and layout of library furniture and equipment
- inspect the building occasionally during construction
- help with the 'takeover' of the building
- carry out post-occupancy evaluation.

> Today's building consultant must be knowledgeable of the requirements for the installation of computers and other new technology, in addition to the traditional planning of functional areas, access for the handicapped, and the esthetics of modern buildings.[53]

Knowledgeable is the right word, for detailed expert advice will come from a computer specialist. The library consultant's job includes understanding the functional, spatial and ergonomic implications of ICT provision.

THE INTERIOR DESIGNER

The architect may design the interior of the building or this may be left to an interior designer from within or from outside the architectural practice. If from outside the practice and picked by the client, then much the same process and criteria as for the selection of the architect can be used. The chosen interior designer must demonstrate an appreciation of the purpose of the public library and understand the nature of the image the librarian wants it to project. They should therefore be knowledgeable about modern library service as well as trends in interior design.

It is expected that the interior designer's design proposals will harmonize with, indeed enhance, that of the architect. For as the architect Andrea Michaels has written:

> Only by choosing a talented architect and interior designer can a uniform, beautiful environment be created out of the complexity of a modern library interior.[54]

Importantly, Michaels suggests that memories of a library building are mostly of the inside and that interior designers can 'have much to do with how patrons perceive the library and its services'.[55] Interior designers can be called upon, for instance, to:

- design special items of furniture not available as standard
- coordinate and organize visual communication – signage, colour schemes, graphics, display facilities and lighting

- specify finishes and fabrics
- select works of art.

There is no doubt that those few UK public libraries that have employed an interior designer for such matters as space identification, colour schemes and graphics are rewarded by an interior above the ordinary – Wavelengths (London, Lewisham), Stratford (London, Newham) Anniesland (Glasgow) and Lowestoft (Suffolk), for example. All too often, without the services of an interior designer, librarians make do with inoffensive colour finishes and a conservative choice of standard library furniture, which, with some imagination, might be enhanced by a degree of customizing. Often there is a distinct contrast between the imaginative architecture of a public library exterior and the rather bland feel of the interior that neither offends nor excites.

THE DESIGN TEAM

The team approach to the planning and design of a library means that various individuals will join the architect's design team, such as the library consultant and interior designer, as and when is appropriate. At various stages in the process, this can also include the librarian and other library staff (the project librarian, for example), representatives of user groups, a building cost consultant, structural, mechanical and electrical engineers, the contractor, computer systems specialist, and suppliers of library shelving, furniture and equipment. In large projects there may be also a separate library building team, allowing representation of and input from library staff into the planning and design process. Input is needed in particular from those responsible for specialist services, such as children or local studies, and who will want to make certain that their views are taken into account in both the library and design team. The link between the two teams (design and library), and represented on both, is the librarian, together with those library staff (the project librarian, for example) with responsibility for the oversight and progress of the scheme.

DESIGN STAGE

This is the stage at which the brief becomes the library building – if only on paper or computer screen. It is composed of three main steps, the first being the preparation of sketch plans (or schematic designs). These allow the architect to investigate, try out and amend various building forms, orientation and internal arrangements for the library within the known site and other constraints. Sketch drawings will cover, therefore, site and floor plans, cross-sections and elevations, and may be produced for one or more options. Particular issues at this point will concern, for example, pedestrian, vehicular and disabled access, the relationship of the library to the surrounding built environment, and the number of floors and entrances. Eventually agreement will be reached with the librarian (the client) as to which of the alternative options best meets the requirements of the brief.

Sketch plans are followed by scheme or design development work which looks in detail at structural systems, heating, ventilation and air conditioning (HVAC), lighting, electrical services, cabling and wiring for ICT, floor, wall and ceiling finishes, types of windows, doors, fixtures, and shelving, furniture and equipment layouts. It should be stressed that a high degree of involvement from the librarian and other staff (and consultant, if employed) is required at this stage, reviewing drawings and examining samples of material, furniture and shelving. The librarian should assure themselves that the qualities demanded of the building (such as flexibility, energy conservation, ICT provision and barrier-free access) continue to be present at this design development phase. As discussed in the next chapter, the librarian needs to be skilled in reading drawings, recognizing symbols (for example, for electrical outlets) and visualizing how the building will work. Once agreed, the brief should not be altered after this juncture. At this stage the work of the interior designer (if employed separately from the architect) should begin.

Working drawings – detailed floor plans, cross sections and elevations – bring the design stage to a close. These are used by the building contractor to erect the library and cover every part and component of the structure. Where not the responsibility of the architect, specialists will provide drawings for structural, mechanical, electrical and computer systems, and landscaping and interior design schemes. The architect's working drawings are accompanied by written specifications which describe the exact materials, systems, products and their installation, and so on, to be used in the building. Similar specifications will be provided by the specialist consultants.

The preparation of drawings invariably makes use of computer-aided design (CAD), which can also be used to plan lighting, the use of colour, and furniture in the library building.[56] Furniture suppliers will offer a layout planning design service and, using CAD, will enable the librarian to see how the layout will work in practice and how items of furniture appear in situ.[57]

Following this design work, bills of quantities – statements of the quality and quantity of all the materials to be used and accompanied by specific pricing – are prepared. Tenders are called for from builders (indicating at what cost the tendering contractors can construct the building), and one tender is accepted and the contract awarded. The contract may include the provision of shelving, for example, thereby having the main contractor responsible for access to the site, the successful installation of equipment, and so on.

CONSTRUCTION STAGE

The management of a project requires excellent planning and control, and is particularly complex for a large building. Sophisticated techniques, such as computerized project management, will be necessary. Phases in the erection of the library building can be summarized as follows:

- foundations
- structure
- enclosure – creating the building shell
- services
- finishes
- furniture and fittings.

The librarian should watch the progress of the building, as the design becomes a physical reality that now can be understood more fully. Permission should be sought to visit the site, where the librarian must identify themselves, respect safety requirements, not touch anything nor interfere, but take all problems up with the architect. Where problems arise, change may be possible at an insignificant cost or none at all; where absolutely necessary they have to be executed regardless of cost.[58]

MOVING IN AND MAKING THE BUILDING OPERATIONAL

Moving in suggests one of three scenarios:

1. Moving new furniture, shelving, equipment, book stock and other materials into a completely new building. Furniture, shelving and equipment can be moved directly into the library but the book and other stock will need preparation at another location before being moved into the building. Most new libraries have more stock than in a previous building and just-in-time delivery from the bookseller is ideal, although this presents certain logistical problems as regards receipt, and so on. Alternatively new stock can be delivered in advance of the library opening – acceptable for the classics but less so for stock in-the-news. The timing of orders is therefore critical in relation to the building's completion date, although there is usually a gap between the completion date and the formal handover of the building.
2. Moving library stock from an old building into a new library, possibly from more than one location, and merging it with new stock. The move may include some items of old furniture, shelving and equipment for use in the new library. Unwanted items may be sold or, by agreement, left behind for the building's new occupants.
3. The movement – possibly more than once – of stock, furniture, shelving and equipment within a building to allow for either refurbishment, remodelling or an extension, or possibly all of these. It is likely that this will also involve replacement and additions to stock, shelving and other items of furniture and equipment.

Moving a library ... is a mammoth task that requires precise long-range planning. Moving the library's collection is particularly demanding and requires a specialized methodology.[59]

This stage of the building process, however, is about more than moving in book and other stock and installing furniture, shelving and equipment. In making the building ready for its library users and staff, the following matters, listed in Figure 7.7, need to be considered. Two of these (moving the library's stock and installing computer systems) are given more detailed treatment below. Depending on the size of the library six to twelve months' planning time may be needed.[60]

- Installing furniture and equipment
- Moving the collection and the requisition and the shelving of new stock
- Computer systems and other machinery installed, tested and made operational – telephone and data lines should be ready to be activated on the move date
- Staff familiarization programmes – building, equipment and procedures
- New and changed services and facilities require the formulation of new policies, regulations, rules and procedures
- Anticipating extra use
- Arranging for dedication and opening ceremony[61]
- Publicizing the new facility – preparation of printed and website information
- Planning for visits by librarians, architects and other interested parties

---

Figure 7.7   Moving in and making the building operational

MOVING THE LIBRARY STOCK

Depending upon the size of the task, moving the library's stock may need the appointment of a move director and a move committee to advise and support the director. In a very large library there may be also a number of committees responsible for particular parts of the move. In the move into the Birmingham Central Libraries in 1973, each department had a move-coordinating officer. This move involved bringing together material from ten bookstores in various parts of Birmingham into the new library.[62] As throughout any project, the need for planning – indeed early planning – needs to be emphasized for a move. A basic requirement is to understand the scale of the task and 'to generate an accurate inventory of existing and projected collection holdings'.[63] Other matters will include determining how long the move will take, investigating the use of computer software to assist in planning the move (the use of a spreadsheet collection allocation model, for example), and publicizing details of the move.[64] These matters are part of the planning issues described below.

- The scale of the task – determining the number of volumes and other library materials to be moved – should be known from the architect's brief: professional movers, however, will be more interested in knowing the scale of the task in terms of linear metres or feet.

- Selecting the movers – these could be library staff or other personnel, temporary staff (hired for the task) or volunteers. For all but the smallest moves, however, professional library movers are preferred, as they are specialist experts and also insurance and health and safety issues can pose problems when using the other groups noted above.[65] For large libraries, two companies may be employed, one to move library stock, the other to move shelving, furniture and equipment.
- Selecting the time – this is usually when the slackest period for the library occurs; librarians will try to avoid major interruptions to service; staff and users should be kept informed if material is to be temporarily unavailable.
- Selecting a method for the move – library moves have been carried out by hand, using book trolleys or special equipment, but the most widely used method is packing items into boxes or crates. For a do-it-yourself move involving hiring crates, their size, strength, ease of handling and the protection they afford, along with cost, will all be important. Professional library movers will, of course, provide their own crates. A trial run of the chosen method could be helpful in improving the method and resolving problems.
- Arranging transportation – deciding what is needed to transport material from one part of a building to another, or from one site to another, and whether there is a need for ramps, and so on: professional movers will naturally provide their own transport.
- Allocating responsibilities – as noted above, a move director, a committee (or committees), and move coordinators, as appropriate.
- Preparing written instructions – these would include dates or times for moving (13 weeks were allowed for the Birmingham move in 1973); a system for marking containers and shelves, that might involve colour coding; the creation of stock layout plans (material may be organized differently in the new location and it may be decided that shelves will be partially filled and/or some left empty); decisions as to the order of the move (Birmingham filled from the bottom of the building upwards, allowing early use of lower floors).
- Preparing for the move – clean and weed stock and deal with conservation issues.
- Preparing the new location for the move – clean shelves; mark up new location; place bookends to allow half to a third shelf occupation if required or alternatively leave bottom and top shelves vacant.

INSTALLING COMPUTER SYSTEMS

The authors of *Planning for integrated systems and technologies* note the key events in implementing a system. These include hardware and software installation, system training, acceptance testing, going live (leading to the library's acceptance that the system works as it should), and finally a declaration that the system is operational. The writers record the need for 'a detailed plan and schedule for implementing the system ... a consultant or project manager to help guide your library during the implementation phase'. An implementation plan agreed with the system vendor will involve:

- the key events
- who is responsible for the events – the library, the vendor, or both
- when the events will take place.[66]

UP AND RUNNING

Part of the final stage in creating a library will include planning for the opening, preparing publicity and organizing tours for local people, visiting librarians and other interested parties.[67]

This chapter has provided a planning and design framework to help the librarian understand and confidently take part in the stages involved in creating a public library building. While the perfect and ideal library will never result, because all planning and design necessitates compromise due to constraints imposed by site and funding, for example, this should not prevent the librarian planning from an ideal standpoint. A good library building depends not just on adequate funding and a good site, but on a librarian who can satisfactorily articulate the purpose of the proposed building and the needs of those who will use it. The architect is then able to design a building to respond to that purpose and user needs, and a builder is employed capable of construction work of a high standard. Library design is of critical importance in making 'tangible statements about the role of the library in the 21st century'.[68]

Earlier in this chapter the outline of the contents of a brief included a section devoted to describing the design qualities of the proposed library building. This important feature of the brief forms a major part of the next chapter, which will also consider 'qualities' to be avoided. Assessing whether these desirable qualities have been achieved – and undesirable ones avoided – will be part of the post-occupancy evaluation of the public library building. This and other forms of evaluation used during the planning and design process form the second part of the following chapter.

NOTES

1   Wheeler, J.L. and Githens, A.M. (1941), *The American public library building*, Chicago: American Library Association, 13.
2   'Council windfall dooms library', *Library + information update* **3** (12), 5.
3   Kniffel, L. (1991), 'Sacramento's $20 million gem can't afford to open on time', *American libraries* **22** (6), 475. Library's opening postponed six months due to budget problems.
4   Williamsburg Regional Library (2001), *Library construction from a staff perspective*, Jefferson, North Carolina: McFarland, Chapter 3, 'Renovating old', 48–63.
5   Eley, J. (2003), *Creating excellent buildings: a guide for clients*, London: CABE.
6   Holt, R. (1990), *Wisconsin library building project handbook*, 2nd rev. edn by A.C. Dahlgren, Madison, Wisconsin: Department of Public Instruction, Chapter 1: 'Creating improved library facilities – an

overview'; Martin, R.G. (ed.) (1992), *Libraries for the future, planning buildings that work*, Chicago: American Library Association, 'Outline of the building, planning process', 14–29; Thompson, G. (1989), *Planning and design of library buildings*, 3rd edn, London: Butterworth Architecture, Chapter 3: 'Begin at the beginning', 20–32, which gives a table from the architect's point of view.

7   Eley, J. (2003), 68–9.

8   Briggs, M.S. (1959*), Everyman's concise encyclopaedia of architecture*, London: Dent, 107.

9   Much of this section is covered in Dewe, M. (ed.) (1989), *Library buildings: preparations for planning*, Munich: Saur.

10   *The public library service: IFLA/UNESCO guidelines for development* (2001), Munich: Saur, 24–5, 78–9. See also Zauha, J., Samson, S. and Christin, C. (2001), 'Relevancy and libraries in the consumer age', *PNLA quarterly* **66** (1), 8–14.

11   Pateman, J. (2003), *Developing a needs-based library service*, Leicester: National Institute of Adult Continuing Education (England & Wales), 2.

12   Gee, P.D. (1989), 'Market research for the planning of library buildings: assessing user needs', in *Library building: preparations for planning*, edited by M. Dewe, Munich: Saur, 63–76: 63.

13   Cheshire Libraries and Museums (1978), *Runcorn District Library market research study*, Chester: Cheshire County Council.

14   Gee, P.D. (1989), 64.

15   Cheshire Libraries and Museums (1985), *The Cheshire library survey. 1: New town: new library*, Chester: Cheshire County Council.

16   Wills, H. (2004), 'An innovative approach to reaching the non-learning public: the new Idea Stores in London', in *Libraries as places: buildings for the 21st century* edited by M-F. Bisbrouck and others, Munich: Saur, 103–16: 104.

17   Wills, H. (2004), 108.

18   Wills, H. (2004), 116.

19   Roberts, N. (1986), 'The Cheshire Library Survey in the context of public library user studies', in *What kind of library? A seminar of the Cheshire Library Survey and its implications*, Boston Spa: British Library, 41.

20   Astill, M. (2004), 'Who wants to be consulted?', *Public library journal* Autumn, 9–10. Used by Warwickshire Library & Information Service with other consultation methods for a modernization programme.

21   Nesbitt, H. and Nield, B.V. (2000), *People places: a guide for public library buildings in New South Wales*, Sydney: Library Council of New South Wales, 20–33. This publication is summarized in Jones, D. (2001), 'People places: public library buildings for the new millennium', *Australasian public libraries and information services* **14** (3), 81–9.

22   Hammond, H. (1996), 'Norfolk and Norwich Central Library: the emerging phoenix', *New library world* **97** (1130), 24–31: 29.

23   Baget-Juleff, K. and Miscamble, L. (2003), 'Vibrant places – people spaces: a vision for Camden Council Library Service 2010', *Australasian public libraries and information services* **16** (4) 156–68.

24   Ledger, M. (2003), 'Connecting its community: the Cambridge Library building Western Australia', *Australasian public libraries and information services* **16** (3), 100–109: 103–5.

25   Shirane, K (2004), 'Library that started together with local residents' (in Japanese), *Toshokan Zasshi* **98** (1), 28–30.

26   www.birmingham.gov.uk/lob.

27   Nankivell, C. (2003), 'Consultation involvement in the Library of Birmingham', *Library and information research* **27** (85), 26–36.

28   Bryson, J., Usherwood, B. and Proctor, R. (2003), *Libraries must also be buildings? New library impact study*, London: Resource, 8.

29   Dewe, M. (1989), 'The documentation of library building activity at the national and international level', in *Library building: preparations for planning*, edited by M. Dewe, Munich: Saur, 77–87.

30   www.designinglibraries.org.uk.

31   Adapted from Langmead, S. and Beckman, M. (1970), *New library design*, Toronto: Wiley, 42.

32   Leather D.J. (1990), 'How the focus group technique can strengthen the development of a building program', *Library administration & management* **4** (2), 92–5.

33   Faulkner-Brown, H. (1972), 'The initial brief for an academic library and its development', in *Colloquium on university library buildings, 1971*, Birmingham: Ligue des bibliothèques europeénnes de recherche, 13–27. Although Faulkner-Brown is writing about university library buildings, these can equate in size to a large public library.

34   For a succinct account, see Kaser, D. (1991), *Preparing the building program document*, The Hague: IFLA Section on Library Buildings and Equipment.

35   A detailed contents list for an architect's brief is given in Holt, R.M. (1989), *Planning library buildings and facilities: from concept to completion*, Metuchen, New Jersey: Scarecrow, 219–25.

36   Finney, L.C. (1984), 'The library building program: key to success', *Public libraries* **23** (3), 80–81.

37   Mayo, D. and Nelson, S. (1999), *Wired for the future: developing your library technology plan*, Chicago: American Library Association. The quotation is taken from page xiv. See also Vaughan, J. (2002), 'Preparing for technology: systems planning and implementation in Lied Library', *Library hi tech* **20** (1), 33–46.

38   Batt, C. (1997), 'Designing freedom, *Public library journal* **12** (4), 88–91.

39   'CILIP takes the lead with WiFi conference' (2004), *Library + information gazette* 3 December, 1–2.

40   Langmead and Beckman (1970), 49.

41   The control of capital and maintenance costs was the subject of the 9th Seminar on Library Buildings organized by the IFLA Section on Library Buildings and Equipment, Bordeaux, 1989. The seminar papers remain unpublished but copies are held at the Thomas Parry Library, University of Wales Aberystwyth.

42   To assist in this process the RIBA issues *Guidance notes for clients*; quotations in this section are taken from this document. See also www.ribacompetitions.com.

43   Natale, J. (1991), 'The jury is in: public library design competitions', *Illinois libraries* **73** (1), 90–94 92.

44   Natale, J. (1991), 90–94. (Matteson and Evanston public libraries).

45   Table adapted from Hemsley, R. and Lake, J. (1995), 150.

46   Hemsley, R. and Lake, J. (1995), 'Inviting designs', *Library Association record* **97** (3), 150–51; Spetz, E. (2002), 'Oslo public library looks for an architect', *Scandinavian public library quarterly* **35** (3), 8–9.

47   Waters, R.L. (2001), 'So, design me a box – part three', *Public library quarterly* **20** (3), 29–37.

48   Jones, D.J. (1994), 'Picking a winner: the selection of a design team for a library project', *Australian library journal* **43** (1), 28–34.

49   Jones, D.J. (1994), 34.

50   Curry, A. and Henriquez, Z. (1998), 'Planning public libraries: the views of architects and librarians', *Library administration & management* **12** (2) 80–90.

51   All case study quotes are from Curry, A. and Henriquez, Z. (1998), 88–9.

52   Thompson, G. (1989), *Planning and design of library buildings*, 3rd edn, London: Butterworth, 24–5.

53   Parker, J.S. (ed.) (1986), *Information consultants in action*, London: Mansell, 112.

54   Michaels, A.(1987), 'Design today: [the role of the interior designer]', *Wilson library bulletin* **61** (6), 34–5,79: 79.

55   Michaels, A. (1987), 34.

56   Bengtson, J. and Bell, T. (2001), 'Building design made easy', *Library Association record* **103** (1), 42–3.

57   'See before you buy with new design service' (2004), *Library + information gazette* 5 November, 3.

58   Carroll, R.E. (1987), 'Building a library: the librarian/architect relationship', *New Zealand libraries* **45** (5), 85–9: 89.

59   Habich, E.C. (1998), *Moving library collections: a management handbook*, Westport, Connecticut: Greenwood, vii.

60   Woodward, J. (2000), *Countdown to a new library: managing the building project*, Chicago: American Library Association, 190.

61   Williamsburg Regional Library (2001), 105–16.

62   Wright, D. (*c.* 1973), *On the move of Birmingham Central Libraries*, Birmingham: Birmingham Public Libraries.

63   Habich, E.C. (1998), viii.

64   The library move is dealt with succinctly in the booklet by McDonald, A. (1994), *Moving your library*, London: Aslib. Book-length later monographs include: Tucker, D.C. (1999*), Library relocations and*

collection shifts, Medford, New Jersey: Information Today, and Wells, M.S. and Young, R. (1997), *Moving and reorganizing a library*, Aldershot: Gower.

65 Tanner, S. (1993), 'Help the removal company to help you', *Aslib information* **21** (1), 18.

66 Cohn, J.M., Kelsey, A.L. and Fiels, K.M. (2002), *Planning for integrated systems and technologies*, 2nd edn. adapted for UK by D. Salter, London: Facet, 110–12.

67 Hagloch, S.B. (1994), *Library building projects: tips for survival*, Englewood, Colorado: Libaries Unlimited, 51–69.

68 Bryson, J., Usherwood, B. and Proctor, R. (2003), *Libraries must also be buildings? New library impact study,* London: Resource, 8.

8 Key qualities in design and evaluation

Post-occupancy evaluations of buildings ask questions and provide answers on how buildings actually work in technical, social and management terms for the end-users.

Suzanne Enright, 2002[1]

In preparing the architect's brief, the librarian will want to describe the qualities that they would expect to find in the finished building. The formulation of those qualities might be based on the 'ten commandments' drawn up by Harry Faulkner-Brown, the architect of the much praised 1960s Jesmond Branch Library, Newcastle upon Tyne, and a number of university library buildings at Nottingham, Loughborough, Newcastle and elsewhere. Andrew McDonald, although writing about academic libraries in the late 1990s, says that Faulkner-Brown's 'commandments' are still 'relevant to planning good libraries today' but that 'some of the words now have rather different meanings and that emphases have changed considerably' and so he offers a new version of the 'commandments'. Both Faulkner-Brown and McDonald's versions of these dictums are discussed in detail later.

As well as guiding planning and design, these desirable library building characteristics might also be used as an evaluation tool, along with other methodologies as appropriate, during and after the building project. Equally, 'key issues' intended as a tool for the evaluation of completed library facilities might also be used to help in their planning and design. These 'key issues', devised by two American architects, L.H. Schneekloth and E.B. Keable, also include a concern for the important matter of 'managing the processes of change' – change being a major feature of any library building project. The design quality indicator (DQI) assessment methodology, that looks at build quality, functionality, and impact, can be used also to evaluate the library building, as well as helping with the brief, for example.[2]

Knowing what to avoid when creating a library building is perhaps as important as knowing what a building's good qualities should be. The 'seven deadly sins of public library architecture', presented at the Public Library Association's national conference in the US in 1998, provide guidance as to what librarians might wish to evade in their libraries. This approach, advanced also by some other commentators, can be used also to help with planning and design and later with the evaluation of the physical facility.

Evaluation of one kind or another can occur at a number of stages in the creation of a library building: assessing the old building; reviewing and analysing the architect's drawings, and to correct building faults, for example, as well as carrying out a post-occupancy evaluation (POE). This latter process has been described as dealing 'with the physical and social aspects of the building and the relationship between the two'[3] – in other words, whether the building works for and pleases its users. However, post-occupancy evaluation, whether soon after opening or at a later date, does not appear to be a common practice: 'It is ... unusual for anyone to take a formal look at how the building works and then share that information with a broader community'.[4]

THE 'TEN COMMANDMENTS': DESIGN QUALITIES FOR LARGE LIBRARIES

Faulkner-Brown has suggested that a large library building, whatever its type, should have the following ten desirable qualities:

- *flexible* – with layout, structure and services which are easy to adapt
- *compact* – for economy of movement of readers, staff and books
- *accessible* – from the exterior into the building and from the entrance to all parts of the building, with an easily comprehensible plan needing minimum supplementary directions
- *extendible* – to permit future growth, with minimum disruption
- *varied* – in its provision of book accommodation and of reader services, to give wide freedom of choice
- *organized* – to impose appropriate confrontation between books and readers
- *comfortable* – to promote efficiency of use
- *constant in environment* – for the preservation of library materials
- *secure* – to control user behaviour and loss of books
- *economic* – to be built and maintained with minimum resources both in finance and staff.[5]

Earlier versions of these 'commandments', which have been in use since the 1970s, had a slightly different wording and the tenth was originally 'indicative of use' rather than 'economic'. This change reflecting perhaps the difficulties of achieving the former and the ongoing significance of the latter. Anyway, the 'eleven commandments' doesn't quite have the same ring.

In brief, the qualities described by the 'ten commandments' result in an open-plan library, preferably a cube in shape (to reduce travel distances in the building), with an easy and identified route from the entrance and on to the main elements of the building without needing too much signage. The library's site and construction should facilitate an extension, planned in advance so as to extend easily the original design. Faulkner-Brown writes of his 'commandments' that some 'can be bent, some diluted, but this one should not be abandoned'.[6]

Discussions of the library's interior organization in a later chapter will cover the 'varied' and 'organized' qualities and it is hard to believe that modern libraries can be anything but 'comfortable', but this may be so if there is unsatisfactory heating, ventilation, air conditioning and lighting. The preservation of library materials, except in the broadest sense, is not a major issue in the many public libraries without significant reserve or historical collections. Their long-term preservation, however, depending on the different formats involved, suggests different conditions to the constant climate proposed by the 'commandment' for the main body of the library.

If a building is to be economic, as Faulkner-Brown suggests, running costs can be assisted by ensuring that the ratio of wall area to floor area is low (another argument for the cubic form), by small window openings, with the total window area not exceeding 25 per cent of the total wall area, plus wall and roof thermal insulation.

THE TEN COMMANDMENTS REVISITED

McDonald's new list of nine (rather than ten) qualities is clearly based on a revision of those proposed by Faulkner-Brown.[7] Although concerned with academic libraries, McDonald acknowledges the relevance of his qualities to public library buildings. In his version of the 'commandments', which aims to create libraries that are functional, easy to use and economical to operate, these qualities are described as:

- *adaptable* – flexible space, the use of which can easily be changed
- *accessible* – social space which is inviting, easy to use, and promotes independence
- *varied* – with a choice of learning environment and between different media
- *interactive* – well-organized space which promotes contact between users and services
- *conducive* – high-quality 'humane' space which inspires people
- *environmentally suitable* – with appropriate conditions for readers, books and computers
- *safe and secure* – for people, collections, equipment, data and the building
- *efficient* – economic in space, staffing, and running costs
- *suitable for information technology* – with flexible provision for users and staff.

Of the two versions of the 'commandments', Faulkner-Brown shows an equal concern for materials and readers but with less mention of staff. McDonald shows more concern for people generally (users and staff) and their environment.

The main new elements introduced by McDonald relate to the human and inspirational aspects of the library building (what he calls its conducive quality), greater recognition of different media, and the facility's suitability for technology. The inspirational quality he attributes to the result of such matters as imaginative architecture, varied internal spaces, the provision of works of art, and the control of noise. Suitability for technology, according to McDonald, implies a cabling infrastructure that enables a fully networked computer with an appropriate environment anywhere in the library building, but he recognizes the design tensions and problems that may result.

With some additional requirements, that the building be civic (to demonstrate its status through design), that art be featured and the premises 'retail'-oriented, the above qualities form a major component of the 2003 brief for the Castle Cary Library (Somerset). In France, a 1992 law requires that buildings be compact, flexible, offer ample space for multimedia, and their use by a varied and regular flow of users. These principles are demonstrated, for instance, in the public library at Reims – the Médiathèque Cathédrale (6,716m^2).[8] The city library of The Hague (1995) was designed round a version of Faulkner-Brown's ten commandments,[9] which have some similarity to the French requirements.

In his detailed discussion of his nine qualities, McDonald also brings out many issues of concern to library planners, such as the questioning of flexibility, good provision for staff and users with disabilities, the use of natural ventilation, and the challenge posed by ICT. In writing about library qualities both authors are more seemingly concerned with economic space provision rather than adequate or even generous provision. *Better public libraries* also advances a number of design qualities that introduce other factors such as appearance, context, and continuity and enclosure, that place the library building within its local surroundings.[10] These aspects are addressed elsewhere in this book.

FLEXIBILITY

Of all these ten qualities, librarians will invariably require that the library be flexible – almost above all else – believing that this permits future change through the reorganization and interchange of the interior spaces of the library for readers, staff, library materials and equipment. The resulting open plan also allows for self-service and the economic deployment of staff. However, there is little published evidence that the advantages of an open-plan building are fully utilized and result in a radical reorganization and exchange of library space. The cost of complete flexibility, including that for ICT, is likely to add to the cost of the library and the cost-benefit of such flexibility might be questioned if that flexibility is under-used, not utilized or proved later to be mistaken.

Phoenix Library interior (Arizona, 1995) has an industrial look to it, as wires hang from the ceiling. Subfloor wiring races (as installed at Chicago and San Francisco) permit changes, but Phoenix's architect thought this too costly and would require furniture to be moved. This was a part of a commitment to a low-cost but flexible structure.[11]

220

Visually, the absence of interior walls can create large barn-like interiors, which, in the interests of an economic layout and standardized furniture, can be uniform, regimented and overcrowded, and not as distinctive as the architecture that might enclose them. With more imagination much more could be done to make open-plan library interiors more varied, interesting and attractive.[12] Fixed-function library buildings, while not perhaps contemplated today, make for more interesting and varied interiors, and old fixed-function libraries have been capable of spatial change and reorganization. Interestingly, the San Antonio Public Library (1995, 22,110m^2) was constructed as a series of small, connected rooms and designed to encourage visitors to wander from one intimate area to another.[13]

Nevertheless there is no doubt about the advantage of an open-plan library from a staffing economy point of view, although unstaffed parts of large floors (or indeed complete floors) are hardly the sign of proactive library and information work. However, strategically placed information points linked to a staffed desk can help here.

A review of a collection of mid-1990s symposium papers on UK academic libraries and those in other countries said that attempting to guess the future in a rapidly changing technological world was a linking theme: 'as much flexibility as possible while trying to avoid producing a bland shoebox' was the usual requirement, although there is recognition that this is not easily achieved and that 'flexibility is no longer the unquestioned goal in all cases'.[14]

How can we plan for the future? The uncertainty has increased the emphasis on flexibility, a quality stressed by all library planners. Flexibility is not cost-free, however, and there is a danger that such flexibility, as noted above, will be under-used or not used at all. The desire for such all-pervading flexibility results from the mistaken view that the library buildings are always built to last and many are not. It demonstrates also, perhaps, a lack of decision-making, and an attempt to second-guess the unknown, as well as an inability to acknowledge that, as in nature, natural selection operates in respect of buildings. Future generations will decide what it is about a building that merits its ongoing use or its replacement.

EXTENDIBILITY

Faulkner-Brown states that the one 'commandment' that should not be abandoned was extendibility, and that the library building should be so sited and designed so as to be capable of extension. He had academic library buildings in mind, it is thought, when making this statement and a historian of American public library buildings wrote in the early 1990s that since 1946 only a few libraries had been planned for future extension, although a few had been built in phases, as in the UK. The library historian also thought that the placement and design of modern libraries made later extensions problematical and costly.[15]

Where a library building is planned for future extension, it can be achieved in a number of ways:

- linear expansion – extending the building on one or more sides, site permitting
- in-filling – filling in courtyards or other parts of a building's form
- vertical expansion – the library is designed to be structurally strong enough to take one or more additional levels
- overbuilding – building more space than is required at present and renting it out until needed
- underground expansion – where the preservation of adjacent open space is in force.

A few UK public library buildings have been deliberately designed to be built in phases: Bexley Central Library was designed and built in two phases in 1980 (982m²) and 1989 (1,000m²). A further extension (phase 3) can be constructed on the top of the existing building and a phase 4 is possible.[16] Additional phases may not be solely for library purposes: phase 2 of Thurrock's Central Library (1972) was for a theatre and museum;[17] Kidderminster Library (1997) has been constructed so that an arts building can be added at a later stage.

But for many modern public libraries, locations in a high street or within shopping centres mean the ability to extend may not be possible, unless adjacent redundant retail space can be acquired, into which the library can spread. Older library buildings, located elsewhere, may be much better off in this respect. Interestingly, McDonald's revision of the 'commandments' makes no recommendation about the requirement for expansion.

SEVEN 'KEY ISSUES' FOR LIBRARY DESIGN

Research and a literature survey carried out in the early 1990s into major issues in library design, management and evaluation concluded 'that there [are] seven key issues that describe the comprehensive nature of these design considerations'.[18]

1. *Managing the process of change in library facilities*: from needs assessment to moving in; good management of change can increase the satisfaction of staff with the resulting building.
2. *Design issues*: describing the library's relationship to its physical and local authority context, flexibility, entry and control points, future changes in function and technology, building image, and so on.
3. *Resolution of public, private and interface functions*: areas for public access, secure and separate staff areas and areas for staff and user interactions at enquiry desks and issue counters, for example.
4. *Behaviour settings*: 'places such as study areas, circulation desks and staff workstations occupied by specific groups of people in which recurring and predictable patterns of behaviour occur ... Misfits between people, place and behaviour result in poor working conditions, discomfort, inefficiencies in building use, and other problems'.[19]

5. *Environmental controls*: 'lighting, temperature and humidity controls, noise, wiring, fire safety and security affect people's health and well-being, task performance, and material preservation'.[20]

6. *Interface with technology*: microform and computer technology require new types of space and infrastructure. Power and cabling, workstation ergonomics and lighting, for example, are influenced by ongoing changes in technology.

7. *Materials processing*: how library materials are acquired and processed through the organization and the building has implications for staff, space relationships and security.

These 'key issues' provide a fairly complete approach to the planning and design of the library building. In doing so they touch on many of the matters that are considered more fully elsewhere in this book, such as health and safety and preservation. In contrast to the 'commandments', they spell out in much more detail the many design issues that lie behind such broad headings as 'behaviour settings' and 'environmental controls'.

THE DESIGN QUALITIES FOR SMALLER LIBRARIES

In planning smaller libraries, the librarian must make a judgement as to which of the 'commandments' or 'key issues' are appropriate to a given planning situation. It is likely that issues relating to extendibility, preservation and materials processing, for example, are of less or no significance, although this will depend upon the size of the building as determined by the community and upon its role within the library service as a whole. Does it have administrative or storage remits, for example?

The following characteristics were specified by Lancashire Library Services for a new series of branch libraries designed in the 1980s:

- low construction costs
- low cost in use
- conservation of finite resources – such as maximization of free energy and light
- permanent construction, with a minimum useful life of 40 years
- robust – to combat vandalism
- inclusion of multi-purpose areas – enabling the overall library area to be reduced
- capability for combined use – normal library service plus additional activities
- fulfilment of minimum standards for library accommodation
- reflection of both unity (with the library service) and diversity (local needs).

These characteristics were summarized as

> ... a building low in construction and running costs but robust and flexible and capable of adaptation to local needs without loss of identification with the library service as a whole – i.e. unity with diversity.[21]

Some of these characteristics, such as robust nature, provision of multi-purpose areas, and reflection of unity and diversity are new to this discussion and are perhaps more appropriate to public library design than other elements in the Faulkner-Brown and McDonald lists. Others, like low construction and running costs, have much in common with Faulkner-Brown's 'ten commandments', although neither he nor McDonald mention standards, which are perhaps a planning tool rather than a quality.

All of the lists and 'keys' discussed so far provide a useful framework for the planning and design of a library building as discussed in the previous chapter. They could be used also later to help appraise and evaluate a proposed design solution and then the resultant physical structure itself.

THE 'SEVEN DEADLY SINS' OF PUBLIC LIBRARY ARCHITECTURE

In contradistinction to Faulkner-Brown's 'ten commandments', Fred Schlipf and John Moorman, two American librarians, compiled their 'seven deadly sins' of public library architecture in 1998, and an outline description of the 'sins' appears on the Web.[22] The compilers point out that their list (really a handout to accompany an illustrated lecture and giving just main headings and sub-headings) is not complete and records what they consider to be the most common mistakes. As they write:

> We haven't explained [on the website] why we think they are mistakes, how they can be avoided, and what can be done once the mistakes have been made.

The 'sins' quite naturally include some of the opposites to the 'commandments': inflexibility, bad security and complex maintenance. Two other transgressions are more specific, being concerned with bad lighting and insufficient work and storage space, both, as will be seen, frequent sources of complaint in libraries. Two final crimes, and ones not covered by the positive injunctions of the 'commandments', are bad location of the public library and what the authors call 'signature architecture', covering such matters as 'excess ceremonial space' and 'unexpected problems with untested architectural systems'.

While all the main headings covered by the 'sins' are important matters that need to be considered, either when choosing a site or preparing the architect's brief and during the design process, there is a danger that the detailed points in the list, devoid of context, are individual bad experiences that become prejudices and dogma. Skylights, architectural solutions to furniture problems, a location too close to schools, multiple entrances, and ornamental free-standing staircases might all pose problems or spell disaster. On the other hand they might lead to success and distinction in a given situation. Sometimes even librarians must take chances and support change and experimentation.

Maurice Line calls his collection of library 'sins' a users' 'hate list'. While mainly aimed at university and research libraries, there is universality about most of the points he makes. His hate list starts with 'the sacrifice of function to aesthetics (or just fads?)' and continues via poor signage, insufficient lifts, narrow stairs, cramped seats and too few toilets (and other 'hates') to 'drabness'.[23]

NEW BUILDING INADEQUACY

Over twenty years earlier, architects Elaine and Aaron Cohen had drawn attention to similar issues catalogued by the 'seven deadly sins'.[24] In their view new libraries quickly became inadequate because space was wasted on magnificent entrance halls, huge atriums and so on, which were stealing space from the collections, and because of architects' design concepts that overshadowed the purpose of the building: a return to the form and function debate of Chapter 2.

The Cohens draw attention once again to the lack of work and off-duty space for staff, commenting: 'they've donated their work space to the cause of architectural beauty'. They point to the simple fact that staff morale is tied to the day-to-day functioning of the library and that new buildings (usually bigger than the old one) require extra staff and extra space to house their activities. Without adequate space provision for these increases, the library returns 'to square one, but now in a bigger, newer and more expensive building'.[25]

Based on their findings in 1976, the Cohens concluded that American library buildings less than five years old were designed against human use; provided inadequate space; had poor circulation, and that the move to the new building did not justify the costs. Clearly people-centred places with good traffic flow patterns and with adequate (even generous) space provision would have qualities that would reflect the tenor of the ten or nine 'commandments', avoid at least many of the 'deadly sins', and go a long way to justify the investment in a new library.

The Cohens suggested, however, that problems outlined above could be avoided if all librarians, whether in old or new buildings, spent time in self-evaluation 'on an ongoing, thorough and systematic basis'. Checklists can be used and space inventories compiled for the children's library, staff offices, and so on, listing what needs improvement or immediate attention and at what costs. A thorough check of the building would cover:

- the physical structure, its condition and health and safety issues
- heating, ventilating and lighting
- use of space – the need to weed collections; unnecessary displays
- movement patterns
- vandalism and theft.

The Cohens's wide-ranging article concludes:

> There is no reason why so many library buildings in the United States should become inadequate so fast ... many could have a longer and more useful life if they were carefully evaluated and maintained on a systematic basis.[26]

The neglect and lack of maintenance of library buildings, particularly in the UK, are considered in Chapter 5.

EVALUATION OF THE BUILDING

As will be seen, evaluation can be taking place during the planning, design and construction process and, as emphasized in this chapter, in the post-construction period. Both qualitative (subjective) and quantitative (objective) information will be used, making use of people's views, standards, as well as verifiable and statistical measures. The following evaluative criteria have been suggested for libraries:

- space – books, equipment, staff, users
- flow – books, equipment, staff, users
- flexibility – adaptable, expandable
- environment – psychological, social, physical
- aesthetics – exterior, interior
- equipment – equipment, furniture
- cost – construction, maintenance, operation.[27]

The criteria, although formulated some time ago, reflect the fundamental requirements discussed in Chapter 2 and many of the more particular qualities described earlier in this chapter.

While one would not disagree with the Cohens' stress on the necessity of ongoing, systematic maintenance, formal evaluation cannot perhaps be treated in quite the same way as it requires a greater time lapse between evaluations; needs clear objectives; can involve outside experts, users and non-users, as well as staff; and might employ a variety of methodologies.

Evaluation might be applied at many stages in the process of creating a library in order to assess what is being proposed or has been achieved by a building project. *Better public libraries* advocates the use of design quality indicators (DQIs), noted earlier, also as an assessment methodology for evaluating the final building.[28] And most commonly evaluation is thought of in terms of evaluating the building when that process is complete and the library occupied and in use. Such post-occupancy evaluation (POE), except for the necessary correction of building and other faults, seems to be infrequently carried out, mainly because of the lack of time, money and the skills for the task. Project 'fatigue' and the risk of mistakes being revealed are other possible factors, as is the time that must elapse (at least a year) before a significant review can be carried out, and by then other jobs may be more pressing.[29] Given the scale of capital expenditure and the modern requirement for accountability, it is odd that funding authorities do not see this as an obligatory finale to the public library building project, for which a substantial budget has been allocated. Various kinds of planning and building evaluations are described below but with the emphasis on POE.

EVALUATION OF THE EXISTING BUILDING

Whatever its other defects, the desire for new or improved library accommodation is usually prompted by a lack of space for library materials, users and staff, a space deficiency which also prevents the implementation of desirable new facilities and services. It was suggested in Chapter 7 that part of the pre-planning stage should include a formal space assessment of the existing library building which 'documents those perceived deficiencies by comparing the present facility against present and future needs'.[30] The evaluation should not just be concerned with deficiencies and inadequacies but with identifying any good features the library may possess. As well as questions of space provision, it must be concerned also with the adequacy of building services, such as heating and lighting, and the image the building gives to library users, actual and potential. An evaluation of this kind helps strengthen the case for better provision of accommodation, enables a more informed approach to alternative paths, such as an extension or remodelling and refurbishment of the existing building, as well as helping with the writing of the architect's brief.

The *Checklist of library building design considerations* is a useful tool for this kind of evaluation, as one of its aims is 'to enable the evaluation of existing buildings as part of a library's Needs Assessment Process'.[31] The checklist helps, for example, in the evaluation of the existing library's site, as well as the exterior, interior organization and other matters, such as communications, building systems, and safety and security.

PLAN EVALUATION

Designing a library building from the architect's initial concept to the finished design results in drawings of increasing detail as the process runs its course. At each stage the librarian will want to review and evaluate the architect's proposed plans, which may include models, mock-ups and computer simulations, as well as drawings. The key document in this review is the librarian's brief because a judgement will be made as to how well this is reflected in the architect's design proposal for the library. As has been pointed out, plan evaluation is fundamentally an intellectual activity, as plans can never mirror the eventual human reaction to the physical presence of the library, although the reviewer may attempt to do so, for

> This is the opportunity to correct mistakes and to make sure that the building will be efficient and logical from both the staff and the users' perspectives.[32]

Depending upon the particular stage in the design process, the architect's plans may be reviewed by library staff (in particular those charged with managing the project), users' representatives, the general public and the funding authority.

The successful interpretation of library plans requires considerable practice, as well as getting used to using a ruler: examining the plans of an existing library building known to the reviewer can help this process. A full understanding of what the architect is proposing means that the librarian will need to see a complete set of plans (site, perspective, elevations and cross-sections), as this enables him/her to relate the building to its location, for example, and the exterior features of the library to the interior. When in doubt, however, about a plan and its interpretation, the architect should be asked for an explanation.

In reviewing the architect's plans, it is important in the early stages to ensure that the aesthetic aspects of the design are not detrimental to function[33] and that the architect's concept reflects an appropriate library image and purpose and the specified qualities (such as flexibility and accessibility) for the building.

Certain questions and issues will predominate the plan review process at the various stages of the design and these can include the following:

- Are all the required spatial elements of the stipulated size present?
- Are the specified spatial relationships, and the resultant traffic flow patterns, appropriate for library users, staff and materials?
- Are there any proposed building features that should be queried, discussed or rejected, such as apparent wasted space or narrow galleries, or ones that might pose possible maintenance difficulties?
- Can individual spaces accommodate the required shelving, furniture and equipment and have appropriate critical distances been observed?
- Where are electrical outlets located?

Computer-aided design (CAD) allows the librarian to view the building from any direction, permits a walk-through of the library, and enables the easy exploration of different layouts and the enlargement of plans for easier study. It is an important aid to plan review and evaluation, although its versatility can delay decision-making and its screen displays can seduce the evaluator. Where the furniture supplier also designs the library layout using CAD, there is the danger of it being designed to satisfy the supplier rather than the customer.

Andrea Michaels has compiled a checklist to be used as a guide for visiting libraries in the pre-planning process but says that it can be used for evaluating plans.[34] Its merit is its brevity (compared with the *Checklist* mentioned earlier) and the detail it adds to some of the questions noted above. It covers such topics as site, structure, architecture, finishes, signage and display. It also notes things to avoid – 'sins' such as unsupervised areas, and noisy areas near quiet ones.

POST-OCCUPANCY EVALUATION (POE)

This falls into two categories, formative and summative. Formative evaluation is concerned with improving and refining the new library building, does not usually involve structural or expensive alterations and is usually carried out by library staff. Summative evaluation, however, examines the effectiveness of the building, endeavouring to discover the reasons for its success or failure. It is usually carried out by independent assessors and for reasons of accountability may be a requirement of the funding authority. Additional aims will be the avoidance of mistakes in later buildings and to assist others planning new or other library building projects. Post-occupancy evaluations are usually found to have both formative and summative content.

Lushington and Kusack have described the preparation and planning (including clarification of purpose and objectives), and the tools (standards and statistics) and methodologies (questionnaires, observation and focus groups, for example) that might be employed for a POE. The authors note the need for the study to be impartial, objective, systematic and fair, and that it must result in practical recommendations for action. Finally it is recommended that the POE exercise itself be evaluated as a way of improving both the procedure and outcomes.[35]

In the UK the construction industry uses Post-Occupancy Review of Buildings and their Engineering (PROBE) methodology for post-occupancy evaluation, and the higher education sector uses Higher Education Design Quality Forum (HEDQF) methodology for evaluating academic buildings including libraries. There is no such formal appraisal methodology for public library buildings but, as noted in Chapter 2, libraries, including public libraries, may be evaluated by their inclusion and success in various award and prize schemes made by architectural associations, organizations concerned with the built environment and the library profession.

The SCONUL award scheme for academic libraries makes use of the 'ten commandments revisited' discussed earlier, but adds that the library should be 'functional (fit for purpose and facilitate delivery of the library's mission and services)'.[36] The criteria finishes with a kind of 'Wow' factor: 'a further indefinable quality which balances all these to provide inspiration and satisfaction, capturing the minds of those who use the library'.

The post-occupancy evaluation of some public library buildings in the UK is carried out by a judging panel of the Public Libraries Group of CILIP through its biennial, commercially sponsored Public Library Building Awards scheme. The panel takes a holistic view of the library building and its services within the community. Each self-nominated library is asked to supply information under a series of headings: site; exterior appearance, interior appearance and layout; accessibility; public services; ICT provision; furniture (including shelving and counter); non-public areas; mechanical, electrical and security systems; planning for future developments; and other special features. The headings allow librarians not only to provide facts but to offer explanation of design issues that were important for that particular building and describe innovatory features and services.

Shortlisted libraries are visited by the judges and the visits include discussions with the library staff and sometimes with users and the architect. This panel too looks for the

229

'Wow' effect in the libraries it visits. Presentation of the awards takes place at the annual Public Library Authorities Conference and usually provides an opportunity for members of the panel to say something about the social impact of public libraries and design trends. Adjudication is a difficult, sometimes contentious, but always a rewarding task, and awards do not always go to the 'obvious' candidates. The new categories for the award scheme, described in Chapter 2, will doubtless involve different criteria from those formerly used when judging the nominated libraries.

Library buildings in the United Kingdom 1990–94

A contribution to the evaluation of public library buildings has been made by the *Library buildings* series mentioned earlier. The third volume in its present format is in a series with origins in the 1940s. The 1990–94 volume, which includes academic libraries (not all earlier volumes did so), covers major refurbishments as well as new, extended and converted libraries, using a team of librarian reporters.[37]

For its five-year period, the volume lists a total of 325 projects (of which 103 are described) from 127 library authorities: 134 were entirely new buildings. The introduction remarks that there was 'every sign of effective partnership between architect and librarian'. The editor describes the trends of the period from CCTV to themed kinderboxes in children's libraries and stresses that the libraries chosen for description are only some of the best completed in the period.

While statistical and other basic information is supplied for each library in a standard format, the written accounts are not patterned on any particular set of criteria. Generally speaking these are descriptions and appreciations, rather than critiques, although occasional criticisms creep in. The series provides a valuable resource in that it is a conspectus of what can be achieved in designing public libraries of various sizes in a variety of locations.

CONTRACTOR AND SUPPLIER EVALUATION

Prior to opening and at the handover of the building by the contractor, it is probable that some things have not been completed on time and that some items of furniture and equipment have not been received.[38] Thompson writes that the librarians should receive a list of outstanding items from the architect and note their completion or arrival as the case may be. Record-keeping of a high standard is called for as considerable time can go by before everything has been dealt with.[39] The work could involve correcting obvious faults to the fabric and other elements of the building and fine-tuning operations. There will be equipment and building failures that will need the return of the contractor to correct and a call on warranties.

It will take a year or so to provide experience of all weather conditions that will enable fine-tuning of the building's heating, cooling and ventilation systems.

OTHER KINDS OF EVALUATION

User surveys have been a regular feature of public librarianship for many years and are probably one of the most used methods for a POE study. However, user surveys are often more concerned with the use made of the library service than the building, although sometimes this might feature as part of the survey.[40] A study of branch libraries in Cleveland in 1991 included users' suggestions for improvements to buildings and facilities, often about enlarging libraries and improving access.[41]

Today library users are often encouraged to make informal comments about the library service point that they use, including the building itself, by completing a suggestion form or making an entry in a suggestions or comments book, to which a reply will be posted.

Following completion and opening of a new building, the library may carry out a community impact assessment or report, which will be particularly concerned with monitoring the expected increased use. One of the most demanding jobs subsequent to a library opening, particularly in a major building, is dealing with the upsurge of new readers and a big increase in loans. And naturally much will be made of this success. An informal American study of 25 new main American libraries opened prior to 1982 showed an 44 per cent average increase in circulation: the highest was 127 per cent. Circulation does not necessarily plateau at the higher level – small libraries show bigger gains – and in some cases there may be impressive gains in subsequent years, although a building cannot count on sustaining such growth. There may also be an increase in the use of meeting rooms and the number of enquiries, for example.[42] In connection with the opening of San Francisco Public Library in 1996, for example, it was said that 'the successful opening of a new central facility can be overwhelming'.[43]

A 2003 UK new library impact study found that issues reached a peak or plateau 12–24 months after opening.[44] The task for the library is to sustain such increased use over time as the excitement of the new building abates.

An examination of borrower records will help determine whether a new building is attracting new users and usage figures show changes in the level of use of services. If this information shows 'the library coming closer to meeting community needs, the move was a success', otherwise; 'it's time to plan for another kind of change'.[45] Increased use, however, is only one measure of the impact of the public library. Impact standards in preparation in the UK are likely to focus also on widening participation, and the library's impact on individuals, communities, library authorities and national priorities.[46]

Outside the professional literature, building studies appear from time to time in the architectural press, Croydon (1994),[47] Bordon and Southampton, for example, which may include some evaluative detail. That for Sutton Central Library,[48] published in 1980, was in the nature of a POE, as it was a serious architectural study carried out five years after the building's opening. As well as discussing the building's siting, concept ('a department store for leisure') and arrangement, the study covered topics like light, flexibility, visual environment and the provision for workers.

As well as formally evaluating individual libraries in some detail, some public library systems have included a basic review of service points and their adequacy in development plans for a given period. In West Sussex, a ten-year development plan listed and described individual library service points, giving floor areas as a percentage of a recommended standard (80 per cent of IFLA standards) and commented on service point adequacy, noting planned capital expenditure and offering recommendations for the improvement, extension and so on, of particular libraries. The need to create annual library plans for submission to the Department of Culture, Media and Sport (now no longer required) saw an increase in this basic evaluation of their buildings by library services, but these were usually professional assessments rather than the result of formal consultation with staff and the community.

One of the most regular (and well-produced) service point appraisal documents is that from Somerset Library Service. The aims of the 1997 edition are those originally set out in 1980: comparison with national and international standards; priorities for capital projects in times of financial difficulty; and establishing strengths and weaknesses of library provision. A particular goal is 'to ensure that every library building, vehicle and service is equally accessible by all potential users and perceived as a "community resource" by all'.[49] The appraisal provides a library-by-library account and notes floor area (as a percentage of the IFLA standard), catchment population, membership, hours of opening, annual and hourly statistics, circulation system and catalogue. Where appropriate a recommendation is made for extension, the provision of a dual-use library, moving the library, easier maintenance and structural alterations and improvements.

Case study: Riverside Public Library, California (1970)[50]

The Riverside staff questionnaire found staff to be happy about the layout of the public spaces but less happy about their own. Specific complaints included inadequate staff parking, overcrowded staff areas, insufficient storage, the location of restrooms, noise, and the absence of windows and natural light – it is a virtually windowless library.

Case study: Berkeley Library System, California, 1972

User surveys were used to evaluate three libraries (two older buildings and one from the 1960s) in the Berkeley Library System from the viewpoint of user behaviour and satisfaction so as to discover the design implications for this kind of library.[51] In these libraries, ranging in size from just over 200m² to 277m² and 325m², four questionnaires were used, of which three were also put to staff. The questionnaires covered the following topics:

- library use indicator – patrons were asked to tick any of 12 activities, from 'check out a book' to 'make new friends', which applied to them
- general environment – patrons and staff were asked to grade specific aspects of the library environment (lighting, ventilation and privacy, and so on) on a three-point scale
- distractions – from a list of 14 possibilities, patrons and staff indicated what annoyed them in their library
- semantic differential – this questionnaire was designed to learn which concepts (that is, whether the library was pleasant, convenient, and so on) were most frequently associated with the building; 30 pairs of adjectives (for example, good/bad, warm/cold) were used on a five-point scale.

The research found that each branch had a distinct activity pattern and that people were generally favourable about the macro-environment (ceiling height, and so on). However, 25 per cent thought the libraries were too small and, in the older libraries, 20 per cent considered walls and bookshelves were dull, drab and institutional-looking; there was a higher rating for these matters at the newest library. Patrons were more critical of their own micro-environment, with around 25 per cent feeling that there was neither enough space to spread out nor to store belongings. A third of respondents commented on the lack of privacy, both audio and visual, and it was found that noise levels related to the number and type of library visitor at a given time. Staff were much more critical of the environment (poor ventilation and noise from non-human sources), reflecting the time they spent in the building and their own particular tasks. Patrons were distracted by noise, in general required a higher level of concentration than staff, and found uncomfortable furniture a major distraction.

Case study: Ferguson Library, Stamford, Connecticut (1983)

In 1983 the Cohens published a critique of the Ferguson Library, a 1911 brick edifice with a marble-sheathed 1980s international-style addition. They pointed out that the 'theme of the old highlighted by the new is played over and over again', the original interior being essentially kept as it was. However, linking old and new was not without problems when the original three floors became seven. It was felt that rooms did not flow easily into one another, that there was a great deal of traffic space, and security was difficult. In spite of these drawbacks they were very positive about the building.[52]

Case study: Dallas Central Library, Texas (1982)

Under the rubric 'Dynamic Dallas', the American architect Raymond Holt evaluated the central library shortly after its opening. He noted the building's strong architectural statement and put its success down to the brief prepared by the library staff, although he personally found it rather short for such a complex building. Future expansion is catered for by compact shelving on most floors and a design that allows for a later additional wing.

A pedestrian walkway divides the entrance approach into two, with group-use facilities (for example, the auditorium) on one side of it and the library proper on the other. There are subject floors from the third to the eighth floors and a number of rooms (for special collections, and so on) and other facilities which 'make Dallas Central Library Building a very extraordinary place'.

The critic found the entrance walkway not completely successful as a people place: it was an imposing space but overlooked user orientation and masked the point of entry to the library. There was also criticism of the circulation counter, terminal stands, conspicuous cabling, traffic routes, the location of particular collections (at variance with the brief), underestimation of use by children (requiring more space and a change of location), and confusion caused by incomplete signage. The library itself recognized various difficulties of major significance (for example, possibly too few public lifts) and of minor importance (such as messy soap dishes in the toilets). Holt felt, however, that the buildings's shortcomings were overshadowed by its many excellent features.[53]

Case study: Runcorn Shopping City Library (1985)

Runcorn may be almost unique in the library world in that its effectiveness 'in terms of what people said they wanted [in 1977] before it was built' was surveyed in terms of 'they have actually done [during 1981–84] since it was built'.[54]

Runcorn's appraisal confirmed the success of its Shopping City Library (1981) and demonstrated that the new building (2,230m^2) exceeded the estimated scale of use by 25 per cent. This reflected the problems of predicting new service point use but also the success of the library professionals in developing the library service. The survey, however, was principally concerned with people's attitudes to libraries generally and their use of Runcorn Library and its services in particular rather than the building itself. There is a description of the layout, facilities, design and construction of the library but the survey is mainly concerned with site constraints and services provided. Disappointingly, opinions were not sought about the building and its atmosphere, although favourable responses were expressed towards libraries in general, their environment, services and staff.[55]

Case study: Fairfax County, Virginia (1990)

Because of an ambitious building programme, Fairfax County Public Library put a POE process in place 'to help assess the effectiveness of the new facilities in meeting the needs and expectations of library patrons and staff'.[56] The POE programme started by looking at three regional libraries, newly built or renovated, but having different design and site constraints. The objectives of the POE were:

- to help library staff and architects design better libraries
- to gather information about how new buildings are functioning and to identify problems needing correction
- to share findings with other libraries
- to develop a POE model for use by FCPL and other libraries.[57]

Four evaluation techniques were used for the POE:

- self-administered questionnaires (adult library users and staff)[58]
- interviews with children
- observation of library users
- testing environmental conditions – monitoring temperature and lighting levels at various locations in the three buildings during the week of evaluation.

Results of the evaluation found that staff were more critical than library users of interior building features such as noise level and temperature, and some reported a lack of space and conversational privacy, poor air circulation, too few electrical outlets and insufficient storage space. It was also determined that renovated libraries should have a new lighting layout and not make do with the old and that parking configurations 'must be carefully arranged and adequately lighted for both staff and patrons'. Generally speaking all the POE's objectives were met and future projects would benefit from the results of exercise and the POE process would be applied to all FCPL building projects 18 months after opening.

Case study: San Francisco Public Library, California (1999)

Always a controversial project, the San Francisco Public Library was opened in 1996 and after that high-profile event there were various criticisms, such as insufficient space for books. Some three years later the new building was already full. An independent post-occupancy evaluation was commissioned and a draft report presented in August 1999. The major problems associated with the building had been identified by staff before construction and by library users soon after. The POE came to the conclusion that the library

> ... designed to be a grand public space, does not function as effectively as it should or as effectively as peer institutions do in several major aspects.

As *Library journal* put it: 'Staff and public input is useless when it's ignored'.[59] Points from the POE include:

- insufficient collection space because 'the usable area is severely compromised by multiple floor openings'
- a building that was difficult to use due to floor layouts, entryways and poor signage
- movement of materials through the library impeded by the location of sorting rooms, for example
- 150 items from the construction remained unfinished or flawed.

In order to help remedy these problems, the POE report recommended that more space be provided for collections and services; older material be moved out to an archival service department nearby; better utilization of existing space; the relocation of non-public services to an offsite location; and the replacement of many closed stacks with open shelves.[60]

CASE STUDY SUMMARY

While there are drawbacks peculiar to particular buildings, a number of common issues emerge. Some of these are:

- inadequate staff space
- lack of privacy; inadequate personal space for users, for instance
- too much circulation space
- noise
- poor user orientation.

It is important to ensure also that problems from the old building do not migrate to the new, such as the lack of a quiet study area. Other common design and planning shortcomings and deficiencies that have been identified in the US are:

- poor-quality lighting
- inflexible building design
- ineffective functional relationships
- non-compliance with the accessibility mandates of the Americans with Disabilities Act 1990, or ADA (comparable with the UK's DDA)
- no plan for future expansion
- lacks energy efficiency
- inadequate energy distribution
- little attention to maintainability.[61]

There is a failure, clearly, to observe the 'commandments' in a number of cases and it would seem that major libraries can make similar mistakes to their smaller cousins. An evaluation of the Bibliothèque de France revealed, amongst other things, the need for improvements to signage, eating facilities for the public, staff work space conditions, and movement within the building.[62]

Describing the desired qualities of a public library building for an architect is a major contribution to creating successful premises. Success can be assessed through the use of post-occupancy evaluation, with a view to fine-tuning the building, its services and operation and remedying any faults. Case studies in this chapter have exemplified this approach, pointed up common problems and demonstrated its usefulness. Suzanne Enright has helpfully summarized the uses of POE as:

- creating a feedback culture
- demonstrating that money was well spent
- 'introducing appropriate record management, technical information, support and training of technical staff'
- 'help[ing to] address occupant dissatisfaction/complaints'
- preparation for building alteration, refurbishment or new build.[63]

Accountability for funds, the satisfaction of the library's occupants, improved record management and preparation for the future would, for example, all seem to make POE a worthwhile investment.

NOTES

1   Enright, S. (2002), 'Post-occupancy evaluation of UK library building projects: some examples of current practice', *Liber quarterly* **12** (1), 26–45: 26.
2   www.dqi.org.uk.
3   Lushington, N. and Kusack, J.M. (1991), *The design and evaluation of public library buildings*, Hamden, Connecticut: Library Professional Publication, 118. This is a substantial contribution to the literature of library post-occupancy evaluation and has been drawn upon heavily for the content of this chapter.
4   Lushington, N. and Kusack, J.M. (1991), 118.
5   For a recent and fuller account of these design qualities see Faulkner-Brown, H. (1999), 'Some thoughts on the design of major library buildings', in *Intelligent library buildings*, edited by M-F. Bisbrouck and M. Chauveinc, Munich: Saur, 9–31.
6   Faulkner-Brown, H. (1999), 16.
7   For a fuller account, see McDonald, A. (2000), 'Planning academic library buildings for a new age: some principles, trends and developments in the United Kingdom', in *Advances in librarianship*, volume 24, edited by E.A. Chapman and F.C. Lynden, London: Academic Press, 51–79.
8   Roy, R. (2003), 'Reims: the consecration of the resource centre' (in French), *Bibliothèque(s)* (10), 62–4.
9   Anghelescu, H. (1999), 'Libraries without walls or architectural fantasies: a turn-of-the-millennium dilemma', *Libraries and culture* **34** (2), 168–74: 70.
10 *Better library buildings* (2003), London: CABE and Resource, 22, 25.
11 Wiley, P.B. (1997), 'Phoenix's arch architect', *Library journal* **122** (3), 112.
12 Diamond, J. (1982), 'Beyond technology, or computers are not enough', *Canadian library journal* **39** (4), 206–9. Argues for a 'variety of parts'.
13 Boehning, J.C. (1995), 'San Antonio splashes its red library across downtown', *Library journal* **120** (20), 60–61.
14 Winkworth, I. (1996), review of *Building libraries for the information age* (York: University of York, Institute of Advanced Architectural Studies, 1995), in *Journal of librarianship and information science* **28** (1), 58–9: 58.
15 Oehlerts, D.E. (1991), *Books and blueprints: building America's public libraries*, New York: Greenwood, 133.
16 Harrison, K.C. (ed.) (1990), *Library buildings 1984-1989*, London: Library Services, 89-90.
17 Ward, H. (ed.) (1974), *New library buildings 1974 issue* [buildings opened 1970-72], London: Library Association, 34.
18 Schneekloth, L.H. and Keable, E.B. (1991), *Evaluation of library facilities: a tool for managing change*, Champaign, Illinois: Graduate School of Library and Information Science, University of Illinois, 4.
19 Schneekloth, L.H. and Keable, E.B. (1991), 5.
20 Schneekloth, L.H. and Keable, E.B. (1991), 6.
21 Bullet points and quotation taken from documentation supplied to the author by Lancashire Library Service.

22   http://urbanatreelibrary.org/tredarch.htm.

23   Line, M. (2002), 'Library buildings: a user's viewpoint', *Liber quarterly* **12** (1), 78–87.

24   Cohen, E. and Cohen, A. (1976), 'Do our library buildings have to be discarded every fifteen years?', in *Library space planning: issues and approaches*, edited by K. Nyren, New York: Bowker, 56–60.

25   Cohen, E. and Cohen, A. (1976), 56.

26   Cohen, E. and Cohen, A. (1976), 60.

27   Evans, G.E. and others (1971), *Library environmental design: physical facilities and equipment*, [Los Angeles]: Institute of Library Research and others, University of California, 111, 114.

28   *Better public libraries* (2003), 26.

29   Lushington, N. and Kusack, J.M. (1991), 120. Much of this section is based on this account and it is recommended for those wanting to investigate more fully the theory and practice of post-occupancy evaluation.

30   Dahlgren, A. (1996), *Planning the small library facility*, Chicago: American Library Association, 4.

31   Sannwald, W.W. (1997), *Checklist of library building design considerations*, 3rd edn, Chicago: American Library Association, vii.

32   Lushington, N. and Kusack, J.M. (1991), 117.

33   Cohen, A. (1987), 'Analyzing architectural and interior design plans', *Library administration and management* **1** (3), 91–3.

34   Michaels, A. (1987), 'Design today', *Wilson library bulletin*, **61** (5) 50–51.

35   Lushington, N. and Kusack, J.M. (1991), 157–60.

36   Enright, S. (2002), 37.

37   Harrison, D. (ed.) (1995), *Library buildings in the United Kingdom 1990-1994*, London: Library Services.

38   Batt, Chris (1993), 'The cutting edge 21: the key to the door', *Public library journal* **8** (6), 186–9.

39   Thompson, G. (1989), *Planning and design of library buildings*, 3rd edn, London: Butterworth, 105.

40   User satisfaction survey at Weobley Castle Library (Birmingham, 1991); for details see Harrison, D. (ed.) (1995), *Library buildings in the United Kingdom 1990-1994*, London: Library Services, 84.

41   Crookston, E.M. (1991), *The branch library service – a survey of users' views and experience*, Middlesbrough: Cleveland County Council.

42   Suvak, D. (1982), 'Opening day: what to expect in a new library', *Wilson library bulletin*, **57** (2), October, 140–41.

43   Wiley, P.B. (1997), 'Beyond the blueprint', *Library journal* **122** (3), 110–13.

44   Bryon, J., Usherwood, B. and Proctor, R (2003), *Libraries must also be buildings? New library impact study*, London: Resource.

45   Suvak, D. (1982), 190.

46   Poulton, A. (2004), 'Leadership and marketing are keys to the future', *Library + information gazette* 3 December, 11.

47   'Public library revitalises Croydon' (1994), *Architect's journal*, 5 January, 29–39.

48   van der Wateren, J. (1980),'Central Library, Sutton', *Architects' journal*, 5 November, 887–900.

49   Froud, R. (1997), *Public library service point provision in Somerset*, Bridgwater: Somerset Library Service, 3. Other service point surveys have been produced by, for example, the City of Edinburgh (1988), and Hereford and Worcester (1992).

50   Lake, A. C. (1970), 'The new building after five years: an evaluation', *California librarian* **31** (1), 7–11.

51   Durkin, M. and Sommer, R. (1972), 'User evaluation of three branch libraries', *California librarian* **33** (2), 114–23.

52   Cohen, E. and Cohen, A. (1983), 'A critique of the Ferguson Library, Stamford, Connecticut', *Public library quarterly* **4** (3), 23–36.

53   Holt, R.M. (1983), 'Dynamic Dallas: a building critique', *Public library quarterly* **4** (4), 67–84.

54   Cheshire Libraries and Museums (1985), *The Cheshire library survey. 1: New town: new library*, Chester: Cheshire County Council, para 12.1.1.

55   Cheshire Libraries and Museums (1985), paras 8.2.1, 12.1.6.

56   'Does this building work?' (1990) *Virginia librarian*, **36** (3), 16–17: 16.

57   'Does this building work?' (1990), 16–17.

58   For brief details of patron and staff questionnaires see Clay, E.S. and Hlavka, G. (1987), 'Does this building work?', *Library administration & management* **1** (3), 105–6: 105.

59   Berry, J.N. (1999), 'The key lesson from San Francisco', *Library journal* **124** (15), 6.

60   'Study finds major flaws in San Francisco Main Library' (1999), *American libraries* **30** (9), 16.

61   Brawner, L.J. and Beck, D.K. (1996), *Determining your public library's future size: a needs assessment and planning model*, Chicago: American Library Association, 4–5.

62   Bicket, J-L. (2001), 'From necessity to reality: journal of the Bibliothèque Nationale de France Project', in *Buildings in a changing environment*, edited by M-F. Bisbrouck, Munich: Saur, 163–75: 165.

63   Enright, S. (2002), 41.

9 Identity, communication and style

All buildings demonstrate a body language – planned or accidental – which people intuitively respond to and form relationships with.

Gerald Melling[1]

The days are gone when a public library, large or small, might be readily identified through its civic architecture, whether gothic, classical, Edwardian Baroque or neo-Georgian, and by its name chiselled in the external stonework. However well-regarded many of these older libraries might be today (because of their period architecture), they are usually thought to provide the wrong image for a modern public library – considered monumental, perceived as institutional, deemed old fashioned and, because of their fixed function characteristics, uneconomic to operate and change. They may now also be wrongly sited. Given the opportunity, librarians are often keen to desert the old – the Morgue of Culture, the Great Stone Face, the Stuffed Shirt (as Wheeler called them back in the 1960s[2]) – for a more modern 'with-it' building.

As was demonstrated in Chapter 5, older purpose-built library buildings, suitably modernized and possibly extended, can (and do) continue in use for many years. Buildings of a similar vintage (or even older) and not originally constructed as libraries, may be successfully converted for library use. These older buildings, whether originally built as public libraries or not, often offer a quality of craftsmanship and materials that is too rarely seen in today's public buildings.

Whether housed in a new, refurbished, extended or converted premises, the librarian will be concerned that the building is readily identifiable as a library and with the image it conveys, both externally and internally, to its potential users. But communication with users does not cease at the library entrance, however, and attention must be given to guiding and signs, colour schemes, furniture, decorative features and public art, for example, as means of reinforcing the library identity and image.

IDENTITY

In *Open to all?* it is claimed that UK public libraries need to change so as not to seem municipal, bureaucratic, unwelcoming and as passive state institutions.[3] Although public libraries cannot escape their local authority affiliation, they are probably the least bureaucratic, and most welcoming and proactive of many public organizations: that is the story of their development over the last 50 years. This is not to say that there is no room for improvement or that all public libraries display all these virtues equally.

Open to all? suggests that the remedy for the failings it identifies is to rename and rebrand public libraries.[4] It could be argued that renaming and rebranding has taken place in a limited way already. Both the 'public' and 'branch' parts of the library title are usually dropped from external library signs and often the name of the place the library is located is also omitted: 'Library' is all that remains.

As was seen in an earlier chapter, many libraries also now call themselves a community, neighbourhood or learning centre. In other instances the L-word has been entirely rejected and libraries have become an Idea Store or Discovery Centre, with all the branding that this entails. This is in response to the view that 'rebranding the traditional library name' ensures a 'new image ... of a proactive, friendly, relevant and easily accessible environment'.[5] But the brand must live up to a sustained reality.

PUBLIC LIBRARY LOGO

Part of the rebranding story is also the search for a national public library logo that could be used to identify library buildings, amongst its other uses. County libraries in the past were identified by the flaming torch symbol: something more modern and suitable for all public libraries was required. Other countries, such as Germany and the Netherlands, had a national library symbol and it was thought that this should be the case also in the UK.[6] A library symbol was created for the UK and at one time it seemed to be well used on public library signs, vehicles and on printed material. It was developed as a symbol for all types of library but, because it was sponsored by the Public Libraries Group, it became more closely identified with public libraries, largely because only they took it up. It now appears to be much less used and some library authorities have their own logo and brand image. Libraries may be obliged, however, to adopt the corporate marketing scheme of their local authority, rather than having their own distinctive identity and image. In 2002, it was proposed that a cheap and simple way of promoting Europe's 'invisible' public library network of 40,000 or so libraries would be to create a Eurologo.[7] The idea of a public library symbol is viewed here as both of national and European importance and, it might be added, could have international application.

IMAGE

Given the comments about the use and appeal of older buildings, whether purpose-built as libraries or not, does the question of library image have any real meaning? It would appear that users are prepared to accept and use buildings that are well located and identified as a public library, without them necessarily being new and of hi-tech design. Interestingly, the design-build competition for the Chicago Central Library ($c.70,000m^2$) resulted in the choice of a classical design from a post-modernist architect, Thomas H. Beeby. The choice both surprised and disappointed, as the monumental style of the proposed building was seen by some as representing the nineteenth-century 'cathedral-of-learning' stereotype. The design had many supporters (including staff), however, and was seen as being in harmony with downtown Chicago architecture.[8]

For the library experience is not just about the building but also about the quality of the staff, the appropriateness of its collections, the range of services provided and so on. The 'Give'em what they want' philosophy espoused by Baltimore County Public Library (BCPL), for example, emphasizes relevant and useful materials (high-interest fiction and non-fiction) and services (such as information provision, accessibility and good parking) seemingly above excessive expenditure on physical facilities, such as a flagship central library. BCPL appears to show a greater concern for maintenance and repair and the interior of its buildings – signs, layout and retail store design features – than for the exterior and the 'image' it gives.[9]

Nevertheless *Open to all?* suggested that

> The physical appearance of libraries needs to be audited to check that they are not forbidding from the outside and that the internal layout is easy to understand.

This question of layout is discussed in the next chapter. Better signing, more self-help public access terminals and the removal of enquiry desks, it is suggested, can all help overcome barriers to use experienced by some excluded people.[10]

DYSFUNCTIONAL AND FUNCTIONAL COMMUNICATION

Gulten Wagner emphasizes this view – the need for the physical appearance audit – by seeing both external and internal design features of public libraries as meaning systems and as responsible 'for possible acts of dysfunctional communication' – design giving off the wrong messages. Her external signs of dysfunctional communication include a local authority architectural style, the lack of a unified style of public library building, inaccessibility, lack of signage and opacity. Wagner was writing about libraries in the Perth (Australia) metropolitan region in the early 1990s and it could be contended that in the UK the potential for 'dysfunctional communication' due to inaccessibility, lack of signage and opacity have been addressed generally by modern public library buildings.

Service points within a library system are likely to be a mix of old and new buildings and of architectural styles. Whether libraries need to have a style that readily identifies them as public buildings, or more closely as public library buildings, seems unlikely. Great emphasis therefore must be placed on the other signifiers by architects and librarians, such as access, signage and transparency, to ensure 'functional' rather than 'dysfunctional' communication with potential users. The Ideas Stores approach, discussed in Chapter 7, emphasizes this functional communication with its users and particularly potential users.

Where public libraries are co-located with or part of a local authority building or complex, there is perhaps greater possibility for 'dysfunctional communication' – the library is seen as a local authority institution. Yet the library's relationship to the other building or buildings and the quality of its functional architecture, that allows a display of library purpose and activity, can combat this tendency.

WHAT SHOULD A LIBRARY LOOK LIKE?

Endeavouring to design a public library, or a series of libraries, with some idea of a standard, all-purpose image in mind (as with Tower Hamlet's Idea Stores), is, perhaps, a mistaken quest, leading as it does to soulless high street uniformity to which many object. Wielding all the usual stereotypical phrases about libraries – old-time, passive, find-it-if-you-can book repositories – G. Holt says that what is needed is 'modern libraries that delight'. He offers a number of 'potential for delight' criteria:

- distinctive exterior appearance
- classy, distinctive, retail interiors
- cleanliness
- money: 'the cheapest-possible library is hardly ever a delightful library'.

He also adds the need for convenient parking and a trained and appropriate staff.[11] But even if all these criteria are met, commercial-style branding is hardly ever likely to lead to public library buildings that 'delight'.

Image is tied up with a view of the public library's role and its aims and objectives. Not all – users or librarians – will see it as part commercial enterprise, part fast food chain or as a book supermarket, but all will want it to be non-elitist, easy to use and representative of an open mind: 'too often defensibility is allowed to dominate design, giving the building a closed-in feeling'. It should be a public space for all, but one whose 'civilising influence remains essentially unchanged'.[12]

A major problem with image and branding is that it requires regular adjustment and change. The commercial world responds to this in a way publicly funded organizations, like libraries, might find difficult, except when new building projects are in hand, when some or all of the following elements discussed in this chapter and the next might be part of the planned library accommodation.

MARKETING THE BUILDING

The library image is not just a matter of what the building looks like but, as one writer puts it, of marketing libraries through their physical environment and using that 'to instil a sense of anticipation and of participation in something special'.[13] People, it is said, need to be enticed to and into the building through attractive and useful external and internal spaces even though initially they may use the space in their own way and ignore traditional library use: 'If they leave the library later with some need satisfied ... the likelihood of a repeat visit is increased'[14] and they may understand more fully what libraries can do for them. The physical elements of the library building, such as the approaches to the building, its setting, the entrance area, windows, and activity space can all be used as part of a marketing strategy.

> There is no reason that the word 'fun' cannot become a synonym for 'library'. Today, when only a fraction of our library building's use has anything to do with our collections and traditional services, we should exploit all of our resources to increase use ... library space both within and without can be put to an amazing number of creative and beneficial uses.[15]

Although this perhaps overstates the case, and a note of desperation may even be detected, it emphasizes the need to actively market the physical environment.

THE LIBRARY VISITOR'S EXPERIENCE

While there is greater political influence over the external sign system of a library (in other words, what it looks like), library professionals create the 'control sign systems ... in constructing the logic of internal space'. Here Wagner is writing about such issues as open versus closed domains, the separation of noisy and quiet areas and the amount of space given to children and young people.[16] These questions of library arrangement will be considered in the next chapter.

Some external signifiers, such as signs and guiding are also important internally. Other features of the library building and its environment are also likely to encourage use, such as gardens and courtyards, public art and the use of colour, and can be seen as positive library signifiers. The cumulative effect of good lighting, comfortable furniture, attractive flooring and the good use of colour and textures create the distinctive character of the library interior.[17] The importance of this cumulative effect is strengthened by a small-scale academic library study which found that 'although individual factors in the library do affect a user's perception, it is the total environment that has the greatest effect'.[18]

Another small-scale survey from Australia discovered that 'most people suggested that, correctly applied, colour and lighting aid in the establishment of an overall pleasant environment'. However, they put greater emphasis on lighting as '"library" implies the undertaking of sight dependent activities'.[19] In the above-mentioned academic library survey just over half did not notice the library's colour scheme, although others strongly disliked it.

245

DESIGN CONCEPTS

In creating a public library, it can help to have a particular concept for the proposed building: the library as a department store, for instance, as at Turku Library, Finland.[20] A concept may reflect the purpose, organization or character of the building and is a way of giving a focus to both planning and design. Earlier ideas of the public library as a 'temple or cathedral of learning' may be considered unfashionable now but that description, and the library as the 'university of the people', are underlying themes of modern concepts concerned with lifelong learning and social inclusion. The choice of one concept may well give a general direction to a building project but, because of the varied purposes of the public library, it may be necessary to have subsidiary themes or design concepts for different elements.

An exercise for architectural students, based on a proposed central library building for St Albans, produced four concepts and anticipated some later, similar proposals. The concepts were of the library as:

1. A series of libraries. 'Not one building, but a series of buildings, each with vastly differing requirements, all linked by vertical or horizontal communication lines.'[21] Within each 'building' there would be transient areas capable of constant change.
2. An all-in-one pavilion. This would help to deal with the issue of overlap and boundaries (such as between the children's library and the adult lending library), permitting flexibility, and separating functions by visual and acoustic insulation where needed.
3. A market place. 'The multi-purpose hall [the marketplace] distributes the traffic to various departments and pulls them together; they are otherwise isolated due to their different functional requirements. It is also used as the main exhibition and display area.'[22]
4. A place of introversion. An environment that could add something to people's lives: 'it could give them a quiet place where they could retreat into themselves ... Or it could give people the feeling of jointly searching for knowledge, reaching towards the universal which can be very exciting ... a place where you discover things you never knew would interest you.'[23]

With the exception of the idea of an all-in-one space, these 1960s concepts are largely concerned with compartmentalized libraries, in three cases they encompassed outdoor courtyards. Only the last one shows a concern for the varieties of library experience, the others being mainly concerned with a concept to underpin a particular arrangement of internal spaces. The marketplace is a theme that has been repeated in the design of other public libraries, in Scandinavia, for example, and has some similarities to the following idea.

THE LIBRARY STREET CONCEPT

The idea of an indoor library street, as a means of moving visitors through the library to various destinations, can be seen in libraries as far apart as Canada, Hungary and Sweden. The 'street' may run through the centre of the library, across the library diagonally or close to one edge of the building. At the Békéscsaba County Library, Hungary, the internal street

> ... does not serve exclusively the library traffic ... it integrates many library functions ... and functions as the marketplace of the library where we can meet friends, make acquaintances, have a rest with a coffee, enjoy an exhibition, buy ... cakes or flowers.[24]

Case study: Hillerød Library

An example of the library street concept is at Hillerød, Denmark, where in 1999 it was decided to create a Knowledge and Culture Park, on a site close to the town centre, making use of existing buildings. The scheme included a library and involved the renovation and extension of the existing building: a park linked the library and the other cultural buildings. It was hoped that the proximity of other cultural institutions would inspire more activity and cooperation by the library.

Key aspects of the design were openness, attractiveness, information provision and quiet contemplation, summarized as 'knowledge, information and culture' and reflected in the way the library and its contents are organized. From the outside there is access to a lobby, which includes the issue desk and is ideal for exhibitions.

> It runs through the entire building, as a kind of internal distribution mall [70 metres long], connecting the departments in the adjacent buildings. There is direct access from the lobby to the park.[25]

As well as demonstrating the street concept, the design's concern for 'quiet contemplation' reflects the 'introspective' concept described earlier. It is one that finds resonance in the proposed Library 21 in Stuttgart. This will have a centrally placed room (500m^2), called the 'heart', for 'meditation and communication'.[26] The design of Shanghai Public Library has also shown a concern for serenity, both in the building and through the inclusion of a garden.[27]

THE MARKET SQUARE CONCEPT

The library as a public, indoor marketplace (or square) has been seen both as a separate concept and as a possible feature of a library street. The idea seems to have originated with Werner Mevissen, the German writer on library buildings. He emphasized the need for openness in libraries and saw the marketplace (front hall or entrance) as a fairly large room housing all those services that precede borrowing library material: reading newspapers, exhibitions, café, or lectures after closing, for instance.[28] Some such services and facilities may be housed in areas immediately adjoining the market place or front hall.

Case studies: two Swedish libraries

The market square concept realized in the Skara Diocesan and County Library, Sweden, took Danish examples as its model. Built during 1986–87, Skara Library brings the visitor through a fairly low, unpretentious entrance with reception desk into an indoor space – the information square. Surrounded by brick walls, with a limestone floor and generous headroom with toplighting, the square creates a feeling of an outdoor environment, encircling the 'tree of knowledge' which supports the sloping disc of the roof.

The indoor square contains information material – reference works, newspapers, publications of the local authority and national government, consumer and computerized information. It is equipped with street lamps and signs that point to the colour-coded reading rooms that lie behind the arched openings in the brick walls of the square. The open square also has payphones and coffee dispensers and provides flexible space for cultural activities.

The modest two-storey Skara library contrasts strongly with the Sundsvall Centre or Cultural Store, which is four storeys high and about 100 metres long. Four old buildings around a street crossing (now glazed in) have been made into one unit consisting of library, museum and archives. The public entrance takes the visitor to what was originally the crossing of the two streets, where reception, café and museum are located. Beyond the crossing is the lecture hall, with museum and library entrances to the right and left of the crossing. The library entrance leads to the information street, with access to the ground-floor library departments and other parts of the building on the upper floors on either side of the street. The higher floors on either side of the street are linked by bridges, providing access to public and staff areas. Although Sundsvall is designed as a 'street' library, the central location of the street in the building, and the way it leads to departments either side of it, has some similarity to the role of the square at Skara. One commentator has described the library in the Sundsvall cultural centre as

> ... not ideal – nobody ... would have given it this form: ... Such are ... the conditions a rebuilding entails ... [that] a library has been created that resembles no other, a library of great environmental merits... It is above all the light in the space between the beautiful old buildings which is the great adventure at Sundsvall.[29]

LIBRARIES AS RETAIL OUTLETS

Librarians have been asked to make their libraries more like bookshops and for some time there has been an increasing similarity between the two (although cafés were a feature of libraries long before they were commonly found in bookshops). It will be clear from earlier chapters that the library as a retail outlet or even a supermarket are also ways of looking at the public library in whole or in part. Libraries may endeavour to imitate the display and other merchandising techniques of both bookshop and supermarket.

Persuading people to buy a goodly quantity of books (that may go largely unread) may make for profitable bookselling. Increasing library usage by, amongst other things, simply getting 'patrons to borrow more per visit', as John Stanley suggests, has usually been seen as crude librarianship and poor economics.[30] It treats the library visit purely as a shopping trip and the reader as a consumer concerned with the latest trends – the best-sellers – and as someone who is encouraged to take (consume) more than is perhaps needed (listened to, viewed or read).

The merchandising approach suggested by Stanley and others, often with large bookshops in mind, implies that public libraries are unconcerned about image and atmosphere, customer service, partnerships, genre shelving, signs, separate 'zones' for different readers and purposes, and displays.[31] It also ignores the efforts that librarians have made, since the 1940s at least (as described in the next chapter), to arrange and display their multimedia stock in a helpful and informative way.

This is not to say that librarians cannot learn from others and there is no doubt that many librarians are attracted to the retail outlet/bookshop concept of library service. This is most readily achieved in a new library building project and might be seen as especially appropriate when the library is located in a shopping centre. As with the adoption of all such concepts, it remains to be seen whether public libraries can sustain them or keep up with developments in the private retail sector. Imitation may be the sincerest form of flattery but it may not be the most worthwhile approach in the long run and may seem to blur the many differences that should exist between public library and the bookshop or other retail outlet.

OTHER CONCEPTS

Borrowed time? mentions the Scandinavian idea of the indoor square and street concepts, with their covered courtyards, as symbolizing the public function of libraries. There is also the idea of the library as the community's or society's living room – 'as a place where everyone can feel at home and comfortable'. It is suggested that 'these themes are intended to provide high quality public spaces in the everyday environment of the library'.[32] The public living room concept in Scandinavia dates from the 1970s when interior design had to overcome the institutional feel of the library and promote cosiness and interaction. People expected to listen to audio material in the library, as well as silently browse and read; a café was a standard facility and a place for people to meet, and there were new media, new shelving layouts and guiding. It has been said that the living room concept was too successful and with the 'disorder' that resulted the library lost its intended cosiness.[33]

Bournemouth main library (2002) has been described as a street corner university, while another, Croydon Central Library (1993), has been seen as a department store.

The store concept is reflected also in Tower Hamlets' description of its libraries as Idea Stores where, as has been seen, there is an emphasis on a retail style in its current and proposed buildings.[34] But this is more branding than content related – they are essentially libraries and learning centres. The name on its own is uninformative, although arousing curiosity, and needs explanation. Time and appropriate promotion and publicity may well reverse this.

Alan Bundy has collected together the many ways that libraries are described these days, reflecting their various roles and perhaps suggesting ways in which the design of the public library building might be conceptualized in whole or in part. Examples include the following: knowledge warehouse; info gas station; the new village green; imagination's stronghold; cultural café; and equity building blocks.[35] Two further case studies from Finland and Germany show how particular design ideas for a library building come to dominate both their form and function.

Case study: the wood grouse as a library form

A Finnish public library that has attracted worldwide attention, especially because of its form and materials used, is Tampere Main Library (1986, 6,630m²).

> The architect's visions – of the post-Ice Age rock landscape, of a Celtic pin-brooch, and ultimately of that essentially Finnish bird, the wood grouse – have been transposed into a working library.[36]

The round shape of the wood grouse, its beak, wings and feathers, are all part of the building's form.

> The round shape of the building minimized the need for space-consuming corridors and produced an economic ratio of net to gross floor area. The internal routes branch out radially from the entrance hall to the various sections.[37]

The 'wood grouse' consists of a ground floor, entrance floor and mezzanine. Given the solid massing of shelves in the adult lending library, and the non-library occupancy of part of the ground floor, there is a feeling that the grouse concept does not readily contain the library it was constructed to accommodate.

Case study: Stuttgart Library

Stuttgart Central Library is currently housed in a former palace, built about 150 years ago and, at around 5,000m², too small for today's needs. The new building – 'Library 21' – is a prize-winning design by Korean-born Eun Young Yi and is in the form of an immense cube of glass bricks surrounded by water. The library can be entered from all four sides. Work on the building is planned to start in 2005.

The spatial organization of the proposed building would seem to be dictated by the concept of the 'heart' at its centre, a 14 metre high room (500m²) for contemplation, inspiration and silence. The promenades around the heart provide 'strolling paths' to other parts of the building. There is an 'open end' area and a café (the entrance hall) with newspapers, computer terminals and circulation desk planned to be open from 7.00 a.m. to 12 midnight. Other features of the library include eight learning studios (covering topics of interest), a children's media centre, auditorium, art department and music library.

Although the 'cube' is loved, the librarian admits there are weak points from a functional viewpoint that will be discussed with the architect: the location of the children's library and 'cyberspace ring' of computers, and problems with the 'open end' area, as well as lack of balconies and gardens.[38] Another problem may well be that, given the size and central location of the heart, it dictates the arrangement of the rest of the library's interior.

A REVIEW OF CONCEPTS

Where concepts describe the overall physical arrangement of the library or the character of its design – in Malmö's public library (1997–98), the new library building west of and linked with the old library is called the 'Calendar of Light', emphasizing the effect of daylight in the building – then perhaps they have some meaning. Where they describe the purpose of the library, they are perhaps less helpful, although perhaps emphasizing a strong element of the library's work, such as education. As Chapter 2 demonstrated, public libraries perform a variety of roles and offer a variety of services and facilities to realize them. So no one concept, even a very general one, like 'a space for all', is liable to encapsulate all a library might stand for. It could be argued that what is wanted is a mix of concepts. An article, 'Ten ways to look at a library', illustrates the public library's diverse roles by calling it, amongst other things, a study hall, distribution centre, museum and part-time parent.[39] *Borrowed time?* points out that

> The public library is a complex social space, that at different time of the day, at different times of the week serves changing needs and interests.[40]

Lunchtime concerts, after-school activities and regular cultural and community events represent the kinds of changing needs and interests that could be catered for.

EXTERNAL FEATURES OF THE LIBRARY BUILDING

Modern buildings are often devoid of external and internal decoration, as the architect may consider that this detracts from the purity of the architecture on display. Indeed, some architects may even react against a sign on the building that declares its location and purpose.

EXTERNAL SIGNS

Awareness of the proximity and location of a library building can be facilitated through street signs and banners. Although an elementary way of promoting the library, these can be easily overlooked. Then it makes sense for the building itself to bear its place name and function, perhaps in neon at night-time, rather than the single word 'library' on the building. The exterior sign, which could also include the library service logo may, especially if illuminated, require planning permission. Where there is some hesitation about signs on the building itself, then an imaginative, easily-seen, free-standing sign should be provided: Peterborough Library has a simple but almost sculptural free-standing pavement sign outside its building bearing the word 'library'.

ENTRANCES

The library entrance should not be difficult to find, or mean in its proportions, as this does little for the library's wish to be welcoming and encourage people to enter. It is helpful to clearly identify the entrance or entrances, as in some libraries people may approach the entrance area, foyer or lobby from different directions. Decorative features, like the dragon plaque at Taunton Library (Figure 9.1), or distinctive lettering close to the entrance can also help make its location clearer.

The entrance area should not be just a space to pass through but should have a purpose both functionally and aesthetically. It 'provides both a physical and a psychological transition from one environment into another'[41] and, bearing in mind the concepts described earlier, offers opportunities, for example, for reception, book return, information-giving, directional signs to departments, rooms and facilities, a café, as well as exhibitions, displays and small-scale events.

A new cultural centre is planned for Arnhem in the Netherlands, which will include a public library. In the meantime the current building has been upgraded and now offers a more welcoming entrance and a café.[42] Vimercate Library, Italy (1993–94) has an entrance area that contains display panels, interactive information points and specially lit book exhibitions.[43]

VIEWS INTO THE LIBRARY INTERIOR

Library services and activities can also be publicized to the passer-by, or would-be user, by offering them views into the interior of the building. The public library in Codrolpo, near Udine in Italy, whose building hallmark is transparency, includes an unusually large window of 300m^2 looking out over a rural landscape.[44] Windows are important for bringing natural light into the building and for offering a view of the interior – and by readers of the outside – but are also a way of marketing services and events. Resources are needed, however, to ensure high quality and changing displays.

Figure 9.1   Taunton Library, Somerset (1996): terracotta sculpture of a Dragon by Philip Thomason
Source: Pauline Rook

Views of the interior are likely to be particularly appealing and effective at evening time when the building is in use and the library ablaze with light. During those hours of darkness, particularly when the library is not in use, floodlighting can remind people of the library's existence and the quality of the building, as well as being a security feature.

SYMBOLISM

The author has seen a French library building where the spine of a book has been used as a repeated symbolic feature of the building façade. Inside the same building wall lampshades were shaped like an open inverted book. The public library at Mejanes, Aix-en-Provence, housed in a former match factory, has two large sloping 'books' forming part of its facade. The exterior of the Osaka Prefectural Central Library is said to resemble stacks of books piled up horizontally on top of one another. Symbolism is seen at its most extravagant in the form of the four controversial towers (representing open books) of the Bibliothèque de France, bringing form and function into conflict. The four towers dominate the design and were considered to have drawbacks for the storage of library materials from both operational and preservation points of view. At great expense, wooden shutters were added to the windows in the storage towers to overcome doubts about preservation and there was a reduction in the number of floors. The appeal of the overall design solution may overcome present-day reservations about the Très Grande Bibliothèque (TGB) and it will be loved, it has been suggested, like the TGV (Train de Grand Vitesse).

DECORATION

Decorative features have often added character and appeal to older library buildings, both externally and internally. While some of the features clearly related to the architectural style, the subjects of others emphasized the literary nature of the building or more broadly associated it with the arts, science and commerce.

Victorian and Edwardian architects, it might be argued, went too far in their decoration of the exterior, with features such as:

- the name of the library carved in stone, often above the entrance, and sometimes with an uplifting phrase for good measure here or elsewhere in the building
- the coat of arms of the borough
- statues of literary figures like Shakespeare, Milton, Bacon and Spenser and, at certain celebratory periods, Queen Victoria
- low-relief sculpture representing arts, science, literature and commerce
- standard architectural decorations, such as swags and festoons
- a clock or weathervane.

The interior of the public library might contain:

- stained glass
- decorative plasterwork
- carved woodwork
- busts and statuary.

In his book, *A vision of Britain*, Prince Charles makes a plea for the use of decoration and provides various examples. One such example is the façade of Islington Central Library by Henry T. Hare (1907), which, while not the most appealing of models, illustrates many of the features noted above.[45] Probably one of the most lavishly decorated public libraries is New York Public Library,[46] only equalled in Britain perhaps by the John Rylands Library, now part of the University of Manchester.

Where today libraries are designed to include external decoration on the façade of the building, these are unlikely to be sculptures of literary figures or symbols of art and commerce, as in the past. One of the last UK examples was probably Grimsby Central Library (1968) which featured sculpted figures of the Guardians of Knowledge. Chicago has (amongst other decorative features) its owls, symbolizing wisdom, at the top of its massive building. Much more usual is the decorative mural, either of an abstract nature or depicting a local scene, past or present. Examples include Sutton Coldfield Central Library (1974), which has a mural depicting themes of local historical significance, and the older Pontardawe Library (Neath Port Talbot) which now has three exterior murals (2002).[47]

The much-praised Wellington Central Library, New Zealand (1991, 14,000m²), ranged on six levels, received a number of building awards. A distinctive decorative feature of the building is the series of metal palms that frame the entrance and form a colonnade down one side of the building.[48] Although a German academic library, Eberswolde Library, by Herzog and De Meuron of Tate Modern fame, has an unusual decorative exterior and has been described as 'a simple cube of concrete and glass panels ... tattooed from top to bottom with a pattern of images – like the body of a Papuan'.[49] Another, earlier academic building, the University Library, Ciudad Universitaria, Mexico City, (1953) uses its walls for substantial mural decoration that mixes signs and symbols, both old and new.

FREE-STANDING STATUARY

Although modern library buildings usually no longer incorporate statues in their building façades, sculptors may well be commissioned to create such works as free-standing library symbols or representations of individuals, named or unnamed. The exterior of the library may also be considered the right place for pieces of art, whether abstract or representational. Examples include Tel Aviv, with its 'totem pole' pile of books of different colours; Holywood Arches Library, Belfast, which has a statue of C.S. Lewis (complete with wardrobe see Figure 9.2); and Hamilton, Canada, that has a statue of the librarian (male, of course, and wearing a frock coat). Outside Halsteren Public Library in the Netherlands there is a statue of a young girl reading, seated next to a small pile of books. Not least, there is the example of an impressive statue, Paolozzi's four-metre depiction to Newton, in the forecourt of the British Library.

Figure 9.2 Holywood Arches Branch Library, Belfast (1997): C.S. Lewis sculpture by Ross Wilson, 1998
Source: Belfast Education and Library Board

PUBLIC SPACES AND LANDSCAPING

Depending upon its siting, the public library building may face onto a landscaped garden area, paved or hard-surfaced public space. It may have some enclosed space of its own that both public and staff can use. Settings like this have the advantage of drawing attention to the presence of the library, as well as providing space for seating, planting, statuary, works of art and opportunities for library and non-library events. Such open spaces also become recognized as useful meeting places for locals and visitors alike, where buskers and performers might entertain. Two notable examples from outside the UK are the steps of the New York Public Library (NYPL) and the plaza of the Pompidou Centre, Paris.

NYPL has taken commercial advantage of the steps – there are cafés in mild weather – these 'provide users with various places that can support active engagement with the setting and other people there, or quiet reflection and rest'.[50]

At the Pompidou Centre half the site is devoted to a public square as part of a network of pedestrianized surrounding streets. Here people sun themselves, eat, talk, read, sleep and rest or join in with the singing and dancing to live music. The square attracts many street performers, who have to be of a good standard to maintain the interest of the crowd. The square is a Paris attraction, as much as the building itself: 'Even though it is largely a concrete pavement, the square seems to be a comfortable place ... a magnificent stage'.[51] The Pompidou Centre demonstrates the drawing power of the building, creating a context for the use of the square. This use flourishes through a simple space (not overdesigned), which has open-minded management, policies and planning to guide it in use, allowing for the expected and the unexpected.

The NYPL is an example of where a library has taken advantage of the unexpected use by the public of part of its monumental building. The Pompidou Centre's square was deliberately created to fulfil many roles – relaxation, entertainment and social intercourse, for example. However, landscaping, whether garden, open space or public square, should not be added on to a building as an afterthought, nor used solely to ameliorate a poor-quality environment and undistinguished architecture. Ideally, it should be a collaborative effort between all members of the design team.[52]

Examples of libraries with public spaces include:

- Birmingham Central Library facing the stepped Chamberlain Square.
- Barnstaple Library looks onto a square with seating and statuary and a green area is close by.
- March Library, Cambridgeshire – Chris Drury (the celebrated land artist, working with art and nature) worked on the landscaped gardens surrounding the building and the setting is often used for wedding photography, as the registrar has offices in the library.
- Calne Library, Wiltshire – one approach to the building allows the enjoyment of a landscaped area alongside a stream together with public art.

- Norfolk and Norwich Millennium Library – 'The invitation is not only to a library but a collective space, both within the Forum, but also outside, into the square and the market. It creates a social environment many feel comfortable lingering in.'[53]

A recent library impact study, which collected information on 70 libraries, found that a significant number provided for gardens or green spaces in the design of new building projects.[54] A colonnade, offering a covered walkway around part of the building and adding to its setting, is also an attractive feature in a small number of libraries; for example, Wigton Library, Cumbria (1975) and Barnstaple, Devon (1988).

Great public spaces are seen as having access and linkage; comfort and image; uses and activities; and sociability. In addition to the Pompidou Centre and NYPL two further examples of note in North America are Multnomah County Library, Portland (US) and Beaches Branch Library, Toronto (Canada).[55] Much of this approach reinforces the idea of the public library as a meeting place, as discussed in Chapter 1.

INTERNAL STRUCTURAL FEATURES

ATRIUMS AND VOIDS

The atrium can be used to bring light to the inner parts of a building, to put the different levels of a large building on display and to house stairs, escalators or lifts. It is a feature of many large modern buildings including libraries and generally speaking is not much liked by library building experts. Like the architectural void it may be seen as a waste of space, creating inflexibility, and having the potential, unless enclosed, for allowing noise to travel through the building. Writing about the atriums in the Los Angeles, Phoenix and San Francisco public library buildings, Lowell Martin notes that

> They may lift the spirit but ... also complicate the disposition of books and reading rooms ... Users may be impressed but they may be unsure where the material and staff they need are located. The relative simplicity of the earlier Baltimore plan has been lost.[56]

As the Cohens have amply demonstrated, if an atrium or void(s) is part of an architect's library design, then the most important factor is its placement if problems are to be avoided or minimized. If the central or other placement of the atrium or void(s) divides the interior floor space into a number of unequal sections, then problems will occur.[57] Atriums placed along the front or sides of a building, although possibly narrower in design, will be less problematical. Examples of UK libraries with atriums or voids are listed in Figure 9.3. However, a difficult site may encourage the use of a central void or atrium to provide light and to introduce a feeling of spaciousness into the library building.

Ilford Central Library, London, Redbridge, 1986 (void over entrance desk)
Uxbridge Central Library, London, Hillingdon, 1987 (split level floors and central void)
Barnstaple Library & Record Office, Devon, 1988 (off-centre circular void)
Jersey Library, 1989 (large void though upper floors)
Willesden Green Library Centre, London, Brent, 1989 (atrium as central walkway)
Bradford-on-Avon, Wiltshire, 1990 (large corner void)
Weymouth Library, Dorset, 1990 (central void)
Hartlepool Central Library, Cleveland, 1991 (atrium over front section of ground floor)
Brixham Library, Devon, 1993 (atrium over entrance)
Ipswich Library, Suffolk, 1994 (large atrium over part of adult lending library)

Figure 9.3   Atriums and voids in UK library buildings

MEZZANINE FLOORS

A mezzanine may be the raised part of a library floor, in which case the matter of easy access for all to the upper level will need to be planned for. More usually it is a part upper floor over a lower floor. This library feature also gets a bad press. It is seen as offering little aesthetic gain; creating a fixed function area; increasing the cost of construction; giving access difficulties and problems of moving library materials up and down. Why not have a full floor? says one critic.[58]

Mezzanine floors work best when they are allocated an important part of the library service that attracts users in good numbers, when satisfactory access is provided (as is required today), and where, whatever their size and height and placement, they do not adversely affect the space below them. Wheeler thought them most advantageous in small libraries where space and cost were project constraints. He thought their use could be abused by architects wanting to create a 'well' effect with an encircling balcony.[59]

An interesting example of the use of a small, oblong centrally placed mezzanine occurs at Ross-on-Wye Library (Hereford, 1988), where access from the counter area leads up to the staff workroom, office, and so on. Bridport Library, Dorset (1997, 480m^2) has a first-floor mezzanine for adult non-fiction, reference material and local studies, with access by stairs and lift. Worcester Park Millennium Library, London Borough of Sutton (2000, 262m^2) has a mezzanine floor because of the limited size of the library site. Two twenty-first century Irish public libraries provide contrasting examples of the use of the mezzanine: Blanchardstown Library, Dublin (2,610m^2) and the smaller Cootehill Library, Co. Cavan, both opened in 2001.

GALLERIES

An early modern library plan was the Scandinavian gallery type plan (now no longer in vogue) pioneered by the Central Public Library, Fredriksberg, Denmark (1935). The adult lending department, in the centre of the building, was a large hall with wall shelves and a shelved gallery above accessible to readers. Today the gallery, or balcony around one or more walls of the library, is not a common feature of the modern public library building, except in buildings converted to library use where this may have been an original feature. Examples of such conversions include Hexham Library and Arts Centre (Northumberland, 1981), Coventry Central Library (1986), Denbigh Library and Museum (Clwyd, 1986) and Leamington Spa Library (1,300m², 1999). Where such balconies or galleries are sufficiently spacious they may, for example, house a number of subject areas or reference and local studies facilities.

Many of the comments made about the mezzanine apply to the gallery or balcony. In small or medium-sized libraries they may occasionally be used as a bookstore gallery, as at Shildon Branch Library (County Durham, 1981) and Pershore Library (Worcestershire, 1975), or more probably for reference and study facilities (Petersburn Library and Drop-in Centre (Monklands, 1991). At Evesham Library (Worcestershire, 1990) its dramatic interior is enhanced by a balcony which houses a grand piano, amongst other things.

CEILING HEIGHT AND WINDOWS

In Victorian and Edwardian library buildings, the public rooms often had tall windows and high ceilings, usually decorated with ornate mouldings. Light and airy rooms were required as much for ventilation as for aesthetic effect. By contrast the low, flat-roofed, rectangular buildings of the 1960s often had fairly standard ceiling heights, except where required to accommodate a gallery or mezzanine floor. Extensive glazing of one or more walls might also be a feature, especially at the entrance frontage. Where wall space was at a premium, narrow windows above the bookshelves were often used as a solution. As today, internal glazing would be used to separate different library areas, while still allowing some oversight, or to enclose planting or define an internal courtyard. As at any period of library history, not all single-storeyed libraries conformed to this description. Libraries with pitched roofs and high internal ceilings were also to be found.

Today even small libraries are likely to have high ceilings, with exposed roof trusses, whether of metal or wood, forming part of their aesthetic appeal. Glazed walls of some size may also be a feature of their library design.

STAIRS, LIFTS AND ESCALATORS

Early public libraries relied entirely on stairs for reader access to their upper floors. Today lifts and, in bigger libraries, escalators (such as those in Birmingham, Sunderland

and Croydon) are an important feature of multi-storeyed library buildings, libraries with mezzanines and galleries, or those sited at first floor level.

Peterson noted in his survey of main library buildings that open stairways, while possibly aesthetically pleasing, can impede traffic flow, reduce flexibility and create administrative difficulties. He felt that there were advantages in placing such things as stairways, book lifts and lifts for people in a building core and that escalators, like stairways, also needed to be carefully placed, and in a way that allowed for supervision. One library director wanted better control by placing public elevators in a bank, rather than scattered, and having them located in the entrance lobby. Also public service lifts should not go to non-public areas and lifts for closed areas should be outside public areas of the library.[60] Lifts can be major internal design features, as in Metropolitan Toronto Library for instance, as can escalators, as deployed in Rotterdam Central Library.

GARDENS AND COURTYARDS

The use of plants in libraries, as in commercial and other public buildings, is not unusual, but since at least the 1960s, many public libraries have been built with interior gardens or courtyards as a major or minor feature of the overall design. This may be a small, centrally placed, full-height glass-enclosed planted area, as at Newtown Library, Powys, or a raised bed of planting running the length of part of the library. Metropolitan Toronto Library has a garden feature that includes indoor pools, and Helsinki City Main Library includes a water pool in the centre of the principal public area.[61]

The internal courtyard may form part of the interior design for a variety of reasons: to break up and thus add variety to the library space; to give natural light in a deep building, or to provide an outdoor area for sitting, reading and library activities. Courtyards may not necessarily be an interior feature of a building but may be an enclosed space to the side, front or rear of the library, as at Lochthorn Library (Dumfries and Galloway, 1995). Other British examples include:

- Hornsey Central Library (1965) – incorporates a garden court and pool
- West Norwood Library – the courtyard was redesigned in 2000
- Lincoln Central Library – the 1996 refurbished and extended building (described in Chapter 5) contains a courtyard.

INTERNAL DECORATIVE FEATURES

Construction materials and features, such as brickwork, steelwork (sometimes coloured), timber beams and cladding, glass and plaster, as well as light fittings, can all lend distinction to the library interior. Non-structural decorative features added to the library interior include banners (which can also be used outside the library), murals and other works of art, such as paintings, prints, free-standing sculpture, wall hangings, and stained or engraved glass panels. Traditionally, library art is created by local artists and is usually commissioned for the building. Works of art are usually funded by the setting aside of a percentage of the cost of the building or by seeking external funding available for public art.[62] Linton Library, Cambridgeshire (1999, 150m²) installed artwork designed by local people, and at Muirhouse Library, Edinburgh (2000, 737m²), 1 per cent of capital was allocated to works of art.

Local artefacts may also be displayed in the library, both for their historic interest as well as their aesthetic value. Whether artefacts or works of art, renewing and rotation is important if they are not to become invisible over time. In selecting or commissioning works of art, librarians must beware of adopting a conservative, reassuring and nostalgic approach and be willing to be more adventurous.[63] As experience from the US shows, public art, in one case murals planned for Albuquerque Public Library, can sometimes cause controversy. Resolved in this instance by compromise amongst the artists, architect and city official involved, the murals were painted on panels and attached to the walls of the library.[64]

Examples of decorative features include:

- banners: Croydon Central Library (outside the building)
- murals: Wath upon Dearne Library, West Riding of Yorkshire (1970); Ardkeen Library (2002)
- works of art: Uppsala Library, Sweden (1986)
- inscriptions: Kensington Central Library (1960) has a 'Wisdom and understanding' quotation; Sunderland and Ardkeen libraries have inscriptions on glass and wood
- window designs: Glastonbury Library, Somerset (2000) has a specially commissioned pair of circular windows at either end of the building using designs that reflect the history of the town and of the library site
- artefacts: Buncrana Library has a small boat of local type suspended from the ceiling in the adult lending library
- exhibitions and displays: where there is appropriate space and equipment, they can also add colour and variety to the library interior.

The library impact study noted earlier indicated that over half of the 70 new libraries surveyed made provision for public art in their buildings.[65]

COLOUR SCHEMES

On the whole British librarians are not adventurous when it comes to the use of colour, whether for interior finishes to the building or for furniture and soft furnishings. Indeed the impact of an exciting and colourful exterior may be somewhat lessened by a rather restrained, undifferentiated interior – all pastel colours. The children's library or teenagers' section might be a little more colourful. By contrast, Stratford Library, Newham, benefiting from the advice of interior designers, makes use of a palette of strong colours – blue, yellow, red in the children's library and green, as well as graphics. A similar strong palette of colours was used in the refurbishment of Lowestoft Library by employing the same interior designers. At Portsmouth Library (1976) the use of red and black for soft furnishings created a rich effect.

At Huizen in the Netherlands, the library is part of what has been described as a UFO-like building with an unappealing and unwelcoming library entrance. The library proper, however, makes use of a striking colour scheme featuring red, blue and silver in its public areas. The bold use of colour and stylish furniture is deemed to have created an outstanding library.[66]

In a small-scale survey in Australia it was found that people's preferred colour was blue: 'yet when asked to indicate the preferred colours to adopt in library interior design, light and neutral colours became the overriding preference'.[67]

GUIDING AND SIGNS

Like hospitals, supermarkets and department stores, libraries rely on signs to help users find their way around. Library signs and guiding may be completely or partially overlooked at the planning and design stages and that omission only made good to a greater or lesser extent when the building is opened, sometimes in a makeshift fashion. This poses practical difficulties for users, who may be confused and discouraged from self-help, as well as being detrimental to the image of the library. Guiding as an afterthought has to be deplored and should be given due consideration in the brief, as the guiding system should not be considered in isolation but integrate with and contribute to the aesthetics of the interior, as well as carrying out its functional task. Signs and guiding are part of the library's system of communication with its users and potential users: this includes its printed materials, and so on, as they help market the library and contribute towards its brand image.

Signs and guiding perform three main tasks:

- to inform – for example, plans, directories, warning and prohibitive signs and notices showing opening hours, also instructions for the use of equipment or procedures during fire or other emergencies
- to direct – that is, arrow signs pointing the way to particular destinations, such as reference library, learning centre or local studies department
- to identify – indicating when a destination has been reached; for example, fiction, toilets, information desk.

There is usually a hierarchy of signs leading from those that inform to those that direct and identify. In libraries on more than one floor or level, guiding will be needed at junctions, stairs and lifts, and consideration will need to be given as to which system of floor naming and numbering is to be used. 'Cake' plans, showing each library floor, provide an easily understood map of what is where in a multi-level building and may be made more useful by means of colour coding.

Signs may be wall-mounted (flat or projecting), hung from the ceiling or free-standing, others may be attached to shelving and doors or located by furniture and equipment.

PLANNING AND CHOOSING A GUIDING SYSTEM

The guiding system needs planning, not only to decide on the required signs and their location, but to take into account such matters as the following: choice of lettering (Helvetica is very popular), colour, size, the use of symbols, method of fixing, illumination (if required over service desks and counters, for example), flexibility (easy to move or update), protection against tampering and vandals, and maintenance. 'Maintaining signs is much like maintaining the collection; it is ongoing. No signage system is ever completed.'[68]

In choosing a guiding system it may be decided to use (or adapt) a commercially available system, or to have one custom designed for the building. A suitable guiding system may be in use already, however, in a public library service's other buildings. Where this not the case, a custom-designed system may be preferred as providing a distinctive house style. Quality and consistency of guiding can be ensured by the creation and updating of a library sign manual. Once installed, the effectiveness of guiding and signs need to be formally evaluated.[69]

The provision of too much by way of guiding, however, may mean that the library is not organized in the most helpful and logical way and the layout should therefore be examined.

In addition to signs, almost anything can help in guiding the reader; for example, the positioning of plants, sculpture or other non-verbal means (such as letters, numbers, symbols, pictograms, colour coding, and the way furniture is placed).[70] Other methods can include prominently displayed floor plans of the library, showing where staff points, sections of the collection, photocopiers, and so on, are located. A computerized version – relating class marks to library locations – is another possibility, although as with floor plans it can suggest a static layout. Video screens or computer terminals can also be used to inform users about library and other events, new services, changes to library arrangements, notice of closure and so on, or to provide answers to frequently asked questions about using the library, its services and equipment. Terminals might also be used to provide a virtual tour of the library. In all such instances most information is easily changed and updated.

Computers can not only be used to provide information to users but also to create 'attractive, helpful signs. This is a fast and inexpensive method of producing most temporary, as well as many permanent signs'.[71] There is no longer any excuse for poor, handwritten temporary signs that spoil the look of the library. Even temporary signs should conform to agreed housestyle. A selection of general informal principles adopted by some libraries has been summarized by Ragsdale and Kenney:

- for maximum effect, try to keep the number of signs to a minimum
- keep sign colour, wording, and placement uniform throughout
- have permanent signs manufactured professionally (it is worth the cost)
- invest in sign holders rather than fixing temporary signs to the wall.

Kirby lists nine key points for getting people round the library using signs and guiding. Four of these key points are:

- save the detail until needed
- provide guiding at all junctions and decision points
- repeat floor and 'cake' plans at frequent intervals
- guide the user to the exit and other destinations.[72]

Ragsdale and Kenney also have suggestions on mistakes to avoid:

- too many signs; too many words
- signs which are too big or too small
- not enough colour contrast in lettering and background
- signs which are not tamper-resistant near or in lifts or low traffic areas.[73]

The guiding and signs for those with disabilities need to be carefully considered: voice messages, raised lettering and Braille signs, for example. Avoiding poor colour contrast and eliminating glare will be of benefit to all users, not just the disabled.

An American survey has shown that many different colour combinations are in use, with black letters on a white background considered by many to be very effective. Dark backgrounds with lighter letters were thought by others to be more visible and legible: for example, white letters on black, blue, red, burgundy or brown backgrounds.[74] A system of colour coding for departments or types of material can also be reflected in the signage.

FURNITURE

As with planning the library building, the selection of shelving and furniture may be a completely new challenge to the librarian, although others are likely to be involved in the process. But

> Regardless of who has primary responsibility for furniture selection, active involvement of librarians in the process is necessary to ensure that the completed library interior is functional.[75]

This advice comes from an American publication which relates library planning to the selection process, arguing the need for furniture selection to be part of the design process and not left until it is time to fill out the empty spaces on the architect's final drawings.

In making furniture and shelving selection three major issues are of importance:

- function – What is its purpose? Who will use it and how?
- maintenance – the ability to stand heavy use and ease of cleaning and repair, and so on
- appearance – its attractiveness and its contribution to the overall ambience and image of the library; its compatibility with other furniture.[76]

As with colour, it would seem that UK librarians have an innate conservatism as regards library furniture. White metal shelves with light wood end panels seem almost de rigeur in recent years, even where other finishes and styles are available from library furniture suppliers. Wester Hailes, Edinburgh (1997), provides an example of a different, more open, colourful style in its approach to furniture selection.

In Finnish and Swedish public libraries of the 1990s, furniture could be architect-designed or standard library furniture, sometimes customized by the architect to create something a little different from that found in other libraries. In Denmark much was supplied by the Danish Library Design Centre.[77] As in the UK, library furniture suppliers make a distinctive contribution to the public library environment and image. At Drachten in the Netherlands a furnishing unit was specially designed for the new public library completed in 1991. Used throughout the building to accommodate displays and provide working surfaces, it resembles a child's swing. A reappraisal of the library's layout and furniture at Delft Public Library led to the design of new computer workstations designed to enable users to work together, in pairs, for example. Scaled-down versions are provided for children. Although custom-built, the workstations are cheaper than those from library suppliers.

There is no reason why older, often more solid library furniture cannot be recycled for use in new or converted buildings. Burnley revamped its library shelving when the library was modernized in 1994 and around the same time Southampton created a period atmosphere in its impressive local studies room through the re-use of furniture from an earlier period of the library's history.

The importance of furniture for a library's image is demonstrated by the comments of public relations experts on four Dutch public libraries. In their view the use of wooden shelves and carpeted floors at two libraries created a welcoming image to users, while aluminium shelves and linoleum at another suggested a dull, old-fashioned image.[78]

For both staff and public areas, 'system furniture' has been suggested to create workstations. Parts can be assembled in a variety of configurations. Such furniture includes wire management capabilities, is ergonomic and flexible, and can be equipped with light fittings and acoustic panels.[79]

LIGHTING

There are many issues connected with library lighting: preservation, health and safety, energy consumption and lighting for particular purposes, such as displays, exhibitions, computer use and study. In this chapter, lighting will be considered largely from an aesthetic point of view as a major contributor to the attractiveness and appeal of the library building. This concerns the appropriate use of natural and artificial light and how the two affect the ambience and appeal of the library, as well as providing satisfactory levels of illumination for particular tasks.

It has been said that lighting is a main consideration of library design[80] and, while wishing to bring natural light into the building – it is free, after all – there are certain disadvantages as regards its changing intensity and position. Continuous exposure to natural light is also damaging to library materials. A design which makes much use of glass, and therefore of natural light, without adequate controls (such as external shading or blinds), may subject users to glare and discomfort caused by heat gain in summer and heat loss in winter. While the feeling of spaciousness and airiness that the use of glass can bring to a building is to be welcomed, there should be a balance between building transparency, views into and out of the building, aesthetics, and the practicalities of library use, without returning to library designs that have an over-reliance on electric light.

In using electric lighting there may be a tendency to employ a standard level throughout the building. However, 'Uniform lighting is observed to present a dull overall appearance and should only be required where uniform tasks are undertaken'.[81] A lighting system should not neglect the opportunity to use decorative lighting, spotlights, concealed lighting, uplighting and task lighting to create a more varied and comfortable environment.

The way lighting is designed for use in the library will influence the choice of finishes, provide the right levels of illumination for particular tasks and will help to avoid the discomfort to users of glare and brightness. Lighting design guidance, with appropriate recommendations, has been prepared by the then Chartered Institute of Building Services (now CIBSE).[82]

FLOORING

Until the 1960s library flooring was of the hard and practical kind – wood or linoleum – that needed considerable maintenance through polishing or washing. The luxury, as it was considered, of carpet began in an incremental way, with particular areas of the library being carpeted, such as a browsing or reading area. In due course carpeting the library throughout, often using carpet tiles, was considered the normal way of providing a floor covering.

267

Through its colour and design, carpet adds to the appeal of the library interior, but it is not without its problems of wear and damage that can make the library floor look unsightly and even dangerous; hence the appeal of carpet tiles that allow rapid 'repairs' to the floor covering. However, some librarians are discouraged by the problems associated with carpet and are making use of marmoleum for flooring.

For health reasons, as discussed in Chapter 6, not all librarians and library workers are happy with carpeted interiors, as they are believed to encourage allergies. Scandinavian libraries observed by the author in the early 1990s appeared to avoid carpeted libraries, making use of wood, linoleum and even paved interior surfaces in stone or marble. The question of noise seemed not to be a problem given the soft shoes that are worn nowadays.[83]

ACOUSTICS

Three categories of acoustical problems in libraries have been identified:

- intrusive noise – for example, children's areas, or a building's mechanical systems
- overly reverbant spaces – communication can seem difficult and they always seem 'noisy'
- lack of speech privacy or distraction from unwanted speech, other workstations, carrels or library users.

In overcoming these problems it is suggested that noise and acoustics, matters of particular concern when library buildings are evaluated, are raised at the planning stage, that the subsequent design is assessed to see how they have been addressed, and that options are offered when there are cost problems or design issues involved.[84]

So far, this book has been concerned with the purpose and roles of the public library, the nature of the physical structure erected to fulfil them and the concepts that might underlie their creation. The following chapter considers how the elements of the library – its departments, areas or rooms – can be deployed and organized to reflect library use. In particular it looks at the way the library's stock or collections might be arranged to suit the needs of users and how this grouping influences the library layout and organization.

NOTES

1   Melling, G. (1993), 'The body language of library buildings', *New Zealand libraries* **47** (8), 150–56: 151.
2   Wheeler, J. (1967), *A reconsideration of the strategic location for public library buildings*, Urbana, Illinois: University of Illinois Graduate School of Library Science, 31.

3   Muddiman, D. and others (2000), *Open to all? The public library and social exclusion*, volume 1 *Overview and conclusions*, London: Resource, 62.

4   Muddiman, D. and others (2000), 62–3.

5   Muddiman, D. and others (2000), 62–3

6   Cronin, B. (1981), *A national graphics resource centre for libraries in the United Kingdom*, London: Aslib, 30 and appendices 16, 17 and 18.

7   Berndtson, M. and Ostrom, M. (2002), 'A common European logo for public libraries', (in Finnish), *Kirjastolheti* (3), 23.

8   Plotnik, A. (1988), 'Chicago to build nation's largest municipal library', *American libraries* **19** (7), 565–6.

9   Baltimore County Public Library, Blue Ribbon Committee (1992), *Give'em what they want!: managing the public's library*, Chicago: American Library Association, Chapter 8 'The buildings they want', 122–37.

10 Muddiman, D. and others (2000), 62-3; Wagner, G.S. (1992), 'Public library buildings: a semiotic analysis', *Journal of librarianship and information science* **24** (2), 101–8; Hart, C., Bains, M. and Jones, K. (1996), 'The myth of material knowledge: reading the image of library buildings', *New library world* **97** (1127), 23–31.

11 Holt, G. (1998), 'Libraries that delight', *Bottom line* **11** (4), 180–83.

12 Melling, G. (1993), 150, 151, 152.

13 Simon, M. (1992), 'Marketing libraries through their physical environment', *Wilson library bulletin* **66** (7), 33–5, 120: 34.

14 Simon, M. (1992), 120.

15 Simon, M. (1992), 120.

16 Wagner, G. (1992), *Public libraries as agents of communication: a semiotic analysis*, London: Scarecrow, 48.

17 Kniffel, L. (1992), 'Interior dialogues: library design speaks volumes to users', *American libraries* **23** (4), 281–8.

18 Clee, J. and Maguire, R. (1993), 'Library environment and library usage', *Library management* **14** (5), 6–8: 8.

19 Niedzwetzki, J. (1991), 'Colour and lighting in public libraries', *Australasian public libraries and information services* **4** (2), 103–5: 105.

20 The impact of this concept on the library's design is discussed by the architect in Mäki-Jyllilä, J. (1999), 'Planning a library for the future', *Scandinavian public library quarterly* **32** (4), 21–2: 22.

21 Sturt, R. (ed.) (1963), 'An architectural project: four students' plans', in *New library buildings 1962–1963*, London: Library Association, 453–9: 454.

22 Sturt, R. (ed.) (1963), 457.

23 Sturt, R. (ed.) (1963), 458.

24 Csomay, Z, Hegedus, P. and Kerecsenyi, Z. (1987), 'County Library, Bekescsaba', in *Adaptation of buildings to library use*, edited by M. Dewe, Munich: Saur, 228–38: 229.

25 Bjarrum, C (2001), 'Hillerød Knowledge and Culture Park', *Scandinavian public library quarterly,* **34** (1), 10–11.

26 Jouly, H. (2001). 'Stuttgart: on the way to Library 21', in *Library buildings in a changing environment*, edited by M-F. Bisbrouck, Munich: Saur, 91–7: 91.

27 Delambre, R. and Delambre-Zhou, M. (2004), 'Anatomy of Shanghai Public Library' (in French), *Biblothèque(s)* (13), 22–4.

28 Mevissen, W. (1958), *Büchereibau/Public library buildings*. Essen: Heyer, 56–7.

29 Ellin, I. (1987), 'The market of knowledge and the street of information', *Scandinavian public library quarterly* **20** (4), 39–46: 46. Both Skara and Sundsvall are described in *The library of the '80s: Swedish public library buildings 1980–89* (1990), Stockholm: Swedish National Council for Cultural Affairs, 32–40.

30 Stanley, J. (2003), 'Grow your library', *Public library journal* **18** (4) 94–5.

31 Sannwald, W.W. (1998), 'Espresso and ambiance: what public libraries can learn from bookstores', *Library administration and management* **12** (4), 200–206, 211; Rippel, C. (2003), 'What public libraries can learn from bookstores', *Australasian public libraries and information services* **16** (4), 147–55.

32 *Borrowed time? The future of public libraries in the UK* (1993), Bournes Green, Gloucestershire: Comedia, 78.

33   Hirn, S. (1986), 'Entrance area strategy in libraries', *Scandinavian public library quarterly* **19** (4), 129–31.

34   Wills, H. (2004), 'An innovative approach to the non-learning public: the new Idea Stores in London', in *Libraries as places: buildings for the 21st century,* edited by M-F. Bisbrouck and others, Munich: Saur, 103–16.

35   Bundy, A. (2004), 'Places of connection: new public and academic library buildings in Australia and New Zealand', *Australasian public library and information services* **17** (1), 32–47.

36   Maritikainen, T. (1987), 'The wood grouse takes off – Tampere Main Library in action', *Scandinavian public library quarterly* **20** (4), 19–21: 19.

37   Elonheimo, E. (1986), 'Ready for take-off. The new main library of Tampere', *Scandinavian public library quarterly* **19** (1), 16–22: 17.

38   Jouly, H. (2000), 'The dance of change: staff and user', *Liber quarterly* **10** (2), 160–67: 164. Updated by a later paper: Bussman, I. (2003), 'Library 21, Stuttgart', given at an international seminar, Library architecture and design: European perspectives, Institut Français, 6 May.

39   Rizzo, J. (1992), 'Ten ways to look at a library', *American libraries* **23** (4), 322–4, 326.

40   *Borrowed time?* (1993), 77.

41   Simon, M. (1992), 35.

42   Krol, J. (1999), ' The new Arnhem Library to be housed in Paradise' (in Dutch), *BibliotheekBlad* **3** (18), 12–14.

43   Vidulli, P. (1994), 'On a scale designed for the user' (in Italian), *Biblioteche oggi* **12** (1), 21–31.

44   Vecchiet, R. (2000), 'Where the hallmark is transparency' (in Italian), *Biblioteche oggi* **18** (7), 30–35.

45   Charles, Prince of Wales (1989), *A vision of Britain,* London: Doubleday, 90–92.

46   Reed, H.H. (1986), *The New York Public Library: its architecture and decoration,* London: Norton.

47   *Newyddion,* (60) Sept 2002, [2].

48   McKeon, B, (1993), 'Public library service in New Zealand: Wellington Public Library', *Wilson library bulletin* **67** (8), 38–9.

49   Mack, G. and Liebermann, V. (2000), *Eberswolde Library: Herzog and De Meuron,* London: Architectural Association, 8.

50   Carr, S. *et al.* (1992), *Public space,* Cambridge: CUP, 109.

51   Carr, S. *et al.* (1992), 111.

52   Lyall, S. (1997), *Designing the new landscape,* London: Thames & Hudson, 19.

53   Bryson, J., Usherwood, B. and Proctor, R. (2003), *Libraries must also be buildings? New library impact study,* London: Resource, 39.

54   Bryson, J, *et al.* (2003), Appendix 7.

55   Kent, F. and Myrick, P. (2003), 'How to become a great public space', *American libraries* **37** (4), 72–4, 76. See also, website of the Project for Public Spaces (www.pps.org).

56   Martin, L. (1998), *Enrichment: a history of the public library in the United States in the twentieth century,* London: Scarecrow, 90.

57   Cohen, A. and Cohen, E. (1979), *Designing and space planning for libraries: a behavioral guide,* 67.

58   Peterson, H.N. (1972), 'Developments in the planning of main library buildings', *Library trends* **20** (4), 693–741: 701–2.

59   Wheeler, J. (1966), 'Mezzanines', *Library journal* 91 December 1, 5851.

60   Peterson, H.N. (1972), 706.

61   Lindqvist, E. (1987), 'Helsinki City Main Library', *Scandinavian public library quarterly* **20** (4), 16–18.

62   For public art and local authorities, see www.publicartonline.org.uk.

63   Vogrin, J. (1990), 'Interior public art in libraries', *New Jersey libraries* **23** (1), 7–12: 10–11, 12.

64   Waters, R.L. (2001), 'A brush with compromise ...', *Public library quarterly* **19** (4), 21–6.

65   Bryson, J., Usherwood, B. and Proctor, R. (2003), *Libraries must also be buildings? New library impact study,* London: Resource, Appendix 7.

66   Krol, J. (2001), 'Who is afraid of red, silver and blue?' (in Dutch), *Bibliotheeksblad* **5** (8), 10–11. For another description, with an English summary, see Krol, J. (2003), *New library buildings in the Netherlands,* The Hague: Netherlands Library Association, 30–33.

67   Niedzwetzki, J. (1991), 103.

68   Ragsdale, K. and Kenney, D.(1995), 'Introduction', [2].

69   The major stages in a signing project, the preparation of a sign manual, evaluation of the system, etc.,
      are dealt with in Reynolds, L. and Barrett, S. (1981), *Signs and guiding for libraries*, London: Bingley,
      146–50. For a published example of a sign manual see Henderson, J. (1982), *T.L. Robertson Library sign
      manual*, Perth: Western Australian Institute of Technology.

70   Cohen, A. and Cohen, E. (1979), *Designing and space planning for libraries: a behavioral guide*, New York:
      Bowker, 183–212.

71   Ragsdale, K. and Kenney, D. (1995), 'Introduction', [2].

72   Kirby, J. (1985), *Creating the library identity: a manual of design*, Aldershot: Gower, 90.

73   Ragsdale, K. and Kenney, D. (1995), 5–6. This is a selection (with small changes to wording) of two lists:
      'informal rules' and 'mistakes to avoid'. See also Stanley, J. (2004), 'Signs dos and don'ts', *Library +
      information update* **3** (4), 25.

74   Ragsdale, K. and Kenney, D. (1995), *Effective library signage*, Washington DC: Association of Research
      Libraries, Office of Management Services, 'Introduction' [1].

75   Brown, C. R. (1995), *Planning library interiors: the selection of furnishings for the 21st century*, Phoenix,
      Arizona: Oryx, xiii. A similar work by the same author is *Interior design for libraries: drawing on function
      and appeal* (2003), Chicago: American Library Association. An allowance must be made for US
      legislation, business practice and the use of imperial rather than metric measurement. An earlier and
      somewhat wider-ranging work is Pierce, W.S. (1980), *Furnishing the library interior*, New York: Dekker.

76   A more detailed list of criteria is given in Michaels, D.L. (1995), 'So, just select some furniture', *Library
      administration and management* **9** (3), 140–44.

77   Dewe, M. (1992), 'Compliments, comments and contrasts: a view of Scandinavian public library
      buildings', *Scandinavian public library quarterly* **26** (1), 4–6: 5.

78   Tilburg, L. (2000), 'A bit of fun doesn't harm' (in Dutch), *BibliotheekBlad* **4** (5), 18–19.

79   Novak, G. (1988), Office-landscape furniture systems create order out of computer chaos', *American
      libraries* **19** (4), 270–71.

80   Scherer, J. (1999), 'Light and libraries', *Library hi tech* **17** (4), 358–71.

81   Niedzwetzki, J. (1991), 104.

82   Chartered Institute of Building Services (1982), *CIBS lighting guide: libraries*, London CIBS.

83   Dewe, M. (1992), 6.

84   Wrightson, D. and Wrightson, J.M. (1999), 'Acoustical considerations in planning and design of library
      facilities', *Library hi tech* **17** (4), 349–57.

10 The library interior

A library must be arranged in some kind of order and a list of its contents provided.

James Thompson, 1977[1]

In the brief, the librarian describes for the architect the range of departments, rooms, areas and spaces that are required in the library building, and their preferred relationships. These relationships may also be shown diagrammatically as part of the brief. For a multi-storeyed library, the librarian may (in some circumstances) also indicate those parts of the library which it is preferred should be located on the various floors or levels of the building. The right spatial relationships will ensure that the time and convenience of users and staff is not imposed upon and that the library can be used and operated economically, efficiently and effectively.

Although an indication of the preferred relationships of library departments and areas may appear to dictate the design solution, this is not the case, for the architect must balance the client's ideal requirements with the constraints imposed by the site and its size, finance, and building and fire regulations.

In determining the right spatial relationships the librarian will take into account a number of factors that relate to the use and operation of the library. While some may reflect well established principles of designing library layouts, other factors will be determined by the pursuit of particular policy decisions relating to the library service, its organization and management. Such decisions will be reflected in the internal organization of public and staff spaces and the manner in which the library's collections are organized and displayed.

CYCLES IN LIBRARY PRACTICE

In the long history of libraries and their design, a number of issues have re-occurred over the centuries that affect library organization and layout. Not surprisingly they have been handled in completely contrasting ways at different times. The four main issues are:

- access to the collection
- security of the collection
- the organization of library materials
- the layout of shelving, tables and seating, and similar items.

In dealing with these organizational and intellectual matters, library practice has, over the years, sometimes swung from one position to its exact opposite. Although public libraries have a shorter history than libraries generally – in the UK of just over 150 years – there have been significant changes of direction as regards, for instance, access to library materials and their organization on the shelves – matters that have affected in particular the interior design and layout of the public library.

ACCESS TO THE COLLECTION

Free access to the library collection, allowing readers to move around and choose their books and other materials, has varied over the centuries. Increased number of users and larger stocks in the nineteenth century led to closed access libraries, where material was fetched for readers from the stacks. In the UK, the early public libraries were closed access libraries. James Duff Brown implemented the first open access public library in 1894 and, although widely (if slowly) adopted, closed access lingered on until the 1940s and the early 1950s. In public libraries having a substantial reserve stock, access to the stacks where it is held is generally closed to readers. In some instances, however, access to the reserve stacks could be encouraged and so reflected in the library design and layout.

SECURITY OF THE COLLECTION

> The chains [in medieval libraries] ... were the technology that brought a change in library policy and the granting of direct access to books. They solved the problem of security.[2]

Closed access and records of loans, however, were the methods of ensuring security in the early public libraries. Open access, when introduced later, was generally called safeguarded open access and required a barrier-like counter and wicket gates at the library's entry and exit points. In the early twentieth century many of the wicket gates were removed as not being good for the library image and the security of library books was generally ignored. With the appearance of new formats for loan, the advent of electronic security systems and a realization of probable stock losses, as discussed in Chapter 6, security is once more an issue, and not just for the collection.

ORGANIZATION OF LIBRARY MATERIALS

Classification

'The provision to the public of access to a collection does not in itself ensure effective retrieval of the desired information.'[3] The organization for retrieval of books, other materials and information in libraries has therefore generally relied on a classification scheme for imposing an order on the collection. Initially, where used, it was broad classification, but with the emergence of detailed subject classification schemes, such as the Dewey Decimal Classification and the Library of Congress in the nineteenth century, a more complex system of arrangement for books on the shelves in public libraries was possible. Open access in public libraries demanded a system of arrangement to help both staff and readers locate the required book (or group of books) on a subject, and generally this has come to mean using the Dewey Decimal Classification, where a notation (the classmark or number) represents a subject.

Browsing

Without getting into a detailed discussion about the pros and cons of library classification, it is possible to say that many users are not looking for a particular book, or for books on a very specific subject, and this is probably true for other kinds of material. They may be looking for something to read in a particular fiction genre, such as a romance, a western or science fiction novel, or for something in a fairly broad subject area like travel, biography or sport, or just something interesting to read, listen to or to watch. The library, however, is usually organized to suit those who have a reasonably clear idea of what they want, rather than the browser. In Kent, for example, it was found that borrowers 'were making as much use of the few bays of returned shelves as the tens of bays of A–Z fiction'.[4]

This more casual or serendipitous way of using the library is often pleasant, effective, more rewarding and even more exciting for many readers. How librarians have provided for the browser, by minimizing organizational and physical barriers to browsing, is dealt with later in the chapter.

SHELVING AND FURNITURE

In those early libraries where readers were allowed access to the collection, the need for natural light meant that the placement of windows strongly dictated the library layout. Seating was placed between rows of shelves whose location, at right angles to the wall and between windows, created a kind of alcove arrangement. Where natural light came from higher or clerestory windows then shelving could also be arranged around the library walls. This helped to emphasize the alcove effect and is an arrangement that can still be seen in some modern library layouts. Figure 10.5 shows an interesting modern layout at Alton in Hampshire.

In closed access public libraries, and with the advent of artificial lighting, rows of shelving, now away from readers, could be closer together and bays could be higher. With the advent of open access, the shelving in public library interiors tended to be arranged quite formally in blocks with gangways. Usually the shelving was arranged at right angles (or radially) to the staff counter so that, in theory, it was feasible to oversee readers using the library and this too is an arrangement still to be found in some modern libraries: Epsom Library (2001, 1,393m²) in the Ebbisham Centre has a radial feel to the layout. It could be argued that the use of a numerical classification scheme like Dewey required a formal and orderly library layout.

Shelving patterns can be strongly influenced by the chosen method of stock arrangement; that is, whether there are alphabetical and classified arrangements or reader interest categories. The latter categorized arrangement and shelving layout are discussed later in this chapter.

The use of broad classification for some of a library's stock, the potential for the integration of hitherto separated parts and formats of the public library's collection, and the distribution, rather than segregation, of computer terminals, makes possible the creation of a more informal and varied library interior.

THE DESIGN CONTEXT

Not all public libraries have necessarily adopted precisely the same approach to access, security, shelf arrangement and the library layout. The exact resolution and implementation of these issues for particular libraries has to be set in the context of:

- any overall design concept or philosophy that underpins the whole building project
- the general design principles employed to determine spatial relationships between library areas
- the general design principles applied to the interior layout of individual areas and spaces
- the preferred organization of public spaces – for instance by function, such as lending or information-giving.

SPATIAL RELATIONSHIPS: GENERAL PRINCIPLES

There are a number of principles that might be employed for determining the spatial relationships of departments, areas, rooms and spaces within the library building. The application of individual principles will very much depend on the librarian's view of their significance for the library project in question. Space relationship and traffic flow diagrams will illustrate the nature of the preferred proximity and location of different elements of the building.

Most used departments or areas

These, together with income generation areas, are placed closest to the library entrance. This usually means a progression from the popular to the more purposive and then to the more specialized departments or services. In a multi-storey building this will probably result in an upwards floor progression from the the most-used to the more specialized parts of the library, as is the case in Shanghai Library (1996).[5] In Finland, however, library areas of secondary importance, such as a large auditorium, have been located in proximity to the entrance area, to the disadvantage of library users who must go upstairs in the building for library services.

High exposure

Services and facilities for which the librarian requires high exposure may also be placed near the entrance, such as a 'quick choice' area (as depicted by Figure 10.1), audio-visual material, exhibition and display areas and self-service information facilities. An example

Figure 10.1   Blackburn Library (refurbished 2003): 'quick choice' area
Source: Blackburn with Darwen Borough Council

277

of this approach is Fredericia Library (Denmark), where the entrance area leads up to the music and media department, with children's library, adults' section and the knowledge and information department on the three floors above.[6]

Noise

Noise has been identified earlier as a major library problem. One of the matters raised in a 2004 survey of People's Network users in Hillingdon was the 'lack of control of "noisy" kids'.[7] Noise will be a factor therefore in determining relationships. An open-plan library will endeavour to separate noisy areas – caused by the movement of people, conversation, and the use of machines – from quiet areas. These may contain enclosed carrels or silent rooms for those wishing to engage in prolonged study. One library has found that, 'even with cyberspace, there continues to be a great need for traditional research and reference work'. This has led to a cyber-free haven in the library – a glass-enclosed study and reading space.[8]

In multi-level buildings noise should diminish as readers move upwards in fewer numbers through the building to more specialized services.

Quiet should be planned for, as this is much easier (and less expensive) to do in advance than later having to take later remedial action. Not every noise problem in libraries can be anticipated, the now ubiquitous mobile phone, for example. These can be a source of irritation to some but not to others and so there is a need for a policy about their use in the library. This might provide for one or more dedicated areas where the use of mobile phones is permitted.[9]

Movement of staff and users

Staff will move to and from public and staff areas and from one staff area to another. Users will carry out a variety of activities, such as returning or borrowing a book or other item, consulting a book or other item, making use of ICT and other equipment, and attending a library or non-library activity, such as a meeting, held in the library during or outside library hours. A simple 'design formula', and largely applicable to study areas, suggests: (1) a movement area; (2) a buffer zone; (3) a prolonged study area.[10] The application of such a formula often results in the 'separation' of readers and their materials.

Those advocating a retail approach to the library layout draw attention to the counterclockwise arrangement in stores as being the direction with which most people are comfortable. In bookshops this can mean that customers come into contact first with best-sellers, behind which are located staff recommendations.[11]

Movement of materials

The organization of the library should reflect the movement of materials through the building, such as delivery and sorting of materials, their cataloguing, processing and dispersal to the shelves.

Co-location

Those parts of the library which might be used together (such as the reference library and local studies department, catering and toilet facilities, counter and workroom) should be co-located or in close proximity in the building.

INTERIOR LAYOUT: GENERAL PRINCIPLES

Many of the principles concerned with determining spatial relationships within the building, such as noise and traffic flow, will also govern the interior layout of individual departments or library areas within it; for example, the arrangement of shelving and seating in public areas and the layout of staff work areas. Other factors may include some of the following.

Security

The need for supervision and oversight of particular library areas (the children's and teenage areas, and archive and local studies sections, for example) will have an influence on the location of the counter or staff desk and the arrangement of the shelving.

Interaction

The need to encourage interaction between staff and users will affect the location and prominence of an enquiry information or help desk(s).

Critical distances

The need to take into account recommended clearances for furniture and shelving layouts (for example, the distance between rows of shelving, or between reader seats) will influence the detail of the layout in the library floor plan.[12]

Economical use of space

The need for the economical use of the available floor space may dictate a fairly formal arrangement of seating and shelving, rather than the more varied and informal layout that invites the user to explore.

Disturbance of readers

Disturbance of readers from others who are utilizing materials in an area primarily designated for study, thus creating noise and visual distraction, should be prevented as far as possible. It is suggested that 'at all costs study areas on one side or either side of gangways leading to stacks [or other areas] should be avoided'.[13]

An associated issue here is that of privacy when, for example, people use People's Network computers to conduct their financial and other personal business matters.[14]

Central square concept

The central square idea, put forward by the Cohens, suggests that, whatever the shape of the library building, 'the central square should be the focus of the library from which all user activities radiate, an open place where people and activities converge'.[15] Every floor and every department should have its central square, it is suggested. In some ways the concept has similarities with those of the market square or library street, as well as encapsulating various design principles; for example, areas needing less user interaction between staff and users, or where readers expect not to be disturbed, are situated at a distance from the central square.

Architectural features

Additional factors affecting the interior organization will be those introduced by the architect's design solution:

- the location of the entrance
- the number of floors
- the placing of structural columns
- the location of the service core or cores
- the shape of individual spaces
- fenestration – windows and glazed areas
- floor loading
- architectural features such as atriums, courtyards and galleries, described in the previous chapter.

ORGANIZATION OF PUBLIC AREAS

Public libraries may be physically and intellectually organized or divided up in a number of ways. Division of the library may be by:

1. *Function*: separate lending, reading and reference areas or departments, for example.
2. *User group*: for instance, separate areas of stock and/or services for adults, ethnic groups, disabled users, teenagers, children, under-fives and local historians.
3. *Form*: separate areas allocated to books, newspapers and periodicals, sound and visual recording, and electronic information, for example. This spreads related subject materials around the library building, although this suits those who just want

a given format. There is a danger that when a new format appears a new department is founded, usually because it requires special knowledge, skills and equipment.

4. *Popular and purposive nature*: the division of the library stock into popular and 'serious' sections, the popular section usually preceding the serious one in the library layout. This can be described as a two-part library, in contrast to the three-part division described below. In the UK, this concept was developed by A.W. McClelland in the 1950s, based on earlier work by Ernest Savage at Edinburgh in the 1930s. At his Tottenham Library, McClelland divided readers' interests into 'purposive' and 'diverting', creating what was known as 'service in depth'. Readers passed from a bookshop-like area, with fiction, non-fiction displays and a subject arrangement of current and classical material (the 'diverting' part of the library) to the 'purposive' area of a large non-fiction collection arranged by subject.[16] In Brent two methods of stock division were considered: separating popular material from more in-depth items on the same subjects, or creating a leisure oriented library from popular subjects and a 'serious' library from the other material. The latter choice was made and a Leisure Library created on the ground floor and an in-depth library on the first floor – The Upper Library.[17] At Hoddesdon Library the stock was divided into Family (recreational) on the ground floor and Subject (or purposive) on the lower ground floor.[18]

5. *Level of use*: the so-called tripartite library, dating from the 1970s, and used in some German public libraries, such as Gütersloh and Reutlingen. In one commentator's view, the three-part division in a large building is not good for users.[19] In this model the library areas are divided into three:
   - the near area – that holding current unclassified, uncatalogued items on non-standard bookshelves: this may well be a multimedia mix of items and changing displays, reflecting seasonal change and demands, and it can be the setting for discussion and for meeting friends
   - the middle area – that displaying less-used items in the more usual library manner
   - the remote area – the stored library materials only available via the catalogue.

6. *Subject*: the setting up or transformation of a general library into a library with a number of subject divisions or departments. These would be supported by a popular library with fiction and non-fiction, provision for children, possibly a general reference library, and probably functional units dealing with circulation and the acquisition of library materials, and so on. Such an arrangement is usually found in large libraries which permit a number of subject floors. Large open plan libraries on fewer floors may take a similar approach by dividing each floor into a number of subject areas.

Libraries may choose to use a mix of all of these characteristics of division – function, subject, and so on – to create separate departments, sections or areas in the library building. For example, Otterup Library, Denmark, has a 'supermarket' section, a lending library divided into areas defined by genre format, function (games area) and age group zones, and a classified part for material not included in the genre arrangement.[20]

Case study: Gütersloh Library

Jointly funded and administered by the town council and the Bertelmann Foundation, Gütersloh Library in Germany opened in 1984. Its library materials are organized as three collections. The first is a browsing collection of heavily used items, the second – the library proper – comprises alphabetical and classified sequences, and lastly a reserve collection. Material is moved between collections according to monitored demand. There is a children's library, as well as a department for the over-12s.

Gütersloh was the first library to use the tripartite concept to underpin the organization of a new library building, which comprises two wings linked by a central area under a cupola. This central area includes a café, behind which is the browsing area. Other materials are located on the first and second floors of the library.[21] The three-tier arrangement is also used at Harburg Branch Library, Hamburg. There, the 'near' area is described as a supermarket section and presents different groupings of material in bookshop fashion. The lending library is divided into areas defined by genres, format, function and users' ages. Books not included in the genre collections are in classified order.[22]

ORGANIZATION OF LIBRARY CONTENT

'Every library should have a policy ... about the arrangement of its stock', taking into account users and their needs and the variety of information formats that it houses.[23] Without such a policy, which can be outlined in the architect's brief, there can be no proper advance thinking about much of the future organization and layout of the library.

FICTION

In many libraries fiction may be kept largely in alphabetical author order. Some popular categories, such as romances, fantasy, spy stories and detective stories, may be shelved separately from this sequence. Other libraries may categorize as much of their so-called light fiction as possible, to include, for example, historical novels and science fiction, keeping these categories – and 26 or more may be used – separate from more literary or serious novels. The reasons given for categorizing fiction by genre, especially where there is a large fiction collection, are:

- to make browsing easier and more fruitful
- to improve access to popular material
- to increase self-service potential.[24]

Libraries could classify their fiction according to a particular classification scheme, of which a number have been proposed, such as those by E.A. Baker (1899) and A.W. McClellan (1978), but seemingly rarely used.[25] A Danish scheme combines fiction in A–Z order with a classified catalogue which it claims 'has increased reader satisfaction ... revived under-used bookstock ... and improved librarians' professional knowledge'.[26] The unwillingness for fiction readers to use a catalogue might be overcome by providing a database with appropriate search facilities, synopses, and an indication whether items were on loan or not.

It is usual to identify categories or genres by some kind of sticker, often pictorial, on the spine of the book. Where this is done, categorized stock need not necessarily be separated from the main collection but can be part of the usual alphabetical order. This may lessen the accusation that librarians are spoonfeeding readers. A Finnish branch library decided to categorize its entire collection into 11 classes, separately housed and each with marked coloured spine stickers. It was recognized that the number and type of categories should be adjusted to local demand and the size of the library. The biggest drawback was for those readers who look for fiction by author but this could be overcome by linking categories with catalogue entries.[27]

NON-FICTION

Non-fiction can be arranged on the shelves according to a classification scheme, invariably Dewey in public libraries, or by subject categories (described later in this chapter) that reflect the interests of library users. In a library on one floor, the numerical order of the classification scheme is usually reflected in the sequential layout of the shelving. A library on two or more floors, and with a large non-fiction stock, faces the problem of how the subject sequence, whether classified or in broad subject categories, should be dispersed over the different floors of the building.

SUBJECT DEPARTMENTS

Where a large library has a number of floors, it is possible to think of some floors as a subject floor or one housing a group of related subjects, with others accommodating the functional divisions of the library. Lowell Martin has described the rise (and decline) of the subject departmentalized library, noting its American origins in the early part of the twentieth century. Subject departments usually emerged when building opportunities came about and in the US these resulted initially in libraries with departments for art and music, local history and business. This trend was reflected in the UK in the 1930s with the opening of new large libraries at Sheffield, Manchester and elsewhere.

> Later development, in larger central buildings [in the US], sought to complete the ... circle of subjects, so that all topics were covered ... The number of subject departments in the full development is usually six to eight.[28]

In the UK, McClellan's 'service in depth' arrangement, described earlier, led a subject specialization scheme at Tottenham as part of this approach. The non-fiction was divided into five broad subject groups with specialist librarians. Mathematical models applied to the subject areas ensured viable stock levels. The resources that were needed and the complexity of McClelland's methodology meant his concept was never fully adopted elsewhere, although it is clear that his ideas continued to influence later stock management schemes and thus the organization and layout of the public library.

This subject approach to library organization in the UK was mainly pioneered in the large public libraries erected from the 1960s onwards in Newcastle upon Tyne (1965), Bradford (1967), Birmingham (1973) and, following its 1981 extension, the Mitchell Library (Glasgow). At Bradford Central Library in the 1960s it was decided to integrate the reference and lending stock in subject departments located on the first six floors of its ten-storey building. Popular and children's libraries were provided on the ground floor.[29] Newcastle upon Tyne, however, hoped 'to achieve the benefits of subject specialisation without incurring the cost of subject departmentalism' through the economic use of staff. Subject specialists would be accessible from the one major enquiry desk serving the demands of both reference and lending users. In a building of five main floors, the only subject department was the Northumberland Room.[30]

At Birmingham the reference library building, with its five subject floors, was linked to a lower structure that contained the entrance, lending library and other departments.[31] Originally, the Mitchell Library had followed the early subject model in its old building, creating three subject departments – music, local history and science and technology – but lack of space prevented further development. Its 13-floor extension in 1981 made it possible to have ten subject departments, including those for general reference and special collections. The only lending department was that for music.

The question of subject departments or areas in the library continues to engage library planners in Britain and elsewhere. The Norfolk and Norwich Millennium Library had as its original basic specification that the stock would be organized in nine subject departments, but this was not implemented in full in the completed building.[32]

The Vancouver Central Library, Canada (1995), is organized into 19 subject areas, 17 of which are public ones. These include language and literature, business and economics, a quick information service, and a youth department.[33] Traditional subject departments were eschewed, however, at the San Antonio Public Library, US (1995), where departments are as follows: telephone reference (non-public), media, circulation (non-fiction in Dewey order on six floors), reference, government documents and special services, periodicals, children, and Texana/genealogy.[34]

The advantages of subject organization are:

- all materials dealing with a subject are housed together
- readers have subject librarians, who build up the collections, to help them.

The disadvantages are seen as:

- expensive duplication of stock
- subject librarians being more difficult to recruit and retain, and more expensive to employ
- a larger staff is required
- use of individual departments is not necessarily constant during opening hours
- readers may have to visit more than one department.

For such reasons Martin notes a trend back towards broader subject divisions, such as the humanities, arts, social sciences and natural sciences. This may require some readjustment of the order of the classification scheme to bring dispersed subjects together in departments with these broad headings. For example, literature and language dispersed in Dewey may be brought together under the humanities banner. Sutton Central Library (1975, refurbished 2005), with three floors (each on two levels), was originally organized into five subject departments, each with its own colour code. In addition to a general and children's library, there were broad subject departments: language and literature (including fiction), music and arts, religion and social sciences, commerce, science and technology, history and travel, local studies and government publications. The refurbished central library is arranged somewhat differently and includes a quick choice area, readers' lounge and coffee bar, a music and film area, facilities for children and teenagers, a large open-plan bookstock area, IT suite and local studies centre.

Martin writes that there is no one right answer to the problem of organizing a complex structure like a large library but whatever is decided should be a user-oriented rather than a library-oriented structure. He also notes the historical movement away from the functional approach and then back: 'the functional foundation usually prevails. Other forms of specialization play more a supplementary and supporting role.'[35]

For the future Martin suggested that the public library be divided by focusing on its roles, resulting in divisions for education, information, recreation and, it might be added, culture. While not without its difficulties, 'there would be shift from function and from collection to purposes and to users'.[36]

Although interest in subject departmentalized public libraries seems to have declined in the US and UK, it is still a live professional issue in Europe, albeit using the broader approach. Including fiction, Malmö describes itself as having five subject sections: art and music; social science; humanities; and natural science and technology.[37] In late 2001, Hamburg Central Library was in the process of changing over to subject departments.[38] Solingen Municipal Library, Germany (2000), is on three floors and has departments for adults, children, teenagers and information. Within these, non-fiction is divided into broad subject groups.[39] In the multimedia library of Limoges (1998), the library is organized as five broad subject collections with a centre for young people. The subject sections are arranged by Dewey: its combination with a reader interest arrangement (see 'Alternative arrangement' below) did not work.[40] Turku Central Library, in Finland,

285

was opened in 2003 in a refurbished building plus a new one, and is divided into four departments. These are a children's library and three subject departments (society; nations and culture; nature, technology and leisure), each department stocking all types of material.[41]

ALTERNATIVE ARRANGEMENTS

Classification serves the purposive reader well but the browser less so. In the early 1940s, Detroit Public Libraries devised a Reader Interest Classification – broad classification for part of its stock – to serve the browser more helpfully. This approach received a great deal of attention in the UK in the late 1970s and 1980s and continues to be of interest both here and abroad. This, and other approaches to stock provision and arrangement, described in this chapter, have the potential to influence the furnishing, guiding and layout of the public library.

In the UK in the late 1970s, a number of library systems, such as Cheshire, Surrey, Brent, Sunderland and East Sussex, broke away from collections arranged entirely by Dewey to ones arranged by broad categories considered appropriate to readers' interests and needs. Associated with what became known as 'stock categorization' were other issues like integrated stock (discussed below), the greater use of paperbacks and, rather than the traditional balanced 'stock', one that was smaller and produced 'a closer "fit" between supply and demand'. There was a recognition also of 'the role of stock in improving the congeniality of public libraries'.[42] Stock categorization was the spur to changing the layout of the library, and improving its atmosphere and attractiveness.

Most libraries that use stock categorization use it for part of their non-fiction stock, the rest remaining in classified order. As with fiction, symbols or colour coding can be used to distinguish the categories, and books can be in classified, author or random order within categories.

In the mid-1990s it was noted that

> None of the public libraries report categorising children's (11-years) books. They remain in the traditional sequences of easy reader, alphabetical author arrangement of fiction and classified non-fiction, which are categories separated from the rest of the collection.[43]

In Cambridgeshire, however, children's fiction was divided into genres such as horse and pony stories, folk tales and legends, and stories to make you laugh.[44] In the same county in the 1980s, service was limited to 'popular' material in demand in the many small libraries in the suburbs of its two cities and the numerous villages in rural areas. At the time it was said that 'the form of service ... is evolving in response to the changing needs of each community' and that it was more flexible than Dewey 'and adaptable to the needs of a changing community'.[45]

Presentation is seen as vitally important to the successful implementation of stock categorization, and consideration must be given to:

- each category having its own bay of shelving
- order within categories
- visibility and thus location of categories in the library layout
- appropriate shelving
- face-on display
- good guiding and signs: the choice of wording is important
- the link with the library catalogue.

One writer has said that 'reader-interest classification [stock categorization] suits the current trend for library orientation from the users' perspective and increased responsiveness to popular and changing needs'.[46] In the UK an account of the widespread and continued use of alternative arrangement is provided by Glasgow City Libraries. In the 1990s ten libraries were operating with categorized stock: fiction is categorized too. Not all libraries use all the categories noted in Figure 10.2 (non-fiction) or Figure 10.3 (fiction).[47]

(1) Art world	(2) Business & industry
(3) Computer world	(4) Crime
(5) Entertainment	(6) Family & health
(7) Famous lives	(8) Food & drink
(9) History	(10) Hobbies & crafts
(11) House & garden	(12) Language
(13) Literature	(14) Living & learning
(15) Music	(16) Natural world
(17) Politics & government	(18) Science
(19) Scotland	(20) Sport & recreation
(21) Supernatural	(22) Transport
(23) Travel	(24) War
(25) Work & money	(26) World faiths

Figure 10.2 Non-fiction categories (Glasgow City Libraries)

(1) Adventure	(2) Crime
(3) Historical	(4) Romance
(5) Science fiction	(6) Sea stories
(7) Short stories	(8) Spy stories
(9) Supernatural	(10) War
(11) Westerns	

Figure 10.3 Fiction categories (Glasgow City Libraries)

CATEGORIZATION BY LEVEL

Another approach to the categorization of adult non-fiction, and investigated in the 1970s, involved classifying books by their intellectual or user level; for instance, as a popular, elementary or advanced publication. In this way, for example, symbols could be incorporated 'in catalogue entries and charging codes indicating the nature, and hence the potential use of each ... title'.[48] It was not proposed that books be arranged by these categories but they might be used as a further refinement of the two-part library organizational method, discussed earlier.

Reader interest classification or stock categorization is used in a variety of ways in other countries such as France, Japan, South Africa, Germany and the Netherlands. In the Netherlands, dissatisfaction with the Dutch classification system used in public libraries led to the formulation of in-house schemes such as those at Leerdam and Weert, and gave rise to the creation of the Presentation System for Information Media (PIM). This is considered 'suitable for collections up to 12,500 items, including non-book materials, and is easily understood by all users'.[49] Bad Homberg von der Hohe Municipal Library has recently reorganized its stock into thematic islands. These consist of thematic groups from the classified arrangement: natural language descriptions rather than class numbers are placed on the spines of books.[50]

AND NOW FOR SOMETHING DIFFERENT

Reader interest subject groupings of non-fiction and the categorization of fiction allow purposeful browsing by readers. Providing for those in a hurry, wanting to take pot luck, needing help with browsing, or wishing to be pointed in new directions requires a variety of different approaches, the tripartite library being one. In the past in the UK the trolleys or shelves of returned books have filled many of these roles. The Norfolk and Norwich Millennium Library has an 'express' choice area in the front part of the library, open longer hours than the rest of the building. Libraries in Suffolk have 'quick choice' areas near the entrance.

At Lausanne Public Library, 3,000 unclassified volumes, combining best-sellers and quality works are arranged on the shelves as in a second-hand bookseller's. This 'disorder', it is hoped, will lead readers to make discoveries – browsing, and finding what they had not known they were looking for.[51] In response to public interest for in-demand titles and topics, Gütersloh Municipal Library created a 'Trends' Department. With 20 per cent of the new acquisition fund, a small team anticipates these trends and demands and focuses on suitable material, of which later use proves quite high.[52]

Sevenoaks Public Library, seemingly wishing to break away from the standard fiction genres, set up a special browsing area called 'Novel ideas'. Fiction was presented under such themes as books made into film; best-sellers past and present; and Africa in fiction.[53]

OTHER LIBRARY MATERIALS

Public libraries also house a variety of non-book material that bring with it questions of arrangement, display and storage, as well as preservation and security. In small libraries there may not be large collections of non-book formats and the arrangement, display and storage of CDs, videos, DVDs, audio tapes, and newspapers and journals, for example, poses no major problems. With the exception, perhaps, of current issues of newspapers and journals, this non-book material is available for loan.

Larger libraries with bigger loan collections of such material, and with subject and special collections, such as the local studies department (which may include archives), will give greater attention to the organization of such collections. Non-book material includes a wide variety of formats: maps, sheet music, photographs, ephemera, microforms, computer disks, framed pictures, three-dimensional items, sound recordings, film, and the other sound and image formats mentioned earlier. Some obsolete formats may pose problems of use and some material is likely to be stored away from readers, available on request and only for use in-house. Even where material has been digitized, or other surrogate form created, or transferred to another medium (such as microfilm), it is usual to retain the originals.

Whether on open or closed access some system of organization for retrieval is necessary and although items may, for example, be stored on shelves, some form of primary container, such as jewel cases and acid-free boxes, will be needed for some items. Other material will require more specialized housing, and rare and fragile material a secure and controlled environment.

It is not possible to deal with all these formats in a work such as this and so this section will confine itself to general remarks about the arrangement of non-book material. Depending on the quantity of these materials, they can be organized by:

- the same classification scheme as that used for book materials
- a different classification scheme, perhaps specially devised for that material: it may be a published scheme, possibly adapted, or an in-house scheme
- broad subject heading – some subdivision, alphabetical or numerical, may be needed within headings: for an outline of the scheme used for recorded sound in Cheshire, see Figure 10.4
- alphabetical, numerical or random order – some materials, such as maps, may have their own numbering system.

SEPARATION OR INTEGRATION OF LIBRARY MATERIALS?

The interior layout and furnishing of the library can be affected by decisions to depart from the traditional separation of public library stock by function, form, age group, and so on. Such departures can entail the integration of different formats of material (books

Orchestral	Easy listening
Concertos	Jazz and blues
Instrumental	Folk and country and western
Classical vocal	Brass and military bands
Children's	Films and shows
Pop	Miscellaneous – spoken word, language courses, etc.[54]

Figure 10.4   Recorded sound categories: sub-divisions omitted (Cheshire Libraries)

with videos and DVDs on the same subject, for example), or the integration of different types of stock (for instance, lending and reference material). Or as in reader interest arrangement (stock categorization), subject groupings can be used which mix different types of book and formats. Examples of separation and integration are described below:

1. Non-fiction: where appropriate, non-fiction is co-located with fiction in reader interest categories: crime, mystery and detection; adventure and spying; the sea; war; and the unknown, for instance. In an attempt to interest more readers in non-fiction, a 'ribbon' of non-fiction shelves in class order may run through the fiction sequence in some libraries. Others may interfile adult and children's non-fiction material into one sequence.

2. Adult reference material: the interfiling of adult non-fiction for loan and reference material into one sequence, with perhaps a small separate quick-reference collection. The subject approach often incorporates this arrangement also.

3. Children's reference material: the interfiling of adult and children's reference material into one sequence.

4. Multimedia: books, videos and DVDs on the same subject may be brought together in the standard classified arrangement, for example.

Other reasons for the separation of library materials include:

- value – items may be stored in locked glass-fronted cases
- preservation – material stored in a climate-controlled environment
- size and shape – resulting in parallel classified or alphabetical sequences: those libraries employing stock categorization usually try to avoid this
- the susceptibilities of some users – items may need to be available only on request
- vulnerability to theft – again, items may need to be available on request only
- special equipment is required for their use; microforms, for example
- restriction to (or more suitability for) certain groups of user or type of use, such as large-print books and equipment for the visually impaired.

At Gütersloh Municipal Library, changes made since 1995 mean that media are integrated under broad thematic headings, some of which change while others are permanent.[55] Cologne too has combined various formats into broad subject displays.[56] In Finland, Vaasa City Library, an extended 1930s building, is divided into integrated subject areas, containing all types of material.[57] The media centre at La Rochelle (1998) divides its collections into subject zones which also incorporate all types of material.[58] Another French library divides its collection by format, with books separated into fiction and non-fiction. Adult and children's fiction is separated but non-fiction is integrated, with children's titles appropriately distinguished. The belief is that children's non-fiction will interest adults and vice versa.[59] Also in France some consideration has been given to the integration of the library's sections for children and adults in a single room. The view is taken that this degree of integration is not just for small or medium-sized libraries.[60]

SHELVING

The layout of shelving in libraries can be of the more traditional kind – serried rows of shelving, with gangways between, supplemented by wall shelving. This linear effect may be relieved in some libraries by the creation of shelved alcoves, which may contain seating. Other arrangements of shelving are possible, and bays of shelving may be placed in an echelon (or staggered) fashion or arranged in a curved or zigzag manner. Danish public libraries, for example, have demonstrated more interesting library layouts for many years.[61] The German library supply organization (EKZ) has also shown how traditional shelving arrangements can be altered to create new innovative shelving patterns that often permit the enclosure of some seating.

While a library may retain some of the traditional shelving elements in its layout, another arrangement may predominate, or there may be a mix of patterns that creates an irregular appearance to its floor plan. Shelving may be arranged, for example, diagonally across the library, at an angle to gangways or grouped in such a way as to create V-, T- or Y-shaped patterns. Cross or star layouts may also be used; anything, it would seem, to avoid straight lines and long runs of shelving.

Stock categorization provides an 'opportunity to change the whole layout and atmosphere of the library to make it more attractive to users'.[62] It has helped in the change to replace regimented ranks of shelving, and books shelved spine on, with more varied layouts, perhaps using shop units, and face-on display. It has helped do away with inaccessible top and bottom shelves and its success has been ensured by the use of large, colourful, readable guiding.

Over-varied layouts, that are without some obvious pattern and logic, can be disastrous, however, in aesthetic and security terms and in their ease of use. They often look better on the plans than they work in practice. Non-traditional layouts seem also to require above average space to be successful, allowing the varied shelving patterns and layout to be readily understood and easily followed by readers.

While the visual impact of the shelving arrangement is important, matters other than aesthetics must be considered during their selection and layout. These include:

- purpose – whether for formats other than books
- shelving construction
- stability
- required floorloading
- whether wood or metal, or a mix of the two, is preferred
- sizes and capacity
- colours and finishes
- flexibility and modularity: the ability to move shelving (on castors) and to adjust shelf height and shelving units whose use can be changed, to display periodicals, for example
- critical distances to be kept between shelving, and between shelving and other furniture (such as seating) to permit ease of movement
- whether compact shelving is to be used (see recent Australian guidelines for mobile shelving for libraries, museums and archives[63]).

OTHER MAJOR LAYOUT ELEMENTS

When arranging the main elements of the library layout – the issue and return counter, enquiry or help desk, shelving, tables and seating, and workstations – there are two major choices. The first segregates these elements into separate blocks of shelving, seating and workstations, with staff desks and counters placed close to where people enter and leave the library or library department. The alternative is to devise a layout where the above elements are integrated, producing areas where shelving, seating and workstations are mixed together in smaller groupings and where staff desks and counters are placed more centrally, to one side, or at the rear of the library or department or appropriately dispersed. Clearly a mix of the two approaches is possible.

ISSUE AND RETURN COUNTERS

Depending upon the size of the library, how it is organized, and the volume of traffic, there may be more than one counter. Decisions to have separate counters for issue and return, for adults and children and for different formats will also affect their number. Counters can be designed in different shapes (a horseshoe, for example), and can include membership and enquiry or help points.[64] As discussed in Chapter 6, self-service is creating changes in this aspect of library operations, although many libraries offer both self-service and staff service to borrowers. As a number of self-service points can be provided, however, the need for a large counter is reduced: even more so if self-issue

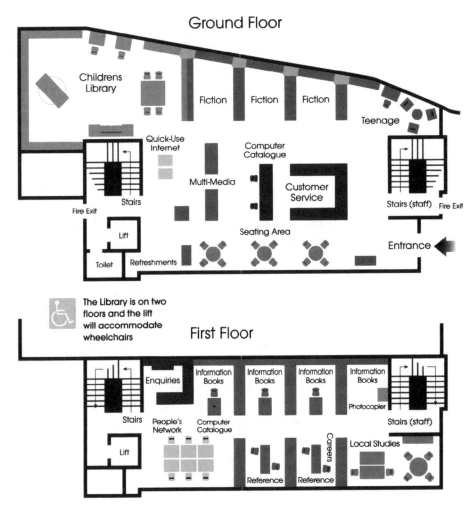

Figure 10.5 Alton Library, Hampshire (2004): floor plans
Source: Hampshire Libraries

and self-return are the norm in a particular library. There will still be a need for some kind of desk or counter, nevertheless, to provide a focal point for those requiring staff assistance. The Malmö approach is noted below, that of Singapore later under 'Interior design trends'.

ENQUIRY OR HELP DESKS

Increasingly the title of readers' adviser or enquiries desk is being replaced by information or help desk/point. In small libraries such positions may be incorporated with the issue desk. In bigger libraries there will be a separate desk, or desks (in larger libraries), and their likely location was noted earlier. Malmö's new public library decided to situate the information and circulation functions side by side at a variety of points round the building – there are also self-issue points. The intention was to do away with desks as barriers and facilitate interaction between staff and visitors. A special desk was designed to accommodate information searches and so on and to deal with staff-assisted returns.[65] Consultation counters, allowing staff and user to sit side by side, were also planned for Vuosaari Library in Helsinki.[66]

TABLES AND SEATING

Whether dispersed, in clusters, concentrated to create a reading room effect, or integrated with shelving (within or at the end of bays), the librarian will have a number of basic issues to resolve in respect of tables and seating. These relate to the total number of tables/seats to be provided, the seating space per reader, the number of different types of seating and tables, and their size and shape. Standards can help with some of these issues and possibly indicate the number and variety of tables and seating that might be required. Where appropriate, this will include seats for listening, viewing (as well as reading), and lap-top use, meeting and conference rooms, auditoriums, and possibly a theatre. Library table and seating needs (bearing in mind also the requirements of children and young people) are:

- lounge – single casual-type easy chairs, sofas and low tables
- study tables and seats – at single tables or multi-seated tables[67]
- study carrels – open (single and multi-user) and closed
- computer workstations – single and multi-user
- bench seating – for computer and microform use
- special tables – for example, for maps or for users with disabilities.[68]

STAFF ACCOMMODATION

The way the library is organized physically and intellectually will determine how staff are deployed in the public areas. The greater the degree of separation of library materials from readers, the greater the expectation by the public that staff are knowledgeable and are able to offer information and guidance in their subject or format area. Behind the scenes, staff may work in open-plan or landscaped (burolandschaft) offices and there may be also a certain amount of group and cellular space.[69] Staff office space may be dispersed around the building but generally most will be centralized in one part.

A non-traditional approach to the workspace of the business office divides it into personal and collaboration spaces, providing different work settings for individuals and groups, according to the dictates of time, task and people involved. There are useful ideas here for the library work environment. Personal space, which is permanent and bookable, consists of cellular offices, desks, carrels and touchdowns. Collaboration space (for the whole staff, customer or team) covers café or restaurant, smart meeting rooms, conference area, project rooms, oasis and informal areas. Varieties of opportunity for staff to work individually, to meet other staff, and to meet library visitors in appropriate surroundings are suggested by this range of spaces. Working, however, in 'a non-traditional office space, just like those who work with new technology, may require instruction and mediation'.[70]

Staff also need adequate sorting space, and workroom/delivery areas should be large enough to accommodate an increasing volume of circulating stock between libraries and for policies allowing books to remain where they are returned. Good employment practice, and the demands of shift work, for example, mean that spacious and pleasant staff rooms, with a good outlook (if possible) should be provided, together with appropriate cooking and food storage facilities. Secure personal lockers, toilets, shower and first aid rooms also need to be considered. At Leamington Spa Library there is a staff balcony overlooking the River Leam.

CLOSED ACCESS STACKS

A major design issue for some public library buildings is the location of closed access material in relation to public and staff areas. In a multi-storey building, one of the following patterns might be used and, where appropriate, repeated on floors throughout the building:

- library above, bookstacks on the floor below
- library on the floor above, and a floor below, the bookstacks in between
- library in the centre, surrounded by bookstacks
- library space in front, bookstacks behind
- centrally placed bookstacks surrounded by library
- bookstacks on either side of library area
- bookstacks in form of a separate tower block.

OTHER SERVICES AND FACILITIES

A public library may provide meeting and exhibition space, an after-hours loans area, bookshop, café, toilet and other facilities. Their location in the building is important if access is required at opening times that are different from those of the library and if certain facilities need to be grouped together.

INTERIOR DESIGN TRENDS

From the previous chapter, and the book as whole, it is clear that the library interior is in a state of flux. It is a state that favours a retail style, but is driven also by changing functions, legal requirements, and communication, information and building services technology. These trends range from the need to provide for media storage and display, and workstations wired for power and data, to greater use of bookstore shelving.[71] They are also part of an effort to reposition libraries in the cultural marketplace, as two examples show.

Singapore has begun to locate its new libraries 'in commercial or institutional buildings in town centres or housing estates'. Their interior design has been influenced by a number of factors:

- self-service loans – this required a redesign of the area round the library entrance
- book-drop – this required work space behind the book-drop to process returned books
- radio-frequency identification (RFID) tagging of library materials – automatically cancels loans when books are returned by the book-drop
- cashless payment – more space required near entrance
- multimedia and Singapore One service – digitized material received from a central server; only workstation space is required at the libraries
- double-sided browsing shelves – books returned via the book-drop are placed on public-facing book shelves within 15 minutes
- video and CD-ROM lending service – space and shelving provide for their attractive display.[72]

As with Singapore, the Idea Store concept was also much concerned with lifelong learning. A network of seven such stores is proposed in the London Borough of Newham, each one to be located in one of its shopping districts. The prototype at Bow was not ideal – an old library building plus an imaginatively converted adjacent council building – but quality design was implemented. Design issues considered in planning the Idea Store included:

- a café and newspapers first rather than an issue desk or security gates
- best practice as regards accessibility (better than that required by legislation, for instance), with attention paid to furniture height, circulation route widths, and so on
- seamless provision of library and learning activities rather than obvious separation in the building
- 'retail' rather than 'library' wherever possible – no notice boards or racks of leaflets but use of plasma screens and a videowall, for example
- a design that allows for easy updating in the way that shops change every few years
- self-help – self-service issue terminals.[73]

Further Idea Stores are planned at Canary Wharf, Isle of Dogs, Watney Market, Bethnal Green, Poplar (2004) and at Whitechapel (2005), which at 3,600m² will be a larger version of the brand than the Bow prototype.

THE OPEN SPACE LIBRARY

Modern public library interiors, with their large open-plan interiors, contrast with the compartmentalized libraries of decades ago. When discussing the organization of the library interior, it is important to draw attention to the disquiet that has been expressed over the way such space is organized because of the effect it has on people's attitudes: enclosed 'living room' space (personal space) versus the open-plan 'supermarket' (common space). In the latter environment people feel alone and there is less pressure to make contact with others. Consequently in open space, which brings with it greater problems of supervision, the onus is on the librarian to make contact with the user (as in the Idea Stores), although such moves may be rejected. In small, one-room libraries the initial contact between staff and reader upon entry is thought to lead to better communication. The placement of furniture

> can create psychological 'rooms' even in an open space situation. This enclosed space then becomes an area of accountability to both patron and the librarian.[74]

Libraries can never entirely succeed through a good interior organization and layout, unless they further good communications between staff and readers – communications for which staff must take a proactive stance.

The optimum organization of the library interior, both physically and intellectually, combined with environmental qualities described in this and other chapters, will have a significant impact on users and staff. Readers and borrowers may well rate the public library interior, with a responsive and proactive staff, its ability to meet their library and information needs, and to offer a pleasant and rewarding ambience and experience, above a building's 'grand design'.

NOTES

1   Thompson, J. (1977), *A history of the principles of librarianship*, London: Bingley, 222.
2   Shoham, S. (2000), *Library classification and browsing: the conjunction of readers and documents*, Brighton: Sussex Academic Press, 61–2.
3   Shoham, S. (2000), 88.
4   Sear, L. and Jennings, B. (1991), 'Organizing fiction for use', in *Managing fiction in libraries*, edited by M. Kinnell, London: Library Association, 101–19: 108.
5   Wu, J. (2000), 'Constructing the new Shanghai Library', in *Building libraries for the 21st century: the shape of information*, edited by T.D. Webb, Jefferson, North Carolina: McFarland, 32–40: 37.

6   Lauridsen, J. (1996), 'New library on 5 floors' (in Danish), *Bibliotekspressen* (20), 584–8.

7   'PN users survey' (2004), *Library and information update* **3** (6), 12.

8   Jacob, B. and Morphew, C. (1997), 'The quiet room: a cyber-free haven in the community library', *Public libraries* **36** (4), 216–17.

9   Rogers, M. (1999), 'Communication overload', *Library journal* **124** (12), 66–7

10   Marples, D.L. and Knell, K.A. (1971), *Circulation and library design: the influence of 'movement' on the layout of libraries*, Cambridge: Cambridge University Engineering Department, 2.

11   Stanely, J. (2003), 'Grow your library', *Public library journal* **18** (4), 94; Rippel, C. (2003), 'What public libraries can learn from superbookstores', *Australasian public libraries and information services* **16** (4) 149.

12   For details of layout and critical sizes, see Thompson, G. (1989), *Planning and design of library buildings*, 3rd edn, London: Butterworth, Chapters 13, 14 and 15; Department of Education and Science (1981), *Designing a medium-sized public library*, London: HMSO, 26, 28.

13   Marples, D.L. and Knell, K.A. (1971), 1–2.

14   Wozniak, S.J. (2002), 'Soapbox: Lack of privacy is just one of the problems in using the People's Network PCs', *Library + information update* **1** (9), 16.

15   Cohen, A. and Cohen, E. (1979), *Designing and space planning for libraries*, New York: Bowker, 68.

16   Overington, M.A. (1969), *The subject departmentalized public library*, London: Library Association, 119–120.

17   Morson, I. and Perry, M. (1982), 'Two-tier and the total stock arrangement in Brent', in *Alternative arrangement: new approaches to public library stock*, edited by P. Ainley and B. Totterdell, London: Association of Assistant Librarians, 101–18: 105.

18   Reader, D. (1982), 'User orientation in a Hertfordshire branch', in Ainley, P. and Totterdell, B. (eds) (1982), 34–41: 37.

19   Hirn, S. (1986), 'Entrance area strategy in libraries', *Scandinavian public library quarterly* **19** (4), 129–31: 131.

20   Lind, S. and Dalsgaard, J. (1990), 'Everyone knows what a library looks like ...' (in Danish), *Biblioteksarbedje* **11** (30) 7–13.

21   Oerom, A., and Thorhauge, J. (1986), 'The tripartite library' (in Danish), *Bibliotek* **70** (8), 245–9; Henning, W. (1984), 'The opening of the new municipal library in Gütersloh' (in German), *Buch und Bibliothek* **36** (5), 361–3, 366–70.

22   Hansen, P. (1999), 'Stock presentation at Harburg Library' (in German), *Buch und Bibliothek* **51** (5), 330–32, 334–5.

23   Booth, P. (1991), 'Together or apart: the problems of stock integration', *Library work* (13), 7.

24   Sear, L. and Jennings, B. (1991), 109.

25   Atkinson, F. (1981), *Fiction librarianship*, London: Bingley, 49–50.

26   Sear, L. and Jennings, B. (1991), 115.

27   Saarti, J. (1992), 'Experiments with categorising fiction in Lohtaja Library', *Scandinavian public library quarterly* **25** (4), 22–4, 29.

28   Martin, L. (1996), *Organizational structure of libraries*, rev. edn, Lanham, Maryland: Scarecrow, 180.

29   Bilton, H. (1968), 'Planning a new central library (i) Bradford', *Public library conference proceedings 1968*, London: Library Association, 29–31.

30   Tynemouth, W. (1968), 'Planning a new central library (ii) Newcastle Upon Tyne', *Public library conference proceedings 1968*, London: Library Association, 32.

31   Berriman, S.G. (1974), 'A view of paradise: Birmingham Central Libraries', *Library Association record* **76** (3) 37–41.

32   Hammond, H. (1996), Norfolk and Norwich Central Library: the emerging phoenix, *New library world* **97** (1130), 24–31: 29.

33   www.vpl.vancouver.bc.ca.

34   Zapatos, C. (2000), 'The San Antonio Public Library', in *Building libraries for the 21st century: the shape of information*, edited by T.D. Webb, Jefferson, North Carolina: McFarland, 41–52: 50–51.

35   Martin, L. (1996), 203.

36   Martin, L. (1996), 204.

37   *A library for all times* (1997), Stockholm: Swedish National Council for Cultural Affairs, 107–12.

38   von Steinaecker, C. (2001), 'No stone is left unturned ... ' (in German), *Buch und Bibliothek* **53** (10/11), 656–60.

39   Eisner-Overberg, C. and Stamm, S. (2000), Solingen's new centre' (in German), *Buch und bibliothek* **52** (10), 650–53.

40   Duperrier, A. (2001), 'Subject focal points at Limoges Library' (in French), *Bulletin des Bibliothèques de France* **46** (1), 88–90.

41   Heikkila, I. (1998), 'The new Turku Central Library' (in Finnish), *Kirjastolehti* (9), 269; Näätsaari, I. (1999), 'Planning a library for the future: the librarian's perspective', *Scandinavian public quarterly* **32** (4), 19–20.

42   Ainley, P. and Totterdell, B. (eds) (1982), 9, 11.

43   Sapiie, J. (1995), 'Reader interest classification: the user friendly schemes', *Cataloguing and classification quarterly* **19** (3/4), 143–55: 149.

44   Chandler, D. (1982), 'Self-service libraries: providing for the smaller community in Cambridgeshire', in Ainley, P. and Totterdell, B. (eds) (1982), 47–59: 55.

45   Chandler, D.J. (1985), *The service from the smaller library in Cambridgeshire: a popular approach*, [Cambridge]: Cambridgeshire Libraries and Information Service, 6.

46   Sapiie, J. (1995), 152.

47   Miller, A. (1992), 'Alternative arrangement in Glasgow City Libraries', *Public library journal* **7** (5), 131–3.

48   Jones, A. and Pratt, G. (1974), 'The categorization of adult non-fiction', *Journal of librarianship* **6** (2), 91–8: 91.

49   van der Heijden, D. (1999), 'PIM – an alternative shelving system for non-fiction: the NBLC develops a comprehensive package for updating collection display' (in Dutch), *BibliotheekBlad* **3** (1), 6–8. Quotation from LISA abstract.

50   Gotz, M. and Strohmenger, K. (2003), 'Themes in worlds – without classification ...', *Buch und Bibliothek* **55** (1), 31–4.

51   Lador, P-Y. (2001), 'Results of placing part of the collection in "free stabling" ' (in French), *Bulletin des Bibliothèques de France* **46** (1), 54–6.

52   Mensching, U. (2001), 'The quest for titles, topics and temperaments' (in German), *Buch und bibliothek* **53** (3), 166–71.

53   Jennings, B, and Sear, L. (1989), Novel ideas: a browsing area for fiction', *Public library journal* **4** (3), 41–4.

54   Astin, J. (1982), 'Cheshire: alternative arrangement and beyond', in Ainley, P. and Totterdell, B. (eds) (1982), 13–33: 19.

55   Stein, A. (1999), 'New forms of stock presentation at Gütersloh' (in German), *Buch und Bibliothek* **51** (5), 340–42.

56   Schmick, B. (1999), Cologne fragments ...' (in German), *Buch und bibliothek* **51** (5), 342–4.

57   Verho, S. (2001), 'New ideas in Vaasa City Library building' (in Finnish), *Kirjastolehti* (7), 8–9.

58   Carbone, B. (2000), 'Multimedia at La Rochelle' (in French), *Bulletin d'informations de l'Association des Bibliothècaires Français* (186), 90–92.

59   Jacobsen, H. (1994), 'Young people's section/adult section: why separate?' (in French), *Bulletin d'informations de l'Association des Bibliothècaires Français* **165** (4), 15,

60   Jacobsen, H. (1999), Children's and adult's sections – should they be integrated?' (in French), *Bulletin des Bibliothèques de France* **44** (3), 76–9.

61   Dewe, M. (1981), 'Interior landscape and the public library building', *Library review* **30** (1) 4–12.

62   'Summary and conclusions' (1982), in Ainley, P. and Totterdell, B. (eds) (1982), 119–35: 133.

63   *Guidelines for mobile shelving for archives, libraries and museums* (1997), [Dickson, ACT, Australia]: Australian Archives, Standards Australia and Standards New Zealand.

64   Examples of counter design are given in Thompson, G. (1981), 167–9; Department of Education and Science (1981), 14–19.

65   *A library for all times* (1997), 55–9.

66   Aaltonen, H. (2000), 'A counter', *Kirjastolehti* (7), 24–5.

67   Study facilities are helpfully described in, Department of Education and Science (1981), 46–51.

68   For further details of tables and seating, including layout, see Thompson, G. (1981), 161–6.

69   Dewe, M. (1981), 6, 8.

70   Davenport, E. and Bruce, I. (2002), 'Innovation, knowledge management and the use of space', *Journal of information science* **28** (3) 225–30.

71   Sager, D. (ed.) (2000), 'Interior design trends in libraries', *Public libraries* **39** (3) 137–42.

72   Ngian, L.C. (2001), 'Designing library interiors in a changing environment: the Singapore experience', in *Library buildings in a changing environment*, edited by M-F. Bisbrouck, Munich: Saur, 155–62: 157–8.

73   Wills, H. (2004), 'An innovative approach to reaching the non-learning public: the new Idea Store in London', in *Libraries as places: buildings for the 21st century* edited by M-F. Bisbrouck, Munich: Saur, 103–16: 109–110, 114.

74   Hildrich, S.R. (1978), 'Problems of the open space library', *Connecticut libraries* **20** (4), 42–4: 44.

11 Anything it needs to be?

The public library will provide enrichment well into the twenty-first century. And it will do so primarily with the medium of the printed page. Without it we will all be the poorer. The history of the public library highlights an essential role that will be needed more, not less, in our future.

Lowell Martin, 1998 [1]

There is still a need for library premises. Amidst all today's machines, people long to be social, and experience libraries as places for both being and doing.

Maija Berndtson, 2001 [2]

The prophesied death of the book and the demise of library, including the public library and its building, is the starting point of this final chapter. In part, the public library's predicted demise in the UK is attributed to its supposed inability to change, and so demonstrate its appeal and relevance in today's world. The nature of those required changes to UK public library services, and the implications they might have for their buildings, have been considered in earlier chapters and reference made to the changing library scene elsewhere in the world. As discussion of these changes in the public library has shown, conflict can result: over combining the old and the new, between the young and old, over self-service and personal service, between the serious and the popular, over solitude and group activity, over consumerism and commercialization, and over noise and calm. Resolution of these conflicts and clashes lies at the heart of making change successful and this can be helped by appropriate public library buildings.[3]

One thing is clear: the present and the future of public libraries, including the design of their buildings, is intimately bound up with their deployment of ICT (Information and Communications Technology) – yet this is supposedly another argument for their coming demise. Access to a computer terminal at home, at work, at school and at play will, it is thought, obviate the need to visit a building like the public library to seek information, to borrow books and other formats, to look at an exhibition, to attend a discussion group, or to do the many other things that libraries have on offer. Current library functions will all be fulfilled by access to a networked computer which will provide the library in all its virtual facets. The demise of the public library, and with it the *public* provision of ICT, assumes that everybody has access to the technology, including the latest technology, and that the library's future purpose is purely a technological one. This scenario is predicated also on the demise of the book and thus the need to acquire, display and store them.

CHANGE AND CHALLENGE FOR PUBLIC LIBRARIES

THE END OF THE BOOK?

The supposed threat of modern technology to libraries containing books is not a new one. In 1944, the American librarian, Freemont Rider, advocated the use of microcards as a cost-effective, space-saving storage solution. Rider found, however, that many took his proposal as 'forecasting the doom of libraries of books'.[4] Talking about the future of the book around ten years later, Lester Asheim concluded that, while the book had (and would have in the future) many rivals, 'we need have no fears concerning its future'.[5]

Since that date others have predicted the death of the book and there is no doubt that electronic versions of some reference works and journals, for example, are making some printed material redundant today and that this is a growing development. But the death of the book, and of libraries containing books, is hard to reconcile with the increase in the number of published titles, the growing number of literary prizes, the popularity and presence of the modern bookshop, and buoyant book sales. However, paradoxically, there is an educational concern over levels of literacy and a perceived decline in reading, accounting for the 'books and reading' theme in *Framework for the future*. Books continue to make up a substantial proportion of a public library's stock but nowadays co-exist with a variety of other formats, creating multimedia collections.

THE DEMISE OF LIBRARIES?

There are those, librarians and others, who forecast that the end of libraries is in sight, because of the increasing availability of ICT and the services it offers. By implication, this means the end of the library building. As with the demise of the book, librarians have been here before. The much vaunted completely electronic 'library' and the paperless office have not materialized and modern electronic technology co-exists with traditional library resources and older technologies, such as the microform and the photocopier. While a powerful information tool, the use of ICT has completely altered also many of the operations and procedures of library work such as inter-library loans, circulation and acquisition work, with implications, as has been seen, for library design.

In *Future libraries*, Crawford and Gorman argue against the all-electronic future, including the demise of the library as a physical entity. They say that

> This 'vision' is an irresponsible, illogical, and unworkable nightmare ... a future in which all
> problems disappear as if by magic. It is, like most phantasies, an escape from reality and not
> a serious attempt to deal with the world as it really is.[6]

Larry Dowler puts the opposing views like this:

> Perhaps no claim is more likely to provoke hoots of derision by the technically sophisticated,
> or more fearful and defensive reactions by the literate than the notion that the library will or
> won't be a physical entity.[7]

Without the death of the book (and of other formats) in their current physical form, it is difficult to see the disappearance of the library building. And the evidence of the many building projects mentioned or discussed in this book does not seem to suggest the demise of the public library and its buildings. Librarians should not be complacent about the balance – books and electronic services – continuing to be maintained: libraries on the Web mean it will not always be necessary to visit the library, where the librarian will be more important perhaps for their work behind the scenes than to the virtual or physical self-service visitor.[8] As discussed in Chapter 1, the library can come to be, however, a good meeting place: 'public librarians ... have responsibility [to] offer a physical as well as a virtual meeting place. Both types of space are important and must be nurtured'.[9]

The accepted view at present is that the public libraries will be a mix of the old and new, as regards services, formats and equipment, and will still operate from a library building.[10] The 2003 library impact study concluded that

> Although the virtual library has a role to play ... in the 21st century libraries must also be
> buildings ... [and] this project demonstrates the value and impact these buildings can have on
> local communities.[11]

A public opinion survey on public libraries in the US, commissioned by the Kellogg Foundation, found strong support for this technological and traditional mix, although providing a library building was ranked third after providing children's services and books. This balanced attitude to past and present, and the relevance of the library building, may reflect older people's lengthier experience of the public library. The younger generation would appear to have no such attachment to a physical structure. Those surveyed in the 18–20 age group were

> least enthusiastic about maintaining and constructing library buildings. They are also the least
> enthusiastic of any age group about the importance of libraries in a digital future.[12]

A conclusion from this is that the public library will not survive without attracting the younger age group who will become its future users and supporters. The danger is that the public library becomes too strongly 'yoof'-oriented at the expense of other age and user groups. For example, Lowell Martin draws attention to the challenge to provide services to the growing number of elderly people.[13] In the UK, the popularity of local and family history research amongst older (particularly retired) people has led to improved library facilities as a response to the needs of this group, in some instances leading to separate local studies or local history centres, as discussed later in this chapter.

THE CHANGING ROLE OF THE LIBRARIAN

The demise of the librarian, as well as the book and the library, has also been forecast, or if not demise, a change of 'role from custodians of culture to knowledge navigators', as *Better public libraries* has it.[14] It must be many a decade since public librarians saw themselves as 'custodians' and would probably squirm at being called 'knowledge navigators', or other fanciful terms, such as 'cyberlibrarians' or 'answer network technicians'. Nevertheless, library services and buildings cannot change without staff changing too: 'the more we digitize, the more we miniaturize, the more we technologize, the more we need to provide assistance, mediation, instruction, and analysis'.[15] This means spending more time with people, helping them to understand and use ICT, advising on reading and information needs, offering customized services, disseminating information outside the library walls, and going out to the user, for example.

However the role of the librarian crystallizes, designing for their presence in the library to facilitate communication and interaction, as discussed in the previous chapter, is an ongoing challenge.

THE PACE AND COURSE OF CHANGE

While there seems to be a continuing future for the public library, UK commentators nevertheless forecast its end in Britain unless there is change; of priorities, in the role of the librarian, and in their buildings, for example. The commentators seem not to appreciate that libraries have always initiated and accommodated change: self-service, computerization, and cafés were all library features long before the retail models held up as examples of modern practice, such as shops and bookshops, employed them. Public libraries have been the subject of evolution rather than revolution and it might be mistaken to believe that this evolution will not continue. However, its process is likely to be what Chris Batt has called 'drip, drip' rather than 'bang, crash'.[16] As Susan Kent has written:

> In reality, libraries and librarians have been on the leading edge of change for many years, change that has been quietly transforming the public library.[17]

Some of this pressure in the UK for instant, rather than evolutionary, change is in the hope that it will encourage greater use by a wider range of people. The call for public libraries to 're-invent' themselves can be put down to some extent to the 'curse of the consultants'; individuals who map out the future path for public libraries but may lack historical perspective, have a tendency to dismiss the past (traditional is 'bad', modern is 'good'), re-invent the wheel, and create a new vocabulary to dress up old ideas as new. Rather than creating a climate for change, a climate of conflict is produced amongst different users with different library and space needs.

In portraying the need for change when planning library space, librarians too can be guilty of polarizing supposed alternatives – 'the changes from collection to access and from preservation to communication'[18] – when all four of these matters must continue to be considered in one way or another in the planning and design of many library buildings. And, while recognizing the changes that have taken place, librarians can be guilty of colouring the past as 'morgue-like' days of elderly readers, rigid staff and departmental demarcation, the Browne issue system and vagrants nodding off in the reading room.[19]

The charge that change has been uneven in UK public libraries is more acceptable and is a consequence of a locally funded and administered public service where choices have to be made about purpose and audience for the public library. Much of the demand for change relates to the quality of library buildings and sustaining that quality but, equally important for designing accommodation, is resolving the question as to the purpose and roles of the public library and its targeted audiences, as aired in Chapter 1.

Internationally the profession seems divided over the purpose of the modern public library. Is education or information services to be its future strength, or its recreational and cultural roles? Perhaps in the UK, as Bob Usherwood suggests, there is an emphasis on 'doing' rather than 'thinking'; failing to contemplate 'the philosophy, values and beliefs that should underpin our professional practice'.[20] Lowell Martin sums up his philosophy of public library service with the word ' "enrichment", with the dictionary definition in mind, "to make richer in quality" '.[21]

As described in the opening chapters, more is demanded of the public library today than its educational and other roles; helping to combat social exclusion, for example. But in all of this there is a danger that the public library is being asked to make good some of the deficiencies of educational, welfare and recreational provision, rather than offering a place of 'enrichment'.

While the public library may reach out to particular groups in society, like any institution it will have its regulars, a very important but miscellaneous group – people characterized by Martin as 'individuals seeking enrichment'.[22] In targeting particular groups, public libraries must continue to do their utmost for the self-motivated person, whatever their background, who seeks an 'enrichment' that is meaningful to them.

SEPARATE PROVISION

Nevertheless, two user groups in the UK – children and young people and local and family historians – are given special considerations in library buildings because of their particular space requirements, sometimes in separate purpose-designed accommodation. This is also one way of resolving some of the conflicts between the needs of different groups mentioned earlier. In a discussion about the nature of the central library in Chapter 3, the matter of separate building provision for particular services, subjects and user groups was raised, and the 'lifestyle' and 'boutique' library concepts deployed in Singapore were touched upon. The separate provision described below, both in the UK and elsewhere, reflects these concepts but perhaps in a less upbeat fashion.

LIBRARIES FOR CHILDREN AND YOUNG PEOPLE

Library provision for a community's children and young people is usually to be found in the local public library building which also caters for adults. Although there is a long history of successful children's provision, *Better public libraries* rather dramatically suggests that 'children's services will grow in importance, as the library becomes a secure, electronic safe haven in the city'.[23]

As with provision for local and family historians, the question arises as to whether the needs of children, and particularly young adults, are best catered for in separate accommodation, either as part of or adjacent to the public library building, or located elsewhere. Catering for different age groups is the issue here and, like education provision, suggests a range of approaches to provide for the very young, older children, teenagers and young adults.

A number of recent UK examples of provision for children and young people is given in Figure 11.1.[24]

Peterburn Library and Drop-in Centre, Airdrie, 1991 (designed to attract and
   serve teenagers and young adults)

Children's Library, Croydon Central Library, 1993 (large children's section with
   decorative features and a nautical theme)

Children's Library, Kirkby Library, Knowsley, 1998 (refurbished children's section
   with maritime theme)

Children's Library, Stratford Library, London, Newham, 2000 (colourful and
   spacious children's section)

Play and Learn Library, Britwell Library, Slough, 2003 (library addition and
   garden area)

Figure 11.1   Library accommodation for children and young people in the UK

Within the library building

As will be seen, library provision for children and young people is usually offered in one of three ways; most commonly, however, through accommodation within the main body of the library, often as one or more distinctive areas in an open-plan library. It is this openness that may be the cause of antagonism between different user groups. Nevertheless, physical separation from services to adults can be achieved by, for example, locating children and young people's provision on a different floor, in the wing of an L-shaped building, for instance, or in a separate room.

A UK survey into the design and location of the children's library in relation to the adult library – open-plan or separate department – generally boiled down to a compromise between likely advantages and available resources. Perhaps not unexpectedly, users who were interviewed preferred the arrangement with which they were familiar.[25] The radical idea of integrating adult and children's libraries, rather than emphasizing their separateness, has already been touched on in Chapter 10.

Increasingly, however, distinct provision is made for children (including very young children) and teenagers, because of the different demands of the two groups as regards library materials and ambience. In Sarezzo, Italy, (2000, 900m^2), the children's section specializes in meeting the needs of the six-and-under age group.[26] Also in Italy, Viadna's children's library (250m^2) has a special room for the under-fives and a fun reading room for the 10–14s with music CDs, DVDs, comics and appropriate fiction.[27]

Where to locate the children's library in a building of more than one floor is often an issue. The Centre for the Child in Birmingham Central Library (1995), which meets the needs of children (including teenagers) and their carers, is located on the ground floor close to the entrance.[28] In the Evereux Médiathèque (1995, 3,500m^2) of red brick, glass and oversailing zinc roof, the children's library is located on the ground floor which in addition houses the entrance, the current affairs library – the informal hub of the building – and garage.[29] In the refurbished and extended Putney Library London, Wandsworth (1998), the children's library is located on the first floor. At Limoges (1998) too the children's library is on the first floor and accommodated in a rectangular space with an elliptical centrepiece housing the story-hour room and the salle d'animation (activities room). Provision for the youngest to teenagers progresses around the room, encircling the central elliptical space.[30] In Verl, near Gütersloh, where 22 per cent of the population are under 18, the children's library is housed in a restored half-timbered building next to the main library.

In a building consisting of linked units of accommodation, the children's library may be located in an independent block with its own entrance but, for example, joined to the main library building by a short corridor. Wester Hailes Library (1997, 1,200m^2), Edinburgh, has a youth library in an upstairs location with its own entrance to the right of the main entrance. The library is aimed at the 12–22 age group – separate provision is made for younger children in the main building – in a district where 46 per cent of the population is under 25. Following consultation, a comfortable environment was created, with a strong youth identity. Soft seating, magazines, music listening points, board games and appropriate stock are provided, along with free and easy access to PCs.[31]

Catering for young people or teenagers within the library building is a major challenge and two American libraries have responded by creating special areas. The

Teen'Scape library and resource centre at Los Angeles Public Library is considered one of the most advanced technologically. There is a cyberzone area of terminals and a comfortable lounge for reading, watching television or playing board games.[32] Phoenix (Arizona) has a Teen Centre with sections for reading and computers and a lounge area. There are lots of PCs and a homepage for children.[33] Other initiatives in the UK include that at Camden, where a combined library, learning and youth resource centre is being built. The refurbishment of the central library at Blackburn and Darwen (2003) has provided online learning for basic skills for young people, including a café and a young persons' drop-in centre.

Separate buildings or accommodation

The provision of a separate building or accommodation for children and young people located away from that providing services to adults is professionally controversial. Examples, however, can be found in France (Paris), Greece (Thessaloniki), Spain (Barcelona), and the former USSR had a large network of branch libraries for children and teenagers. St Petersburg today, for instance, has 192 public libraries of which 64 are just for children.[34] Corregio (Italy) created a leisure centre for families and children in 1997 to promote play and the enjoyment of reading. The centre consists of a young people's library, children's library, video library and studio. In 2003 the centre was relocated to a building in a park.[35]

In the UK, a number of separate children's branches were constructed in the 1950s and 1960s, for example, the Dick Whittington Junior Library (Islington, 1962), but few since that period. One example is the Wiend Centre Children's Library, Wigan (1987, 470m²), considered both exciting and unusual at the time.[36]

Singapore demonstrates what can be done for the 18–35 age group by providing separate accommodation. One of the most well known examples of a separate building for children, with its distinctive cylindrical architecture, is that at Clamart in Paris (1965, 550m²), surrounded by gardens covering about 600m², and funded privately by La Joie par Les Livres foundation. It is a building with lending library, separate reading rooms for younger and older children, storytelling room, small hall, activities room and gardens. Another French example is La Bibliothèque Enfantine de Choisy-Le Roi (1971, 580m²).

The Al-Qattan Centre for the Child, Gaza, is another complete building dedicated to library service for children and teenagers and funded by the Qattan Foundation. While this is not a unique approach – and there are other examples in the Arab world – it is rare for such a building to be of such a scale (the library element is 1,100m²), to offer such a wide range of services and facilities (which includes a multi-purpose hall), and appeal to such a wide age range. The Centre is aimed solely at children and young adults aged up to 15 in a region where around half the total population are under this age. The building is designed to provide distinctive library areas for three age groups (5 and under, 6–11 and 12–15), as well as children with special needs, parents and carers. A feature of the interior is a central street, lit from above, separating and yet linking the different parts of the open plan centre.[37]

Shared accommodation

Libraries for young people may be found also in accommodation offering music, sport and social facilities. In the UK, for example, the Powerhouse (2000) in Manchester is targeted exclusively at young people, but the main users are Afro-Caribbean males in the 18 to 25 age group. It is a youth centre located in a deprived inner-city area and jointly run by the city libraries and the youth service. A library, providing books, magazines, music and computer access, is at the heart of the centre which also houses a café, crèche, residential wing, art and music studios and a basketball court. Young people came up with the chosen model for the centre and then the architect was commissioned.[38]

Two Scandinavian examples of shared buildings are those at Nacka, on the outskirts of Stockholm, which is home to the Diesel Work Shop, a community centre that includes a library for children and young people. At Morkov (Denmark), a library and youth club are provided under one roof but occupy different ends of the building. The club includes books for young people and a basement music room for all ages.

Separately located accommodation for children and young adults has certain practical and perceived disadvantages, particularly for younger children. There is the problem for families of parents and children being catered for at separate locations, and children and teenagers may not feel encouraged later to move on to use adult facilities located elsewhere. Nevertheless, where circumstances dictate, perhaps because of the large numbers of children and young adults, for example, such a solution can be worthwhile and can result in innovative services and buildings.

LIBRARY PROVISION FOR LOCAL AND FAMILY HISTORIANS

Collecting materials about the library's locality – creating a community memory – has been a feature of public libraries in the UK since their inception in the mid-nineteenth century. Local collections were fairly commonplace by the 1880s and were usually housed in the reference library. In the 1930s, local history collections (as they were called then) began to be provided with better accommodation. Since the 1960s many new buildings have included separate areas or departments, often with specialist staff, for what is now called the local studies collection. In some local authorities today, the library service has a responsibility for archives and/or museums and these may be housed also in the public library building rather than elsewhere. An interesting Irish example of local studies and archives provision, along with other services, in the one building is to be found in the refurbished and extended Dublin City Library and Archive (2003). It is both a research facility, housing the Dublin and Irish studies and city archive collections, together with lecture and exhibition rooms, and a branch library, as well as an administration and management headquarters.[39] In other UK local authorities archives and museums are separately administered and located.

LOCAL STUDIES CENTRES

The idea of a local studies centre, incorporating the printed materials of the public library, archival records and museum objects, became the subject of professional debate in the UK in the early 1970s. In some places, circumstances have permitted the bringing together of all three collections. The Wiltshire History Centre, for instance, due to open in 2007, will house the record office, local studies library, museum and conservation services. More commonly it is the printed and archival materials that are housed jointly, although not always as an integrated service. A distinctive feature of this development is the location of the local studies centre in a separate building to the public library. Sometimes this is a converted building of architectural or historical significance, the former post and telegraph office at Oldham, for example, but from time to time it is new purpose-built accommodation.

As in other instances of shared use, there are a range of benefits, but in the case of local studies centres, the fears of overcentralization and the need to continue to use existing premises, for example, may prove deterrents to a development not always viewed favourably by the three professions concerned. From the user's point of view, however, the approach is logical and provides them with an integrated and complete resource in one place.

The idea of combining printed material and archives in a separate building from the public library seems to be on the increase in the UK. Apart from the benefits and disadvantages noted earlier, it reflects the ever-growing numbers and demands made by local and family historians. Examples of this combined approach can be found elsewhere in Greece (Thessaloniki History Centre, 1995),[40] for example, but it does not seem widespread outside the UK. Some examples from both UK urban and county authorities are described briefly below.

- Shropshire Record and Research Centre comprises the former Shropshire Record Office and the Local Studies Library. These were brought together in a purpose-built repository in Shrewsbury in 1995.
- City of Westminster Archives Centre brings archives and local studies collections, formerly held in two libraries, together in a new building opened in 1995.
- Touchstones, in Rochdale, is based in the town's former 1884 central library and was opened in 2002. It houses a new museum and local studies/archive centre, art galleries, tourist information centre, bookshop, café and education centre.
- With the aid of lottery funding, the Centre for Buckinghamshire Studies also opened in 2002. The centre houses the county record office and local studies library in new premises on the corner of the new county offices.

310

Figure 11.2   Surrey History Centre, Woking (1998)
Source: Surrey History Centre

- Surrey History Centre (1998) is housed in purpose-built premises (Figure 11.2) and replaces the former Surrey Record Office and the Surrey Local Studies Collection Library, parts of which were in five different buildings. It also accommodates the county's Archaeological Unit and is home to the Museums Development Officer. 'The Centre has been designed to provide the best possible conditions for preservation and public access and also to be a focus for promoting awareness and understanding of Surrey's history.'[41] The research space is called the Surrey Room, and other public accommodation includes a small refreshment area, and an exhibition and lecture room for educational work with schools and adults. In contrast to Shrewsbury Records and Research Centre, for example, there is one reading room for both printed and archival material and people using either are helped by the same staff.
- The Tameside Local Studies and Archive Centre opened in a building linked to the former Ashton-under-Lyne Central Library in 2004 and which includes a purpose-built archive store. The impact of the resulting structure can be gauged from Figure 11.3.
- Examples in Wales and Scotland include the A.N. Palmer Centre for Local Studies and Archives at Wrexham, and the Angus Local Studies Centre. The former was opened at Wrexham County Museum in 2002, making it a one-stop heritage facility

311

Figure 11.3 Tameside Local Studies and Archive Centre, Ashton-under-Lyne (2004)
Source: Tameside MBC; Jim Standring of Cruickshank & Seward, architects; Shona Coppin, artist

housing museum, archaeology, archives and local studies services under one roof. A joint searchroom for archives and local studies is provided.[42]

The trend is not always towards bringing printed and archival material together. The two were housed in the same library building at Norwich. After the library fire, however, the local studies collection is now located in the Forum building but Norfolk Record Office, together with the East Anglian Film Archive, is now housed in the Archive Centre (2003). This forms part of the county hall site and allows use of its shop and restaurant by centre visitors.

A COMMENT ON SEPARATE PROVISION

Providing separate and distinct accommodation within or away from the public library building is a way of serving the needs of teenagers and young adults in what should be a stimulating environment. Very young children, however, are likely to be best served in the same library as that for adults but the 'play' environment and its location in the building needs careful consideration to respect the needs of others. Local studies centres not only provide the right environment for readers (and the preservation of materials), but provide one where the demands for personal service from librarians and archivists is likely to be high.

Separate accommodation helps librarians deal with some of the conflicts and tensions in their library buildings and demonstrates the public library's ability to respond to the demands and cater for the needs of particular users.

RESPONDING TO THE CHARGES

In view of the fact that public libraries have generally been successful in the process of 'hybridization', mixing the old and the new, how are they meeting the charges that they need to re-invent themselves and that their buildings give the wrong image, are of outmoded design and poorly located?

LOCATION

The issue of location was thoroughly explored in Chapter 4 and doubts expressed about the suitability of the integrated shopping centre location in terms of the kind of space it can provide, the image it gives and the view engendered of the library as just another shopping trip. Drawbacks to such a location stem from libraries at first-floor level (although not such a problem with adequate lifts and escalators), a lack of a distinctive interior (perhaps a universal space of walls, columns and windows), often inadequate space, and accommodation which is not purpose-designed. The use of art, decorative features and a greater variety of finishes, colour schemes and layout can help overcome some of these aesthetic drawbacks but not those relating to the amount of space. But there is no doubt that libraries in shopping centres have advantages of cost, increased use and car parking. In 1990, in the introduction to *Library buildings 1984–1989*, K.C. Harrison noted 'that increasing numbers of public libraries are being provided as parts of shopping centres ... So these, strictly speaking are not *library* buildings at all'. He asked whether it witnessed 'the beginning of the end of the public library building *per se*?'[43]

As Chapter 4 showed, there is a long history in the UK of libraries forming part of buildings that include other public services and facilities. Nevertheless, Harrison clearly felt that this was a significant trend of the late 1980s worth commenting upon. A poor economic climate in the US, it was observed, was also encouraging a move to multi-use facilities in 2002–03.[44] The shared use of buildings is an approach encouraged by *Better public libraries*: 'future libraries will be developed in partnership with other services' with the aim of spreading capital costs with partners.

Following its experiences with a new branch library, built as part of multi-purpose accommodation, the London Borough of Newham decided not to erect any further

313

library-only buildings. The branch, called 'The Gate', also accommodates the housing benefit office and in spite of the difficulties of reconciling the cultures of the two services, the positive results are considered encouraging in an ethnically diverse and poor borough.[45] On a larger scale, and associated with leisure provision, is the concept for the ten millennium centres, the first of which opened in Washington in 1998. The centre contains a library, electronic village hall, ICT learning centre, a multi-use outdoor games area, indoor multi-use sports hall, youth information centre, meeting rooms, creche, café and disco area. The centre received funding from the Millennium Commission.[46]

Local circumstances – social and economic – may well dictate a multi-purpose building but doubts about this as a standard approach in all situations have been expressed in Chapter 5. In rural villages, however, the library may well be in a position to take on or accommodate some of the roles and features of the church, pub, post office or shop that are now missing from the community – the library becomes a major element in a community centre, shopping and meeting place.

IDENTITY AND IMAGE REVISITED

Libraries should have an identity that reveals who they are, the affiliation of individual service points and their relationship with their local authority, and various ways of achieving this were discussed in Chapter 9. From 1992 to 1997 Logan City Council Library, Queensland, Australia, opened five new libraries, all with the same corporate colour scheme, interchangeable shelving, furniture and signage. As well as establishing an identity, substantial savings were made by rotating items among libraries. One library had a pick-up and return drive-through facility.[47] But does the Logan approach make for boring, 'samey' buildings?

Many aspects of identity may be readily changed but changing an image – 'the general idea that the public has of a product, brand or company'[48] – may be a lengthier and more costly process.

There is a feeling today that the 'library' brand does not resonate with the general public and needs to be changed. Some of this rebranding concerns qualifying or adding to the library title or renaming the library entirely. However, one of the strengths of the public library is that everybody knows what it stands for and it is seen as 'the most popular and loved of local services'.[49] Edwards and Fisher reinforce this view of the 'library' brand and add that:

> If society ceases to use the word 'library', it will lose sight of function, form, construction and meaning in libraries themselves ... 'Library' is, therefore, a term we must protect in spite of the fundamental change to the media, upon which it is increasingly based.[50]

Cerritos Public Library in California, opened in 2002, believes in the real adventure of coming to the library and calls itself the 'Experience Library': that is, the library is

314

experienced by and appeals to users through their five senses.[51] The library has become an environment, not just a building.[52]

Often branding is associated with making the library like retail outlets or bookshops in the belief that this makes them more attractive to users, particularly those thought of as socially excluded. The reason the library is not more like a bookstore

> ... is that libraries and bookstores have different missions ... We are still a better bargain than ... a bookstore but it never hurts to improve our image [perhaps with a coffee shop] and work to keep it strong and positive.[53]

The Change in Store? research project demonstrates that people feel that bookshops and libraries should be different but that both should promote books and reading and make books exciting and appealing. The project concludes that a public library service for all should pay attention to the attitude and behaviour of young people and middle-income earners and seek a balance between education and recreation – 'purpose and pleasure'.[54]

'Library' is a strong image or brand which is already equipped with features from shops and stores: perhaps what is required is strong promotion of that library image/brand rather than searching for new descriptors for what is often existing library provision. And rebranding the library service, if taken to extremes, could do away with the varied nature and character of library buildings in a given area. If 'library' is to be abandoned, then the adoption of the French 'médiathèque' might make more sense. While the library may have similarities to other places, it should dare to be itself.

Also, a branding approach might prove unsustainable over a period of time in a local authority environment. Will all seven of the proposed Idea Stores in the London Borough of Tower Hamlets be built? And if they are, does the library service wish to be locked into such a concept for an undefined period? Suffolk's strategic approach to upgrading its existing libraries through better layouts, comfortable furniture, use of bright colours and graphics, for example, as evidenced at Lowestoft and Ipswich, seems a more achievable and sustainable target.[55]

OUTMODED DESIGN?

The charge that public libraries are of outmoded design is easily made, but is it really true and does it always matter? The public library building stock has been built up over 150 years and its buildings reflect the architecture and librarianship of the time of their construction. Many of the early buildings have been replaced, as have some of more recent vintage. The best, as has been shown in Chapter 5, have been reorganized and refurbished and sometimes extended for present-day use. Suitable non-library buildings, often of architectural and/or historical interest, have been converted also to libraries.

As the volumes in the *Library buildings* series demonstrate, the period after the Second World War saw an expansion in service point numbers, particularly from the

1960s onwards, with new and replacement buildings, as well as refurbishment, conversions and extensions. Thus many are of quite recent date. Available figures for the UK show that from 1984 to 1989 there were 452 reported public library building projects (207 new buildings), and between 1990 and 1994, 325 reported projects (134 new buildings).[56]

It would be wrong to say that they and later buildings (some celebrated by award schemes, as noted in Chapter 2) are all outmoded and lack innovative solutions and that there is a lack of well-designed and welcoming buildings. Rather than outmoded they may not fit current architectural fashion or particular view of the library image. There is a danger, however, that over-fixating on the architecture, rather than library service, leads to a demand for a building that is a feature in itself, where the unusual and bizarre may be preferred above all else – the building being more important than its contents and activities. And, harking back to Chapter 1, Chris Batt points out with regard to buildings generally that 'too frequently the architect tries to produce a work of art which fulfils needs having nothing to do with the occupants or building's uses'.[57]

This is not to say that all library buildings are completely adequate and appealing but great efforts have been made over a long period of time to make them so and to provide the important ingredients of good stock and helpful staff. All library buildings cannot therefore be of the early twenty-first century and its times.

The problem faced by librarians, however, is not just of creating good accommodation but keeping it that way. The opportunity to completely 'refresh' a library building may only occur once every 20–30 years, unlike the commercial and retail premises with which libraries are being compared. Also, badly maintained buildings, particularly in urban areas, give libraries an air of make-do and neglect that can deter use. New and refurbished service points, it is argued, will attract increased use and membership – sometimes an unexpectedly large increase – but this has to be sustained over time to be judged a long-term success. Without refreshment and proper maintenance, the most well-regarded buildings can go downhill and become a problem. The issue is not outmoded design but a lack of regular capital investment that prevents public libraries being provided and maintained to a standard which people encounter in the private sector. Space or facility management must be resourced and be a regular professional activity.

Another criticism that might be levelled at today's public libraries is their unadventurous approach to colour and the furniture with which many are equipped. One of the influences, often a determining influence, on what public libraries look and feel like, is the result of the choice of library supplier of shelving and furniture. In recent years, libraries have not confined themselves to suppliers in their own country. Outside the UK, the Danish Library Design Centre, Btj in Sweden, and EKZ and Schulz Speyer in Germany have been particularly influential – the latter furnished the central library in The Hague.

THE ARGUMENT FOR MORE SPACE

Chapter 6 emphasized the importance of the quality of the library environment for users, staff and collections, as well as their safety and security. It is these factors plus the library features and décor discussed in Chapters 9 and 10 that seem to be more important to the visitor than the external appearance of the building, about which views can be divided. In a review of public library buildings of the late 1970s and early 1980s, Godfrey Thompson commented on Portsmouth Library (1976) that it was 'hideous outside ... but solid and satisfying inside'.[58]

A major criticism of the modern UK library interior – compared with older buildings and modern European and other examples – is its lack of spaciousness. Generous space provision not only makes a library feel more open, light and attractive but also allows for the better provision of library services as well as the amenities and facilities that are seen as essential in today's libraries.

Early British public libraries devoted more space to reading on the premises, particularly newspapers and magazines, than to the lending of books. Later, with the shift in emphasis to book loan, the space previously devoted to reading was usually taken over to expand that for open access book display and loan and then to include other formats as well, the lending service eventually becoming *the* major core public library service. Space allocation for reading on the premises declined except for specific purposes such as study and reference.

Access to computer facilities – to surf the Net, send e-mails or word process, for example – forms the modern version of 'reading' on the premises, and makes considerable space demands. Whatever gains might be made from providing smaller collections of books and other formats, workstation space needs will absorb them. One of the conclusions drawn by the 1997 study tour was 'that the widespread take-up of new media and telecommunications [meant] more rather than less space is required'.[59]

The danger, however, is that libraries come to resemble anonymous typing pools or factory lines. Considerable thought needs to be given, therefore, to humanizing the electronic environment, perhaps by breaking the interior down into smaller and more agreeable groupings.

As with the provision of facilities and amenities, such as a café, a library of adequate size is required to be able to offer a variety of spaces and resolve potential conflicts. ICT conflict, for example, may have to be resolved by having an Internet café separate from serious ICT study areas.[60] ICT will still be available everywhere in the library, including café and outside areas,[61] but thought needs to be given as to what kind of use is being catered for in different areas.

New methods for the display and arrangement of an increasing range of library materials, including the use of stock categorization, has led to public library interiors that are similar to the atmosphere, practices and layout of the bookshop, supermarket, department store or even the marketplace. More space is required if more varied layouts are desired, if there is the continued addition of new formats, and if a best-seller, rather than a Man Booker prize approach, is taken to display. Space for children and young people is often inadequate and needs to be improved upon.

In Finland the specification for the library floor area has been redefined as 100m^2 per 1,000 inhabitants. Helsinki had previously used 50m^2 per 1,000.[62] This newer allowance, which could become something of an international standard, is much more generous than the 28m^2 per 1,000 population standard for Wales – the only quantitative standard for library buildings currently in use in the UK.

ROLE MODELS FOR TODAY (UK)

There are a number of UK libraries that have attracted professional and media attention and, as described in Chapter 2, some have received awards from various bodies for their library building. Many of these have been mentioned in this book and are seen as setting examples of good practice. In *Better public libraries* CABE draws attention to such examples: these include Hetton-le-Hole, shared with other service providers (Sunderland); the dual-use facility for Blyth Community College and Cowpen Library (Northumberland, 2002); and Bridport Library, a converted nineteenth-century house (Dorset, 1997).

Bournemouth Central Library, however, was seen by the Libraries Minister, Baroness Blackstone, in 2002 as 'a role model for what I want to see all over the country'.[63] The library is part of the regeneration of the Triangle area of Bournemouth. It includes some shopping space with the library arranged on two open-plan levels forming a horseshoe which overlooks a foyer café. A north-facing glass wall allows views from the street into the library. Inside, the upper floor is reached by a curving staircase which gives views of the street and town hall. The information and issue desk is on the first floor at the top of this stairway, and all main lending functions are situated here. The large second-floor mezzanine contains reference section, music library, local history section, gallery and staff offices.[64]

Those library buildings in the pipeline, such as Newcastle upon Tyne Central Library, or recently opened, may also provide models of good practice for libraries of varying sizes and suited to differing circumstances.

The proposed Library of Birmingham,[65] due to be completed in 2007, has already been mentioned many times in this book. One commentator has written:

> The scheme envisages a landmark building that is alive with new technology and designed to open itself up to the widest possible audience, with books, galleries and exhibition spaces, restaurants, an auditorium and conference suite, which is topped and tailed by sky gardens and parkland.[66]

The elliptical building will be 300 metres long and will have around 36,000–40,000m^2 of floor space. A glass curtain wall on the north-west side will overlook a new park extension to the existing park. Protecting the library from rail noise and the sun on the south-eastern side will be a curved building which will probably accommodate shops, offices and cafés. This creates a semi-enclosed street between the building and the library and is somewhat reminiscent of Vancouver. The roof-top garden forms part of a canopy sheltering open areas around the library, and provides a place for reading and study. It remains to be seen how practicable this roof-top garden will prove to be for the suggested purposes.

In reviewing all the options in mid-2005 for creating the Library of Birmingham, the city council's preferred option was now however, that the library should have two centres. One in the west end civic quarter, not far from the existing central library, and the other in Eastside at Millennium Point. The latter site would house the Library of Birmingham Archives and History Centre, the other would provide lending, reference, information and learning services.

Opened in March 2005, the PFI-funded Brighton Library (5,000m²) displays three times the stock of the old library. The ground floor contains adult fiction, children's area, young people's space, a sound and vision collection, exhibition space, a shop and café. Information stock and space for quiet study is located on the upper floor, along with a rare books reading room, learning centre and computer suite. A mezzanine floor accommodates staff offices and a conference suite and permits literary and arts events to take place. Self-issue terminals are used in the library and the requirements of people with special needs are fully met.

On a smaller scale is Alton Library, Hampshire (2004, 740m²), arranged on three floors, with public areas on the first two (Figure 11.4). The red brick building has windows on all floors at the front to provide natural light and a view into the library. Retractable awnings and timber louvres shade the glazing on this south side of the building. Underfloor heating permits the maximum space for shelves and seating.

The ground floor houses fiction, multimedia, quick-use Internet, refreshments area and a teenage section – at the opposite end of the floor to the children's library. The first floor provides information books and reference material, a local studies section and People's Network area. Staff areas are on the top floor, which also houses a meeting room accommodating groups of up to 20 people and bookable by the local community.

Other recent UK examples not mentioned earlier include Ballymena Central Library (2004, 1,500m²); Dereham Library, Norfolk (2005); Hackney Technology and Learning Centre, (2002), housing the central library and Hackney Museum; and Cambourne Library, Cambridgeshire (2004, 221m²) in a shared-use building in which the library service operates the main reception desk. Libraries in the pipeline include Crawley Library, West Sussex, following a RIBA-managed competition, and Lewes Library, East Sussex, due for completion in 2005.

Figure 11.4   Alton Library, Hampshire (2004): exterior
Source: The author

ROLE MODELS FOR TODAY: NON-UK EXAMPLES

Library buildings in other countries can provide helpful models and, as preparation for new buildings, two international library tours were carried out by Australian librarians in 1996 and 2002.[67]

NORTH AMERICA

As might be expected the tours featured major American libraries, as the 1990s saw the appearance of a number of large library buildings in American cities: Chicago, Los Angeles, Denver, Phoenix,[68] San Antonio,[69] San Francisco and Rochester, for example.

Lowell Martin considered their exteriors 'for the most part undistinguished and even traditional', preferring the exterior of Moshe Safdie's Vancouver Central Branch Library (1995),[70] visited by both Australian groups, one also visiting other Canadian public library buildings in Toronto, Burnaby and Richmond.

Vancouver Public Library (35,150m²), conjuring up an image of the Colosseum, is in the form of a rectangle within an ellipse and has three floors of underground parking and nine floors above ground. The two top floors are leased out, allowing for later expansion of the library. A feature of the building is the glazed curving concourse

320

between the glass-walled library and the café and passing shoppers.[71] Safdie is also the architect of the six-storey main library for Salt Lake City, Utah (22,296m²) (Figure 11.5). Reminiscent of Vancouver, it has a curving wall and embraces the public plaza, with shops and services. It has a children's library for dreaming, playing, reading and inventing, and the Canteena, designed to appeal to teenagers.[72]

Figure 11.5   Salt Lake City Main Library, Utah, US (2003)
Source: Salt Lake City Public Library/Paul Richer

Public reaction to the intriguing and colourful 15-storey Seattle Library (33,721m²), for example, has been extraordinary.[73] It is loved by the critics, liked by the staff and besieged by visitors: it has been called the 'best new library of a generation'. The spiral ramp that links four middle floors has raised concerns about use by the disabled and this and other access matters are to be looked at by a consultant. Funds have also been made available in Seattle to renovate the city's 22 branches and build five new ones, with work to finish in 2007.[74]

Other new major buildings in the US include the Minneapolis Central Library, due for completion in 2006, which will have automated book and materials handling equipment and public art,[75] and Jacksonville Public Library, Florida, where the new main library is to be completed in 2005.

In examining the influence of other countries on public libraries in the UK and elsewhere, America ranks highly. Much of our view as to how public libraries and their buildings should change emanates from those shores. It is expected that advances in America, affecting acquisitions, services and the design of buildings, will have an impact also on public libraries in France in the next few years, unless the degree of cultural difference between the two countries produces a somewhat different library future for France.

EUROPE

Helsinki, which is building a new central library (10,000m² is proposed), as might be expected, featured on both Australian itineraries mentioned above, with one tour also taking in the Netherlands (Rotterdam and The Hague)[76] and France (Nîmes), the other Denmark (Aarhus) and Sweden (Norrköping). The two Dutch libraries are major buildings that have attracted international attention and libraries have always benefited from the influence of Scandinavia on their design. The spaciousness of their buildings and the quality of their furniture have influenced UK library design since the 1960s. In the Netherlands, the Libraries 2040 project has been about the future of public libraries and their buildings. Of the seven proposed libraries of the future, the architect's proposal for the Brabant Library (a 230m-tall 'metalibrary'), with space for 5 million books and about 800 glass study booths that move vertically and horizontally, seems very futuristic.[77]

In their visits to the UK, Croydon Library[78] featured in both tours by the Australians; others were Lewisham Central Library (London),[79] and one of its branch libraries (Wavelengths, which is combined with a swimming pool); Chelmsford (Essex); and Sutton (London).

Many of these buildings have been referred to during the course of this book to exemplify a variety of design concepts and issues. They and other modern buildings that have been mentioned, such as Malmö and Münster, provide models of current thinking and practice about library service and buildings that can be investigated by those in the process of creating new premises.

Malmö is not, however, without its critics, some more vociferous than others. One observer found the link between old and new buildings fails to function; that draught had led to the closure of one entrance in the Cylinder; and that dysfunctional furniture had created chaos. Then there was the disproportional Calendar of Light, long access corridors, an elegant but monotonous central hall, and an unimaginative children's library. The writer concluded that staff will have to work hard to make the building fulfil its library function.[80]

Surprisingly neither study tour chose to visit Germany: Dortmund Central Library (8,800m²), described as 'a media department store', is a long rectangular building with a semi-circular glass rotunda in front;[81] and there are new buildings at Darmstadt, Landau, and Ulm. Ulm Central Public Library (2004) is situated in an ideal central location. It has a complete glass shell, the upper half in the form of a pyramid. The floors below the pyramid increase in size as they rise to meet it, the pyramid itself enclosing further smaller floors.[82] Pforzheim Municipal Library is distinguished among other things for its top quality furnishings and the way classical design elements have been combined with modern equipment. In Berlin, the Central and State Library, a merger of the Berlin Municipal Library and the American Memorial Library, is now the largest public library in Germany, and is hoping to acquire a new building.[83]

Nîmes Médiathèque in France was visited by one group but there are also new large libraries from the 1990s at La Rochelle (1998), Limoges (1998), Orléans (1994) and Poitiers (1996),[84] as well as later examples, such as Montpelier (2000, 12,000m²), Toulouse, Nice and others mentioned in Chapter 1 and elsewhere, as well as Fresnes (3,180m²) a three-level library.

Other European countries also provide interesting examples of library architecture completed or planned. In Spain, Granada (11,750m²), and Puerta de Toledo, Madrid, built in association with a social centre[85] (both 1994); Madrid Public Library is to open shortly in a new building.[86]

Norway's Tønsberg Library (1992, 4,900m²) includes conference rooms, learning resources and computer areas. The Deichman Library new building is to start in 2004 in an area planned to house a cinema, art gallery, Nobel Prize Centre, hotel and shops.

Italy's programme is producing excellent examples. Seregno Library, (1990, 4,410m²) is a building of three distinct parts – a courtyard, a vaulted central space and cylindical tower.[87] Comparable sites include the three-storey Montebelluna Library (2002, 3,300m²)[88] and the Rovereto Library (9,000m²) in a city centre complex that also houses an art museum. The latter's architectural features include a inner-court glass pyramid to light the basement and a large glass-window-roofed circular piazza at the entrance.[89] The San Giovanni Library and Multimedia Centre in Pesaro (2002, 2,050m²) in a converted convent is said to rival similar centres in France and Germany. In Turin, a four-storey central municipal library and culture centre (40,000m²) is to be opened in 2007.

The public library in Liberec, in the Czech Republic, is combined with a small synagogue, and this design has attracted international attention as a 'building of peace and reconciliation'.[90]

SOUTH EAST ASIA, AUSTRALASIA AND THE FAR EAST

Other than Singapore, with interesting regional libraries at Tampines and Woodlands, for example,[91] the two Australian tours appear to have ignored libraries in Australasia and in the nearest part of Asia.

Australia itself has the recent buildings of Singleton Public Library, and Swansea Library, City of Lake Macquarie, both opened in New South Wales in 2004.

In New Zealand central library buildings at Auckland, Hamilton (1993, a conversion), New Plymouth, Palmerston North (1996), Paraparaumu (2002) and Wellington (1991) are considered worthy of note. Opening in 2004 is the Procter Library, Kerikeri.[92]

China has its large, well documented Shanghai Library (1996, 83,000m²), with its two towers of 11 and 24 storeys respectively.[93] Other buildings of distinction include Shaoxing Library (1999), the second largest library in China, and Zhejiang Library[94] (2000), which has an imposing four-storey atrium.[95] All three of these libraries are large buildings but their architecture has none of the highly glazed shapes and curves of modern buildings elsewhere.

Hong Kong has a 12-storey new central library (2001, 33,800m²), which undertakes some national library functions. An arch-shaped entrance to the building represents the Gate of Knowledge.[96]

In Japan, the Library Associations Library Architecture Award has recognized a number of public libraries: in 1996, Odhara Municipal Kanome Library and Ichiwaka City Central Library; in 2000, Shimodate and Suomoto municipal libraries. Other Japanese libraries of note include Osaka (1996),[97] Yokohama (1995) and Sendai Multimedia Centre, Tokyo (2001, 21,682m²), with its emphasis on barrier-free access exemplified by services for the visually and hearing impaired and others who are physically challenged.[98]

These non-UK examples of library building are generally of the larger kind, as small libraries receive little attention in the professional literature. One French example is the public library at Mauriac (2002) in the Cantal region. It occupies 450m² and is well sited in the city centre.[99]

THE LIBRARY CAN BE ANYTHING IT WANTS TO BE

When the public library movement began in the UK just over 150 years ago, three main choices were open to it. The public library could form a central part of a club, rather like the workmen's institutes or miners' welfare halls of South Wales that included a library, although they were created by their communities and not by local authorities. Or its building could also house a museum and possibly an art gallery to create a broad-based cultural institution. Or the building could simply accommodate library-only facilities for reading, lending, reference and study. Generally speaking it was the last described model that was adopted, but buildings that also housed a museum and/or an art gallery were also established.

Over the years, with the emergence of extension activities, particularly for children, some aspects of the club environment became part of the public library ethos; a place for both group and individual activity, for participation as well as solitude. The library as an institution continues to have this versatility; to be essentially a library or, for example, to contain and embrace a range of cultural facilities, such as exhibition space, a theatre, and an auditorium, or community facilities like meeting rooms, cafe, crèche and shop. Chapter 4 demonstrated that, as a dual-purpose establishment, the library can be designed to serve both general and educational needs when located in a school or other educational building. It can also form part of a civic, cultural, educational, leisure or shopping complex, whether the various library and non-library elements are housed under the same roof or exist independently on nearby sites. The library can also be co-located or linked with a variety of other public provision, whether it be a housing development, swimming pool or health centre. (Figure 11.6 shows one such successful example in a striking new building.)

Figure 11.6 The Campus Community Library, Weston-super-Mare, North Somerset (2004): a shared building for library, educational, community and sports facilities
Source: Architects/lead designers, David Morley; photographer, Morley von Sternberg

Not only have public libraries been willing to accommodate or be associated with other kinds of public provision, but they have been responsive to social and technological developments and have pioneered changes in attitude, services and methods of operation. Older library buildings have thus had to adapt to change, while new library buildings have the opportunity to embark upon and accommodate change. This pattern is one that repeats itself time and time again. As for the changes that the future might bring, these can only be prepared for in the most general of ways. The library as a building type and cultural institution endures constant renewal and rebirth, but decline, fall and demise, although always possible and predicted by some, does not seem imminent, certainly when a worldwide picture is taken.

For as Crawford and Gorman say:

> The future means both print and electronic communication ... both linear text and hypertext ... mediation by librarians and direct access ... The future means a library that is both edifice and interface.[100]

These concluding remarks and quotation seem to show that the public library can be anything that it wants to be or that conditions dictate it needs to be. The trick is to decide what is right for the present time and circumstances but to know that changes and challenges to the service and its buildings can occur at any time.

NOTES

1 Martin, L.A. (1998), *Enrichment: a history of the public library in the United States in the twentieth century*, Lanham, Maryland: Scarecrow, 196.

2 Berndtson, M. (2001), 'Helsinki City Library – the prize-winner seeking new vistas', *Scandinavian public library quarterly* **34** (2), 29–32: 32.

3 For a summary of such conflicts, see Demas, S. and Scherer, J.A. (2002), 'Esprit de place: maintaining and designing library buildings to provide transcendent spaces', *American libraries* **33** (4), 65–8.

4 Rider, F. (1949), *Compact book storage*, New York: Hadham, 1.

5 Asheim, L. (ed.) (1955), *Future of the book: implications of newer developments in communication*, Chicago: University of Chicago, 105.

6 Crawford, W. and Gorman, M. (1995), *Future libraries: dreams, madness and reality*, Chicago: American Library Association, 87.

7 Dowler, L. (1996), 'Our edifice at the precipice', *Library journal* **121** (3), 118–20: 118.

8 Hodgkin, A. (2003), 'Libraries on the web: collections or services?' *Library + information update* **2** (7), 48–9: 48.

9 Marcum, D.B. (1998), 'Redefining community through the public library', in *Books, brick and bytes*, edited by S.R. Graubard and P. LeClerc, New Brunswick, New Jersey: Transaction, 191–205: 204.

10 Dobbie, A. (2001), 'The library as a physical place', *New Zealand libraries* **49** (5), 163–5, 173: 163.

11 Bryson, J., Usherwood, B. and Proctor, R. (2003), *Libraries must also be buildings? New library impact study*, London: Resource, 10. See also review of this publication by Jones, D. (2003) *Australasian public libraries and information services* **16** (2), 93–6.

12 Marcum, D.B. (1998), 199.

13 Martin, L. (1998), 180–83.

14 *Better public libraries* (2003), London: CABE and Resource, 5.

15   Kent, S.G. (1998), 'American public libraries: a long transformation moment', in *Books, brick and bytes*, edited by S.R. Graubard and P. LeClerc, New Brunswick, New Jersey: Transaction, 207-20: 209.

16   Batt, C. (2001), 'Drip, drip or bang, crash!?', *Public library journal* 16 (2), 51-3: 51.

17   Kent, S.G. (1998), 210.

18   Berndtson, M. (2002), 24.

19   Spencer, O. (2000), 'A very little memoir for the millennium', *Public library journal* 15 (3), 67-8.

20   Usherwood, B. (2004), 'Pragmatism is not enough', *Library + information update* 3 (7/8), 16.

21   This section is based on a discussion of library purpose and roles in Martin, L.A. (1998), 173-7, 188-96.

22   Martin, L.A. (1998), 176-7.

23   *Better public libraries*, (2003), 8.

24   For details of some of these examples, see Dewe, M. (1995), *Planning and designing libraries for children and young people*, London: Library Association, 189-202.

25   Sisson, F. (1999), 'Children's library design', *British Library. Research and innovation report* (166), 254-7.

26   Salviati, C.I. (2003), 'A new library with roots in the past. A visit to Sarezzo library's children's section' (in Italian), *Biblioteche oggi* supplement 21 (10), 40-42.

27   Martelli. M. and Vezzani, M.S. (2003), 'A guided tour of the children's library' (in Italian), *Biblioteche oggi* 21 (8), 30-2.

28   Dewe, M. (1995), 199-202; Everall, A. (1995), 'The child at the centre', *Library Association record* 97 (4) 218-19, 221.

29   Joubert, P. (1998), 'Ship of culture', *Architectural review* 203 (1212), 63-5.

30   Riboulet, P. (1999), 'The space for children in public libraries', (in French), *Bulletin des bibliothèques de France* 44 (3), 70-75.

31   Kilmurry, E. (1998), 'Purpose built', *Public library journal*, 13 (4), 56-8.

32   Persic, P. (2003), 'The Teenscape area for young people in Los Angeles public library' (in French), *Bulletin des bibliothèques de France* 48 (3), 67.

33   Gilling, S. (2002), 'The public library in Phoenix – an oasis in the middle of the desert' (in Danish), *Bibliotekspressen* (10), 302-4.

34   Kouznetaova, V. and Nazarova, J. (1999), 'The main public children's library of St Petersburg', *Library review* 48 (4), 193-4.

35   Masoni, V. and Ronchetti, M. (2003), 'Reading areas and playrooms ... A new, multipurpose library in the park for Correggio' (in Italian), *Biblioteche oggi* supplement 21 (10), 13-16.

36   Lendon, J.W. (1990), 'Wiend Centre', in *Library buildings 1984-1989*, edited by K.C. Harrison, London: Library Services, 323-5.

37   www.qattanfoundation.org.

38   Raven, D. (2001), 'Choose a book: choose a life', *Public library journal* 16 (3), 91.

39   www.iol.ie/dublincitylibrary/buildings.htm.

40   www.thessalonikiCity.gr/English/History_Center.

41   Robinson, D. (1998), 'Surrey's new history centre', *Local history magazine* (70), 23-6: 24.

42   Thomas, J. (2003), 'Local studies and archives – one stop shop', *Y ddolen* (34), 14.

43   Harrison, K.C. (ed.) (1990), *Library buildings 1984-1989*, London: Library Services, ix.

44   Fox, B-L. (2003), 'These joints are jumpin': library buildings 2003', *Library journal* 128 (20), 36-49: 36.

45   Murray, D. and Whittle, A. (2004), 'Through the forest to the gate', *Library + information update* 3 (2), 28-31.

46   'First millennium centre opens' (1998), *Public library journal* 13 (3), 48.

47   Johnson, C. (1997), 'Drive-through library a first', *Incite* 18 (9), 15.

48   Ivanovic, A. and Collins, P.H. (1996), *Dictionary of marketing*, 2nd edn, Teddington, Middlesex: Collins, 101.

49   Batt, C. (2001), 52.

50   Edwards, B. and Fisher, B. (2002), *Libraries and learning resource centres*, Oxford: Architectural Press, 209, 211.

51   Williams, J.F. (2002), 'Shaping the "Experience Library"', *American libraries* **33** (4), 70–72.

52   Boone, M.D. (2002), 'Library design – the architect's view: a discussion with Tom Findley', *Library hi-tech* **20** (3), 388–92: 392.

53   Leonhardt, T.W. (2004), 'Future trends in libraries', *Technicalities* **24** (1), 4–5: 5.

54   Cartwright, H. (2003), 'Change in store?', *Library + information update* **2** (7), 52–3, 55.

55   Jenkins, G. (2004), 'Winning by design', *Public library journal* Spring, 10–12.

56   Harrison, K.C. (ed.) (1990), *Library buildings 1984–1989*, London: Library Services, 12; Harrison, D. (ed.) (1995), *Library buildings in the United Kingdom 1990–1994*, London: Library Services, 11.

57   Batt, C. (1997), 'Designing freedom', *Public library journal* **12** (4), 88–91: 88.

58   Thompson, G. (1988), 'Public library buildings: a review article', *Journal of librarianship* **20** (1), 60–65: 64.

59   Awcock, F.H. and Dungey, P. (1997), 'Buildings for the new millennium: a study tour of recent library buildings', *LASIE* **28** (3), 34–41: 37.

60   Wozniak, S.J. (2002), 'Soapbox: Lack of privacy is just one of the problems in using the People's Network PCs', *Library + information update* **1** (9), 5.

61   Boone, M.D. (2002), 390.

62   Berndtson, M. (2001), 29.

63   'Bournemouth at cutting edge' (2002), *Library + information update*, **1** (6), 8.

64   'Bournemouth library opens' (2002*), Public library journal* **17** (3), 78. After opening, the library experienced an 80% increase in visitors and 5,000 people took out membership. See also Shonfield, K. (2003), 'Reading room', *Architect's journal* **217** (11) 30–35.

65   Dolan, J. and Khan, A. (2002), 'The Library of Birmingham', *Library + information update* **1** (5), 34–6. The *Birmingham Post* (4 December 2004) reported the possibility that the new library would not go ahead.

66   Bradbury, D. (2003), 'Read all about it', *Telegraph magazine*, 15 March, 50.

67   Awcock, F.H. and Dungey, P. (1997), 34–41; Clifford, N. (2003), 'International public library trends', *Australasian public library and information services* **16** (3), 115–22.

68   Edwards, R.M. (2000), 'A new central library for Phoenix', in *Building libraries for the 21st century: the shape of information*, edited by T.D. Webb, Jefferson, North Carolina: McFarland, 156–67.

69   Zapatos, C. (2000), 'The San Antonio Public Library' in *Building libraries for the 21st century: the shape of information*, 41–52.

70   Martin, L.A. (1998), 90.

71   *Library builders* (1997), London: Academy, 178–81; MacPhee, J. (1996), 'Architecture and libraries: a Canadian perspective', *Feliciter* **42** (2), 20–24. MacPhee describes the colourful Lillian H. Smith Branch of Toronto Public Libraries, as well as Vancouver Public Library.

72   www.slcpl.lib.ut.us/details.

73   See http://seattletimes.nwsource/news/local/library.

74   Kniffel, L. (2004), 'Seattle opening draws huge crowds', *American libraries* **37** (7), 12–13.

75   www.mplib.org/newcentrallib.asp.

76   Denver, San Francisco, Rotterdam and The Hague are discussed in Bisbrouck, M-F. and Chauveinc, M. (eds) (1999), *Intelligent library buildings*, Munich: Saur.

77   Bruijnzeels, R. (2002), 'Libraries 2040: the first seven libraries of the future', *Scandinavian public library quarterly* **35** (4), 4–9.

78   *Library builders* (1997), 202–5.

79   'Access is priority for new Lewisham central' (1994), *Library Association record* **96** (5), 248.

80   Lauridsen, J. (1999), 'More collision than collaboration between the library function and the architecture' (in Danish), *Bibliotekspressen* (4) 22 February, 126–9; Ehlin, I. (2000), 'Malmö City Library', *Scandinavian public library quarterly* **33** (1), 24–9.

81   Engelkenmeier, U. and Jedwabski, B. '"That's something! The new one ...". The central library of Dortmund Municipal and State Library in a new building' (in German), *Buch und Bibliothek* **52** (2) 130–36.

82   Lange, J. (2004), 'The new building of the Central Public Library of the City of Ulm' (in German), *ABI-technik* **24** (3), 190–99.

83   Lux, C. (1998), 'The Central and State Library Berlin – two libraries become one' (in German), *Bibliotheksdienst* **32** (3), 490–95.

84   For details of some of these buildings and other French libraries from 1981–1991, see Jean, R. (1993), *Bibliothèques: une Nouvelle Génération*, Paris: Réunion des musées nationaux.

85   McGuire, P. (1994), 'Drum role', *Architectural review* **196** (1174), 23–7.

86   Bertolucci, C. (2004), 'Cave of knowledge', *Architectural review* **215** (1283), 22–8.

87   For details of this and other buildings of the early to mid-1990s, see *Library builders* (1997), London: Academy.

88   Buosi, B. and Resta, A. (2003), 'Montebelluna: a building designed to be a library' (in Italian), *Biblioteche oggi* **21** (3), 15–21.

89   Baldi, G. (2003), 'A 9000 square metre blend of modernity and tradition' (in Italian), *Biblioteche oggi* **21** (2), 29–34; Sandro, A. (2003), 'A modern piece of architecture' (in Italian), *Biblioteche oggi* **21** (2), 34–7.

90   Kousal, R. (2000), 'Library Liberec', *Liber quarterly* **10** (2), 208–12; Vahlídalová, V. (2000), 'Building of peace and reconciliation', *Liber quarterly* **10** (2), 198–207.

91   The Singapore experience is described in Chia, C. (2002), 'Riding the beast', *Public library journal* **17** (1), 19–20, 23; Pruess, J. (1995), 'Tampines Regional Library, Singapore', *Asian libraries* **4** (3), 8–12.

92   Bundy, A. (2004), 'Places of connection: new public and academic library buildings in Australia and New Zealand', *Australasian public library and information services*, **17** (1), 32–47. Includes a list of recent outstanding building projects in Australia and New Zealand, including dual-use libraries; Stanley, J. (2004), 'Retail therapy in New Zealand', *Library + information gazette* 19 November, 11; Tindale, J. 'Exchanging jobs' [Paraparumu Library], *Library + information update* **3** (5), 22–5.

93   Ma, Y. (2001), 'The development of library buildings in Shanghai', in *Library buildings in a changing environment*, edited by M.-F. Bisbrouck, Munich: Saur, 31–8; Wu, J. (2000), 'Constructing the new Shanghai Library', in *Building libraries for the 21st century: the shape of information*, edited by T.D. Webb, Jefferson, North Carolina: McFarland, 32–40; Wu, J. (ed.) (1999), *New library buildings of the world*, Shanghai: Shanghai Scien-Tech, 148–51; Wang, R. and Wu, J. (1998) 'A palace for knowledge: the new building of Shanghai Library', *Asian libraries* **7** (cumulative issue), 196–9.

94   Cheng, X., Ying, C. and Lin, Z. (2001), 'To create an atmosphere ... On the new building of the Zhejiang Province', in *Library buildings in a changing environment*, edited by M-F. Bisbrouck, Munich: Saur, 177–90.

95   Intner, S. and Tseng, S.C. (2001), 'Polished stone with soul: four public libraries in China', *American libraries* **32** (7), 46–50.

96   Deselaers, S. (2002), 'The newly opened central library in Hong Kong' (in German), *Buch und Bibliothek* **54** (2), 95–9. www.hkpl.gov.hk/hkcl/eng/.

97   Tomie, S. (2001), 'The process and development and the transition of method for facility planning in Japanese public libraries', in *Library buildings in a changing environment*, 61–78. Includes descriptions and plans of Hino City Library, Hekinan City Central Library and Osaka Municipal Central Library.

98   www.smt.city.sendai.jp/en/.

99   Faucher, K. (2004), 'Success at Mauriac in the Cantal' (in French), *Bibliothèque(s)* (13), 58–60.

100   Crawford and Gorman (1995), 180–81.

Appendices

APPENDIX 1
BIENNIAL UK PUBLIC LIBRARY BUILDING AWARDS, 1995 ONWARDS

NOTES

1. In 1995 and 1997 awards were made in two categories, for (a) a new building and (b) a converted, extended or refurbished library. Thereafter four awards were made to large and small libraries in each of the two categories.
2. 'Converted/refurbished' in the listing below may also include a library extension. All three or just one or two of these elements may be present.
3. As noted in Chapter 2, the award categories have been changed for 2005.

1995 WINNERS

New: Wavelengths Library (London, Lewisham)
Converted/refurbished: Burnley Central Library (Lancashire)

1997 WINNERS

New: Lochthorn Library (Dumfries and Galloway)
Converted/refurbished: Sunderland Central Library

1999 WINNERS

New (large): Kidderminster Library (Worcestershire)
New (small): Holywood Arches (Belfast)
Converted/refurbished (large): Putney (London, Wandsworth)
Converted/refurbished (small): Bridport Library (Dorset)

2001 WINNERS

New (large): Stratford Library (London, Newham)
New (small): Brixworth Library & Community Centre
Converted/refurbished (large): Leamington Library (Warwickshire)
Converted/refurbished (small): Buncrana Community Library (Donegal County, Ireland)

2003 WINNERS

New (large): Clayport Library (Durham)
New (small): Cootehill Public Library and Arts Centre (Cavan County, Ireland)
Converted/refurbished (large): Lowestoft Library, Record Office and Learning Centre (Suffolk)
Converted/refurbished (small): Ardkeen Library (Waterford, Ireland)

2005 WINNERS

Partnership award: Jubilee Library, Brighton (Brighton & Hove)
Architect meets practicality award: Hamilton Town House (South Lanarkshire)
Interior design award: Swiss Cottage Library (London, Camden)
Heart of the community award: Waterford City Library (Waterford City, Ireland)
Mary Finch accessibility award: Hamilton Town House (South Lanarkshire)
Delegates' choice: Jubilee Library, Brighton (Brighton & Hove)

APPENDIX 2
US LIBRARY BUILDINGS AWARD PROGRAM, 1991 ONWARDS

These biennial awards have been jointly sponsored by the American Library Association's Library Administration and Management Association and the American Institute of Architects since 1963. They 'recognise distinguished accomplishment in library architecture by an American architect for any library and without regard to location or type'. Public library buildings attracting awards since 1991 are listed below – in 1991 they were all public libraries – and, in the spirit of the awards program, 1991 also included a library building in Berlin by American architects. Libraries are new buildings, unless otherwise stated and library size is generally indicated. An illustrated article featuring the award-winning libraries for that award year is usually found in the April issue of *American libraries* and in the summer or fall issue of *Library administration and management*. The latter has usually fuller descriptions, statistics and plans. The libraries are also briefly described at: www.ala.org/ala/lamaawards/aiaalalibrarybuildings.hmt.

1991 WINNERS

Las Vegas Clark County Library and Discovery Museum, Las Vegas, Nevada (112,000ft^2/10,405m^2)
Buck County Free library and District Center, Doylestown, Pennsylvania (41,500ft^2/3,855m^2)
Stillwater Public Library, Stillwater, Minnesota (Renovation)
Humboldt Library, Berlin, Germany (30,000ft^2/2,787m^2)
Headquarters Library of the Clayton County Library System, Jonesboro, Georgia (32,500ft^2/3,019m^2)
Buckland Branch Library, Atlanta, Georgia (20,000ft^2/1,858m^2)

1993 WINNERS

Hope Library, Alaska (1,300ft^2/121m^2)
Parlin Memorial Library, Everett, Massachusetts (Renovation and addition)
Howell Carnegie District Library, Howell, Michigan (Renovation and extension, 31,000ft^2/2,880m^2)

1995 WINNERS

Lake Shore Facility, Cleveland Public Library, Ohio (Conversion, 135,650ft^2/12,602m^2)
Los Angeles Public Library, Los Angeles, California (Renovation and extension, 539,000ft^2/50,073m^2)

Amanda Park Timberland Library, Washington (2,200ft²/204m²)
Bellevue Regional Library, Washington (130,000ft²/12,077m²)

1997 WINNERS

Great Northwest Branch, San Antonio, Texas (13,150ft²/1,222m²)
New York Public Library, Tottenville Branch, Staten Island (Renovation, 6,645ft²/617m²)
Phoenix Central Library, Phoenix, Arizona (280,000ft²/26,012m²)
San Francisco New Main Public Library, San Francisco, Calfornia (398,908ft²/37,059m²)

1999 WINNERS

Main Reading Room, Humanities and Social Sciences Library, New York Public Library
    (Restoration, 23,000ft²/2,137m²)
Carmel Mountain Ranch Library, San Diego, California (13,102ft²/1,217m²)
Queens Borough Public Library, Flushing Branch, New York (76,000ft²/7,060m²)

2001 WINNERS

Friend Memorial Library, Brooklin, Maine (Renovation and addition, 2,294ft²/213m²)
Robertson Branch Library, Los Angeles, California (10,000ft²/929m²)
North Mason Timberland Library, Belfair, Washington (14,000ft²/1,300m²)
Denver Public Library, Denver, Colorado (Renovation and extension,
    540,000ft²/50,166m²)
Woodstock Branch Library, Portland, Oregon (7,450ft²/692m²)
Multnomah County Regional Library, Portland, Oregon (Reconfiguration and addition,
    125,000ft²/11,613m²)

2003 WINNERS

Lee B. Philmon Branch Library, Riverdale, Georgia (14,000ft²/1,300m²)
South Court, New York Public Library (42,500ft²/3,948m²)
Seattle Public Temporary Central Library, Washington (Renovation, 13,000ft²/1,208m²)

2005 WINNERS

Carnegie Library of Pittsburgh, Brookline Branch, Pennsylvania (Renovation,
    12,418ft²/1,154 m²)
Issaquah Public Library, King County Library System, Washington (15,000ft²/1,394m²)
Salt Lake City Public Library, Utah (240,000ft²/22,296m²)
Seattle Central Library, Washington (362,987ft²/33,721m²)

Bibliography

This select bibliography is limited to books, reports, etc. that are principally concerned with (or are particularly important for) the planning and design of library buildings. Journal articles and items that are mainly concerned with other matters, such as public library purpose and roles, and social conclusion, are listed in the chapter notes.

Ainley, P. and Totterdell, B. (eds) (1982), *Alternative arrangement: new approaches to public library stock*, London: Association of Assistant Librarians.

Alire, C. (2000), *Library disaster planning and recovery handbook*, New York: Neal-Schuman.

Audit Commission (2002), *Building better library services*, London: Audit Commission.

Audit Commission (1997), *Due for renewal: a report on the library service*, London: Audit Commission.

Baltimore County Public Library, Blue Ribbon Committee (1992), *Give'em what they want!: managing the public's library*, Chicago: American Library Association.

Barker, M. and Bridgeman, C. (1994), *Preventing vandalism: what works?* London: Home Office Police Department.

Beckman, M. (1993), *Public library buildings for the 21st century: a handbook for architects, libraries and trustees*, Munich: Saur.

Berriman, S.G. (ed.) (1969), *Library buildings 1967–1968*, London: Library Association.

Berriman, S.G. and Harrison, K.C. (1966), *British public library buildings,* London: Deutsch.

Better public libraries (2003), London: CABE and Resource.

Bisbrouck, M-F. (ed.) (2001), *Library buildings in a changing environment*, Munich: Saur.

Bisbrouck, M-F. and Chauveinc M. (eds) (1999), *Intelligent library buildings*, Munich: Saur.

Bisbrouck, M-F. and others (eds) (2004), *Libraries as places: buildings for the 21st century*, Munich: Saur.

Borrowed time? the future of public libraries in the UK, (1993), Bournes Green, Gloucestershire: Comedia.

Brawner, L.B. and Beck, D.K. (1996), *Determining your public library's future size: a needs assessment and planning models*, Chicago: American Library Association.

British Standards Institution (2000), *Recommendations for storage and exhibition of archival documents*, London: BSI.

Brown, C.R. (2003), *Interior design for libraries: drawing on function and appeal*, Chicago: American Library Association.

Browne, M. (ed.) (1981), *Joint-use libraries in the Australian community*, Canberra: National Library of Australia.

Bryson, J., Usherwood, B. and Proctor, R. (2003), *Libraries must also be buildings? New library impact study*, London: Resource.

Building blocks for library space: functional guidance (1995), Chicago: American Library Association.

Burrows, J. and Cooper, D. (1992), *Theft and loss from UK libraries: a national survey*, London: Home Office Police Department.

Chaney, M. and MacDougall, A.F. (eds) (1992), *Security and crime prevention in libraries*, Aldershot: Ashgate.

Charles, Prince of Wales (1989), *A vision of Britain*, London: Doubleday.

Chartered Institute of Building Services (1982), *CIBS lighting guide: libraries*, London CIBS.

Coates, T. (2004), *Who's in charge? Responsibility for the public library service*, London: Libri Trust and Laser Foundation.

Cohen, A. and Cohen, E. (1979), *Designing and space planning for libraries: a behavioral guide*, New York: Bowker.

Cohn, J.M., Kelsey, A.L. and Fiels, K.M. (2002), *Planning for integrated systems and technologies*, 2nd edn, adapted for UK by D. Salter, London: Facet.

Commonwealth Schools Commission (1983), *School/community libraries in Australia*, Canberra: The Commission.

Connolly, P. (ed.) (1999), *Solving collection problems through repository strategies*, Boston Spa: IFLA Offices for UAP.

Crawford, W. and Gorman, M. (1995), *Future libraries: dreams, madness and reality*, Chicago: American Library Association.

Dahlgren, A.C. (1996), *Planning the small library facility*, Chicago: American Library Association.

Dahlgren, A.C. (1988), *Public library space needs: a planning outline*, Madison, Wisconsin: Wisconsin Department of Public Instruction.

Department of Culture, Media and Sport (2001), *Comprehensive, efficient and modern public libraries – standards and assessment*, London: DCMS.

Department of Education and Science (1981), *Designing a medium-sized public library*, London: HMSO.

Department of Education and Science (1973), *Abraham Moss Centre*, London: HMSO.

Department of Education and Science; Library Advisory Council (England); Library Advisory Council (Wales) (1971), *Public library service points: a report with some notes on staffing*, London: HMSO.

Department of National Heritage (1997), *Reading the future: a review of public libraries in England*, London: DNH.

Dewe, M. (1995), *Planning and designing libraries for children and young people*, London: Library Association.

Dewe, M. (ed.) (1989), *Library buildings: preparations for planning*, Munich: Saur.

Dewe, M. (ed.) (1987), *Adaptation of buildings for library use*, Munich: Saur.

Edwards, B. and Fisher, B. (2002), *Libraries and learning resource centres*, Oxford: Architectural Press.

Fraley, R.A. and Anderson, C.L. (1990), *Library space planning: a how-to-do-it manual for assessing, allocating and reorganizing collections, resources and facilities*, 2nd edn, New York: Neal-Schuman.

Framework for the future (2003), London: Department of Culture, Sport and Media.

Graubard, S.R. and LeClerc, P. (eds) (1998), *Books, bricks and bytes: libraries in the twenty-first century*, New Brunswick, New Jersey: Transaction.

Habich, E.C. (1998), *Moving library collections: a management handbook*, Westport, Connecticut: Greenwood.

Hagloch, S.B. (1994), *Library building projects: tips for survival*, Englewood, Colorado: Libraries Unlimited.

Harrison, D. (ed.) (1995), *Library buildings in the United Kingdom 1990–1994*, London: Library Services.

Harrison, K.C. (ed.) (1990), *Library buildings 1984–1989*, London: Library Services.

Harrison, K.C. (ed.) (1987), *Public library buildings 1975–1983*, London: Library Services.

Holt, R.M. (1990), *Wisconsin library building project handbook*, 2nd rev. edn by A.C. Dahlgren, Madison, Wisconsin: Department of Public Instruction.

Holt, R.M. (1989), *Planning library buildings and facilities: from concept to completion*, Metuchen, New Jersey: Scarecrow.

Hopkins, L. (ed.) (2000), *Library services for visually impaired people: a manual of best practice*, London: Resource.

How to deal with sick building syndrome: guidance for employers, building owners and building managers (1995), Sheffield: Health and Safety Executive.

Jean, R. (1993), *Bibliothèques: une Nouvelle Génération*, Paris: Réunion des musees nationaux.

Jones, T. (1997), *Carnegie libraries across America: a public legacy*, New York: Wiley.

Kahn, M. (1998), *Disaster response and planning for libraries*, Chicago: American Library Association.

Kennedy, J. and Stockton, G. (eds) (1991), *The great divide: challenges in remote storage*, Chicago: American Library Association.

Kirby, J. (1985), *Creating the library identity: a manual of design*, Aldershot: Gower.

Koontz, C.M. (1997), *Library facility siting and location handbook*, Westport, Connecticut: Greenwood.

Krol, J. (2003), *New library buildings in the Netherlands*, The Hague: Netherlands Public Library Association.

Leadbeater, C. (2003), *Overdue: how to create a modern public library service*, London: Demos.

Library builders (1997), London: Academy.

A library for all times (1997), Stockholm: Swedish National Council for Cultural Affairs.

The library of the '80s: Swedish public library buildings 1980-89 (1990), Stockholm: Swedish National Council for Cultural Affairs.

Lueder, A.C. and Webb, S. (1992), *An administrator's guide to library building maintenance*, Chicago: American Library Association.

Lushington, N. (2002), *Libraries designed for users: a 21st century guide*, New York: Neal-Schuman.

Lushington, N. and Kusack, J.M. (1991), *The design and evaluation of public library buildings*, Hamden, Connecticut: Library Professional Publication.

McCabe, G.B. (2000), *Planning for a new generation of public library buildings*, Westport: Greenwood.

McDonald, A. (1994), *Moving your library*, London: Aslib.

Marples, D.L. and Knell, K.A. (1971), *Circulation and library design: the influence of 'movement' on the layout of libraries*, Cambridge: Cambridge University Engineering Department.

Martin, L. (1998), *Enrichment: a history of the public library in the United States in the twentieth century*, London: Scarecrow.

Martin, R.G. (ed.) (1992), *Libraries for the future: planning buildings that work*, Chicago: American Library Association.

Mayo, D. and Nelson, S. (1999), *Wired for the future: developing your library technology plan*, Chicago: American Library Association.

Mevissen, W. (1958), *Büchereibau/Public library buildings*, Essen: Heyer. Bi-lingual text.

Ministry of Education (1962), *Standards of public library service in England and Wales*, London: HMSO.

Morris, A. and Dyer, H. (1998), *Human aspects of library automation*, 2nd edition, Aldershot: Gower.

Morris, J. (1986), *The library disaster preparedness handbook*, Chicago: American Library Association.

Morris, J. (1979), *Managing the library fire risk*, 2nd edn, Berkeley, California: University of California.

Myllylä, R. (ed.) (c. 1992), *Ten Finnish libraries*, Helsinki: Finnish Library Association.

National Assembly for Wales (2001), *Comprehensive, efficient and modern public libraries for Wales: standards and monitoring*, Cardiff: National Assembly for Wales.

Nesbitt, H. and Nield, B.V. (2000), *People places: a guide for public library buildings in New South Wales*, Sydney: Library Council of New South Wales. This document and supplementary material at www.slnsw.gov.au/plb.

New library buildings 1962–1963 (1963), London: Library Association.

Office of the Deputy Prime Minister (2002), *Building regulations: explanatory booklet*, London: ODPM.

Overington, M.A. (1969*), The subject departmentalized public library*, London: Library Association.

Powell-Smith, V. and Billington, M.S. (1999), *The building regulations explained and illustrated*, 11th edn, Oxford: Blackwell.

The public library service: IFLA/UNESCO guidelines for development (2001), Munich: Saur.

Ragsdale, K. and Kenney, D. (1995), *Effective library signage*, Washington DC: Association of Research Libraries, Office of Management Services.

Review of the public library service in England and Wales ... (1995), London: Aslib.

Reynolds, J.D. (ed.) (1967), *Library buildings 1966*, London: Library Association.

Reynolds, J.D. (ed.) (1966), *Library buildings 1965*, London: Library Association.

Reynolds, L. and Barrett, S. (1981), *Signs and guiding for libraries*, London: Bingley.

Robinson, W.C. (1976), *The utility of retail site selection for the public library*, Champaign, Illinois: Graduate School of Library Science, University of Illinois.

Sanin, F. (1994), *Münster City Library*, London: Phaidon.

Sannwald, W.W. (1997), *Checklist of library building design considerations*, 3rd edn, Chicago: American Library Association.

Schneekloth, L.H. and Keable, E.B. (1991*), Evaluation of library facilities: a tool for managing change*, Champaign, Illinois: Graduate School of Library and Information Science, University of Illinois.

Shuman, B. (1999), *Library security and safety handbook: prevention, policies, and procedures*, Chicago: American Library Association.

Stephenson, M.S. (1990), *Planning library facilities: a selected, annotated bibliography*. London: Scarecrow.

Swartzburg, S.G. and Bussey, H. (1991), *Libraries and archives: design and renovation with a preservation perspective*, Metuchen, New Jersey: Scarecrow.

Taylor, J.N. and Johnson, I.M. (1973), *Public libraries and their use*, London: HMSO.

Thompson, A. (1963), *Library buildings of Britain and Europe*, London: Butterworth.

Thompson, G. (1989), *Planning and design of library buildings*, 3rd edn, London: Butterworth.

Tomorrow's library: views of the public library sector (2003), Belfast: Department of Culture, Arts and Leisure in Northern Ireland.

Tucker, D.C. (1999), *Library relocations and collection shifts*, Medford, New Jersey: Information Today.

Vale, B. and Vale, R. (1996), *Green architecture*, London: Thames & Hudson.

Wagner, G. (1992), *Public libraries as agents of communication: a semiotic analysis*, London: Scarecrow.

Ward, H. (ed.) (1976), *New library buildings: 1976 issue,* London: Library Association.

Ward, H. (ed.) (1974), *New library buildings: 1974 issue,* London: Library Association.

Ward, H. and Odd, S. (eds) (1973), *Library buildings: 1972 issue,* London: Library Association.

Webb, T.D. (ed.) (2000), *Building libraries for the 21st century: the shape of information,* Jefferson, North Carolina: McFarland.

Wells, M.S. and Young, R. (1997), *Moving and reorganizing a library*, Aldershot: Gower.

Wheeler, J.L. (1967), *A reconsideration of the strategic location for public library buildings,* Urbana, Illinois: University of Illinois Graduate School of Library Science.

Wheeler, J.L. (1958), *The effective location of public library buildings*, Urbana, Illinois: University of Illinois Library School.

Wheeler, J.L. and Githens, A.M. (1941), *The American public library building*, Chicago: American Library Association.

Williamsburg Regional Library (2001), *Library construction from a staff perspective,* Jefferson, North Carolina: McFarland.

Woodward, J. (2000), *Countdown to a new library: managing the building project*, Chicago: American Library Association.

Worpole, K. (2004), *21st century libraries: changing forms, changing futures,* London: CABE and RIBA,

Wu, J. (ed.) (1999), *New library buildings of the world*, Shanghai: Shanghai Scien-Tech.

Index

Only a small number of the many named library buildings from the different countries mentioned in this book are included in the index. The sub-heading, 'public library buildings' below a country heading, however, draws together references to buildings in that country not specifically named in the index. The main country entry (e.g. Canada) is used for other, non-building references, such as library legislation and funding.

References to illustrations, plans and lists of buildings (e.g. refurbished libraries) are printed in bold type.

346